The Light of the Gods

The Light of the Gods

The Role of Light in Archaic and Classical Greek Cult

EVA PARISINOU

Duckworth

First published in 2000 by
Gerald Duckworth & Co. Ltd.
61 Frith Street, London W1D 3JL
Tel: 020 7434 4242
Fax: 020 7434 4420
Email: enquiries@duckworth-publishers.co.uk
www.ducknet.co.uk

A catalogue record for this book is available
from the British Library

ISBN 0 7156 2912 3

Typeset by Ray Davies
Printed in Great Britain by
Redwood Books Ltd, Trowbridge

Contents

Στους γονείς μου,
Με αγάπη

Acknowledgements

This is a thoroughly revised and expanded version of my London Ph.D. dissertation (1994-98). It has benefited from many people whose contribution I am very happy to acknowledge here. My greatest debt is to my Ph.D. supervisor, Dr C.A. Morgan, whose academic advice and practical support have been much more than generous throughout the years of my study. Warm thanks are owed to Dr A.W. Johnston who read several drafts of this work and made valuable comments. I have, on many occasions, benefited from the expertise of Professors P.A. Cartledge and R. Parker and Dr S. Price, whose help in shaping the literary side of this work is much appreciated. I wish to thank Professor J.N. Coldstream for his many useful comments and suggestions concerning the earlier lighting material, and also for his discussions of the lamps from the sanctuary of Demeter and Kore at Knossos. Constructive criticism and comments have also been received from Professor G.B. Waywell and Dr K.W. Arafat. Special thanks are owed to my department – the Department of Classics at Royal Holloway and Bedford New College – for its continuous support and encouragement in academic and practical matters.

I am indebted to the Managing Committee of the British School at Athens for having granted me permission to study material and to consult archives of the School's earlier excavations at the sanctuaries of Demeter and Kore at Knossos, Artemis Ortheia at Sparta, Aetos on Ithaka and Athena at Emporio on Khios. Similarly, Dr J. Maran kindly granted me permission to examine lighting material from earlier excavations of the German School at Tiryns. Dr N. Bookidis discussed with me the lighting material from the sanctuary of Demeter and Kore on Akrokorinth and also allowed me to examine a number of lamps from the sanctuary in the storerooms of the American School at the site. I am grateful to Dr G. Steinhauer for having granted me permission to study the lamps from the sanctuary of Artemis Mounukhia at Piraeus Museum, and also to Mrs A. Axioti for facilitating my work in the museum and for bringing to my attention a number of unpublished lamps in the museum storerooms from earlier rescue excavations of the Ephorate. I wish to thank Dr L. Parlama for her permission to examine lighting material (both published and unpublished) from the earlier excavations at the sanctuary of Demeter at Eleusis. Special thanks are owed to Mrs P. Papageli for having greatly facilitated my work at that site and to Dr K. Kokkou-Viridi for her generous information about the pyres at Eleusis. The staff at the museums of Sparta, Nafplion and Ithaka as well as of the British School at Knossos and Athens have always been helpful. I thank them all for the facilities with which they provided me.

Many scholars have kindly supplied information through private communication which has been valuable for comparative reasons: Dr U. Hübinger, Dr Th.G. Schattner, Professor H.J. Kienast, Dr S.G. Miller and Dr A. Bammer. The discussions with Dr J. Binder and Dr D.M. Bailey in the earlier years of my study in Britain have been particularly useful (mainly in connection with the lighting material from the town-site on Amorgos, Cyclades). Thanks are also due to the staff of the Beazley Archive in Oxford. Finally, I should not forget my University teacher at Ioannina, Professor L. Marangou, who, as early as my undergraduate student years, first saw that lamps would be a good topic for me.

My research would have been impossible without a scholarship from Royal Holloway and Bedford New College throughout my Ph.D. studies. My on-site examination of material at a number of museums in Greece was realised with the financial aid of the Central Research Fund Committee of the University of London (Irwin Trust), to which I wish to express my gratitude.

For permission to reproduce published illustrations, I wish to thank the following: Soprintendenza Archeologica delle Province di Napoli e Caserta; Soprintendenza BB.CC.AA. Siracusa; Soprintendenza Archeologica Firenze; Musée du Louvre; Ny Carlsberg Glyptotek; Hermitage Museum; Museo Civico Archeologico, Bologna; Metropolitan Museum of Art, New York; Martin von Wagner Museum, Universität Würzburg; Antikenmuseum Berlin – Staatliche Museen Preussischer Kulturbesitz; Greek Archaeological Society; Staatliche Kunstsammlungen Dresden; Bibliothèque Nationale de France; École Française d'Athènes; Hirmer Fotoarchiv, Brill NV, München; Ashmolean Museum, Oxford; Trustees of the British Museum; British School at Athens; Society for the Promotion of Hellenic Studies; Archäologische Sammlungen im Reiss-Museum, Mannheim; Institut für Klassische Archäologie, Johannes Gutenberg Universität Mainz; Deutsches Archäologisches Institut; Athens National Museum; Antikenmuseum Basel und Sammlung Ludwig; Musées Royaux d'Art et d'Histoire, Brussels; Archäologisches Institut, Eberhard-Karls-Universität Tübingen; Badisches Landesmuseum, Karlsruhe; Museum of Fine Arts, Boston.

Finally, I am happy to acknowledge the support and encouragement of my family, friends and colleagues, in both Greece and Britain, who made this task immeasurably lighter. My husband, Roland, has been a much greater part of this work than he can probably imagine, not least because he has always been a source of creative inspiration to me; for his unfailing patience and encouragement, I cannot thank him enough. Nor can I fail to thank my brother, Priamos, who has made hard things seem small to me, so many times, with his endless sense of humour. This work is dedicated to my parents with love and gratitude.

Illustration Sources

Plates

1. Vathi Museum 292. Reproduced with permission of the British School at Athens.

2. Berlin, Staatliche Museen 1962.33. Reproduced with permission of the Antikensammlung, Staatliche Museen zu Berlin – Preussischer Kulturbesitz.

3. St Petersburg, Hermitage 2215. Courtesy, State Hermitage Museum, St Petersburg.

4. Würzburg, Martin von Wagner Museum L 492. Reproduced with permission of the Martin von Wagner Museum, Universität Würzburg.

5. Mannheim, Reiss-Museum Cg 123. Courtesy, Archäologische Sammlungen, Reiss-Museum Mannheim.

6. Dresden Museum inv. Z.V.1050. Courtesy, Skulpturensammlung, Staatliche Kunstsammlungen Dresden.

7. Paris, Cabinet des Médailles 219. Courtesy, Bibliothèque Nationale de France.

8a-b. Mainz, University 116. Courtesy, Institut für Klassische Archäologie, Johannes Gutenberg Universität Mainz.

9. Syracuse, Museo Archeologico Nazionale 21186. Courtesy, Soprintendenza BB.CC.AA. Siracusa.

10. Warsaw, National Museum 142290. Courtesy, Muzeum Narodowe w Warszawie. Photo: Z. Dolinski.

11. Boston, Museum of Fine Arts 68.46. Courtesy, Museum of Fine Arts, Boston. John Michael Rodocanachi Fund.

12. Berlin, Staatliche Museen F 2530. Courtesy, Antikensammlung, Staatliche Museen zu Berlin – Preussischer Kulturbesitz. Photo: Jutta Tietz-Glagow.

13. London, British Museum D 11. Courtesy, Trustees of the British Museum.

14. New York, Metropolitan Museum 28.57.23. Reproduced with permission of the Metropolitan Museum of Art, Fletcher Fund, 1928.

15. Bologna, Museo Civico Archeologico P 236. By courtesy of C. Morigi Giovi, Museo Civico Archeologico, Bologna.

16. Athens, National Museum H 19605 (1414). Courtesy, Athens National Museum.
17. Athens, National Museum 11036. Courtesy, Athens National Museum.
18. St Petersburg, Hermitage St.1792. Courtesy, State Hermitage Museum, St Petersburg.
19. Florence, Museo Archeologico 75748. Courtesy, Soprintendenza Archeologica per la Toscana, Firenze.
20. Athens, National Museum 1443. Courtesy, Athens National Museum.
21. Brussels, Musées Royaux A 10. Courtesy, Royal Museums of Art and History, Brussels inv. A10. Photo: ACL.
22. Karlsruhe, Badisches Landesmuseum F 1926. Courtesy, Badisches Landesmuseum, Karlsruhe.
23. Naples, Museo Archeologico Nazionale 81908 (H 3010). Courtesy, Soprintendenza Archeologica delle Province di Napoli e Caserta, Napoli.
24. Paris, Louvre Ma 2849. Courtesy, Musée du Louvre. Photo: P. Lebaube.
25. Würzburg, Martin von Wagner Museum L 535 (H 4307). Reproduced with permission of the Martin von Wagner Museum, Universität Würzburg.
26. Athens, National Museum 126. Courtesy, Athens National Museum.
27. Würzburg, Martin von Wagner Museum H 4906. Reproduced with permission of the Martin von Wagner Museum, Universität Würzburg.
28. Tübingen, University Museum 1518. Courtesy, Archäologisches Institut, Eberhard-Karls-Universität Tübingen.
29. St Petersburg, Hermitage B 3368. Courtesy, the State Hermitage Museum, St Petersburg.
30. St Petersburg, Hermitage 673 (B1918). Courtesy, the State Hermitage Museum, St Petersburg.
31. Basel, Antikenmuseum BS 1412. Courtesy, Antikenmuseum Basel und Sammlung Ludwig, inv. BS 1412. Photo: Claire Niggli.
32. Copenhagen, Ny Carlsberg Glyptotek 2696. Reproduced with permission of the Ny Carlsberg Glyptotek.
33. Athens, National Museum 1950. Courtesy, Athens National Museum.
34. Athens, National Museum 4540. Courtesy, Athens National Museum.
35. Oxford, Ashmolean Museum 1980.31 (V 289). Courtesy, Department of Antiquities, Ashmolean Museum, Oxford.
36. London, British Museum E 432. Courtesy, Trustees of the British Museum.
37a-b. Paris, Louvre CA 598. Courtesy, Musée du Louvre. Photo: M. et P. Chuzeville.

38. Berlin, Staatliche Museen F 2531. Courtesy, Antikensammlung, Staatliche Museen zu Berlin – Preussischer Kulturbesitz. Photo: Jutta Tietz-Glagow.

39a-b. Naples, Museo Archeologico Nazionale H 2419. Reproduced with permission of the Soprintendenza Archeologica delle Province di Napoli e Caserta.

40. Athens, National Museum A 537 (5825). Courtesy, Athens National Museum.

41. Naples, Museo Archeologico Nazionale 2412. Reproduced with permission of the Soprintendenza Archeologica delle Province di Napoli e Caserta.

42. Parthenon, east frieze (slab V31-35). Reproduced with permission of Hirmer Fotoarchiv, München.

Figures

1. After Persson (1942), 105 fig. 113.

2. After Beazley (1940), 34 fig. 12; 29 figs. 5-6.

3. Vathi Museum 293. Reproduced with permission of the British School at Athens. After Benton (1953), 332 fig. 26.

4. Reproduced with permission of the École Française d'Athènes. After Marinatos (1936), pl. 26.

5. After Cesnola (1991), 336 (fig.).

6a. After Dell (1934), pl. 20. Reproduced with permission of the Deutsches Archäologisches Institut.

6b. After Fergusson (1880), pl. 1.

7. After Travlos (1971b), 218.

8. After Tsountas (1928), 311 fig. 286.

9. Erekhtheion, inv. no. NM X7038. Reproduced with permission of the Greek Archaeological Society. After Pittakis (1862), 92.

10. Aachen, Sürmondt-Ludwig Collection. After Metzger (1951), pl. 46.

11. Lamia, Archaeological Museum AE 1041. Reproduced with permission of Brill NV. After van Straten (1995), fig. 88.

12. Warsaw, National Museum 142290. After Cook (1914), 424 fig. 305.

13. Berlin, Staatliche Museen 2634. After Cook (1914), 224 fig. 165.

14. Eleusis, Archaeological Museum 1215. Reproduced with permission of the Greek Archaeological Society. After Kourouniotis (1937), 240 fig. 12.

15. London, British Museum F 68. After Cook (1914), 221 fig. 164.

16. After Cook (1914), 426 fig. 308.

17. After Papachatzis (1980), 337 fig. 336.

18. St Petersburg, Hermitage St. 1792. Reproduced with permission. After Cook (1914), 220 fig. 163.

19. St Petersburg, Hermitage St. 525 (B 1657). Reproduced with permission of Brill NV. After van Straten (1995), fig. 22.

20. After Cook (1914), figs. 53-4.

21. Paris, Cabinet des Médailles 424. Reproduced with permission of the Bibliothèque Nationale de France. After Cook (1914), pl. 20.

22. Athens, National Museum 1442. Reproduced with permission of the Greek Archaeological Society. After Stais (1886), pl. 1.

23. Athens, National Museum 1519. Reproduced with permission of the Athens National Museum.

24. After Winter (1903), 250.

25. After Kekulé (1884), 117.

26. After Kekulé (1884), 117.

27. Berlin, Staatliche Museen F 1881. Reproduced with permission. After Stark (1868), pl. 9.

28. Naples, Museo Archeologico Nazionale H 3240. Reproduced with permission of the Deutsches Archäologisches Institut. After Salis (1910), pl. 4.

29a. Paris Market; Ex Collection Hamilton, then Feuardent. Reproduced with permission. After Beazley (1939), 621 fig. 2.

29b. Athens, National Museum 1167 (CC1339). Reproduced with permission. After Beazley (1939), 637 fig. 13.

30. After Gabrici (1927), fig. 163.

31. Reproduced with permission of the Greek Archaeological Society. After Kern (1890), pl. 7.

Abbreviations and Conventions

Abbreviations for ancient authors, journals and works of reference follow the *Oxford Classical Dictionary*³ (Oxford-New York 1996). For the following journals, *L'année philologique* (Paris 1996) has been used.

ASMG	*Atti e Memorie della Società Magna Grecia.*
CB	*The Classical Bulletin.*
EMC	*Échos du Monde Classique.*
PCPS	*Proceedings of the Cambridge Philological Society.*
QUCC	*Quaderni Urbinati di Cultura Classica.*
RIA	*Rivista dell' Instituto Nationale di Archeologia e Storia dell' Arte – L' Erma di Bretschneider Roma.*
SCO	*Studii Classici et Orientali, Giardini, Pisa.*

In addition to the above, I have also used:

ABV	Beazley, J.D. (1956) *Attic Black-Figure Vase Painters.* Oxford.
Add.²	Carpenter, T.H. (1989) *Beazley Addenda. Additional References to ABV, ARV² and Paralipomena.* Oxford.
ARV²	Beazley, J.D. (1963) *Attic Red-figure Vase Painters.* Oxford (2nd ed.).
Para	Beazley, J.D. (1971) *Paralipomena. Additions to Attic Black-figure Vase Painters and to Attic Red-figure Vase Painters.* Oxford (2nd ed.).

The dates of texts, inscriptions, iconographical material and archaeological finds cited in this work follow the dating suggestions of the publications to which I refer in each instance. All dates given in the text are BCE unless otherwise indicated. Bold numbers in the text refer to the Catalogues of Vases and Sculptures at the end of the book. Transliterated Greek terms used in the text are italicised only on their first occurrence in each chapter in order to avoid constant repetition of italicised words.

Introduction: Aspects of 'Divine' and 'Earthly' Light

The association between light and the divine seems as old as the Greek pantheon itself. As an inextricable component of divine nature, brightness identifies, surrounds and reflects the presence of a god. It often becomes a passage between heaven and earth by which gods intervene in human affairs. While Greek literature is suffused with bright images of the divine, representations of deities in art reveal a deeper involvement of light in the creation and development of the divine persona. Here, divine brightness is no longer an abstract component which miraculously derives from the god, but instead takes concrete forms resembling the lighting devices employed by humans. Artistic and literary images of gods with torches, or, less commonly, lamps in hand, are at least as plentiful and varied as the connotations that they bear. In several instances, lighting devices are related to the broader realms over which the gods preside, and often offer glimpses of certain rituals involved in their worship.

Light and fire are connected with a variety of human activities inspired by the gods, in both a metaphorical and a realistic way. Emotions such as destructive passion, love or anger 'burn' in Greek literature, and are again released through brightness (e.g. the destructive brightness of torches in war, or the 'fire in the hair of maenads' as described in the *Bacchae* (ll. 757-8), reflecting their ecstatic state during the worship of Dionysos). Light and fire are essential components of literary images of divine wars and are often used to convey images of destruction in the world of mortals. Several rituals of secular character that are heavily dependent upon divine power, such as marriage and childbirth for women, or the founding of a colony and the maintenance of political stability for men, were marked by light and fire mainly provided by torches, lamps and hearth-fires. Human life began and ended with fire rituals; torchlight and hearth-fire purified the newly born from what preceded life, while a torch would ignite a funeral pyre to consume what was left after death, thus sealing the irreversible passage between the living and the dead. However, the use of the torch does not terminate here; brightness, and more specifically torchlight, strongly flavour the image of life after death as experienced in the Eleusinian Mysteries and attested in Dionysian eschatology.

Contact with the gods, on the other hand, required 'earthly' light, contained in human artifacts of which lamps and torches are the most obvious. These served as a common gift to the gods and assumed a more or less regular place in both nocturnal and daytime rituals. As votive offerings, lamps of various types have been unearthed from most excavated sanctuary sites alongside other categories of votive pottery and small finds, and are often marked with dedicatory inscriptions. Lamps of precious material, for example bronze and silver, are among the treasures recorded in temple inventories (such as those of the Parthenon), while other metal or clay specimens could have formed part of temple furniture, used regularly for both practical and ritual needs in and around the temple. Conspicuous examples of the latter are the golden lamp of Kallimakhos which allegedly burned day and night in the Erekhtheion and similar 'eternal' lights in other temples (e.g. the Argive Heraion). The use of lamps and torches in initiatory rites which involved ritual purification may be surmised from artistic depictions and a few archaeological finds. Less conventional types of light-carriers which were particularly linked with special ritual occasions of certain cults are the *amphiphôntes*, the circular cakes bearing thin torches all around them, which were dedicated to Artemis and probably Hekate. Furthermore, a range of open vessels, with or without a spout, could have served as a more primitive type of lamp with a floating wick, as seems to have been the case in the Early Iron Age and Archaic periods. Obviously, considering the multi-functional shape of such a vessel, it would not have had an exclusive role as a source of light.

A basic question that arises is the timing of the rituals in which light was required, and more specifically whether its use was restricted to nocturnal cult activities when natural light was limited or completely absent. Most of the available literary and iconographical evidence points to the primary use of artificial light as a substitute for daylight in nighttime ritual. However, there is also some literary evidence suggesting that light was involved in a number of daytime occurrences, such as divine epiphanies and images of victory or beauty, as well as in many daytime rituals, such as the 'eternal' flames in temples or public buildings and some purificatory rites. To these we should add ritual activities that took place around sunset, or in any case before nightfall, such as wedding processions to the couple's new home. In such cases, torchlight enhanced natural light, even though the latter would probably have sufficed to cover the practical need for illumination. However, taking into account the later stages of the wedding ritual – which included transmission of fire by means of torches from one *oikos* to another – we are indeed often obliged to look for possible further roles for light. It must be remembered that, as in the example of the Attic wedding, it is often hard to draw a clear defining line between the function of torches as purely cult objects, intended to contribute symbolically to the broader religious environment, and their service as light-carriers in the simple material sense, to illuminate nocturnal activities. On the other hand, one should also be aware of instances where, although torches appear in divine hands (often as an attribute), they do not necessarily allude to any nocturnal ritual in honour of the divinity who holds them. For example, the torches held by birth deities (especially Eileithyia, Artemis Lokhia and, on certain occasions, Hekate) may well be symbolic of the function of these deities in bringing children into the light of the world, rather than being reflections of an actual nocturnal ritual.

This study discusses the full extent of the involvement of light in Greek ritual and belief of the Archaic and Classical periods. Light is treated both as a concept associated with the divine persona in Greek literature and as an artifact in the hands of the gods or during human worship. This synthesis is based on an interdisciplinary approach, combining literature, art and archaeology in order to define the complex nature and function of light in Greek cult. Most of the primary evidence dates between the seventh and fourth centuries, but occasional reference is made to later sources whenever they shed light upon earlier rituals or demonstrate possible continuities in cult-practice. No geographical restrictions are imposed on this study. It is nonetheless important to emphasise that since most of the evidence available relates to Attika, there is an inevitable bias towards this region.

The primary evidence for this study is truly diverse in nature, abundant and geographically scattered. The broad title of 'light' covers a complex and multi-faceted series of cult-concepts, ranging from the abstract concept of brightness as a divine characteristic, through its opposition to darkness, to concrete objects made by humans and designed to illuminate cult-activities. Light and fire are particularly closely linked in literature, with flame being understood as the very seed of brightness, and in practice they also produce similar results, with one often being an extension of the other. On another level, the concept of light becomes less abstract when associated with the particular means that produce it, the 'fire-containers', such as lamps, torches and bonfires. Despite the profound scholarly interest in light and its effects, usually evident in the appearance of short discussions within broader works or in a plethora of archaeological publications of lighting devices (predominantly lamps), a synthetic work devoted to lighting effects and methods by which they were created is much needed. In addition, the valuable contribution of lamps to the dating of archaeological strata, due to their relatively well defined life-span, is still the main factor underlying the numerous purely typological studies of lamps. Torches are only occasionally mentioned in archaeological publications, mainly because they are hard to trace in the material record. Although they occur frequently in red-figure and less often in black-figure Attic iconography of different divine circles, they have not so far been the object of a separate study, and therefore their role in Greek cult remains to be ascertained.

A considerable part of this book consists of a systematic examination of the divine iconography of the main torch-bearing deities (especially Deme-

ter, Persephone, Hekate, Artemis and En(n)odia) as well as of gods associated with other forms of light in art or literature (notably Athena, Dionysos
and Zeus). Particular emphasis will be laid upon factors such as type, form
and number of lighting devices, combined with the status and sex of the
figures who hold them, the position in which they are carried and whether
they are alight or not. The number of light-bearing figures (divine or
human) and their likely interactions with other figures in the scenes are
another important element for the interpretation of possible ritual acts.
The different lighting devices are thus studied *in context*, combined with
other objects or figures which may possibly affect their interpretation.

I hope this book will contribute to the better understanding of an
important aspect of many Greek rituals, both nocturnal and daytime, in
the Archaic and Classical periods, recognising that this aspect is by no
means confined to the cults and/or the periods discussed here. At the same
time, the synthesis of a variety of sources of different kinds constitutes a
new approach to the study of lighting material, moving beyond usual
concerns with lamp-typologies or subject-specific treatments of the use of
torches.

I

Light in Early Greek Religious
Thought and Practice

1. The Lamp of Athena in Homer

The earliest reference to a lamp in Greek literature (*lukhnos*) is found in Homer (*Od.* xix, 34). A golden lamp was held by Athena in her secret epiphany to Odysseus and Telemakhos at the scene of the removal of weapons from the walls of the palace, in preparation for their revenge on the suitors: 'Pallas Athene herself took the lead, carrying a golden lamp, which shed a beautiful radiance over the scene' (trans. Rieu 1965). This single occurrence of a golden lamp in the poems of Homer has raised several questions ranging from the source of Athena's light, her role as light-carrier, and the type of object held, to broader issues concerning the authenticity and date of this part of the text.

One of the main philological arguments used to support the assertion that the part of the text which includes this reference to the lamp was a later interpolation, points to an apparent inconsistency in the narration of the preparations to kill the suitors.[1] A further point which has been used to strengthen the argument against the originality of this particular passage focuses on the uniqueness of Homer's mention of a lamp in Athena's hands. Both D. Monro and H. Lorimer rejected the passage mainly on the grounds that the lamp does not fit into the broader historical background of the poem in the eighth century, but rather suggests a later date in the seventh century.[2] Wishing to keep to an eighth-century date for the composition of the *Odyssey*, R. Pfeiffer sought the roots of this negative view which dissociated the lamp from the historical background of the poems in the Alexandrine interpretation of the Homeric texts, which was also repeated by ancient scholiasts.[3] This view was adopted by later Greek authors, such as Eustathios and Athenaios (*Deipnosophistai* xv, 700E): 'The lamp is not an ancient invention; for light the ancients used torches of pine and other woods' (trans. Gulick 1957). Pfeiffer's proposal combines the traditional view of the date of the *Odyssey* with the assumption that this scene of shifting the weapons formed an integral part of the plot. He accepted an unbroken religious tradition in the cult of Athena on the Athenian Akropolis from Mycenaean times onwards, and saw the lamp as a recollection of a Mycenaean trait of Athena, emphasising that the lamp

mentioned in the *Odyssey* had nothing to do with either votive offerings or
lighting utensils.[4]

This idea of 'continuity' has been advanced by others too. Highlighting
the role of Mycenaean elements in Homeric poems, M. Müller cited an
example from the *Odyssey* which, according to her, alluded to the Mycenaean mountain goddess (*Od.* vii, 81).[5] Likewise, H. Rose spoke of
continuous use in cult 'of some archaic and venerated objects', affirming
that 'it is unthinkable that the priests had all forgotten what it [the lamp]
was and how it was used'.[6] The archaeological underpinning of these
arguments is weak, since no examples are cited to demonstrate this
continuity. Furthermore, what exactly is meant by 'continuity' is vague, in
respect of both the period concerned and the type of vessel used for
lighting. In fact, the archaeological evidence available from the Athenian
Akropolis does not allow any conclusive argument for an early cult of
Athena here, at least until the late seventh century, if not later.[7]

In his commentary on *Odyssey* xix, A. Heubeck explains the mention of
a lamp as a striking piece of imagery to highlight the impact of Athena's
help.[8] It is likely that the lamp was employed by the poet because it
belonged to the imagery of Athena in oral tradition, even if that is not
confirmed by the archaeological evidence. Recently, J. Bennet saw the
golden lamp of Athena as one of many Mycenaean survivals which once
reflected status, and which, in the humble world of Homer, could only be
the possession of a god.[9] The possibility of the golden lamp signifying a
torch placed in a heavily ornamented golden candelabrum or a holder of
some sort was discussed and rightly rejected by A. Persson and by U.
Jantzen and R. Tölle, mainly because of the use of the term *lukhnos* rather
than *daïs*.[10] Yet this would accord with lighting practices found elsewhere
in the poem, such as the golden figures of boys in Alkinoos' palace, who
stood on bases and held torches in their hands (*Od.* vii, 100-2): 'And golden
youths stood on well-built pedestals, holding lighted torches in their hands
to give light by night to the banqueters in the hall' (trans. Murray 1995).
Although the authors did not openly rule out the possibility that lamps
were used alongside torches in Homeric times, they admitted a far more
widespread use of torches (*das, daïs, detê*) and braziers (*lamptêres*) both in
secular and sacred contexts.

The brightness emanating from Athena's lamp, or even from the goddess herself, combined with its precious metal, restricted to the possession
of gods, underlines her supernatural presence and emphasises her role in
the action. Flooding light is an almost indispensable feature of divine
epiphany in Homer,[11] while in Athena's operations both gold and light are
frequently present.[12] It is made plain in subsequent verses (*Od.* xix, 36-40)
that the miraculous effect of Athena's light derives not so much from the
lamp's lighting capacity as from the very presence of Athena herself, who
guarantees the victory of the heroes and foreshadows the restoration of
moral order in the palace of Odysseus.[13] That the passage seems to be

incorporated in the plot of the poem may also be demonstrated by the earlier question posed by the maid Eurykleia, who was going to carry the light for the secret evening operations of Odysseus and Telemakhos (*Od.* xix, 24): 'But come, who then shall fetch a light and bear it for you, since you would not allow the maids, who might have given light, to go before you?' (trans. Murray 1995). In this way, the interference of the supernatural is justified since it fulfils a practical purpose.[14] The picture of the goddess holding a light to help in the difficult task of hiding the weapons in the palace of Odysseus has often been interpreted by modern scholars[15] and ancient commentators[16] alike as reducing her to a servant's role. Yet this seems to overlook a unique dramatic technique that convincingly offers justification for the presence of a lamp, the light of which was to have such a beneficial effect on the humans concerned. One the other hand, one should not forget the extensive involvement of light (as a concept) in the Homeric poems, especially in connection with the Homeric perception of the divine.[17] The lamp, the most sophisticated light-carrier with a long tradition before Homer (as will be shown in the discussion of the material evidence in I.2a), is only a medium through which divine radiance reaches humans. The gift of Athena's brightness is harnessed in a human artifact in a way which would have helped Odysseus and Telemakhos to visualise her presence more effectively. Her involvement in a servant's task, complemented by Eurykleia's question, stresses the practical side of holding a light and at the same time underlines the particular symbolism of the goddess's light.

The mention of a lamp in the hands of Athena should therefore be taken primarily as a vehicle symbolic of her favour and support. It is a feature through which the goddess operates and is successfully employed by the poet. No description of the lamp is given, which reinforces the importance of the *abstract* idea of light emanating from the goddess, rather than the *lamp* (as object) itself. However, its extraordinarily bright effect, implying the presence of the goddess, was considered by Homer as worth describing in the ensuing lines (*Od.* xix, 36-40): 'Father, surely this is a great marvel that my eyes behold; certainly the walls of the house and the lovely panels and the crossbeams of fir and the pillars that reach on high glow in my eyes as if with the light of blazing fire. Surely some god is within, one of those who hold broad heaven' (trans. Murray 1995). Clearly, in this particular scene, the object while familiar to the audience[18] fulfils a secondary role, since it is the light that serves as a divine sign and not the lamp. The presence of the lamp in this context would probably have helped the audience, familiar with the object from their everyday life, fully to visualise the imagery surrounding the goddess. The flooding light that illuminates every corner of the *megaron*, reaching up to the high timbers of the ceiling, certainly does not reflect the real lighting capability of a humble artifact belonging to the world of mortals.

The following discussion will examine the much disputed existence of lighting devices in the form of lamps in the 'real' world of humans in early Greece on the basis of surviving material evidence from Greek sanctuaries.

2. Lighting devices in early Greece

a. Eleventh to eighth century

The apparent lack of archaeological evidence for the use of lamps in the period following the destruction of the Mycenaean palaces has been attributed by scholars to various factors.[19] Some emphasise the single mention of a lamp by Homer in contrast with the abundance of references to other lighting devices,[20] namely torches, hearths and braziers, while others point out the absence of recognisable lamp-types (of the nozzled form) from sanctuary contexts of this period. Earlier interpretations attributed the absence of lamps of conventional types to extensive migration, poverty or decline of olive-tree cultivation.[21] However, on the basis of the archaeological record – as it currently stands – it is clear that such explanations are inadequate.[22] The analysis of flora from Mycenaean settlements that survived into the Early Iron Age, such as Nikhoria, Methana, Lefkandi and Iolkos, suggests that there was no dramatic change in the subsistence crops cultivated during the so-called 'Dark Ages'.[23] On the contrary, agrarian activities, especially those that did not require high levels of labour, appear quite widespread. Olive trees and their products which, according to the Linear B tablets from Pylos and Knossos, formed a considerable part of the agricultural economy of Mycenaean times,[24] did not decline. In fact, as far as can be detected from organic remains such as pollen, olive-stones or charcoal, it may have actually increased.[25]

Leaving aside for the moment the issue of the types of combustible material available during the 'Dark Ages', let us first consider the necessary form of the lamp itself. Two elements are essential for a lamp to serve its purpose: a fuel-container and a wick. These can assume a variety of forms as long as the basic function of the vessel is fulfilled. An example of a lamp consisting of a simple open clay container and a floating wick is recorded by Herodotus (ii, 62) from a purely ritual context;[26] its role was central to an ancient nocturnal feast called *lukhnokaïê* in the Egyptian town of Sais. This basic observation was the starting point for P.N. Ure and R.M. Burrows,[27] who denied that specific conventional vessel-forms (e.g. nozzled, open vessels) were necessary for a lighting function to be adduced. Accordingly, they accepted a function as lamps for a wider variety of open vessels, such as the *kothon*-vessels. Soon afterwards, other types of vessel (remote from the conventional nozzled form of later lamps) began to be considered by scholars as possible light-containers. For example, S. Benton[28] did not rule out a lamp-function for the ring-shaped vessels excavated at the sanctuary of Aetos on Ithaka, despite the remote resemblance of these vessels to the standard shape of lamps.

Although one need not agree with these interpretations in their entirety, it is clear that the shape of the earliest 'primitive' lamps shows direct influence from vessels such as saucers, bowls, and similar forms. In view of these considerations, nothing precludes an uninterrupted lighting function for the series of open, often crudely made containers, which have been unearthed in considerable numbers during excavations of both sanctuaries and settlements in Greece (e.g. Tiryns, Korinth, Perakhora, Troizen, Tegea, Rhodes).[29] These are mainly simple clay bowls or saucers, hand- or wheel-made, often with painted crossed or hatched ornaments on the interior and sometimes also on the exterior; in most cases, however, no decoration is noted. The wheel-made specimens are of a more advanced form, with a flat base and an incurved or flat rim to prevent the spilling of oil and often with one or two handles, for easier transport. Those modelled by hand have a simpler and cruder form without the technical improvements at the rim and base and in most cases they lack a handle. Their date ranges from the Bronze Age down to the fifth and fourth centuries, a period which coincides with that during which lamps of the conventional nozzled forms are absent from archaeological contexts. Traces of fire are not always a distinctive trait of these vessels, as a flame on a floating wick would not always reach the walls, though darkened surfaces are not missing altogether around the rim and occasionally deeper, inside the walls of the vase.[30] However, it must be emphasised that this type of vase almost certainly served a variety of other functions in addition to that of a lamp.[31]

Given the evidence for trade-links between Greek mainland and the East from at least the Early Iron Age and probably, on a more occasional basis, since the Bronze Age, it is not surprising that unbroken series of similar vessels are also found at several East Mediterranean sites;[32] the latter include Syria, Phoenicia, Egypt, Asia Minor and Cyprus. The basic form of vessels found in the East, to which a lighting function may be attributed, is an open, crudely made container which is occasionally furnished with a slightly pinched wick-rest; these vessels date from as early as the Late Bronze Age.[33] Alongside these simple lamp-types, more complex examples, comprising a clay, bowl-shaped light container, decorated with moulded female or animal heads (usually of bulls) are found from as early as the Late Bronze Age and continue through to the seventh century, though not in any large quantity. Sanctuaries which yielded such specimens include the temenos of Apollo at Dali and the sanctuary of Artemis at Kition on Cyprus.[34] Despite the apparent lack of any systematic attempt to locate simple, bowl-shaped lighting devices from this period on the Greek mainland, isolated instances of comparable vessels have been found, such as a probable example from a late Proto-Geometric child's tomb in Mycenae.[35] Recent excavations at Oropos yielded eighth- and seventh-century comparable examples,[36] while open, crudely formed and

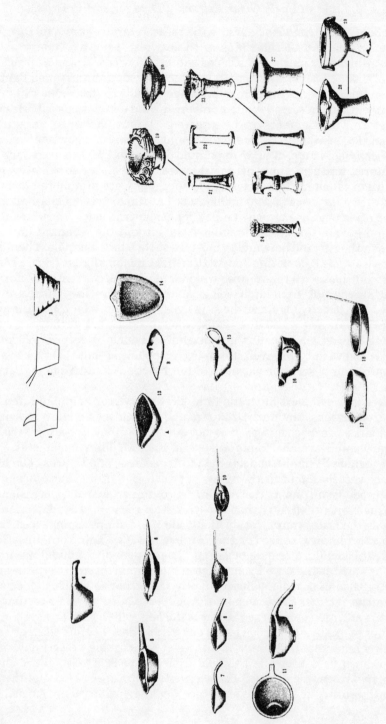

Fig. 1. Selection of Minoan and Mycenaean lamp-types.

unglazed specimens are known from Dreros and Arkades[37] on Krete, as well as Aigina[38] and Tiryns.[39]

The open lamp of the seventh century could well have been a successor to the portable Mycenaean type, such as the handled, spouted, shallow bowls[40] from Dendra or examples from the Athenian Akropolis in the form of conical spouted vases[41] which sometimes take the shape of kylikes (**Fig. 1**).[42] The seventh-century types furnished with first open and later bridged nozzles,[43] appear to be a natural development towards more practical and technically improved forms. This technical improvement may be observed on a series of marble and other stone lamps (dated to the seventh and sixth centuries) which have been found in different places around the Mediterranean, including the Greek mainland, Aegean islands and coast of Asia Minor, South Italy and Sicily (**Fig. 2**).[44] Their elaborate manufacture and sophisticated forms, which combine practicality and ornament, surely betray a long formative period of use and experiment. It seems unlikely that such works of art emerged out of complete ignorance of lighting technology in its basic form of a simple, open container, filled with oil and furnished with a floating, fibrous wick or a wick designed to rest on the walls of the vessel. Furthermore, the find-spots of most of these elaborate lamps imply their use in cult, since most of them come from sanctuaries and tombs; if this is true, it may then be a sign of a long religious tradition, comparable to that of the Minoan and Mycenaean lamp-series.[45] It appears that the negative archaeological argument for the absence of lighting devices in the form of lamps in the 'Dark Ages' is rooted partly in the expectation that there should have been a standard type with a distinct nozzle for the wick, and partly in the often summary treatment of minor objects from excavations.

The lamp as a possession of Athena in the *Odyssey* could well have belonged to that long archaeological tradition of lighing devices of a basic bowl-shaped form, the existence of which should therefore be assessed separately from the broader question of the historical background of the *Odyssey*.[46] In one form or another, the need for a source of light must surely have defined the type of the object destined to fulfil it, and this need does not appear to have ceased in the 'Dark Ages'. As a well known everyday utensil, Athena's lamp was employed by the poet primarily to add vividness and reality to a scene which would otherwise be too abstract and thus perhaps difficult for the audience to visualise. The light surely reflects the divine radiance of the goddess, which was expressed via a human artifact in everyday use at the time of the poem.

b. Seventh century

All kinds of lighting device increase considerably in sophistication during the seventh century. Despite the limited quantity of lighting material from Greek sanctuaries, the seventh century undoubtedly marks a transforma-

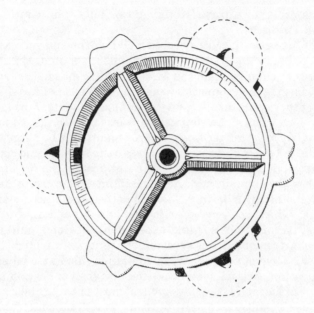

Fig. 2. Examples of archaic marble lamps.

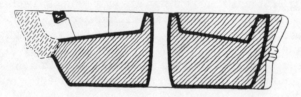

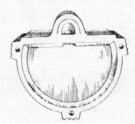

tion in the lighting practices, and more generally the level of investment, required for contact with the gods. It is now that the first recognisable lamps appear, furnished with a wick-rest in an open or bridged form, and often provided with a handle too, and this new, technically improved form is henceforth consistently associated with a lighting function. Costly materials such as bronze, marble and other kinds of stone begin to be used in the manufacture of light-carriers, which now assume more complex forms, since, apart from lamps, torch-holders and candelabra are also reported among finds from sanctuaries. The size of lighting devices often increases and sometimes they (especially stone-lamps) may bear elaborate decoration, such as human heads in the daedalic style (**Fig. 2**) and heads of animals such as rams, while floral decoration is more commonly found on metal candelabra. In the case of clay torch-holders, painted decoration and occasionally painted inscriptions (*dipinti*) may be added (notably examples of seventh- and early sixth-century date found at the sanctuary of Aetos on Ithaka) (**Fig. 3; Pl. 1**).[47]

The strata belonging to the earliest shrine of Demeter Malophoros at Selinous (the so-called 'first megaron') contained two semi-circular, marble, hanging lamps, decorated with daedalic heads. One of these lamps was found among other offerings at the northwest corner of the first megaron, probably very close to where it once hung. To these, a few smaller marble circular lamps should be added from the same sanctuary, but no details of their find-spots are given.[48] A late seventh-century clay imitation of a marble lamp was found in the earliest strata of the votive deposit of the sanctuary of Demeter at Predio Sola in Gela.[49] It is almost triangular

Fig. 3. Figurative decoration of 'torch-holder' from Ithaka (Vathi Museum 293).

in shape and bears rams' heads alternating with human heads on the sides. Traces of painted linear decoration are clearly visible on the exterior of the lamp, while the interior was glazed.[50] *Xoanon*-like clay figurines, over a hundred one-nozzled clay lamps mainly with central tubes, and Korinthian pottery were among the plentiful votives found in the lower stratum (1) of the votive deposit, which dates to the seventh and sixth centuries. Lamps were singled out by P. Orlandini as the most characteristic ex-voto of the Archaic deposit, with the earliest examples belonging to the so-called Syro-Phoenician type, open at the top and with a pinched-out rudimentary nozzle.[51] Clay one-nozzled lamps of seventh-century date are also noted among the finds from the votive deposits of the sanctuary of Demeter at Akragas.[52] The Thesmophorion at Bitalemi was a rich source of lamps which were found in nearly all strata of the excavation from as early as the end of the seventh century (trench 5). The context contains large quantities of hydriai, hydriskai, hydriaphoroi, kernoi, long series of pottery (e.g. Korinthian, local, Attic and East Greek), as well as metal objects and jewellery, and remains of sacrificial meals.[53]

Moving to the Greek mainland, we find a few marble lamps decorated with daedalic heads from the Athenian Akropolis that provide some of the earliest examples of Attic marble sculpture.[54] A date of around the end of the seventh and the first half of the sixth century must be assigned to a marble lamp decorated with lion-heads from Brauron.[55] From the Athenian Agora a number of seventh-century clay lamps with single, open, pinched out nozzles, flat bases and handles are identified by R. Howland as the earliest from the site (Type I).[56] Among their contexts (mainly wells), one is a votive deposit (H 17:4). More specifically, the main lamp-types contained in these deposits range from flat-based specimens with incurving rim and an open wick-rest to more developed types with bridged nozzle, and rare examples, such as a lamp of triangular shape bearing painted decoration of thin bands and schematic water-birds. The lighting material from the sanctuary of Demeter at Eleusis remains unpublished. A limited quantity of lamp-fragments[57] may be identified in the Eleusis deposits; these lamps are unglazed, with one open wick-rest and flat bases. In some examples, traces of burning may be observed on different parts of the side walls of the lamps as well as on their bases. Similarly, the rich lamp-finds from the sanctuary of Demeter and Kore on Akrokorinth await publication. Their presence is observed in virtually all areas of the sanctuary, with the earliest examples most probably dating to the late seventh century. This may be surmised by their discovery in some of the earliest pottery deposits, such as those associated with the building M-N:20-26 from the lower area of the dining rooms of the sanctuary.[58] The sanctuary of Hera at Tiryns yielded early clay, bowl-shaped handmade examples with open nozzles, probably of seventh-century date.[59] A few seventh-century pieces of the usual form for this period are among the votives from the Heraion at Perakhora.[60] Two examples of possible late seventh-century date come from the 'large circular pit' of the sanctuary of Poseidon at Isthmia.[61] Further examples are reported from the temple site of the Aphaia sanctuary on Aigina, while early lamp-types with open nozzles come from the sanctuary of Apollo on the same island.[62]

A plain, undecorated marble lamp was found during the excavations of the sanctuary at Hephaisteia on Lemnos,[63] while simple, unslipped one-nozzled lamps of seventh-century date are included in the rich votive deposits of the Temenos of Artemis Polô on Thasos. These latter were found together with female seated and standing figurines, local and imported (for example Attic and Korinthian) pottery as well as fragments of small bone and ivory objects dating from the seventh to the second quarter of the fifth century.[64] More early specimens are known from another sanctuary of a female deity, probably Artemis, at Sanê in Khalkidike, within mixed votive deposits which date between the seventh and the fourth century.[65]

An early Archaic clay lamp was reported to have stood on the *keraton*-altar of the temple of Artemis and Apollo at Dreros, Krete. Next to the lamp, small-scale images probably of the temple's patron deities were placed;[66] these are of *sphurêlaton* technique in bronze and dated as early as the mid-eighth century (**Fig. 4**).[67] The date of the lamp cannot be decided independently, since the material associated with it comprised four plain cups, along with bones and teeth of goats, sheep and pigs, which are even more difficult to date precisely. Although the cups were not discovered directly on the altar but 'under the slab in front of the bench and under the three little stones of the keraton',[68] their presence may also be explained in connection with the sacrifices that used to take place there. More single-nozzled clay lamps of simple type were found in front of the temple, according to the excavator, S. Marinatos.[69]

The excavations at the Samian Heraion yielded seventh-century clay lamps (which so far have not been fully published), while a circular marble lamp with central spike-hole and fragment of daedalic decoration also comes from the site (**Fig. 2**).[70] Such early marble lamps were found in other East Greek sites such as Miletos, Ephesos, Troy and Rhodes.[71] During the excavations of the sanctuary of Athena at Koukounaries on Paros, an archaic three-nozzled lamp is reported among the finds from the votive deposits which included more lamps along with a variety of pottery and small bronze finds dating from the Late Geometric period to the fourth century. However, no further specific information is given about the dates of the lamps.

The sanctuary of Demeter at Troy was another rich source of votive material, which contained clay lamps of diverse types, the earliest of which date to the seventh century.[72] Two seventh-century marble lamps came from the sixth-century Artemision (the so-called 'Croesus temple');[73] namely a circular lamp with a spike-hole and partitioned oil-chamber which was deposited in a hole in the southeastern part of the cella,

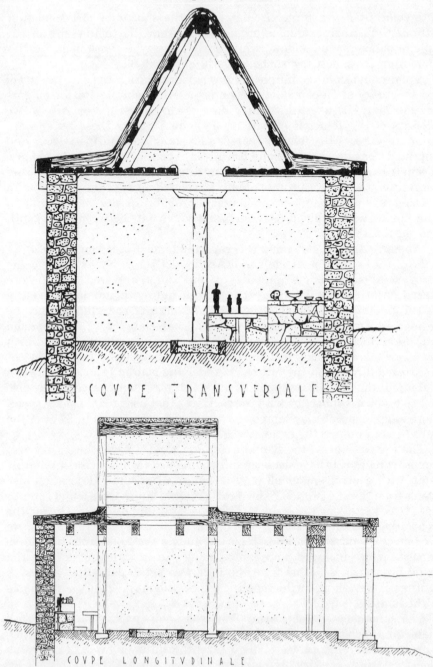

COVPE TRANSVERSALE

COVPE LONGITVDINALE

Fig. 4. Reconstruction of the interior arrangement of the cult room (including the keraton-altar) from Dreros on Krete (Marinatos).

together with another lamp of steatite which was discovered 'near the round marble one'.[74] Simple clay lamps, many with central tubes, are also reported from the Artemision as well as from the temple of Apollo at Ephesos.[75] A few more examples are known from the sanctuary of Athena at Smyrna around the end of the seventh century.[76] At Kyrene, the great abundance of clay lamps and their presence in virtually every sector of the extramural sanctuary of Demeter and Persephone are underlined by D. White.[77] Extending chronologically from the seventh to the fourth centuries, they are proof of the continuous cult activities in the sanctuary throughout this period. Among the earliest, a few stone lamps are mentioned. Finally, the archaic deposits of the sanctuary (probably of Demeter and Kore) at Tokra in Kyrenaika yielded a few seventh-century lamps of the 'cocked hat' type and the open 'pinched nozzle' type, with another dated early in the century bearing painted band-decoration on the rim.[78]

Bronze candelabra with floral decoration (most belonging to the so-called 'Cypriot' type) have been found in a number of sanctuary sites, such as Isthmia, Samos, Rhodes and Olympia (**Fig. 5**).[79] A clay lamp-stand in the form of a standing female holding a two-nozzled lamp on her head has been dated to the seventh century and is among the rare elaborate clay examples from this period. Examples of torch-holders are not absent from this period with a few elaborate clay pieces published from the sanctuary at Aetos on Ithaka. These specimens were meant to stand, since their hollow stem broadened towards the bottom and bore a handle and painted band decoration, while one example is inscribed with a *dipinto* recording the name of its local maker, 'Kallikleas' (**Pl. 1**).[80] Early archaic lamps and torch-holders have also been reported from Palaikastro on Krete;[81] here, the torch-holders were of a type designed to be carried, as may be inferred from the absence of base and handle and their long narrow stems, easy to grip.[82] Finally, we may note a rare example of a torch-holder in the form of a plank-like female,[83] although, unfortunately, this piece has no secure sanctuary provenance. The figure is probably a goddess and wears a short elaborate tunic and laced boots; the torch would have been fitted into her right hand, which is bent at the elbow, while a suspension hole at the top of the figure provides secure hints of how it once hung.

The variety of types and contexts of illumination devices reveals an extensive involvement of light in Greek cult from the seventh century onwards, despite the limited amount of published lighting material from sanctuaries. We may therefore suggest the need for a light – usually provided by a lamp – as temple-furniture inside the sacred building, probably to illuminate the cult-image.[84] Stone or clay lamps could have been suitable for such a function, especially the large-sized examples or those with a partitioned oil-chamber, since these features prolong the burning-time available to light the holy image. The marble lamps from the Akropolis may have served to illuminate the interior of cult-buildings,[85] while a distinct case may be made for the keraton-altar of Dreros where

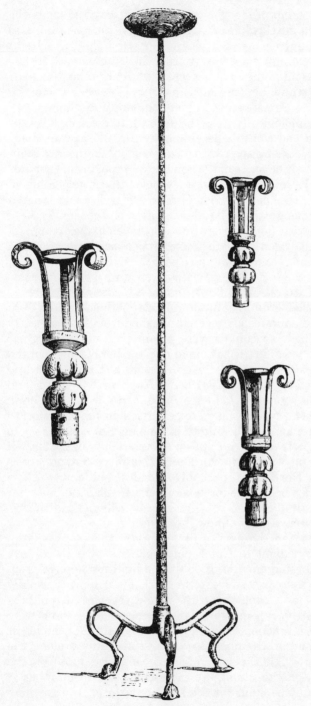

Fig. 5. Bronze lukhnoukhoi of the Cypriot type.

both lamp and holy images of the deities worshipped probably shared a common find-context (**Fig. 4**). The few lamps with central holes may also have served as temple furniture, possibly set on spike-supports which widened towards the base. The Cypriot clay hanging lamps and torch-holders (**Fig. 5**), where the lighting function is combined with moulded decoration at least from the Late Bronze Age, may have been possible sources of influence for the later seventh- and sixth-century East Greek marble and elaborate clay hanging examples with daedalic heads (**Fig. 2**).

A votive function for light in Greek sanctuaries is certain, but the object of dedication to the divine was apparently the bright effect rather than the container itself. This is emphasised by the fact that there seem to be no strict rules regarding the form of light-containers designed for such a function. At the same time, lamps and torches could have served as portable sources of light which were taken away from the sanctuary after their use in ritual. Evidence for most of these functions of light in Greek sanctuaries may be found in greater variety and quantity from the sixth century onwards, when the role of light in Greek cult becomes increasingly complex.

II

Keeping a Flame 'Alive'

1. The ever-burning Lamp in the temple
of Athena Polias

Pausanias offers explicit information regarding the significance attached to continuously burning flames in temples on the occasion of his visit to the Athenian Akropolis. In his description of the contents of the ancient temple of Athena Polias, he mentions for the first time an ever-burning lamp: 'But the holiest of all images which was universally recognised for many years before the Athenians came together out of their country towns, is Athene's statue on what is now the akropolis, though then it was the whole city. Rumour says it fell from heaven. Whether this is true or not, I shall not argue about it. Kallimakhos made a golden lamp for the goddess. They fill this lamp with oil, and then wait for the same day in the following year, and all that time the oil is enough to feed the lamp though it shines perpetually night and day. The wick in it is Karpasian flax, the only kind of flax fire will not consume' (Paus. i, 26.6-7: trans. Levi, 1971).

Pausanias goes further to single out certain striking features of the lamp and its setting: 'Over the lamp a bronze palm-tree climbs to the roof and draws up the smoke. In the shrine of Athene of the City is a wooden Hermes which they say was dedicated by Kekrops, invisible among myrtle branches. Some of the dedications are notable, among the antiques a folding stool by Daidalos and a piece of Persian spoils, the breastplate of Masistios, who commanded the cavalry at Plataia, and a Persian sword they say belonged to Mardonios' (Paus. i, 27.1: trans. Levi 1971).

This is the second literary reference, after Homer, to the goddess Athena as associated with a golden lamp. The temple of Athena Polias must have been a major draw for visitors in Pausanias' time, due to the marvellous items it housed. The first two objects (the ancient image of Athena[1] and the golden lamp) are clearly singled out by Pausanias, not least by of their place at the head of the long list of sacred contents from the temple, but also by the relatively extensive description they receive in comparison with the rest of the valuables kept in the temple. Pausanias' comments on the rest of the offerings are much more brief and general, and do not imply any further involvement of any of these votives in the cult of Athena. The cult statue and the lamp owed their significance to the extraordinary features they possessed, as Pausanias explains; these were, for the former, the tradition that it fell from heaven, and for the latter, that it burned incessantly and needed to be rekindled only once a year.

The peculiar ability of the holy lamp to sustain its flame for a whole year appears to have made a great impact on other authors too. Strabo refers to it as 'the ever burning lamp' (*Geographica* ix, 16),[2] while Plutarch calls it 'the sacred lamp', underlining the religious significance of its 'eternal' flame; he also recalls the impious events that once caused its extinction (*Sull.* xiii, 3-4; *Num.* ix, 5).[3] The fire-proof wick of the lamp, made of flax from Karpasos, ensured long burning. The place that gave the name to this type of material, known today as *amiantos* or *asbestos*, is situated in northeast Cyprus; however it was also grown in Greece, namely at Karystos on Euboia.[4] Strabo (*Geographica* x, 446) and Plutarch (*De def. or.* 43) referred to it as suitable for towels, nets and head-dresses, and emphasised that the fibres could not be burned by a fire but, whenever they were soiled, they could be cleansed again by being thrown in fire. The fuel of the lamp was oil which may possibly have derived, at least partly, from the olive tree of Athena on the Athenian Akropolis. Olive-wood was after all the material of the image of Athena Polias according to ancient tradition.[5] Although the existence of a (and perhaps more than one) sacred olive tree of Athena on the Akropolis is well attested in literature, its precise location in relation to the temple of Athena Polias has so far been a matter of speculation (rather than secure interpretation), due to the inconsistency of ancient accounts.[6] The consensus of opinion, however, points to the association of the tree with the Pandroseion, in the area just outside the west façade of the Erekhtheion.[7] Such an interpretation seems to be supported by the study of representations of the/a sacred tree of Athena in art, the earliest of which feature in the so-called 'Olive tree pediment' from the Akropolis (*c.* 560-550).[8] The possibility that more than one olive tree existed on the Akropolis, not least to cover ritual needs within the sanctuary including the filling of the lamp, cannot be ruled out. On the other hand, physical remains of such a tree in the vicinity of the Erekhtheion have not been securely identified. W. Dörpfeld's hypothesis that the asymmetrical plan of the Erekhtheion resulted from the presence of the olive tree cannot be proven, while equally unsafe (though attractive) appears to be the proposal of J.A. Bundgaard, who indicated extensive traces of a tree in several areas of the building, especially at its southwest corner.[9]

The question of the location of the golden 'ever-burning' lamp of Athena is part of the complex issue of the place of the votives in the cella of the Athena Polias shrine. The latter cannot be divorced from the broader debate about the location of the cults housed in the Erekhtheion. That the eastern part of the building was dedicated to Athena Polias has been the predominant trend in scholarly opinion, albeit for various reasons. These are chiefly based on architectural details and ancient accounts of visitors to the site.[10] The extended portico all along the east end of the building, its temple-like layout with an eastern entrance towards which the cult statue faced, and the presence of Athena's great altar to the east, all speak in favour of this interpretation. Moreover, the formula '*de*' in Pausanias' account (i, 27.1) when he comes to describe the Persian spoils strongly implies that the latter were simply the next pieces in importance to be noted in the same context, and did not form part of the votive material of any neighbouring shrine. A contrary theory considering the monumental north porch as the main entrance of the temple was put forward by J. Travlos in his attempt to trace the route of Pausanias based on the writer's account.[11] Later, R. Wycherley approached the matter in a similar way, following the steps of Pausanias and also taking into account the preserved foundations of the building northwest of the Erekhtheion, which was tentatively recognised as the residence of the Arrhephoroi.[12] Recently, N. Robertson has argued for the attribution of the western part of the temple to Athena, on the grounds of its larger size and architectural irregularities, in contrast to the conventional style of the eastern chamber.[13] Other interpretations visualise the cella as separated into three compartments,[14] each dedicated to a deity, while the opposite theory of a unified building with a double function (*oikêma* and *naos*) has also been suggested.[15]

Investigations of the architectural form of the Erekhtheion, and in particular its southwest corner, have encouraged the association of some architectural irregularities with the location of the lamp of Athena. The tapering of the west end of the south wall of the west compartment of the building, at a height above the door leading to the porch of Maidens, formed a niche with a platform at its base. This niche, according to research conducted in the course of the Akropolis' restoration programme, must have belonged to the original plan of the building. Its possible function has been variously interpreted, with reference to different aspects of the cult of Athena; as a perch for sacred owls, a place for the *xoanon*, a support for her olive tree (traces of which were seen by Bungaard outside the west wall) or a platform for her golden lamp with its bronze chimney.[16] The latest proposal, made by O. Palagia, takes into account the widespread practice of putting lamps in niches, a practice which however seems considerably later than the fifth century.[17] On the other hand, it cannot be ascertained whether Pausanias' mention of the lamp and palm should be understood as a digression from his tour of the temple of Athena Polias, as Palagia supposes in order to justify the presence of the lamp in the western compartment (which is traditionally taken as belonging to Poseidon).[18] The notion that the cult statue was in the cella of the Polias temple in the east compartment, yet the lamp and palm in the west, appears to be contradicted by Pausanias' account.[19] There is no reason to assume that he broke off from his regular tour of the temple to describe objects that merely attracted his attention regardless of their location.[20] Despite Pausanias' silence about the exact location of the votives in the temple (apart from a few vague indications), his account strongly implies that both statue and lamp belonged to the same cultic context honouring the deity whose worship occupied the only 'proper' temple in the Erekhtheion. Moreover, one wonders whether such a precious and holy object, destined to please and venerate the deity in the depths of her temple, would have to be exposed to common view by being placed next to the open southernmost intercolumniation of the west wall.[21] Further difficulties in visualising the palm tree in the niche result from the fact that the upper courses of the back wall are lost and thus no traces of any clamp cuttings survive.[22]

Most of the proposed reconstructions of the interior arrangement of the Erekhtheion appear to have been influenced by the order of description of the holy objects in the text of Pausanias (**Fig. 6a-b**). According to these reconstructions, the statue of the deity is usually placed in an *aduton* before the western wall of the east compartment, facing east. Specifically, it occupies the centre of the west wall so as to be immediately visible from the east entrance of the temple.[23] In Travlos' reconstruction (**Fig. 7**) the statue is placed at a corresponding position in the west compartment.[24] Robertson visualises the lamp beside the ancient image, with the bronze palm above it.[25] These reconstructions generally agree on the placing of the lamp in front of the cult-statue of the goddess (**Fig. 8**); the lamp may either be set on a stand or hang from the ceiling.[26] So, despite the overall diversity of these interpretations, they share a central idea that the lamp was placed in front of, or in any case close to, the xoanon. The lamp with its permanent features (fire-proof wick, palm-shaped chimney) together with the xoanon form an unbroken entity in Pausanias' description, which is distinct from that of the rest of the offerings.[27] Further evidence of the existence of a fire (*to pur*) inside an ancient shrine (*naos*) on the Akropolis is recorded in the archaic Hekatompedon inscription (*IG* I[3] 4B, ll. 6-12).[28] If the shrine mentioned in the inscription is identified with the ancient temple of Athena Polias on the Akropolis, which is a reasonable assumption, then the Hekatompedon inscription may be implying proximity of a fire to the cult-statue. This, according to the proposed dating of the inscription, most probably stood inside the shrine at least as early as the Late Archaic/Early Classical period (possibly between 508 and 480) and, in any case, before the dedication of golden lamp of Kallimakhos to the goddess.

Largely due to Pausanias' silence on the subject, scholars have generally been reluctant to attempt reconstructions of the form of Kallimakhos' lamp and its palm-shaped chimney. N.D. Papachatzis emphasised that the lamp was elaborate (*peritekhnos*), while J. Dell attempted a bold though doubtful reconstruction of a whole system of oil supply for the lamp.[29] The features of the lamp, such as the number of nozzles, its fuel capacity and the way it was displayed, appear to have been heavily dependent on the form of the palm that accompanied it. Proposed reconstructions of the

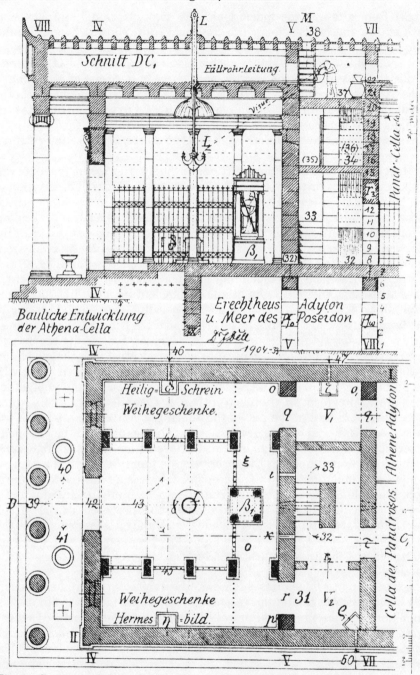

Fig. 6a. Section and ground plan of the eastern part of the Erekhtheion, according to Dell.

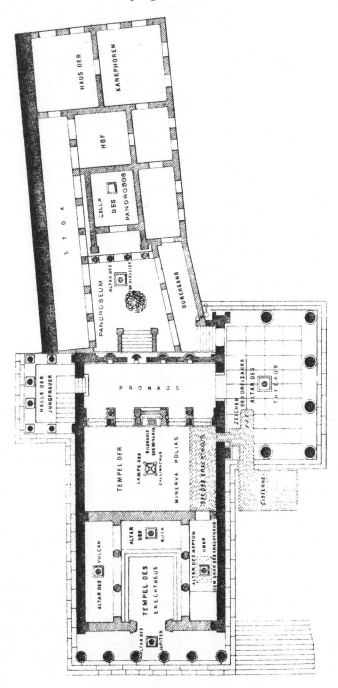

Fig. 6b. Ground plan of the Erekhtheion, according to Fergusson.

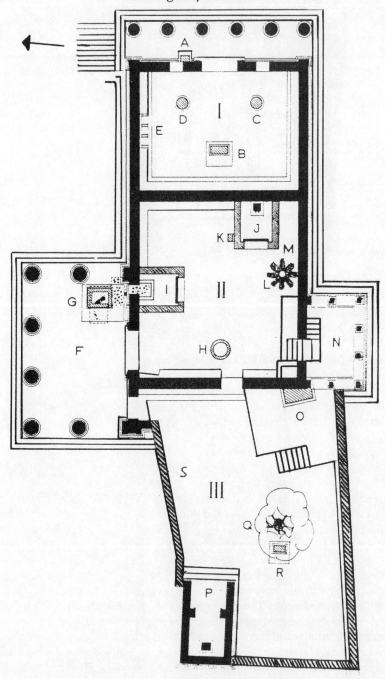

Fig. 7. Ground plan of the Erekhtheion, according to Travlos.

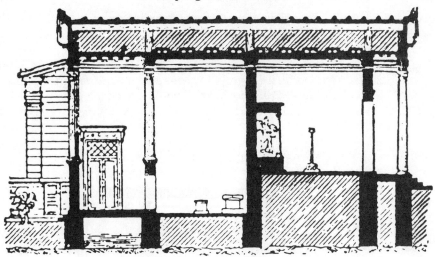

Fig. 8. Section of the eastern part of the Erekhtheion and reconstruction of its interior arrangement, according to Tsountas.

palm-shaped smoke-outlet of the lamp have often been based on Vitruvius' attribution of the invention of the Korinthian capital to Kallimakhos (*De arch.* iv, 1.9). The palm is often assumed to have had the form of a bronze candelabrum on which the lamp stood[30] or under which it hung.[31] Scholars have visualised it as a column in Korinthian style with acanthus leaves.[32] Alternatively, it has been reconstructed in the form of a simple bronze palm tree set on a round base behind the lamp in the niche at the southwest corner of the Erekhtheion.[33] Ancient accounts of votive palms at Delphi and on Delos have apparently influenced these reconstructions, as has archaeological evidence of bronze palms.[34]

In approaching the question of the form of the lamp and palm, one has to be aware of the great importance attached to them as indispensable elements of the ancient cult of Athens' patron goddess. The Athenians would undoubtedly have chosen an exceptional way to glorify Athena and their city and also to impress their enemies. Pausanias' account is very clear on this point: a bronze chimney in the shape of a palm tree reaching up the roof drew off the smoke of the lamp. According to his account, the lamp was set very closely underneath the palm-shaped chimney. The intensive burning of this lamp is suggested by the fact that it required a chimney for the smoke. The myth of its rekindling once a year may be used as an additional argument for its considerable size. The tube of a hollow palm tree trunk would have surely sufficed as a chimney for this purpose,[35] if it was fixed above the lamp. To avoid an awkwardly long tube, the lamp could have hung from the ceiling, on which the palm trunk, with the leaves on top, would have been secured by clamps. It is not possible to know the exact length of the trunk or how high up the lamp would have hung: it would have had to be adjusted according to the height of the cult statue, which probably stood before the west wall of the east compartment of the Erekhtheion. The leaves of the palm could have overhung the roof, so that the smoke could come out of their centre.[36] Everybody could thus have witnessed the undying flame merely by seeing smoke incessantly coming out of the visible 'mouth' of the bronze palm extending over the roof, without having to intrude into the holy space of the temple.[37] The latter seems to have remained in place until Pausanias' visit in the late second century CE.

The lasting popularity of hanging marble lamps on the Athenian Akropolis is archaeologically attested from as early as the seventh century. The relief decoration on some of the earliest examples of these lamps, consisting of human and animal heads, dates them among the earliest pieces of sculpture preserved from the Athenian Akropolis.[38] It seems logical to assume that the type of lamp made by Kallimakhos for the goddess could have not deviated dramatically from these early elaborate forms of lamps, furnished with provisions for hanging. Religious conservatism would undoubtedly have influenced later forms of artifacts which shared a similar function with the early lamps from the site. More than one nozzle is likely to have been required for the lamp of Kallimakhos to ensure prolonged burning. With regard to the decoration of the lamp, one may take into account its creator's reputation for meticulousness and passion for detail, not least among his critics (*katatêxitekhnos*).[39] One would then expect that the decoration of the lamp would have borne some general features of his style. Since it was hanging and therefore seen only from below, it would have borne carvings on its exterior. The position of the lamp in the temple of Athena Polias, and its circular shape as a multi-nozzled lamp furnished with a large fuel container, imply an extensive outer surface for decoration. Themes inspired by myths related to Athena are likely to have been depicted on it. One possibility is the Gorgoneion, which was a recurrent Attic subject encompassing both religious and political symbolism.[40] Representations of the full figure or only the head of the Gorgon Medusa are found repeatedly on a variety of artifacts from the Athenian Akropolis from as early as the seventh century.[41] For example, a bronze cut-out figure of a Gorgon found on the Akropolis (Athens, National Museum 13050, *c.* second quarter of the seventh century) has been interpreted by E. Touloupa as an akroterion of an early temple on the site.[42] The circular form of Gorgon's head, on the other hand, would have been particularly suitable as centrepiece of wider, mainly circular compositions, such as those that are likely to have been required for the decoration of the golden lamp of Athena. The use of a Gorgoneion as lamp-decoration is found again later, when it was copiously reproduced on the discus of Roman mouldmade lamps.[43] If this suggested reconstruction is valid, then the golden lamp of Athena by Kallimakhos would have resembled a unique late fifth-century example of a bronze hanging lamp with sixteen wicks from an Etruscan burial site to the west of the modern city of Cortona.[44] A Gorgoneion is set in the centre of the bowl-shaped oil-chamber of the Etruscan lamp forming the central decorative pattern which is only visible from below; around the Gorgon-head centrepiece a number of zones containing figurative decoration are arranged. These include a variety of themes such as wild animals attacking other animals, wave-patterns and dolphins, winged Sirens and flute-playing Silenoi. Information recorded in the inventory lists of the Erekhtheion seems to add more substance to our earlier hypothesis that the adornments of the golden lamp of Athena may have included a Gorgoneion.[45] In the lists, a golden Gorgoneion is mentioned which once decorated the aegis of the ancient statue of Athena. Although it is not possible to ascertain whether this piece of golden decoration was borne by the statue of the goddess at the time of the dedication of the golden lamp, the similarity of the material of the two artifacts and their common display context might suggest that the decoration of the lamp followed the earlier tradition of the Gorgoneion-emblem.

A further complex issue concerning Kallimakhos' lamp is the obscurity surrounding its commission and subsequent dedication to the goddess. The lack of direct evidence of this has encouraged plausible connections between the lamp's palm-shaped smoke outlet and the popularity of the palm as a votive offering, especially in sanctuaries of Apollo.[46] A famous dedication of a colossal bronze palm tree at Delos by Nikias in 417 (Plut. *Nic.* 3), the round base of which was found to the north of the Oikos of the Naxians in the Delian sanctuary, has led scholars to suggest that both palm and lamp in the temple of Polias were also been his dedications. While the involvement of Nikias in the dedication of the lamp and the palm to Athena is still a matter of debate, there is hardly any evidence to prove that both artifacts, lamp and palm, were offered to the goddess by the same person.[47] However, what cannot be ruled out is the possible 'involvement' of Apollonian symbolism in the conception of the palm-shaped chimney and its intimate connection with the extraordinary golden lamp of Athena. It is very likely that the bronze palm in the Erekhtheion bore direct reference to Apollo, the divine patron of the Delian League, before the latter moved to Athens in 454. From this point onwards, Athena's claim to the patronage of the League (which had rapidly been transformed into an Athenian empire) may have been recalled by the presence of her golden lamp close to the palm in her temple on the Akropolis. One may then argue that these two valuable dedications (lamp and palm) which also probably lay in proximity to each other within the temple of Athena Polias, may well have served as vehicles of Athenian imperial propaganda. The political message promoted through the peaceful and possibly symbolic 'co-operation' of the palm and the lamp surely aimed to legitimise Athens' leadership of the empire, especially during the second half of the century when this leadership was often exercised harshly over her 'allies'/subjects.

On the other hand, the dedication of such a valuable votive to Athena, furnished with the extraordinary capacity to sustain its light perpetually, was surely not a coincidence at that particular moment in Athenian history. The date of the golden lamp (based on evidence for the activity of Kallimakhos, roughly dated in the last quarter of the fifth century, and on the completion date of the Erekhtheion in the last decade of the century)[48] coincides with the restoration of democracy in Athens after the oligarchic coup of the Four Hundred. One of the major political aims during this short-lived period of revival of the democratic constitution was to stimulate public spirit – severely demoralised after the Sicilian disaster and continuous wars against revolting allies – by harking back to the 'good old days' of the empire under Perikles. An obvious way to restore the confidence of the public in their state and to reinforce their hope and courage would undoubtedly have been to glorify the city with new monuments and/or impressive dedications. Such a political project would have not only recalled the great building projects of Periklean Athens, but also visually expressed the promising new era of democracy which had just been restored to its former centre. The completion of the temple of Athena Polias and the dedication of the golden lamp to the patron goddess of the city were clearly part of this political plan, which also included small-scale re-building activity on the Akropolis.[49]

The decision to dedicate a valuable carrier of a perpetual flame to Athena on the Akropolis during a period when the city was striving to recover from war and political instability has wider political connotations. The concept of ever-burning fires in temples and in the heart of city centres – the focus of social, political and often religious activity – was common Greek practice.[50] Tending 'eternal' fires was a particularly important task, usually undertaken by temple priests. The incessant feeding of these fires to ensure their 'perpetual' burning in honour of some god was thought to secure divine favour, which manifested itself as prosperity and political stability at home and success in military operations. In this context, the offering of a perpetual flame to Athena at this particular point in Athens' history would have been entirely justified. Although it appears highly likely that some kind of predecessor of the perpetual fire harnessed in Kallimakhos' elaborate lamp existed on the Akropolis, no ancient testimony supports this speculation. However, references to the burning of the olive tree of Athena during the sack of Athens by the Persians in 480 show that a lamp could have existed there since a source of fuel existed from at least as early as the sixth century. It is tempting to explain the 'miracle' recorded in the sources of the rescue of Athena's olive tree from complete burning during the Persian sack and its subsequent re-growth the next day, as a reflection of a ritual need to preserve the sacred source of the perpetual flame on the Akropolis (Hdt. viii, 55; Paus. i, 27.2).[51]

The sacred lamp of Athena went out once for lack of fuel during the siege of Athens by Sulla in 86, according to Plutarch (*Sull.* xiii, 3-4), our only source for the incident.[52] Sulla's extensive plundering of the treasures of the city was a major disruption of the political and religious stability represented by the continuous burning of the city goddess's lamp. The violent extinguishing of the lamp coincided with the interruption of the lawful institutions of the city. The rarity of literary descriptions of similar unfortunate events of extinction of sacred fires or of letting them burn beyond control is the best 'proof' of the scale of the disturbance. For example, an unfortunate incident with particularly dramatic consequences resulted in the burning of the old temple of Hera at Argos. Thucydides interrupts his narration of military events of the summer of 423 to record this unusual, but apparently no less significant event, which was a result of negligence by the priestess Khryseis (iv, 133). The latter fled by night to Phlious for fear of punishment by the Argives, who immediately afterwards appointed another priestess in her place. The full story of how, while Khryseis slept, fire broke out in the temple of Hera when the wreaths lying near the 'perpetual' lamp of the goddess caught fire, was still being recounted when Pausanias visited the place in the second century CE (Paus. ii, 17.7).

Plutarch explains how a sacred, pure flame (*phlogan katharan kai amianton*) could be rekindled in an entirely natural way, with the aid of concave metallic mirrors placed opposite the sun (*Num.* ix, 5). The ritual annual re-kindling of the golden lamp of Athena is still a matter of dispute. L. Deubner's suggestion that the Kallynteria (in the month Thargelion) offered a suitable occasion for the refilling of the lamp has not been accepted by many later scholars, who prefer to include it in the Arrhephoria at the end of the Attic year.[53]

2. Sacred lights on the Athenian Akropolis

Lamps made of precious materials such as bronze and marble appear to have been popular dedications to Athena throughout the Archaic and Classical periods.[54] A bronze hanging lamp (inv. no. NM X7038) in the form of an Attic warship was found by K. Bötticher in 1862 inside the Erekhtheion, possibly close to its original location (**Fig. 9**). The excavator reports that it was found in the central chamber of the Erekhtheion close to the west transverse wall, while S. Pittakis and I. Roussopoulos spoke of a hole in that wall in which the lamp was carefully placed and buried by the Christians for the later generations.[55] The form of the lamp suggests direct links with the cult of Athena; more specifically, it may reflect the Panathenaic wheeled ship on the mast of which the newly woven peplos of Athena was displayed at the festival of the Great Panathenaia.[56] The association of the find with Athena is confirmed by the incised inscription across the hull of the ship which reads 'Hieron tês Athênas' (*IG* I³, 549bis), indicating that the lamp was a gift to the goddess. The date of the lamp remains questionable; the form of the ship could generally be assigned a much earlier date than the inscription it carries. With the exception of A.

Fig. 9. Bronze ship-shaped lamp from the Erekhtheion (inv. no. NM X7038).

de Ridder's suggestion of a date no later than the mid-fifth century,[57] the consensus of opinion points to a date around the end of the fifth century (*c*. 410-400) but no later than the the third century. A. Göttlicher believes that the shape of the ship may have been a copy of a sixth-century model,[58] but dates it to the fourth or even third century, while J.S. Morrison and R.T. Williams prefer to associate the date of the lamp with the period after the completion of the Erekhtheion in 406, and in any case with a fourth-century date.[59] The study of the letter-forms of the inscription is one of the main reasons for the chronologies proposed so far, since, as Morrison and Williams rightly pointed out, the vessel could well have been an earlier possession of the dedicator before it was inscribed as an offering to Athena in the late fifth or fourth century. Whether the lamp was ever actually in use within the temple of Athena Polias cannot be determined. Pausanias is silent about this particular offering, which was probably placed in the same temple with the golden lamp of Kallimakhos. However, in view of the earlier form of the vessel and its discovery inside the Erekhtheion and probably close to its original location, one cannot overlook the attractive possibility that it was used in the temple of Athena Polias before being replaced by the immeasurably more elaborate golden lamp of Kallimakhos at the end of the century.

The practice of dedicating costly lamps to the goddess on the Athenian Akropolis can be traced back to before the fifth century. Marble lamps bearing elaborate relief decoration of daedalic heads and heads of sacrificial animals began to be manufactured to serve as offerings to Athena on the Akropolis as early as the late seventh century (**Fig. 2**).[60] The earliest example in the series (Akropolis Museum, inv. no. 3869) is contemporary with the first marble sculpture from the site. The suspension holes and size of these lamps suggest that they were not made to be carried around, but more likely to form part of the furniture of sacred buildings on the Akropolis. The traces of burning on the nozzles indicate extensive use. Since their precise find-circumstances within the sanctuary on the Akropolis are missing, one can only speculate about their function. However, the presence and use of such elaborate lighting devices on the Akropolis from as early as the seventh century shows that the later golden lamp of Kallimakhos was a sophisticated development of a long tradition rather than a novelty. A further complex issue inevitably invoked by these valuable early dedications on the Athenian Acropolis pertains to the existence of a sacred building which housed these offerings. Whilst evidence of a first permanent cult building on the Akropolis cannot be firmly established in the seventh century (the date of the earliest marble lamp from the site),[61] nothing precludes the existence of a temporary wooden structure or just a shelter for the basic manifestations of the cult. These would have included an image of the deity worshipped (most probably Athena), a sacred flame contained in a marble lamp from the site (possibly the lamp of inv. no. 3869) and, perhaps, some valuable votives.

Some vague information about a sacred fire of some description in connection with cult-activity inside a sacred building on the Akropolis may be found in the archaic Hekatompedon inscription (*IG* I³ 4B).[62] More specifically, the inscription mentions a ban on lighting a fire while a certain ritual (possibly a sacrifice) is taking place within a cult-building, which should most probably be associated with the cult of Athena. The poor preservation of the text of the inscription does not allow any firm conclusions about the nature of the recipient deity of the ritual or about the specific occasion on which kindling fire within the shrine was prohibited. What is of importance here, however, is that the lighting of a fire seems to be intimately associated with, or indeed dependent on, a particular ritual activity inside a cult-building on the Akropolis. The prohibition on lighting 'the fire' does not encourage further associations with the practice of keeping an 'ever-burning' fire, at least of the type that is found later in the fifth century with Kallimakhos' golden lamp.

References to the association of Athena with a lamp, as a possession of the goddess kept in her temple on the Akropolis, may be found in texts that precede Pausanias.[63] In the *Batrakhomyomakhia* 178-83, Athena complains to her father about the mice, who, among other misdeeds, are accused of having drunk the oil of her lamp:[64] 'I would never go to help the Mice when they are hard pressed, for they have done me much mischief spoiling my garlands and lamps too, to get the oil. And this thing that they have done vexes my heart exceedingly; they have eaten holes in my sacred robe, which I wove painfully spinning a fine woof on a fine warp, and made it full of holes' (trans. Evelyn-White 1929). It seems no coincidence that a lamp is associated with the goddess in a context that includes items belonging to her ancient temple on the Akropolis, namely her wreaths and her peplos. In the Homeric poems both Athena and Erekhtheus are associated with a common temple in Athens (*Il.* ii, 546-51; *Od.* vii, 80-1), while in the *Iliad* (ll. 256-7), it is explicitly stated that Athena reared the child Erekhtheus, whom she then set down in her rich temple in Athens (*Il.* ii, 248).[65] It therefore seems likely that the cult of Erikhthonius was accommodated in the building where he was raised by Athena, namely her temple on the Akropolis. This image of the goddess rearing Erekhtheus appears to have had a long-lasting influence on later literature. Nonnus mentions more than once that Athena secrectly nursed the hero Erekhtheus (most probably meaning Erikhthonius) by the light of her lamp:[66] 'whom [Erekhtheus] Pallas once nursed at her breast, she the virgin enemy of wedlock, secrectly guarding him by the wakeful light of a lamp' (*Dion.* xxvii, 113-17: trans. Rouse 1940). The possibility that Nonnus' text reflects earlier literary tradition is not ruled out by A.S. Hollis, who suggests that the image of the goddess nursing the hero by lamplight may echo a scene from *Hekale* by Callimachus in the third century.[67]

A further possible reference to the lamp of Athena in connection with a sacred basket is made in a fragmentary text by Euphorion (*Coll. Alex.* fr. 9, ll. 3-8), dated to the third century.[68] Although the precise sequence of events in the passage eludes us due to its poor state of preservation, one reads that something that has to do with Athena falls during transportation. The breaking open of a sacred basket (*kistê*) takes place against some divine restriction, while a lamp (most probably that of Athena) is mentioned immediately before this event. The connection between the lamp and the basket is obscure. A relationship between the lamp and the contents of the basket carried by the Arrhephoroi has been suggested by W. Burkert,[69] who argued that the basket contained what was left after the annual purification of the lamp of the goddess on the Akropolis (namely, the remnants of the wick and the fuel), which took place before it was refilled. This is hypothetical but plausible, especially if we consider the secrecy in which the whole ritual was enveloped, since its rules prescribed that the girls were not allowed to look at the contents of the box which they were transporting.[70] According to Burkert's attractive line of thought, these remnants of wool (wick) and oil (fuel) might have been perceived as symbols of Hephaistos' miraculous and mysterious power that gave life to Erikhthonios.[71] This power was, and had to remain, unknown (at least up to that stage) to the young virgins during their service to the virgin goddess. The incident described by Euphorion may bear some distant allusion to the myth of the daughters of Kekrops and the tragic end to their duties as Arrhephoroi.[72]

Based on the hypothesis that the Kekropidai met their deaths as a result of their premature encounter with the mysterious 'power of Hephaistos' (which had taken the form of the remnants of the lamp of Athena), one may be able to explain why the 'ever-burning' fire in the Erekhtheion, like other 'perpetual' fires elsewhere in ancient Greece, used to be maintained not by virgins but by widows.[73] Because of the possible symbolic sexual connotations, the task of keeping a sacred fire alive had to be entrusted to women who had had sexual experience. By contrast, in both art and literature, young virgins tend to be more closely associated with the light of torches in a pre-nuptial context.[74] P. Brulé's suggestion that the Kekropidai took care of the lamp of the goddess as part of their service on the Akropolis seems unlikely, since the virginity of the girls would probably have disqualified them from this duty.[75]

A further interesting issue deriving from the long literary tradition which associated a lamp with the old temple of Athena on the Akropolis is the apparent contrast that this tradition creates with Athena's other major temple on the Akropolis, the Parthenon, which lacked such an elaborate lighting device. This discrepancy can be variously explained. The Parthenon was not the most ancient temple on the Akropolis, nor did it house the first wooden image of the goddess. The concept of an eternal flame particularly suits the character of old-established institutions,[76] such as the earliest form of Athena's cult on the Athenian Akropolis. That the lamp was an ancient feature intimately associated with the goddess in her first temple on the Akropolis is also reflected in literature, notably in the myth of Erikhthonios. From an architectural point of view, the Parthenon, as an expression of the city's glory, was planned from the beginning around the patroness goddess's extraordinary chryselephantine statue. The temple's architectural form, with a relatively wider cella, pi-shaped interior colonnade, two large windows and door, and eastern orientation, ensured that the image of the goddess received the right amount of natural light.[77] This plan reflects the broader 'humanised' concept of the divine in the spatial arrangement of fifth-century temple architecture; according to this concept, apart from better illumination, temples also received richer sculptural ornamentation and more sophisticated spatial arrangement.[78] In the case of the Erekhtheion, the three openings on the east wall of the east chamber[79] allowed less light to penetrate the interior in comparison to those of the west. This was an additional reason behind the earliest reconstructions, which placed the lamp in the east part of the temple.[80]

The Parthenon inventories dating from the period between 434-433 and 405-404 may provide further evidence for lighting needs on the Akropolis, in conjunction with archaeological finds. Two silver lamps weighing thirty-eight and twenty-two drachmas respectively are listed in the *pronaos* inventories among many other treasures mainly of gold and silver.[81] There were surely more uninventoried metal lamps, including bronze examples such as the two-nozzled piece (inv. no. 7045) found to the east of the Parthenon and dated before the middle of the fifth century.[82] Bronze lamp-stands have also been discovered during the excavations, although they are not mentioned in the inventories.[83] It is likely that those lamps were used exclusively in certain rituals and therefore stored in the temple or deposited in the area.[84] Their precious material and find-location strongly hint at such an interpretation. However, their context in the pronaos inventories among other valuable and possibly ritual objects, combined with the standard practice of melting down treasures kept in the temple, do not allow us to form any definite conclusion concerning their use. They may have been 'recyclable' sources not only of holy light, but also of financial support for the city in times of danger.[85]

3. Transferring sacred light: torch-races
(*lampadêdromiai*)

The torch-races that are known to us in some detail are mainly those which took place in Athens, notably those included in the programme of the Great Panathenaia and most probably also in the yearly Lesser Panathenaic festival.[86] The exact day of the Panathenaic torch-race in the programme of the athletic and ritual events of the festival is not yet securely known.[87] Equally obscure is the year in which this type of race was instituted as part of the Panathenaic festival.[88] The starting point of the Panathenaic torch-race is a matter of dispute among ancient authors with testimonies pointing to either the altar of Eros in the Akademy area or to any of the altars of Prometheus or Hephaistos within the Akademy.[88a] This was where the racers kindled their torches; from there, the torches were carried alight by the participants through the Agora, terminating at the Akropolis with a ceremonial kindling of fire on the altar of Athena Polias for the sacrifice (Paus. i, 30.1). Late fifth- and fourth-century Attic inscriptions illuminate aspects of the torch-races, such as their tribal organisation,[89] the participation of *ephêboi*[90] and the prize of hydriai (instead of amphorae) awarded to the winners.[91]

Torch-races formed part of other Athenian festivals such as the Hephaisteia, the Prometheia and the Bendideia, as well as religious celebrations in honour of Pan and Dionysos. The lampadedromia at the Hephaisteia was an annual event, tribally organised from at least as early as 421, the date of the basic document concerning the festival.[92] Earlier information is furnished by Herodotus (viii, 98), who compares the Persian messanger system with the relay torch-race at the Hephaisteia. Herodotus' testimony, along with a fourth-century inscription from Rhamnous recording the victory of the ephebes of tribe Erekhtheis during a torch-race, have been used by N.V. Sekunda to argue that the torch-race at the Hephaisteia must have been the earliest relay torch-race in Attica, practised before 335.[93] The Prometheia were also probably organised on an annual tribal basis and included a torch-race.[94] According to Pausanias (i, 30.2), the altar of Prometheus was the starting point of the lampadedromia in honour of Prometheus which ended at the Akademy.[95] A new type of relay torch-race on horseback was probably instituted in Athens in 429.[96] Plato offers the fullest reference to this race, which took place in the evening in honour of a goddess, probably Artemis Bendis (*Resp.* i, 328A). An early fourth-century votive relief from Piraeus, now in the British Museum (**1.23**), most probably celebrates a victory at a torch-race in her honour. Bendis is depicted in Thracian dress receiving a team of eight naked youths; at the head of the team stand two mature, bearded figures, clad in himatia (probably the gymnasiarchs of the team). Race torches, furnished with the distinct hand-shield, are held by the first of the naked youths and the first of the elder men. Further evidence of torch-races in honour of Bendis is provided by an inscribed fourth-century statue base from Kamariza in Attika, which records a dedication of Daos to Bendis after his victory in a torch-race.[97] Another torch-race was run in honour of Pan in Athens, as Herodotus attests (Hdt. vi, 105; Paus. viii, 54.6-7). This lampadedromia was closely connected with the appearance of the god to the Athenian courier Pheidippides, an event which prompted the Athenians to build a shrine to Pan under the Akropolis and to honour the god with a torch-race and sacrifices.[98] A possible vase-representation of the god Pan running with a burning torch in hand has been proposed by E. Simon; the god figures on the tondo of a black figure cup (**1.24**), painted in the manner of the Haimon Painter and dated to the early fifth century.[99]

A torch-race was probably held in honour of Nemesis at Rhamnous from at least as early as the second half of the fourth century. This is suggested by an ephebic dedication inscribed on a statue base found below the east retaining wall of the sanctuary of Nemesis on the north road leading to the citadel. The dedication was made by the gymnasiarchs and *sôphronistês* of tribe Erekhtheis on the occasion of the victory of their tribe at a torch race. The recipient goddess is not mentioned but should probably be understood as Nemesis, in view of the find-location of the dedication.[100] Two fragmentary votive reliefs from the sanctuary of Nemesis dating to around 330 represent processions of teams consisting of naked youths and elder figures dressed in himatia (**1.25-1.26**).[101] Race-torches with hand-shields are held by one of the two elder men on **1.25** and **1.26** while the naked ephebe who leads the procession of youths on **1.26** also carries a race-torch. The latter also wears a spiked crown, the typical headgear of Athenian lampadephoroi. The recipient deities of the procession of men and youths survive only on relief **1.26**, where two goddesses are depicted; they both stand and one of them leans against the other in a way suggestive of an intimate relationship between them and/or their cults. The identification of the goddesses has been a matter of debate, with the most plausible interpretation in favour of Nemesis and Themis, on the basis of the find-location of the relief and the cult-links of the goddesses within the sanctuary at Rhamnous.[102] A late fourth-century inscribed statue base found at the Kerameikos records a dedication of the victorious ephebes of tribe Aiantis and their sophronistes to the hero Mounykhos, whose cult was housed in the shrine of Artemis Mounukhia in Piraeus. The occasion of the dedication of the inscribed monument to the hero was a torch-race, the details of which are unknown.[103] There is some evidence for inclusion of torch-races in some festivals of Dionysos. Fifth-century representations of torch-racers on khoes (**1.27-1.31**, **1.36-1.39**) may possibly be taken as allusions to such a race during the Anthesteria, while Aristotle's later testimony for some kind of races which formed part of the celebrations at the Dionysia in Lenaeon is too vague to support a case for the inclusion of lampadedromiai in this festival (*Ath. Pol.* 57.1).[104]

Outside Attica, a limited group of fragmentary Korinthian red-figure vases (mainly bell-kraters and a skyphos), may provide evidence for a deity honoured by lampadedromiai in Korinth between the late fifth and the mid-fourth century.[105] Victorious processions of athletes are represented on **1.32**, **1.33** and **1.34**, with a Nike present on **1.32**, as may be inferred by the surviving tip of a wing in front of one of the athletes. The latter are naked or loosely draped in a himation, wear spiked head-dresses and are beardless and short-haired. Their torches have hand-guards, similar in type to their Attic counterparts, but of a cruder form. On **1.35** a youthful Dionysos is depicted with a kantharos and a thyrsos, together with a male bearded companion who dances holding a basket in his left, raised, hand and an extinguished, lowered, torch in his right. Both move to the right, while the god turns back to look at his companion. The reverse of the vase depicts two mantled youths, one of whom carries a torch with a hand-shield. The possible presence of a satyr on **1.33** (if the tip of his tail has been correctly identified) together with the combination of a Bacchic scene with the god himself and the race-torch-bearing youth on **1.32**, and the evidence of a possible cult of Dionysos in the Roman Sacred Spring,[106] are possible indications of a torch-race in honour of Dionysos in Korinth.[107]

J. Pouilloux suggested that lampadedromiai were performed in honour of Herakles on Thasos on the basis of a late fourth/early third-century funerary relief (**1.74**) and two fragmentary inscriptions from the area of the Herakleion.[108] The relief depicts a torch-racer advancing to the right holding a lighted torch in his raised right hand and a club in his left. Because of the position of the club which is used to support the figure, it was earlier interpreted as a staff of some sort. Pouilloux's reasonable suggestion that it is a club bears obvious associations with the iconography of Herakles. Yet, due to the extremely poor preservation of the epigraphical material, it is difficult to accept a regular inclusion of torch-races in the contests of the Herakleia.[109] Numismatic evidence from Amphipolis dating to the fourth century opens up the possibility that a torch-race might have been run there in honour of some god of that city. More specifically, a race-torch of the conventional form furnished with a saucer-shaped hand-shield across its stem figures on several series of tetradrachms and gold coins from the site; in some series the torch is encircled by a laurel wreath, but in most of them this is replaced by a square frame bearing the name of the people of Amphipolis (*'Amphipoliteôn'*).[110] The other side of the coins usually bears the head of Apollo, who, however, does not seem to have been the recipient deity of torch-races. The latter have been linked primarily with the cult of Artemis Tauropolos, who was also worshipped in Amphipolis.[111] Similar race-torches are as one of the main themes of coin-series from the Thracian Khersonesus, Korinth, Hermione, Hestiaea, Dardanus of Troas, Gargara and Rhodes.[112] Most of these are dated to the fourth century, but some go back to as early as the mid-fifth century. Third-century coins bearing representations of a race-torch are known from

Aptera and Kydonia on Krete,[113] but their relation with the local cults remains to be established, which is also the case with the rest of the coin-series bearing this theme. Torch-races are known to have taken place in Teos of Ionia, since the choregy of *lampadarkhia* is mentioned in a late fourth-century decree from the site.[114] Another torch-race appears to have been regularly included in the festival of the Bosporia at Buzantion from at least as early as the third century, according to a surviving inscription recording a dedication of a winner in that contest.[115] Lastly, one may mention two Attic votive reliefs (**1.72**, **1.73**) of the end of the fifth century, on which E. Mitropoulou has recognised Eileithyia and Artemis, and where Eileithyia holds a race-torch with hand-shield. In both scenes, the goddesses, dressed in long sleeveless khiton with overfold, receive women worshippers. It is rather unfortunate that the objects described as race-torches are not well preserved, and therefore their interpretation remains doubtful.[116] Apart from these isolated examples, there is no other evidence for possible torch-races associated with the cult of Artemis-Eileithyia.

a. The iconographical evidence

Attic representations of torch-races share a number of common features, regardless of the deity honoured by the events. Red-figure painters follow certain general iconographical principles in their treatment of the theme. The race-torch (*lampas*)[117] is one of the most distinct elements distinguishing the lampadedromia from any other race. It is short, consisting of multiple wooden stems bound together and set into a probably clay torch-holder (*lampadeion*). The latter is represented by the solid lower part of the race-torch, immediately below the hand-shield. A concave hand-shield was set almost midway along its length, ensuring secure transportation. The provision of a torch-holder with a hand-shield reduces slightly the thickness of the upper part of the torch, and thus facilitates a steady grip, especially at the moment of hand-over of the torch. The race-torch is in most cases depicted as being held upright in the outstretched left hand of the athletes. The spiked crown is the commonest head-dress worn by the racers, who are normally young, beardless, short-haired and naked.[118]

The earliest Attic representation of torch-races is the work of the Bowdoin Painter on a red-figure khous (**1.27**, *c.* 470), where a naked youth runs with a race-torch in hand. Similar simple compositions may be observed on later khoes, such as **1.31** of the late fifth century. Another early black-figure depiction of a torch-racer with two torches appears on a small sherd of a skyphos close to those of the Haimon Group (**1.40**, *c.* 450-400). Around 460, the Altamura Painter offers a unique representation of Dionysos in frontal view, bearded and crowned, clad in a long khiton and a himation with a thyrsos in hand (**1.28**; **Pl. 2**). He turns his head to the left, from where a group of silens run towards a fenced altar, holding race-torches. The silens are less than half the size of the god around whom they run.

From about 430, it is possible to distinguish a number of broad thematic groups within the iconography of torch-races. These range from the moment when the victorious athlete reaches the end (where he is crowned with a wreath or offered a white band by a Nike) and his participation in the sacrifice following the race, to scenes of the race itself, such as the moment of the hand-over of the race-torch between athletes or the depiction of simpler phases of the race (for example, running athletes with a torch). The few surviving representations of the preparation for the race may include athletes other than the torch-racers. Whilst a number of examples may, with some security (**1.1-1.19**), be attributed to the Panathenaic torch-races, the majority of the scenes (since inscriptions rarely accompany them) represent generic 'moments' of the race, widely applicable to a variety of festivals (**Pl. 3**).

The actual moment of the passing of the torch from one runner to another is depicted by the Painter of Louvre G 539 (**1.4**) as early as the last quarter of the fifth century; a nude runner with the torch in his left hand passes it to the right hand of the athlete in front of him, who turns back to receive it. Around the same time, this theme may be found on **1.29** (Painter of Munich 2335) and **1.41**, while in the early fourth century similar representations appear on **1.58**. Two athletes holding burning torches and running one behind the other are depicted on **1.45** (*c*. end of fifth century), while isolated running lampadephoroi repeatedly occur on a closely related group of early fourth-century small Panathenaic amphorae (the Bulas Group, **1.7-1.16**; **Pl. 3**). Another group of fourth-century Panathenaic amphorae depict a race-torch in the hand of a winged Nike figure mounted on the top of a column which flanks the figure of Athena (**1.67-1.71**).[119] The preparations for a torch-race are most probably depicted on **1.54** (Near the Budapest Group), **1.17** (the Jena Workshop; **Pl. 4**) and **1.53** around the end of the fifth and the beginning of the fourth century. A number of examples show simple scenes of a torch-racer, often with a wreath on his head; works of the Kraipale Painter (**1.42**) and the Painter of Ferrara T 782 (**1.51**) depict him standing next to a pillar, while on **1.44** and probably **1.43** (manner of the Codrus Painter) the pillar is omitted.

A work in the manner of the Peleus Painter around 430-420 (**1.1**) offers one of the fullest representations of the moment of the completion of the race by two victorious athletes who hold upright burning torches in their left hands. The end of the race is marked by a burning altar, next to which an elderly bearded man (wearing a richly embroidered sleeveless himation and a laurel wreath on his head) stands making a gesture of welcome the athletes. In front of the altar a hydria is placed probably as a reminder of the rewards of the contest, while a stylised tree behind the altar may perhaps be taken as a hint of the setting of the race on the Akropolis (one is tempted to link it with the olive tree of Athena). The end of the race is depicted on khous **1.30** (*c.* 430), where the finishing point is marked by a pillar. Around 420, Polion depicts a number of torch-racers running around/towards an altar (possibly of Hephaistos), where an elderly bearded man, probably the gymnasiarch of their tribe, awaits them (**1.21**). They are all naked youths with spiked head-dresses and six of them hold the characteristic race-torch with a hand-shield. This theme, with a few variations, including the addition of a Nike figure holding a fillet to garland the victor and the increase of the number of officials who watch the race, may be found on works by the Suessula Painter around 410-400 (**1.47**, **1.48**; **Fig. 10**), the Nikias Painter (**1.22**, and probably **1.46**, *c.* 410-400), and in simpler versions on Kertsch vases (**1.55**) and works of the Erbach Painter (**1.60**) and the Jena Painter (**1.63**) in the early fourth century. Khoes **1.38** and **1.39** (from the Jena Workshop and the Pourtalès Painter or his circle) bear similar scenes of the winners at an altar and their crowning by a Nike. She holds a wreath over an altar, to the right of which a torch-racer stands holding a torch in his left hand and a wreath in his right. To the left, a youth holding a strigil and aryballos watches the scene. Simpler scenes of a racer and a Nike appear on **1.56** (in the manner of the Jena Painter), **1.57**, **1.59** (by the Hare Hunt Painter), **1.61**, **1.62**, **1.65** (the Reverse Group of Ferrara T 463) and **1.66** in the early fourth century. The rewards of the race are sometimes depicted next to the altar, such as on **1.1**, **1.36** and **1.63**.

The Pothos Painter combined different phases of the torch-race on the surviving lower part of a stamnos from the Athenian Agora (**1.3** of *c.* 420-400). These included the handing over of the torch (*diadokhê*) between

Fig. 10. The end of a torch-race: victorious team and Nike. Aachen, Sürmondt-Ludwig Collection (Cat. no. 1.48). Suessula Painter, *c.* 410-400.

two naked racers, a victorious athlete completing the race with his foot visible on the stepped base of the altar, and the leading of a bull for sacrifice by a Nike. A tree is found here again as a topographical indication of the location of the race. The Kekrops Painter presented fuller versions of both subjects, with the handing over of the torch on the reverse side of a bell-krater dated around 425-400, and the bull sacrifice on its obverse side (1.2). On the scene of the sacrifice in which a wingless Nike also participates, the youths are short-haired and wear embroidered himatia loosely wrapped around their bodies. Their spiked crowns are still on their heads but their torches are of the usual long simple type, which lacks the hand-shield; this type of torch is probably included in the scene to indicate the place of the event within the festival activities. As may be inferred from other vase-representations of the sacrifice procession after the torch-race, the race-torches were probably dedicated to the goddess immediately after the victory and were kept somewhere in her temple, since they appear to be replaced by ordinary long torches in the subsequent scene of the sacrifice (1.2, 1.19 and 1.52).[120] Likewise, the kalyx-krater (1.18) in Athens depicts a naked, beardless athlete with a simple long torch; he sits on a hydria facing a Nike with a race-torch in her hand, while a third youth, wearing a short himation and hair-band, is the symmetrical counterpart of the torch-racer. However, neither the krater in Leipzig (1.5, c. 400-370) nor 1.64 (of similar date; Pl. 5) follow this general rule, but depict typical race-torches with hand-shields in the hands of athletes in the scene of the bull sacrifice. On 1.64, the wingless figure who leads the bull to sacrifice has been identified with the personification of the winning tribe and is assisted by a young naked figure, possibly Eros.

From the above review of (mainly Attic) torch-race representations, which range in date from about 430 to the late fourth century, the following shared features may be noted. The participants are shown as young, beardless, short-haired and well trained, as can be seen in the rendering of their anatomy and musculature. Their heroic nudity, or alternatively, the combination of a khlamys as the only garment with a spiked or simple hair-band, wreath, string of beads, shield, strigil and aryballos, reveals their ephebic status, which is also attested in literature.[121] Their representation is often accompanied by scenes taken from ephebic life, such as youths in long himatia conversing, and often leaning on a staff. Aristophanes (*Vesp.* 1202-3) stresses the youthful nature of the lampadephoroi ('*hoti neanikotaton*'), and epigraphical evidence indicates not only that ephebes were very often involved in torch-races but that they also bore torches as military escorts in processions within broader religious festivals.[122] Military contests and pyrrhic dances were combined with the torch-race at the Panathenaia, a procedure which resembles that of other predominantly ephebic (but later) festivals, such as the Theseia.[123]

The cost of torch-races was apparently high for those citizens who organised and sponsored them (*khorêgoi*). Aristotle recommends the abo-

lition of lampadarchy along with other liturgies, such as equipping choruses on the grounds that they are expensive but useless (*Pol.* v,
8.1309a14). Isaeus classes the gymnasiarchy for torch-races in the same
category with the trierarchy and the choregy for tragedy (*de Philoct.
Haeredit.* 60), while a speaker in Isaeus' *On Apollodorus* 36 boasts for his
gymnasiarchy at the Prometheia. A rough idea of the cash-sums received
by victorious torch-racers at the end of the fifth century can be gained from
the testimony of the speaker in Lysias xxi; he mentions that he received
1,200 drachmas as a prize for his victory at the torch-race of the
Prometheia. On the other hand, in Aeschylus' *Agamemnon* 312-14 it is
specified that not only the first, but also the last athlete of the victorious
tribe must be rewarded with a prize, since the race is tribally organised.
This is confirmed by an early fourth-century inscription which records
prizes received by the athletes of the Panathenaic games; here, each
athlete was to receive thirty drachmas and one hydria, while a sum of a
hundred drachmas and a bull would be given to the victorious tribe.[124]

The tribal organisation of the race permitted a considerable number of
young athletes to take part, who thus represented the future Athenian
citizens. The flame of the race-torch carried the traditional symbolism of
the ever-burning fires, which coincided with the aim of the contest.[125] The
inclusion of a lampadedromia in the major festival of the city gave it a
distinct religious 'flavour' until at least the late classical period.[126] This
type of race embodied values such as the well-being of the state, which was
entrusted to the new generation (the ephebes) who were expected to
sustain it respectfully and to perform to the standards of their predecessors. That is presumably why it was thought particularly shameful to
come last in this race, as is revealed by the abuse of those runners who did
so. Aristophanes relates an incident in which an athlete who came last at
the Panathenaic torch-race was beaten (*Ran.* 1086-7). Aristophanes' bitter
ridicule of his contemporary young Athenians who were physically too
unfit to run the race sounds like a criticism of possible inadequacies of the
new generation in other respects too, such as their services to the city.[127]
This line of thought corresponds with and reinforces an earlier interpretation of this passage of Aristophanes by N.V. Sekunda. He contended that
torch-races were a compulsory part of ephebic training by 405, when the
Ranae was performed, since the ridicule of the athletes who came last in
this race would otherwise have made little sense to the audience.[128]
Similar connotations of religious and political continuity are attached to
the ritual act of transferring holy fire from the mother-city to a colony[129]
and are confirmed by Plato's likening of the handing over of the race-torch
between athletes with the concept of the social and religious succession
between a mother-city and its colony, thus linking the colony with the
lawful political and religious institutions of the mother-city (*Leg.* vi, 776b):
'Therefore the married pair must leave their own houses to their parents
and the bride's relations, and act themselves as if they had gone off to a

colony, visiting and being visited in their home, begetting and rearing children, and so handing on life, like a torch, from one generation to another, and ever worshipping the gods as the laws direct' (trans. Bury 1926).[130]

III

Light in Rites of Passage

1. Birth

Fire and light are inextricably associated with the beginning of human existence in Greek literature and art. The transition of human beings from the womb into independent beings is metaphorically 'translated' in Greek literature into images of light and darkness. A long and at the same time miraculous course of preparation of every human life took place within the darkness of the female body. Darkness constitutes the essence of important mythical divine mothers, such as the Earth and the Night.[1] The belief that darkness preceded childbirth, in contrast to the light of the world of mortals, appears to have been widespread considering the abundance of literary references to childbirth as a passage from darkness to light. Being the first experience of human beings on earth, the light of day is the reward of this passage, which is therefore entrusted to divine hands. In the *Iliad* (xvi, 187-8; xix, 103-4, 118-19) the goddess Eileithyia – also called goddess of birth-pangs and labour – assists women in childbirth by bringing children safely to light. Invocations of Eileithyia are often found in Pindar (*Nem.* vii, 1-3; *Ol.* vi, 43-4; *Pae.* xii, 15; *Pyth.* iv, 111) who states that, without her help, people would have been able neither to see and appreciate light nor to understand the meaning of darkness (*Nem.* vii, 2-3: address to Eileithyia): 'Without you we behold neither light nor the darkness of night' (trans. Race 1997). Eileithyia's role during the birth of Apollo was vital in the myth; only when she arrived by the side of the god's mother, Leto, did Apollo spring forth into the light of day thus releasing the birth-pangs of Leto (*Homeric Hymn to Apollo* 119). This transition from darkness to light remains the predominant belief associated with childbirth in tragic drama. Further references to the darkness of the mother in which children grow may be found in Aeschylus (for example, *Sept.* 831), while the concept óf birth as a passage towards light may also be observed in works of Euripides (for example, *Phoen.* 1597).

In art, the torch is a common attribute of goddesses associated with birth. The cult statue of Eileithyia – the birth goddess par excellence – which was seen by Pausanias at Aigion in Akhaia held a torch in one hand (vii, 23.5-6):[2] 'At Aegium is an ancient sanctuary of Eileithyia, and her image is covered from head to foot with finely woven drapery; it is of wood

except the face, hands and feet which are of Pentelic marble. One hand is
stretched out right; the other holds up a torch … The image is a work of
Demophon the Messenian' (trans. Jones 1939). The type of torch carried
by the goddess is not specified. Hellenistic coins from Aigion, Bura, Tegea
and Argos may offer some hints for the reconstruction of the statue, or at
least of parts of it. They depict a statue of a female goddess with one or two
short torches in each hand, who may be identified with an image of
Eileithyia, as S. Pingiatoglou has suggested.[3]

On the other hand, Artemis in her capacity as *Lokhia* presided over
childbirth, during which she revealed her disposition towards women
according to their commitment to her. Death during childbirth was believed to be the work of Artemis, and therefore the clothes of women who
died in childbirth were dedicated to her.[4] Three late fourth- or early
third-century votive reliefs from Delphi (**2.10**),[5] Ekhinos (now in Lamia,
2.15)[6] and the sanctuary of Artemis Lokhia on Delos (**2.14**)[7] depict a
thanksgiving sacrifice to the goddess probably after the successful delivery
of a child. The goddess stands next to an altar facing the approaching
worshippers (**2.14, 2.15**). These are families with young children who hold
offerings for the goddess, together with a sacrificial victim. The torch of
Artemis is over life-size, like a sceptre, and is held in her right hand. The
relief from Ekhinos (**2.15; Fig. 11**) most probably depicts a statue of the
goddess holding in her right hand a long torch in front of her with its upper
part tilting forward, away from the image. The torch has a protective
shield against the dropping embers. The left arm of the goddess, wrapped

Fig. 11. Cult-image of torch-bearing goddess (probably Artemis Lokhia)
approached by worshippers. Lamia, Archaeological Museum AE 1041 (Cat. no.
2.15), *c.* 300.

in a thicker himation, rests, bent, on a pillar, while the top of her quiver emerges from behind her right shoulder. In the background, women's clothes are visible, probably hanging on the wall of the cella.[8] On **2.14** Artemis is simply *daïdophoros*, without weapons, and carries a torch – here without a protective shield – vertically, almost parallel to her body, along her right side. A family with four children lead a ram to the altar; the parents raise their right hands, bent at the elbows, as a thanksgiving or simply a greeting gesture to the goddess. The Delphi relief (**2.10**) omits the altar, but shares iconographical traits with **2.14**, notably the standing goddess with the long torch, receiving a family who brings offerings including a sheep for sacrifice. Next to Artemis, a second seated female deity with a child at her feet is here introduced into this scene, the kourotrophic connotations of which are enhanced by the presence of Hermes, Apollo with his lyre, and four goddesses seated at a table, one of whom holds a horn of plenty.[9] A Thessalian stele from Gonnoi (**2.13**) depicting Artemis *Euonumos* followed by a woman who holds an oinokhoe (probably the person who dedicated the stele to the goddess) possibly alludes to Artemis' capacity as protector of women at childbirth.[10] In this scene, Artemis walks to the right, carrying a life-size torch in her left hand, while next to her, on the same side, stands a female deer.

The fragmentary Delian reliefs **2.11** and **2.12** furnish evidence of another local goddess whose kourotrophic nature may be compared with a significant aspect of the iconography of Artemis.[11] In **2.12**, a female figure holds an over life-size burning torch with both hands in front of her and walks towards a temple, next to which a palm-tree grows. If the building is identified with the Letoön[12] there should be no doubt that the goddess depicted is Leto. Likewise on **2.11**, her identity is revealed by the tree-trunk upon which the torch-bearing goddess leans. The torch is of the same size as on the previous relief, but here it rests on the right shoulder of Leto who holds it loosely by its lower part.[13] Four deities are depicted on an early fourth-century marble relief from Miletos (**2.9**; **Pl. 6**).[14] These are epigraphically identified as Kourotrophos, Leto, Apollo and Artemis. An almost life-size burning torch is carried by the Kourotrophos obliquely across her body as her only attribute. Th. Hadzisteliou-Price suggested a possible identification of the Kourotrophos with the local deity Ino-Leukothea.

In attempting to interpret the significance of the torch in the hand of deities associated with birth, we must first turn to Pausanias' interpretation of the symbolic meaning of the torch of Eileithyia. This evidently echoes earlier perceptions of the power of the torch's flame, as depicted in literature and in art (vii, 23.6): 'One might conjecture that torches are an attribute of Eileithyia because the pangs of women are just like fire. The torches might also be explained by the fact that it is Eileithyia who brings children to light' (trans. Jones 1939). The first of his explanations, that the torch symbolises the pangs of women during childbirth that burn like fire, clearly alludes to the destructive power of the torch.[15] Its flame may become a painful means of punishment in divine hands, which metaphorically 'burns' women in childbirth, many of whom died. Artemis as birth-goddess also carries a torch[16] which is sometimes combined with her hunting weapons, underlining her capacity to deliver a painful death to women in childbirth. The second explanation of the torch, as a symbolic expression of the fact that Eileithyia brings children to light, was a deeply rooted belief which may be detected in literature as early as Homer and Pindar. S. Pingiatoglou sought ethnographical parallels to justify the presence of the torch in the hands of birth deities, and highlighted the significance of the flame as a means of protection for mother and child against evil spirits. This is surely true, considering the importance of the torch possibly as purifier, essential from the very first moment of the founding of a new household upon marriage[17] to the stages after childbirth, to eliminate the pollution of birth.[18] Other interpretations of the torch as a lunar symbol are not, I believe, primarily relevant to the cult of Eileithyia.[19]

W.D. Furley has successfully linked both interpretations of Pausanias with the myth of the birth of Dionysos.[20] Dionysos' mortal mother, Semele, experienced her pains of childbirth under the extraordinary light of Zeus' thunderbolt, which caused not only the premature birth of Dionysos but also her own death (*Bacch.* 1-3): 'I am Dionysus, son of Zeus. My mother was/ Semele, Cadmus' daughter. From her womb the fire/ Of a lightning-flash delivered me' (trans. Vellacott 1972). The image of the bringing of baby-Dionysos to light becomes more concrete and dramatic in Euripides' *Bacchae* (ll. 88-93). At the very moment of the springing of Dionysos from his mother's body, the moment of the sharpest pain for Semele, a celestial fire cleaves the sky in two: 'Once, on the womb that held him/ The fire-bolt flew from the hand of Zeus;/ And pains of child-birth bound his mother fast,/ And she cast him forth immediately,/ And under the lightning's lash relinquished life' (trans. Vellacott 1972). Amidst this divine blaze of light three contradictory events happened: the death of Semele, the miscarriage of the baby and the baby's salvation by his father, who then snatched him[21] and sewed him in his thigh (*Bacch.* 288-9). The mysteries of birth and termination of a life are closely bound up with this light from the beginning of Dionysos' existence, which henceforth became a permanent characteristic of the god. 'Light of Zeus' ('*Dios phôs*') reads a *dipinto* on a black-figure lekythos, which is also the name-vase of the Diosphos Painter (**2.1**, dated *c.* 500; **Pl. 7**). The inscription is set next to young Dionysos as he apparently springs from his father's thigh.[22] The scene is the earliest representation of the birth of Dionysos,[23] and the only one to show him as a child with torches in hand. Zeus is seated holding a sceptre and a thunderbolt, while Dionysos as a young boy stands on his knee holding two torches, one in each hand. Hera attends the birth standing before them.

The associations between the torches held by the child, the painted inscription and the presence of the birth-giving, light-god Zeus are obvious.

2. Nursing divine and mortal children

Once the newly born have seen the light of day, the next stage of their introduction to their new environment involves use of fire, as a supplement to water, for the first purification of the baby. The actual method of purging the impurities of birth is a bath in warm water.[24] A few possible representations of Greek and Etruscan origin are preserved depicting the bathing of small-scale figures which have been interpreted as children by N.M. Kontoleon, while in more recent studies they are connected with the magical practices of rejuvenation such as those employed by Medea for Pelias and then Jason.[25] In the surviving examples a small-scale figure stands in a cauldron set on a tripod, which is placed above a burning fire. The figure in the cauldron is assisted by adult figures who sit or stand flanking the central scene of the ritual 'bath'. A few days following the first bath of a new-born and probably on the fifth or the seventh day after birth, the ritual of *amphidromia* was performed, during which the father carried his baby at a run around the domestic hearth.[26] Whether this ritual was intended to bring the child into contact with the hearth, or whether we should see further symbolic connotations of purging the pollution from birth with the aid of the purificatory qualities of fire, cannot be ascertained from the evidence available.

On the other hand, 'baths' in fire aiming to immortalise children are not unknown in Greek mythology. The unsuccessful attempt of Demeter to turn baby Damophon (the child of King Keleus and Queen Metaneira) into a god at Eleusis by secretly immersing him in a hearth-fire at night is perhaps the best known example (*Hom. Hymn Dem.* 231-41). Similarly, Thetis brings baby Akhilles into contact with fire to test whether he is born a god or a mortal after his father, Peleus.[27] Athena's secret nursing of Erikhthonios by night in the light of her lamp[28] seems not to be too distant from myths which associate light and fire with the nursing of divine children, or with the transformation of mortal children into immortals. All these examples of divine nursing of children happen at night, the nursing deities are female (in two cases they are the natural mothers), and in the myths of Damophon and Akhilles a further common pattern may be observed: the act of secretly dipping the babies into fire is revealed to Metaneira and to Peleus respectively, the first of whom spies on Demeter from her room at night. Based on their mortal experiences of the destructive powers of fire, both Metaneira and Peleus try to stop this 'bath for immortalisation' by surprising the goddesses who perform it and by causing their anger. The immortalisation procedure is interrupted in an almost violent way as the goddesses express their wrath: both Demeter and Thetis leave the baby on the ground.

The long lasting memory of these myths of immortalisation of infants by fire may be found in later Greek and Roman literature. In a story related by Plutarch (*De Is. et Os.* 15-16), Isis on her way to Byblos in search of the body of her son Osiris, became the nurse of the child of the queen. She applied fire to the child to render him immortal but was stopped by the queen who was spying on her, and who thus put an end to the process of immortalisation. Identical versions of the story with names changed also appear in works of Hyginus, Lactanius Placidus and Servius.[29] A questionable representation of immortalisation of an infant or a child by torches may be found on a late fifth-century relief (now in Vienna), which was apparently re-used in the second century.[30] Two female deities bearing most of the iconographical traits of Demeter (seated) and Persephone (standing, two long torches in hand) appear to be involved in an activity which unfolds roughly in the middle of the composition. This activity is watched, or at least attended by, a male bearded figure who stands opposite the goddesses. One of the torches of Persephone is turned towards the ground, where scholars have suggested the presence of a child in a cradle.[31] However, the surface of the relief at this particular area is very poorly preserved, which increases the risk of attempting any interpretations of the action performed by the goddess.

In vase-painting, torches are introduced into the iconography of Dionysos in a number of scenes depicting his childhood. However, they do not appear to refer directly to any specific ritual from among those discussed, but are most probably more general allusions to the use of fire in the cult of the god from its early stages. This is reinforced by the presence of groups of dancing, torch-bearing maenads on the reverse side of vases depicting scenes from Dionysos' childhood. On an unattributed vase dating around 440 (**2.3**) baby Dionysos is held in the arms of a woman who approaches a temple-like structure, denoted by a Doric column. Another female with a lyre attends the scene, which is supplemented by a group of three torch-bearing dancing women, on the reverse of the vase. The Phiale Painter and painters from his circle showed a particular preference for this sort of scene with the baby Dionysos in the arms of a woman or a maenad. On **2.2**, little Dionysos is held by a maenad in a long garment (long khiton with sleeves and himation) and stretches out to another woman in the same outfit who holds a lyre in one hand, while extending the other hand in a gesture of welcome. A small group of women similarly dressed is depicted on the reverse of the vase; they hold a torch, a skyphos and an oinokhoe respectively. A similar combination of scenes is made by the same painter or a painter from his circle around 440, with the birth of Dionysos on the obverse and a torch-bearing maenad on its reverse (**2.4**).

Within an Eleusinian context, the infant or child Dionysos is commonly represented near Demeter next to whom his mother, Persephone – according to the orphic version of the myth[32] – holds two long torches. Thus, for example, the infant Dionysos is received by Hermes from a female figure on the reverse of the Hermitage pelike by the Eleusinian Painter (**2.6**; dated to *c.* 340-330).[33] Here, an ivy-clad cave is visible in the background, from which the child has probably been brought forth. Persephone is seated on a rock in the upper register looking down at the baby; two short parallel torches are positioned on either side of her body. A woman with a *tumpanon* stands next to Dionysos, while Zeus and Hera also attend the scene. On **2.5** (of *c.* 380)[34] the child Dionysos (identified by his dress – a short embroidered sleeveless khiton, topped by a spotted animal skin (nebris) and his Thracian boots) sits in the lap of Demeter. Next to them, Persephone stands with two long torches, looking at the child. Similar arrangements may be observed in red-figure representations of other divine and heroic children, notably Ploutos within an Eleusinian context. On both the fragmentary lid of a lekanis in Tübingen by the Painter of Athens 1472 (**2.7**, *c.* 340),[35] and the Stanford Graham pelike[36] (**2.8**, now lost), the child Ploutos is portrayed naked with a horn of plenty, near the seated Demeter and next to Persephone who carries two long torches.

3. Pre-nuptial rites

Representations on Attic pottery reveal extensive involvement of torches in rituals which marked girls' coming of age and their preparation for marriage. A kind of a ritual run which sometimes involved torches was performed by young girls in the sanctuaries of Artemis in Attika, as may be inferred by the surviving representations on several fragmentary black-figure krateriskoi from Attic shrines of the goddess.[37] The participants in these races were girls, called *arktoi* (little bears), who served the goddess in her sanctuaries in Attika until they come of age for marriage. The name 'arktos' reflects an element of animality which was attributed to them, springing from their 'untamed' virgin nature and their young age.[38] The scenes on the krateriskoi depicting females who run or dance with a burning torch in hand constitute only a small part of the total number of surviving representations of running girls on the krateriskoi. More specifically, running (or dancing) girls with torches appear on two krateriskoi from the sanctuary of Artemis at Brauron, two or possibly three fragments from the sanctuary of the goddess in Mounukhia and one fragment from the sanctuary of Artemis Aristoboulê in the Athenian Agora. All these examples date roughly to the first half of the fifth century.

The torch-bearing female runners move to the right and sometimes turn their heads to look back, as in the examples from Brauron[39] and the Athenian Agora.[40] A fast movement to the right is suggested by the direction towards which the torch-flame burns on the poorly preserved fragments of the krateriskoi from Mounukhia. The latter – which do not include more than the tip of a girl's torch with, in one example, a surviving part of the hand that held it – constitute our only evidence for the practice of these runs with torches in Mounukhia.[41] The location of this activity is vaguely indicated on one occasion; a schematic burning altar is depicted above a handle of an intact krateriskos from Brauron, towards which two naked *parthenoi* move.[42] Whether this altar may be taken as a hint of the sanctuary of Artemis (where the vase was found) is not possible to determine. Further observations on the outfit of torch-bearing arktoi shows that nudity was not a regular feature while performing their run (or dance). Short sleeveless khitons are also worn by the girls, as on the example from the Athenian Agora and a further, unusual one from Brauron.[43] The latter depicts a girl in a dark coloured, sleeveless khiton up to mid-thigh, tight at the waist and held together by means of white striations. Ch. Sourvinou-Inwood has plausibly suggested that the lower edge of the khiton might have been tucked into some sort of briefs underneath the clothes.[44] The absolute age of the parthenoi is a further riddle to solve solely on the basis of the visual evidence of the krateriskoi from sanctuaries of Artemis in Attika. According to the detailed study of Sourvinou-Inwood on the age-groups of the arktoi, as they appear in both Attic literature and art, nudity is the visual code of the older females, those who had reached puberty, while short khitons would be the dress of younger arktoi.[45] One could then claim – on the basis of the few surviving representations of female torch-bearers on the krateriskoi – that the age of the girls who performed these runs or dances with torches must have fluctuated from the older, naked arktoi to the younger parthenoi, dressed in short, sleeveless khitons. Consequently, it could be argued that these female 'athetics' involving torches were included in the programme of pre-nuptial rites or training of more than one age-group.

A further related issue pertains to the nature of these runs and their possible connection with races. The short solid torches of the girls on the krateriskoi contrast with those used in the conventional men's torch-races in Attica; the latter consisted of multiple wooden stems bound together and were furnished with a protective hand-shield.[46] However, a closer observation of the images of the girls' run allows us to see some traits shared with men's torch races.[47] One of them is the presence of ribbons (*taeniai*) hanging in the background, such as those depicted on fragment 546 from Brauron.[48] In the latter, the nudity of some female runners (highlighted in white colour) is an additional feature shared with male torch-racers.[49] If the altars towards which the girls appear to move on the krateriskoi are taken as indications of the end of their run, this would obviously indicate a further resemblance to lampadedromiai for males, the finishing points of which were often marked by altars.[50] However, despite these similarities, the poor preservation of the iconographical evidence of these female runs does not permit any conclusive statement as to whether they runs were races or not.[51] A further point which speaks against the interpretation of all the representations of the running girls on the krateriskoi as races is the presence of examples which do not appear to depict running females at all. Krateriskos fragment 915, discussed above, portrays a girl wearing an unusual type of short khiton, striated in its lower part. She moves to the right while turning her head to look back. Her step is short and elegant and does not resemble the extended, running pose of the other females on the krateriskoi. As L. Kahil suggested, her identification with a dancer appears much more likely than her connection with athletics or races.[52] T.F. Scanlon rightly dissociated the representations of torch-bearing, running females on the krateriskoi from men's torch-races and saw the torches of the girls as an indication of a night-time running ceremony in honour of Artemis *Purphoros* or *Phosphoros*.[53] The possibility that a sort of ritual run with torches took place in honour of Artemis (a goddess particularly linked with torchlight in Greek art and literature)[54] is undoubtedly high. This is reinforced by the observation that this ritual run does not appear to have formed part of the athletics of any particular age group of the arktoi, but was performed by both girls who had reached puberty (the naked ones) and those of younger age (wearing short, sleeveless khitons). That may be indicative of the importance attached to this ritual with the torches (the details of which unfortunately elude us), since it was so widely involved in the rituals of more than one age-group. The role of the torches is then rather be to define a ritual which differs from the rest of the races or runs depicted on the krateriskoi and to highlight the nature of the goddess honoured, who is traditionally linked with torchlight. Whether torches also funtioned as practical devices in the hands of the girls, to illuminate a nocturnal run, cannot be ascertained from the evidence available.

The images of these barely dressed or even naked parthenoi, engaged in strong physical movement in the open (not in the *oikos*), is certainly an unconventional way of representing 'respectable' females in fifth century Athens. However, the girls' young age and maidenhood, combined with the symbolic indication of the sacred space of Artemis within which they act (in the form of palm-trees and altars) and the sanctuary provenance (and probably use) of the surviving krateriskoi which depicted the girls' run, must have justified the unconventionalities of the girls' dress and outdoor activity. Furthermore, in the case of the torch-bearing females, the torch itself might have in some way 'legitimised' their unusual outfit and conduct by serving as an additional point of reference to their future respectable status as wives of Athenian citizens. Accordingly, the torches held by the girls on the krateriskoi should probably be interpreted in the context of their ritual preparation for wedding within the sanctuary of Artemis, and therefore should be seen as pre-images of the girls' nuptial torches. As will be seen in the ensuing discussion (III.4), torches were extensively used in all stages of the wedding ritual. Furthermore, a number of representations of torch-bearing females standing next to (**3.1, 3.8**), or moving towards altars (**3.4, 3.7**), next to (**3.1**), or out of (**3.3**) which palm-trees sometimes grow, also promote nuptial connotations. These examples combine the image of a girl in her pre-nuptial association with the realm of Artemis (indicated by the palm-trees) with that of an altar around which a considerable part of the wedding ritual took place.[55]

A rare scene of a torch-bearing seated goddess in a temple, a figure most probably to be identified with Artemis, is depicted on the body of a red-figure pyxis (**3.6**; **Pl. 8a-b**) by the Oppenheimer Group. The goddess holds a short burning torch in her left hand and is approached by a number of female worshippers (wearing long sleeved khitons and himatia which often cover one arm, and wreaths on their heads) who carry gifts for her, such as flower-wreaths, a necklace, a headband and a vessel resembling a skyphos. Artemis, wearing a hunting dress and holding a short torch, is shown in a work by the Achilles Painter (**3.5**; **Pl. 9**), where the standing goddess faces a young woman who is apparently loosening or even taking off her belt. This ritual act of the woman may be taken as a pre-nuptial offering to the goddess to ensure her favour before her marriage.[56] The presence of a torch as an attribute of the goddess is expected in a pre-nuptial context as an allusion to the next stage in events, the wedding, in the rituals of which it was extensively involved. Combined with Artemis' hunting equipment – which may be turned against animals and humans alike – the torch, as a symbol of destruction, also recalls the vengeful side of the goddess, which was particularly experienced by women in childbirth.[57]

4. The wedding

The wedding marked a transition of vital significance for the life of women, during which their transformation from *parthenoi* to *numphai* (brides) and then to *gunaikes* ('perfect' women) was accomplished. It was the bride's ritual passage from virginity to maturity, from the house of her childhood to her husband's home. Torches are one of the most distinctive features in literary descriptions of weddings. Homer refers to the nuptial torches held by the participants in the wedding scene which formed part of the decoration of the famous shield of Akhilles (*Il.* xviii, 491-3). Jokasta (Eur. *Phoen.* 344-6), Medea (Eur. *Med.* 1024-7) and Klytaimnestra (Eur. *IA* 733) refer to the happy duty of every mother of raising the wedding torch of her child. However, none of these tragic mothers was destined to enjoy this privilege, each for different reasons. The son of Jokasta, Polyneikes, married away from home, in exile, while for Klytaimnestra and Medea this honour vanishes for ever with the premature death of their children. Medea's lament before the murder of her children especially mentions the carrying of their nuptial torches, as a happiness that she would never experience: 'I shall go to another land as an exile before I have the enjoyment of you and see you happy, before I have tended to your baths and your wives and marriage beds and held the wedding torches aloft' (trans. Kovacs 1994).

The suggestion of Agamemnon that he should hold the torches for the fake marriage of his daughter Iphigeneia which formed part of the plot leading to her sacrifice (Eur. *IA* 733), alarms Klytaimnestra who feels that she would thus not perform her lawful duty as a mother. Klytaimnestra's spontaneous reaction does not merely reveal that a father carrying the nuptial torch would be too far distant from the norm. The carrying of nuptial torches here epitomises Klytaimnestra's customary rights as a mother, and her deprivation of these reflects the breaking of a moral code which foreshadows disaster: 'Against all custom! And you see/ nothing wrong in that? I think it right/ A mother give away her daughter' (*IA* 734, 736; trans. Grene & Lattimore 1959). The moral implications of the bride's mother's role as *daidoukhousa*[58] may also be observed in the words used in connection with it in tragic drama, such as *'prepei, nomos-phaul', kalon (esti)'* (*IA* 733, 734, 736) and *'nomimon en gamois'* (*Phoen.* 344). In Euripides' *Ion* 1474-7, Kreusa recalls with sadness that both nuptial torches and dances were absent from her marriage, which resulted in her bringing to light a child outside the conventions of the lawful weddings of her time. The word *nothon* (bastard child) used by Ion reflects a direct association between legitimacy and the performance of certain rituals, which in this case are the carrying of nuptial torches and the celebratory dances.[59] The tragic consequences of a mock-*daidoukhia*, not performed by the mother but instead by the bride herself, are evident in the case of Kassandra (Eur. *Tro.* 308-49). Hekuba hastily removes the torch from her daughter's hands and passes it to the women of Troy, since it is inappropriate for Kassandra to hold it in her maenadic state (*Tro.* 341, 349: *'bakkheuousa, mainas thoazous'*). The presence of one nuptial torch in Kassandra's hand instead of two – as is normally seen in both literary and artistic images of Greek weddings – might have aroused further doubts regarding the torches' appropriateness as a symbol of legitimate marriage in the hand of a maenad. However, apart from the number of the nuptial torches, particular importance appears to have been attached to the way in which they were held. Expressions such as *'anaskhêsei phloga'* (*IA* 732) *'aneche'* (*Tro.* 308) and *'anaskhêsein'* (*Med.* 1027) allude to the lifting of the nuptial torches, while Hekuba's words *'ou gar ortha purphoreis'* might also imply that Kassandra does not carry the torch straight.[60]

In addition to mothers, literary and visual images of weddings show that other people may sometimes carry torches. In Euripides' *Helen* (ll. 722-4), a messenger describes a scene from the nuptials of Helen and Menelaos in which he ran with a torch beside the chariot of the newly wed couple. Shortly before his narration, Menelaos and Helen happily recalled those who lifted the torches at their marriage (ll. 637-40).[61] Similarly, vase-representations of different phases of the wedding ritual, such as the procession to fetch water for the pre-nuptial bath, the bath itself, and the procession from the house of the bride to her new home, often include torch-bearing figures of minor importance (**3.24**, **3.33**, **3.36** and **3.37**). (**Pl. 10**) This brings us inevitably to the question of the actual function of torches during weddings, and more specifically urges us to consider the extent of their practicality for the illumination of a nocturnal ceremony. Although there is no specific information regarding the exact time of day when the various stages of the wedding took place, literary references to wedding nights (e.g. Eur. *IT* 203-5) may imply that the bridal procession and the rituals surrounding the arrival of the couple at their new home happened earlier on the same day (probably the second day of the wedding).[62] Some allusions to the time-sequence of events in a wedding may be found in the fragmentary poem *Partheneion,* a work of the Spartan poet Alcman, if one accepts its interpretation as a *diegertikon* song sung for the newly wed bride at the break of day, after the *epithalamia*[63] that were sung by the maiden-friends of the bride the evening before.[64] Alcman describes a nocturnal celebration of some sort that continues until dawn, in the course of which the Pleiades hold bright torches in the night (*Partheneion* 50-62). Under the light of torches, choral songs are sung for the shining beauty of Agido (*Partheneion* 39-40). A clear allusion to a first wedding night is found in Sappho's fragment LP 30 (ll. 1-5) where night-long singing is offered to the newly wed couple by maidens (parthenoi) who stay awake all night for this purpose. Another possible way to detect the relative time of events in a Greek wedding revolves around the mention of the 'evening star' (*Hesperos*) in Catullus 62, which is often interpreted as having originated from fragment LP 104 of Sappho. If the Sapphic fragment is part of a wedding song, one may then count it an an additional piece of evidence which speaks in favour of evening time as traditional time for weddings.[65]

If one takes into account that the symbolic integration of the bride at the altar of her new home would have taken place after the procession had arrived there, and most probably shortly before their night in the bridal chamber, it may be conjectured that the procession did not necessarily take place in the dark. In this case, torches were enhancing natural light which would probably not have completely gone during the procession. The ritual bath (during which torches were carried, often by more than one person) could have also happened the previous day, which was devoted to preparations, or even early on the second day, before the procession. Such a timing (which is indeed not contradicted by the more secure information about the order of events leading to the wedding night) allows torchlight to supplement the activities without being an indispensable source of illumination. On the other hand, we must not forget the contribution of torches to the happy atmosphere of a wedding, where their light was combined with songs and dances, which in any case 'painted' the predominant literary image for socially 'correct' weddings.[66]

Torches are introduced into the iconography of weddings as early as the second half of the sixth century and are normally held by female figures. These include the mother of the bride, the mother of the bridegroom, and goddesses such as Artemis and Hekate, while male or female participants in the wedding procession with one or two torches in hand are not unknown. A place is reserved for the mother- or goddess-daidoukhousa at the head of the wedding procession. The earliest representations of weddings in Attic black-figure painting include a female figure (possibly a goddess) who holds two short upright torches (**3.9, 3.11-3.20**) and forms part of a wider divine assembly which follows or/and surrounds a bridal chariot (**Pl. 11**). No secure identification is permitted for the daidoukhousa since she is rarely identified epigraphically.[67] However, on **3.11** and **3.20**, the daidoukhousa is followed by a doe, which certainly recalls the iconography of Artemis. The goddess is youthful and wears an elaborately embroidered long khiton and himation with a tainia on her hair, which falls to the shoulders in long curly locks. A four-horse chariot carrying the bridal couple moves to the right amid divinities who are arranged in procession before and behind it. Artemis in her role as daidoukhousa usually stands in the background, partly covered by the horses, and turns her head back towards the end of the procession to face Apollo, who moves to the right holding his lyre. Other divinities in these assemblies include Hermes (**3.9, 3.11, 3.12, 3.17** and **3.19**), who often heads the procession, and Dionysos (**3.9, 3.12, 3.16** and **3.17**).

Before looking at how the iconography of the bridal procession developed in red-figure vase-painting, it is useful to describe briefly the minor processions to fetch water for the pre-nuptial bath of the bride and the groom (**3.24, 3.25** and **3.39**). In these scenes there is generally no rule concerning the sex, age, dress or even the number of torch-bearers. Only **3.24** represents the moment of the bath of the groom, which is attended by female assistants, two of whom hold torches (the Leningrad Painter, *c.* 470; **Fig. 12** and **Pl. 10**). The latter are placed together at the end of the procession; the younger woman carries a short burning torch upright, and her apparently older companion has two long burning torches, one of which is held upright while the other is lowered to the ground. It is tempting to compare this clear up-and-down gesture with burning torches to similar movements performed during other 'rites of passage', such as the Eleusinian Mysteries. Although fire is indispensable for the practical

Fig. 12. Pre-nuptial bath procession including torch-bearing assistants. Warsaw, National Museum 142290 (Cat. no. 3.24). Leningrad Painter, *c.* 470. See also Pl. 10.

purposes of warming the water for the bath, we should not rule out the possibility that the purificatory qualities it shared with water might also have been recalled. The rest of our representations of the procession to the fountain to fetch water for the bride's bath include one to two torch-bearing females; their position in the procession varies, as does the number of their torches, which are usually short and held upright. The adornment of the bride is represented on **3.41** by the Washing Painter, where the torches are held by a woman in a peplos who stands behind the bride.

Red-figure representations of the main procession of the newly wed couple to their new home, mounted on, or about to mount, their chariot, survive among the works of the Peleus Painter (**3.35**), the Marlay Painter (**3.38**) and the Naples Painter (**3.33**), and on two unattributed vases of *c.* 430 (**3.34**) and *c.* 370-360 (**3.48**). The daidoukhousa (peplos or khiton and himation, two upright torches) may stand at the head of the procession close to (**3.35**), or before the chariot (**3.34**), while on **3.33** and **3.48** she follows it. Two young males with one torch each seem to have replaced the daidoukhousa on **3.38**, since they are positioned at the head and the back of the bridal cart. On **3.31** (unattributed, second half of the fifth century) a naked male youth leads the couple to the cart. Processions on foot, where the participants are arranged on either side of the couple, more regularly include daidoukhousai (for example, **3.23** by the Mykonos Painter, **3.27** by Hermonax, **3.30** by the Methyse Painter, **3.40**, **3.42-3.43**, **3.45** by the Washing Painter, **3.44** and **3.46** by the Painter of the Athens Wedding, **3.47**).[68] While the bridegroom is involved in the conventional action of leading the bride by her wrist (*kheir epi karpô*), one or more torch-bearing women shed light on the scene. Polygnotos (**3.36**) introduced two pairs of females each carrying a pair of torches who flank the couple in the centre. The busy wedding preparations which included music and torchlight may be observed on **3.46** by the Painter of the Athens Wedding, where this theme is combined with the bridal procession, headed by a daidoukhousa.

On arrival of the couple at their new home, the procession is welcomed by the bridegroom's mother who stands at the door of her home with two short torches. The Amasis Painter (**3.10**, *c.* 540) offers a unique representation of this moment, with the daidoukhousa arriving on foot at her daughter's new home, accompanied by the couple on a cart drawn by mules and the rest of the participants. The bridegroom's mother apparently moves towards the entrance of her house to meet the procession. A similar scene is depicted in red-figure **3.29** (the Amphitrite Painter, *c.* 460-450; **Pl. 12**), where, while one woman with two torches keeps her place by the door of a house to receive the arriving couple, a young woman with one torch (instead of two) comes last in the procession (instead of leading it as before). The arrival of the procession is combined with a scene of the leading of the bride to the bridal chamber (*thalamos*) on a black-figure pyxis (**3.21**, of *c.* 500) and in red-figure on **3.22** (by the Copenhagen Painter, *c.* 470) and **3.28** (by the Sabouroff Painter, *c.* 460). In a scene of the nuptials of Herakles and Hebe (**3.21**), a woman (perhaps the mother of the bride-groom) waits at the door of the chamber with two raised torches in hand; inside the thalamos, the bridal bed is being prepared by the Kharites. The two remaining examples (**3.22** and **3.28**) depict a similar torch-bearing female figure, probably the bridegroom's mother, just outside the bridal chamber. A peculiarity may be pointed out regarding the torch-bearing figure who receives the bridal procession at the entrance of the house on **3.22**, instead of a torch-bearing female, it is a bearded mature man dressed in a himation (Kheiron), who meets the approaching couple (Peleus and Thetis).

The integration of the bride in her new household is sealed with a ceremonial kindling of the altar of her new home with fire brought from the hearth of her childhood home.[69] This ritual is reflected on **3.26** by the Splanchnopt Painter *c.* 470-460, where two women, probably the mothers of the bride and bridegroom, each with two upright torches, are placed on either side of an altar (**Pl. 13**). Behind the altar, a sceptre-bearing woman, possibly the goddess of the hearth of the house, Hestia, stands looking in the direction of the couple.

5. The day after the wedding (*Epaulia*)

The use of torches continues after the wedding night, as may be inferred from Attic vase-representations of different aspects of the gift-bringing feast (*Epaulia*), which happened on the second day of a Greek wedding.[70] Some distinctive categories of vases bearing representations of gifts being offered to the new couple are loutrophoroi and lebetes gamikoi. Series of early fourth-century small-sized lebetes gamikoi as well as loutrophoroi come from sanctuaries of Artemis in Attica.[71] Regrettably, apart from the examples from Mounukhia, the rest have not yet received publication. Representations of the feast comprise torch-bearing females (often wear-ing a long khiton and himation) among other male or female figures, who hold baskets (kalathoi) such as on **3.52** (the Washing Painter, *c.* 420), alabastra or other vases such as on **3.51** (the Painter of London E 489, *c.* 450) and **3.53** (near the Painter of Athens 1454, *c.* 420) and, on the examples from Mounukhia, pigs or other sacrificial animals.[72] Torch-bearing females sharing common characteristics with flying victories (*Nikai*) often occupy the space under the handles of the vase, as on **3.49** and **3.50**, while on **3.54** (*c.* 420) a winged female with a torch and a ribbon lights the way for the couple as they hold hands, probably in their chamber. A crowded composition is preserved on a mid-fourth-century pyxis (**3.55**) where different stages of the wedding, such as the daidoukhia and the Epaulia, appear in a single common procession. At the Epaulia, a male youth holds an almost life-size torch among female participants.

6. Death and afterlife

a. The journey of Persephone to the underworld and its re-enactment by the initiates at Eleusis

The perception of death as darkness is a commonplace in Greek literature, with the earliest examples appearing in the *Iliad*. Night is described as *'nux'* (*Il.* v, 45; Eur. *Alk.* 269), while *'skotos'* (*Il.* vi, 11) covers the eyes of Phaestus and Akamas as they die on the battlefield in the *Iliad*. The dark bed of dead Agamemnon is mentioned by Orestes in the *Choephoroe* (l. 319) in relation to his attempts to avenge the murder of his father; this act would send a fair light of relief and cheer to the darkness where Agamemnon lies. On her way to death, Antigone looks at the sun for the last time in desperation (Soph. *Ant.* 809) and in her lament she mourns that she will no longer be able to see the light of day (l. 879). Similar is the lament of Iphigeneia as she unwillingly makes her way to sacrifice. In her last words she says farewell to the light of day (Eur. *IA* 1506), which earlier on she described as 'dayspring's splendour' (*IA* 1281). On the other hand, the living enjoy the light of day as an exclusive privilege (*Il.* xxiv, 558; Aesch. *Pers.* 299-301; Soph. *El.* 86).

Torchlight is one of the main components of literary and artistic images which depict the encounter of gods and mortals with death. As in the 'rites of passage' discussed so far, here too gods are not excluded from contact with the source of human mortality, even though they are rarely subjected to it. One of the earliest divine encounters with death in the myth is the symbolic death of Persephone, daughter of Demeter, after her 'abduction' by Hades, ruler of the underworld. During her day and night wanderings in search of her daughter, Demeter abstains from some of her divine habits such as the drinking of nectar and the eating of ambrosia; her 'mortal' feelings of grief and anger for the loss of her daughter are further expressed by her abstinence from activities essential to mortals, such as washing and sleeping, and by her silence and outer appearance, namely her untied hair (*Hom. Hymn Dem.* 40-4). To this image of the desperate mourning mother, burning torches are added. These are apparently indispensable to her since she carries them throughout her search, until the moment she discovers Persephone's fate:[73] 'For nine days then all over the earth mighty Demeter/ roamed about with bright torches in her hands,/ and in her sorrow never tasted ambrosia/ or nectar sweet to drink, and never bathed her skin' (*Hom. Hymn Dem.* 47-50; trans. Athanassakis 1976). The strong association of torches with the image of the mourning Demeter is later recalled by Diodorus Siculus (v, 4.3-4), who specifies that she kindled her torches on Aetna after a first unsuccessful period of search:[74] 'Demeter, being unable to find her daughter, kindled torches in the craters of Mount Aetna and visited many parts of the inhabited world' (trans. C.H. Oldfather 1939). Visual representations of mourning Demeter are limited. In vase-painting, the Kleophon Painter depicted the mourning goddess seated on the *agelastos petra* with a long torch in her left hand; in her missing right hand, she probably held a phiale into which the maiden standing next to her (labelled *'Parthenos'*) poured a libation (**4.13**). On the east frieze of the Parthenon, a long torch is the only object held by the seated goddess, replacing her sceptre (**4.42**). The torch leans loosely against her left elbow, while her right hand is brought to her chin in a symbolic gesture of mourning.

The searches and mourning of Demeter end with the appearance of Hekate, who consoles the goddess and accompanies her to Helios who knows the fate of Persephone. Hekate is described in the *Homeric Hymn to Demeter* as holding torches which shed bright light (*Hom. Hymn Dem.* 52-3): 'Hekate carrying a bright light in her hands, met her,/ and with loud voice spoke to her and told her the news' (trans. Athanassakis 1976). An early classical clay relief pinax from Lokri (**4.41**) alludes to the encounter of the two goddesses; the torch-bearing Hekate stands before a goddess seated on a rock, apparently Demeter, while the protomes of Helios and Eos may also be discerned in the scene. The specification of the early morning setting of the event (*Hom. Hymn Dem.* 51: 'But when the tenth light-bringing Dawn came') makes plain that the repeated mention of torches did not primarily allude to their function as lighting sources to illuminate a dark scene. After all, the natural light of the rays of Helios would surely have rendered torchlight useless. Torches may have only enhanced the early morning light. As 'theatrical' tools of the poet of the Hymn, the torches – combined with other 'mortal' characteristics of gods – are a reflection of the limited knowledge and vulnerability of gods, who, in this particular myth, can neither predict nor prevent death. After all, the role of fire in all forms as symbol foreshadowing destruction is pervasive in literature and art, as will be seen later (Chapter VI.4).

Representations on Attic pottery shed ample light on the nature and extent of the involvement of torches in the contact of the divine with death. Two burning torches are the main attribute of Hekate in the scenes where she attends and assists in the ascent of Persephone from the underworld. The Persephone Painter (**4.11**, *c.* 440; **Pl. 14**) offers one of the most secure representations of the theme, where the figures are epigraphically identified. Among them, Hekate (peplos, barefoot, hair in a bun) with a burning torch held upright in each hand faces Persephone who emerges from the ground. The scene is attended by Hermes (short khiton, cloak, boots, *petasos, kerukeion*) and Demeter, who stands further away from the *anodos*, close to Hekate. Hekate lights the passage of Persephone and at the same time seems to be advancing to the opposite direction, towards Demeter. The earliest black-figure representation of the theme occurs in the sixth century (**4.1**), while works of the the Berlin Painter (**4.3**, *c.* 490) and the Alkimachos Painter (**4.4**, *c.* 470; **Pl. 15**), together with two unattributed vases (**4.8**, *c.* 450 and **4.17**, *c.* late fifth century; **Pl. 16**)

demonstrate a continuing preference to include torch-bearing figures in
the representation of the myth of the anodos of Persephone. In sculpture
similar types of Hekate may have occurred. A running maiden wearing a
peplos and a hairband perhaps from a pediment in Eleusis (**4.39**; *c.*
485-480) has been successfully reconstructed with torches in her hands,
resembling the current fifth-century type of striding Hekate in scenes of
the anodos, with her head turned to the opposite direction.[75] A variation –
probably of no little significance – in the position of Hekate's torches in a
late fifth-century scene of the ascent of Persephone on a red-figure
lekythos should be pointed out (**4.17**; **Pl. 16**). This is a two-figure composition showing Persephone as she emerges from the earth, and a standing
Hekate (wearing a peplos) facing her and moving her torches up and down.
A stage shortly after the anodos of Persephone was chosen for depiction by
the Alkimachos Painter (**4.4**), who introduced a satyr into a scene where
Hermes leads Persephone by the hand. Hekate stands facing them at the
head of the procession, with two short torches held upright. She is most
probably represented here in her role as *propolos*[76] of Persephone, responsible for her reception and her journey to meet her mother, Demeter.

One long torch is held by Hekate in scenes of the abduction of
Persephone by Hades (**4.6**; **Pl. 25** by the Painter of Tarquinia 707, *c.*
460-450 and **4.15** by the Oionokles Painter, *c.* 440).[77] On **4.6** Hekate stands
behind the horses of the chariot of Persephone and Hades, looking towards
the couple. She holds a long torch obliquely, leaning on her left shoulder,
and carries a phiale on her head. Thirty years later on **4.15**, Hekate is
depicted following the cart of the couple at the head of which Hermes is
placed. Other participants in this fragmentary scene include a nude,
long-haired Eros holding a torch and a wreath in the background, and
another female figure behind the chariot, probably an Oceanid. The presence of Hermes in the same context as Hekate is well justified, since both
gods are connected with the liminal points between the two worlds,
guarding the passages between life and death.[78] This is further supported
by the place of Hekate's home in a cave in the Hymn (*Hom. Hymn Dem.*
25). The conspicuous place of torches in scenes of the ascent of Persephone
to the upper world undoubtedly suggests an evening time for the scene;
this is also enhanced by their often being tilted towards the emerging
goddess. This is reinforced by the association with night (well attested in
literature) of both Hekate (e.g. Eur. *Hel.* 569-70) and Hermes (e.g. Aesch.
Cho. 726-8).

The up-and-down gesture with torches performed by Hekate may be
found again in a scene within the same context depicting the anodos of Ge
(**4.30**, *c.* 360-350), represented as a female figure rising from the earth.
Here, it is apparently Persephone who admits her into the upper world
with torches in her hands, which she shakes in the same fashion. Similar
movements are executed by Demeter and other goddesses (such as Hekate)
in rituals connected with the prosperity of land (as will be discussed in

Fig. 13. Departure of Triptolemos attended by Demeter and a torch-bearing Persephone. Berlin, Staatliche Museen 2634 (Cat. no. 4.19). Kadmos Painter, late fifth century.

Chapter VIII; **Pl. 40**), by the female attendant of the pre-nuptial bath of the bridegroom on **3.24** (**Pl. 10**), and by Persephone in a possible representation of her touching an infant with a torch (discussed in Chapter III.2). Simpler compositions consisting of the seated or standing mother (Demeter) and the standing daughter (Persephone) often depict Persephone moving two torches up and down, as on **4.19** by the Kadmos Painter (**Fig. 13**; end of the fifth century), **4.16** by the Calliope Painter (*c.* 440-420), and a relief from Eleusis (**4.40**; *c.* 460). The posture of the two deities recalls the iconographical type of the 'seated master' and 'standing servant', which is often employed in representations of Demeter and Persephone in both sculpture and vase-painting.[79] G. Mylonas saw this up-and-down movement with torches as a respectful gesture which involved the lowering of one of the two torches by the goddess who bears them. This seems doubtful, however, particularly considering the variety of contexts in which it appears.[80] On the relief from Rheitoi (**4.43**, *c.* 421-420) Kore repeats this gesture with two long torches (one of which is almost vertical, leaning loosely against her left arm, the other lowered to the ground) as she stands frontally among other goddesses such as Athena, Demeter and Eleusis.

This up-and-down gesture with torches may further be observed in some of the few preserved representations of the Eleusinian Mysteries. The famous tablet (*pinax*) of Ninnion and **4.25** (both dated to the first half

of the fourth century; **Pl. 17**) depict a youthful long-haired male figure
(wearing a myrtle wreath, an elaborately embroidered knee-length khiton
and boots), traditionally identified with Iakkhos,[81] engaged in moving his
torches up and down while leading a procession of initiates. The latter are
dressed in the typical himation of the *mustai* (initiates), wear myrtle
wreaths on their heads and carry raised staffs (*bakkhoi*). On **4.21** and **4.31**
the initiates are the Dioskuroi mounted on their chariot and the reclining
Herakles. That Iakkhos' torches were not merely held still in an upright
position, but were shaken repeatedly at least at certain stages of the
procession from Athens to Eleusis, is also attested in literature. The verbs
'egeire' and *'tinassôn'* used by Aristophanes (*Ran.* 340) describe a vigorous
movement which Iakkhos executes with his torches. Finally, an identical
movement is performed by the mortal official of the Mysteries on a
fragmentary sixth-century black-figure loutrophoros from Eleusis (**4.2**;
Fig. 14); this is also our first secure representation of a *Daidoukhos*
(torch-bearer at the Mysteries).[82] He is bearded, dressed in a long sleeveless khiton with ornamented edge, and leads a procession of mustai,
including a man, a woman and a child. They wear long khitons and

Fig. 14. Daidoukhos (Torch-bearer) followed by Mustai (Initiates) in procession.
The Daidoukhos moves his torches up and down. Eleusis, Archaeological
Museum 1215 (Cat. no. 4.2). Black-figure loutrophoros, sixth century.

himation, have myrtle wreaths on their heads, and carry a raised bakkhos in their left hands.

It becomes clear that Hekate, Persephone, Iakkhos and the Daidoukhos execute the same gesture within a similar context, loaded with strong funerary connotations, especially considering that the procession of mustai to Eleusis was essentially a re-enactment of the wanderings of Demeter.[83] The literary image of mourning Demeter in search of her daughter, with torches in hand, may have indeed resembled in some aspects at least the processions of initiates at the Eleusinian Mysteries. Emotions such as fear, despair and grief must have been inspired in the mustai during their long nocturnal journey through public burial grounds, including the Kerameikos, on the night of the Mysteries.[84] These strong images of death which the initiates faced during their journey that night, a journey which is likened by later sources to death itself, combine well with Persephone's passage from the underworld to the world of the living.[85] In view of this, it is tempting to recognise a purificatory rite in this up-and-down gesture with torches, which might perhaps have been performed by the Daidoukhos during the actual procession of the mustai. The divinities who perform this rite in art are all well acquainted with death and may possibly make this gesture to repel its pollution.[86] Along with this symbolic movement of the torches, similar apotropaic connotations must probably be sought in the custom of *gephurismos,* the ritual insulting of the initiates during their crossing of the Kephisos bridge.[87]

Another scene of an anodos of a female sceptre-bearing figure in the presence of a frontally standing male with two long upright torches on either side may be seen on **4.10** by the Painter of Bologna 279 (*c.* 450-440). The figures are set among a group of dancing satyrs, some of whom hold hammers. The interpretation of the male as Eubouleus and the female as Persephone may not be ruled out, though other identifications of the figures are equally likely.[88] However, in the context of the Eleusinian anodos this scene is an unusual one since it lacks the solitary and mystic character of the anodos as when attended by Hekate and Hermes. The myrtle wreath on the head of Eubouleus and his raised torches, combined with the dance to the music of a flute-player, demonstrate a festive atmosphere appropriate for the arrival of Persephone. It is possible that an echo of the Orphic myth is detectable here,[89] and this is reinforced by the replacement of the typical deities for rites of passage – Hekate and Hermes – by Eubouleus. The torches are borne high in a gesture of joy and triumph after Persephone's successful journey to Hades, reflecting most probably a similar triumphant gesture performed by the initiates during the pannukhis of the Mysteries. This triumphal dimension of the torch in the hands of a male plausibly identified as Eubouleus may be further observed in scenes depicting the reunion of Mother (Demeter) and Daughter (Persephone) which he attends together with Hermes, Triptolemos and Dionysos on **4.22** (dated to *c.* 400-350). Here, elements from both the

Fig. 15. Array of Eleusinian divinities including torch-bearing figures. London, British Museum F 68 (Cat. no. 4.32). Pourtalès Painter, *c.* 350.

Homeric and Orphic traditions appear to be have been combined.[90] Young Eubouleus raises his two torches with joy, while, on the left, Hermes (identified by his petasos, kerukeion and sandals) watches the scene. The short, sleeveless khiton and boots of Eubouleus and the pose of Hermes (who leans against a pillar to rest) suggest that they may have arrived from a long journey for the recovery of Persephone. Similar connotations are evoked on **4.34** by the Eleusinian Painter (**Fig. 18** and **Pl. 18**),[91] where the same divinities have gathered, perhaps to celebrate the arrival of Kore. The latter is manifested by the torches of a young male – possibly Eubouleus – which still burn after the journey, as also by his boots and short khiton. In crowded compositions, Eubouleus' torches are reduced to one without any other significant alterations in his outfit. **4.32** by the Pourtalès Painter (**Fig. 15**) and **4.33** depict him among the rejoicing Eleusinian divinities after the return of Persephone (**4.33**) and at the welcoming of the Dioskouroi as initiates (**4.32**).[92] In the second scene, he shares both a similar outfit with Iakkhos as well as a corresponding position between gods and initiates. Their torches recall their leading role in the cult-practice of the Mysteries.

Eubouleus' torches justify his special association with Persephone, next to whom he is portrayed on **4.30** (mid-fourth century); the goddess Ge is received by Persephone as she emerges from the earth, while the figure commonly interpreted as Eubouleus walks away with his torches, turning to look back towards Persephone. In possible representations of the gloomy and solitary world of the dead on **4.7** and **4.9** by the Sabouroff Painter (*c*. 440)[93] and **4.12** by Polygnotos (**Pl. 19**), Eubouleus stands frontally between Theos (Hades) and Thea (Persephone) holding out his torches towards them. On **4.12** he looks at Persephone, perhaps alluding to his role of escorting her to her mother, while on **4.7** and **4.9** he seems to be addressing Hades but is about to move in the opposite direction towards Persephone. The way in which he holds the torches in his outstretched hands creates a visual effect implying the separation of the divine pair. At the same time, with his outstretched arms he keeps distance from the dead, while his torchfire may be taken as an agent which repels the pollution of the god of death. On **4.37** (*c*. 330-320) Eubouleus should be identified with the figure who stands next to the grieving, seated Thea; his short khiton, boots and double torch point to this long journey, underlining his significant role among the Eleusinian divinities in the composition.[94]

b. Light in the Eleusinian Mysteries

Persephone is the principal torch-bearing figure in scenes alluding to, or depicting the Eleusinian Mysteries. On the Ninnion pinax (**4.25**; dated to *c*. 370; **Pl. 17**), the female figure usually identified as Persephone walks towards a seated woman (possibly Demeter) dressed in an elaborate garment and holding a sceptre. Although the exact stage of the ritual and its place in the sequence of activities of the Mysteries are open to discussion,[95] this representation corresponds to literary descriptions of the procession of Iakkhos (*Ran*. 340-8).[96] The bright effect of the torches of both Persephone and Iakkhos (despite their different gestures) on the Ninnion pinax recall the bright images of a happy afterlife, promised to those who took part in the Mysteries (*Ran*. 456-9):[97] 'Oh, to us alone is given, when our earthly days are done,/ To gaze upon the splendour of a never-setting sun;/ For we saw the holy Mysteries and heard the god's behest,/ And were mindful of our duty both to kinsman and to guest' (trans. Barrett 1970). This promise of 'light' for the initiates of the Mysteries appears in the hands of Persephone, who is invoked as 'Mistress of fire' (Eur. *Phaethon* 268). Persephone holds torches when she appears in broader arrays of Eleusinian gods alone (such as on **4.23**, **4.29**, **4.31**, **4.33**, **4.36**, and **4.38**; **Pl. 20**), together with her mother (as on **4.44**, **4.45**, **4.47**, **4.52**, **4.54**, **4.28** and **4.24**), among mustai (**4.46**, **4.49-4.51**), and together with a torch-bearing Iakkhos (as on **4.20**, **4.23**, **4.31**, **4.36** and probably **4.53**; **Pl. 20**). Statues of Persephone and Iakkhos (including one of Demeter) are described by Pausanias (i, 2.4) as having once stood close together in a sanctuary of Demeter near the Pompeion by the Sacred Gate in Athens, at the place where public processions started.[98] This statue of Iakkhos with one torch in hand was brought to Eleusis in the nocturnal procession on the twentieth of Boedromion, a procession which started from this point. Iakkhos

(youthful, myrtle wreath on head, short elaborate khiton and boots) normally appears in art in connection with initiates, whom he often leads in
procession. His special relation to the initiates is revealed by his position
between the Dioskouroi on **4.31** by the Painter of Athens 1472, and his
address to them accompanied by a gesture on **4.32** by the Pourtalès
Painter (**Fig. 15**).⁹⁹ His torch rests upright on the ground and is held
loosely (for example in **4.18**), primarily as an attribute alluding to his role
in the Eleusinian ritual. It is the same size as the sceptre of the seated
Demeter next to whom he stands on **4.37** (**Fig. 19**). The interplay between
torch and sceptre is a common feature in representations of Eleusinian
divinities, and on **4.37** it is combined with pairs of seated and standing
figures, underlining the role of each one in the cult. A scene of the ritual
purification of Herakles performed by Iakkhos with his torches may
perhaps be observed on **4.5** by the Painter of the Yale Lekythos (**Pl. 21**) and
will be discussed in Chapter IV.1.

A mortal version of the procession of Iakkhos is found on a work by a
painter in the Group of Polygnotos (**4.14**), where the Eleusinian official
who acted as Torch-bearer at the Mysteries (Daidoukhos) leads a procession of mustai. The Daidoukhos shares iconographical traits with Iakkhos
with the exception that his beard alludes to his mature age. He has long
hair adorned with a hairband and wears a mid-calf length sleeveless
khiton, topped by an elaborately embroidered garment. He is barefoot and
raises his torches upright triumphantly, perhaps suggesting a later stage
in the procession when the passage from death to life had been successfully
accomplished.¹⁰⁰

The accounts of Aristophanes (*Ran.* 310-14, 326-33, 342, 440-7), Sophocles (*OC* 1048-58) and Euripides (*Ion* 1075-7) leave no doubt that torches
were held by the participants during the actual nocturnal celebrations at
the Mysteries. Images such as a brightly blazing meadow (*Ran.* 342), a
torch-lit coast (*OC* 1048), a mystic brightness ('*pheggos*') in the night (*Ran.*
447) and the strong smell ('*aura mustikotatê*') of burning torches (*Ran.*
314) are intimately connected in the sources with the procession of Iakkhos
and the subsequent pannukhis.¹⁰¹ The recurrence of the word *pheggos*
(*Ran.* 344, 447, 454) for the light of torches instead of merely *phôs* confirms
the special ritual significance of their light, over and above its indisputable
practical necessity in the nocturnal ceremonies.¹⁰² Brightness, which in
the context of the Mysteries is the effect of torchlight, is clearly associated
with the initiates' happiness in the afterlife. Torchlight is therefore comparable to the light of the sun which can be enjoyed only by those who have
experienced initiation, in contrast to the darkness ('*skotos kai borboros*',
Ran. 273) that envelops those who did not taste this experience¹⁰³ (*Ran.*
454-9).

This relationship between happiness and brightness was effectively
reflected in the torch-dances at Eleusis, which were accompanied by songs
and the music of flutes (*Ran.* 154), as well as the clapping of hands (*Ran.*

157).[104] A certain kind of ritual dance with torches was included in the procession of Iakkhos, as can be detected from various passages from the *Ranae*. The chorus' invitation to Iakkhos to come and dance with the worshippers in the *Ranae* is maybe the most conspicuous example (ll. 326-33): 'Come, Iacchos, leave your temple,/ Join your celebrants devout!/ Come and dance across the meadows,/ Lead us in the mystic rout!' (trans. Barrett 1970). Reference is made to the dances of the initiates on their way to the Thriasian plain (*Ran.* 448-9): 'Dance on then merrily through the flowery grove;/ let all that have part in our festival tread the sacred precinct of the Goddess' (trans. Barrett 1970).[105] The mention of flutes (*Ran.* 312) in connection with torches, as well as the allusions to the dancing movements of the aged participants (*Ran.* 342) and of Iakkhos himself (*Ran.* 345), leave no doubt that dances were performed also during the actual procession of the Mysteries. Despite the silence of the sources about the kind of dances which accompanied the procession of Iakkhos, Attic red-figure vase representations provide considerable help.

As noted,[106] the up-and-down gesture with the torches performed by Iakkhos at the head of the procession of his mythical initiates indicates a likely ritual dancing movement that was imitated by his followers, at least during the passage through burial grounds. There, the apotropaic and cleansing powers of the brightness and warmth of the torches, supplemented by the specific movements of this ritual dance, would have been particularly effective against *miasma* from the world of the dead with which cemeteries were associated. Apotropaic connotations may be ascribed to the use of obscene language (*aiskhrologia*) and behaviour during the crossing of the Kephisos bridge (*gephurismos*), where another sort of dance with torches must have been performed. The obscene character of these torch-dances may have involved display of the genitalia of those performing it,[107] an act reminiscent of the mythical episode of Iambe in the Hymn, who thus entertained the mourning Demeter (*Hom. Hymn Dem.* 203).[108]

On the arrival of the *pompê* at Eleusis (on the evening of the twentieth of Boedromion), the scene changes to one of blissful joy, with night-long songs and dances of young maidens around the Kallikhoron well. The brightness of the torches creates the principal visual effect of the festivities of the pannukhis. Their use in the female circular[109] dances in honour of the goddesses is attested by Aristophanes (*Ran.* 440-7) and Euripides (*Ion* 1075). The latter treats torches as if they were actual eye-witnesses of the ceremonies around the Kallikhoron well, who stayed awake together with the participants (*aüpnos, ennukhios*).[110] At the conclusion of the initiation procedure (on the evening of Boedromion twenty-first) came the display of the *Hiera* (*deiknumena*) at the Anaktoron[111] by the *Hierophant*. Light was the major component of the most sacred scene of the Mysteries, which left an everlasting impression on the initiates. The extraordinarily bright effect is recorded by many literary sources, which describe it as a great fire ('*hupo pollô puri*', Hippol. *Haer.* 5.8.40), while emphasis is also placed on the alternation between light and darkness ('*skotous kai phôtos enallax autôn phainomenôn*', Dio Chrys. *Or.* 12.33). However, we are left completely in the dark concerning the technical devices which created such an effect.[112]

O. Rubensohn attributed to 'the great fire' the function of merely creating the show, necessary at that particular moment in the ritual, and emphasised that it had nothing to do with the offering of sacrifices. He argued for the existence of a raised built hearth (*hestia*), on which light wood from pines and vines was burnt; this type of wood produced particularly strong flame. Rubensohn supported that torches were used at the same time, but not alone, since he found their light insufficient for such a bright effect.[113] Yet the problem of locating the smoke outlet necessary for such a strong fire in the *Telestêrion/Anaktoron* remains unsolved. Despite Plutarch's reference to an '*opaion epi tou anaktorou*' (*Vit. Per.* xiii, 7), modern reconstructions can hardly validate the existence of such a feature. Without attempting to solve the problem of the existence of a smoke outlet in the Telesterion/Anaktoron, W. Burkert sees the fire in the Anaktoron not merely as the main lighting device but also as the centre of sacrificial activities in the sanctuary. Basing his argument on evidence from parallel activities at other sanctuaries of Demeter, such as at Lykosoura, he points out the early origins of big sacrificial fires that were originally lit in the open air at both Lykosoura and Eleusis.[114]

The inadequacies of this theory are addressed by K. Clinton, who draws a clear distinction between the activities in the Anaktoron and those that took place in the open air.[115] The former are linked with dazzling light coming from the interior of the Anaktoron, which was produced by the burning of 'thousands of torches held by the *Epoptai*'. Clinton's interpretation agrees with the literary sources which are clear on this point: they confine their description to a bright light and not to other effects inevitably linked with sacrificial activities, such as smoke and smell. The latter (on the twenty-second of Boedromion) took place at the altars of the two goddesses just outside the main gate of the Eleusinian sanctuary, where they were easily accessible and visible to the initiates. Further evidence of sacrificial pyres outside the retaining walls of the peribolos of the archaic Telesterion is discussed by K. Kokkou-Viridi. She distinguishes three separate pyres, remains of which have been observed outside gates of the peribolos-wall: two pyres are located just outside the south gate of the geometric and archaic retaining walls and one outside the north gate of the archaic retaining wall of the peribolos of the Telesterion. This is supplemented by the extensive signs of burning on the outer side of this wall, first recorded by D. Philios and also discussed by K. Kourouniotis and G. Mylonas.[116]

Both torches and sacrificial pyres played their part in creating the magnificent lighting effect. Torches of split wood were particularly suitable lighting devices for the scene at the Anaktoron, which required a sudden light effect after the immediately preceding darkness. In the hands of a multitude of people, torches produced ample and even brightness over an extended area, against which the figure of the Hierophant emerged. Their rapid ignition and easily spread flame prevented the accumulation of too much smoke in the Anaktoron before the opening of its doors, so that the viewers' attention would not have been distracted from the main bright effect. The use of lamps cannot be excluded from the scene at the Anaktoron, since they have the additional advantage of being a less smoky means of illumination and a much safer precaution against fire in an interior space. However, their gentle flame would not have been particularly suitable for the creation of such a dramatic, almost theatrical, spectacle, the central effect of which was to turn the darkness into extraordinary gleaming light. By comparison, a sacrificial pyre is confined to one place, takes longer to prepare, and produces much more smoke. In ritual pyres are closely linked with sacrifices, for which their destructive and purificatory powers were essential.

Sacrificial calendars of the fifth and fourth centuries from Eleusis and other Attic demes provide some information about the quantities of wood purchased for Demeter festivals. The purpose of the purchase of wood is sometimes specified.[117] Thin brushwood (*phrugana*) along with normal thicker firewood (*xula*) is specified for the hiera ('*epi tois hierois*').[118] Torches are mentioned on one occasion,[119] under the name of *daïda*, in a sacred law concerning the Mysteries from the Eleusinion in the Athenian Agora.[120] The cult regulations of the Eleusinion in the deme of Phrearrhioi may mention a torch in a rather obscure context, in relation to the procession of Iakkhos.[121] Bare torches (without a holder) made of split wood were handier for the final stage at the Anaktoron, when the effect required was a bright light within a short burning time. The speed of transition from darkness to light depended heavily on the material used, which must mostly have consisted of thin stems of highly combustible wood, bound together to produce a strong flame.

c. Light in the Mysteries of Dionysos

The association of Dionysiac cult with death and the afterlife is encountered several times in literary sources including inscriptions from the fifth century onwards.[122] The capacity of Dionysos as protector of souls in the underworld seems to go beyond his syncretism with Iakkhos,[123] whose mystic rites shared similar traits with mysteries of pure Dionysiac character. Although explicit references to the nocturnal context of some Dionysiac mystic rites are no earlier than Plutarch and Pausanias, it seems likely that the constant opposition between darkness and light in the *Bacchae* is a symbolic expression of the actual experiences of the initiates. The power of Pentheus, which did not exceed the limits of the mortal world, led the god and his followers to dark prison chambers. By contrast, the immortal light of Dionysos offers freedom from any mortal restraint, and is closely connected with life after death. This is symbolically alluded to in the *Bacchae* 623-4, when fire suddenly appears on Semele's grave after the liberation of the god and his followers from the prison of Pentheus.

Speaking about the rites of Dionysos at Lerna,[124] Plutarch (*De Is. et Os.* 364F) briefly mentions the *Nuktelia* which took place at night. The ritual summoning of Dionysos is discussed by Pausanias (ii, 37.6),[125] who also attests that it was annual and nocturnal. These nocturnal rites probably derived from and re-enacted the myth of the fetching of Semele from the underworld by the god (Paus. ii, 37.5).[126] A close parallel to these nocturnal rites is undoubtedly the procession of Iakkhos at Eleusis which symbolically re-enacted, through a series of ritual stages, the search for, and subsequent 'finding' of, Persephone. Without diminishing the role of torches as means of illumination in these nocturnal rituals, one may also recall their function as apotropaic and purificatory devices during contact with the dead, which was symbolically enacted at Lerna. Finally, another – apparently much later – nocturnal rite of Dionysos which took place on the Akropolis of Sikyon (around the temple of the god and near the theatre) is recorded by Pausanias (ii, 7. 5-6). Two statues of the god, one of Dionysos Bakkhios and another of Dionysos Lysios, were carried by the Sikyonians in a nocturnal procession from the so-called *kosmêtêrion* to the temple of Dionysos. Torch-light and hymns to Dionysos were the main features of this nocturnal rite which provided the only occasion in the year on which the two sacred images of the god, normally kept inside the temple, were exposed to public gaze.

IV

Pollution-Repelling Fire

1. Purification from the miasma of death

The earliest explicit reference to the use of torch-fire as a means of purification from the miasma of death occurs in the *Odyssey* (xxii, 481-2, 490-1, 492-4). After the slaying of the suitors, Odysseus asks the faithful maid Eurykleia to bring him fire and sulphur to purify the palace (xxii, 481-2): 'Bring sulphur, old woman, to cleanse from pollution, and bring me fire, that I may purge the hall' (trans. Murray 1995.) Earlier on (xxii, 437-56), Telemakhos, the cowherd and the swineherd had first removed the dead bodies of the suitors from the palace, and then, aided by the women servants, carried out the actual cleansing of the place, including the washing and scraping of the floors, tables and thrones with water and sponges. Between the two purifications, first with water and then with fire and sulphur, further killings took place; the female servants who behaved disrespectfully during the absence of Odysseus remained to be executed. Once this final task had been accomplished, Odysseus purged with fire the hall and the rooms of the palace as well as the court outside. It is worth noting that Odysseus uses fire only after the completion of all the 'necessary' killings. Water apparently serves as an intermediate purging element, to wash away the actual bloodstains and dirt, which are confined mainly to the interior of the palace. In contrast, the capacity of fire and sulphur as purifiers goes beyond that, extending to the space outside the palace, which is precisely where the dead bodies were heaped. The polluted mass of corpses was dragged outside and piled up near the courtyard gate, where Odysseus kindled a purificatory fire (xxiii, 50-1). No further details of the purificatory ritual performed by Odysseus are given, nor are we informed of the exact function of the torches held by the faithful servants later, when they welcome their master in the hall (xxii, 497). Sulphur is mentioned about six times in Homer, four of which are connected with light in the form of a bolt of lightning.[1]

Tragic drama provides further examples of the use of fire in rituals intended to erase the stain of death. The altar of Zeus is the source of the torch-fire held by Herakles in his attempt to purify the house where he slew king Lykus (Eur. *HF* 922-30). The purification procedure involves a sacrifice, prior to which a basket containing barley and a sacrificial knife was passed on between the participants; this is followed by the extinguishing of a burning torch by Herakles in lustral water. It is tempting to see the presence of the torch as part of the purification ritual performed by Herakles – the details of which are not given – since torches were not normally separately mentioned in literary descriptions or visual representations of sacrifices.[2] A few lines later (ll. 936-8) Herakles, in a fit of madness, mentions cleansing fire in connection with another killing that he wishes to attempt, namely the murder of Eurystheus. His question to his dead father, wondering why he should cleanse himself with purifying flame if he has another murder to perform, apparently serves as an explanation for his earlier extinguishing of the torch at the scene of the sacrifice. Since he thinks he will soon be exposed to new pollution, he prefers to kindle the flame for purification after he kills Eurystheus.

A ritual which took place by the hearth-flames of the house of Kirke on Kirke's island is recorded by Apollonius Rhodius (*Argon*. 685-717). After the murder and the mutilation of the body of Medea's brother, Medea and Jason had to purge their pollution by running to the hearth of Kirke's house (ll. 702-3), where she cleanses them by sprinkling pig's blood over them.[3] A similar setting next to the *omphalos* (and therefore the hearth of Apollo) may be observed in both literary descriptions and vase representations of Orestes' purification at Delphi, after the murder of his mother and Aigisthos. Possible purificatory connotations may be identified in the torch of a goddess who stands next to Apollo in a red-figure representation of Orestes by the Naples Painter (*c*. 440-430). Orestes is depicted on his knees upon the omphalos or stone altar of Apollo, while at the same time he raises his sword to repel an Erinys. This scene is calmly observed by the two gods who hold purificatory materials, namely a laurel branch and a torch.[4]

Further possible allusions to ritual purification with the aid of torch-fire may be sought in a scene from the Eleusinian Mysteries depicting Herakles and Iolaos as initiates, on a work by the Painter of the Yale Lekythos (**5.1=4.5; Pl. 21**). They stand on either side of a bearded male figure (usually identified as Iakkhos) who holds out torches towards them. The torch-bearer is barefoot, wears a simple, sleeved, long khiton and himation, and has a myrtle wreath on his head. Both initiates are also barefoot, with myrtle wreath and himation. They respond to Iakkhos with a greeting gesture, holding a *bakkhos* and a myrtle branch; Herakles has left his club on the ground. According to the myth, Herakles' stain of death as a homicide was cleansed by the torches of Iakkhos.[5] Another possible representation of Herakles' initiation may be found on **5.2**, which depicts him (dressed in a similar himation) between Athena and Dionysos in a broader divine assembly, which includes a youthful torch-bearer (possibly Iakkhos) as well as the patron-goddesses of Eleusinian cult.[6] A later depiction of a purification ritual involving Herakles may be found on a late second/early third-century CE Ephesian sarkophagos from Torre Nova near Rome. The

Fig. 16. Scene of purification with the aid of burning torches on the Torre Nova sarcophagus, Naples.

seated and veiled hero (identified from his lion-skin) is approached from behind by a female figure, probably a priestess, who holds two torches lowered towards him (**Fig. 16**). An identical scene may also be found on a fragmentary sarkophagos now in Naples.[7]

The fullest literary account of a purification ritual is given in Euripides' *Iphigeneia in Tauris*. This ritual was planned to precede the awesome task of the sacrifice of Orestes and Pylades which would have to be performed by Iphigeneia, who was the priestess of Artemis in the land of Taurians. Iphigeneia states explicitly (ll. 1224-5) that she will cleanse the image of the goddess from the stain of the matricides with the aid of torchlight ('*selas lampadôn*'). Dramatic tradition associating Iphigeneia with the ritual of purification with the aid of a torch is reflected in representations on Roman sarkophagoi (*c.* second century CE). She is depicted holding the image (*xoanon*) of Artemis in one hand and a burning torch in the other. Her torch is directed towards the ground on one representation, where she stands before the seated Thoas, the Taurian king. An earlier scene on a

Pompeian fresco (dated to the first half of the first century CE) offers a different arrangement of the figures; here, the burning torch is not held by any figure, but is placed at the foot of a burning altar, together with a metal hydria.[8]

One of Iphigeneia's instructions to king Thoas, who would perform the purificatory ritual for her, was to cover the heads of the strangers (Orestes and Pylades) as well as his own eyes to avoid being polluted by the stain of murder; then Thoas would purge the temple with his torch. The practice of the covering of the heads of those already polluted as a necessary precaution to prevent their pollution from affecting the pure light of the sun is an interesting one, since this practice may be found elsewhere in tragic drama. In Sophocles' *Oedipus Tyrannus* (ll. 1425-8), Kreon urges death-tainted Oedipus to move away from the sun and into the house, since his pollution might affect living creatures, who are fed by the sun. A similar concept of impiety springing from exposing the sun to mortal pollution is found in Euripides' *Orestes* (ll. 819-23). The chorus describes with horror how the death-reddened knife of Orestes (stained with the blood of his mother) was lifted to the light of the sun. However, this moral prohibition on exposing the sun to the pollution of those stained with death seems to have been, at least partially, lifted in the case of Herakles (Eur. *HF* 1231-3). Having murdered his children as a result of his madness, Herakles realises the extent of the disaster that he has incurred, and wonders why Theseus did not cover his head to protect the sun from his pollution. On this occasion, Theseus denies the possibility of transmission of human pollution to the divine world. That Theseus' affirmation derives from sophistic influence is a plausible suggestion,[9] since it contradicts an apparently general belief that the sun was vulnerable to human pollution. If this really holds some truth, then one may trace a contrast between the nature and function of torch-light, which is apparently not affected by human pollution, and that of the sun; the latter, despite its immeasurably stronger and brighter lighting capacity, is vulnerable to ritual taint.

On the other hand, the burning of a dead body also repels pollution which may affect the living; Herakles demands the flash of a torch for his funeral pyre (Soph. *Trach.* 1198). Electra mentions the cleansing of the corpse of her murdered mother in the funeral fire (Eur. *Or.* 39-40), while the polluted status of Orestes is expressed by his abstinence from water (since he does not wash) and food, and by his isolation 'huddled under his cloak' (ll. 40-2). A few lines later, a series of prohibitions which practically place matricides in the margins of society clearly reflect public attitudes towards this form of pollution; matricides were to be debarred from shelter, fire and contact with anyone. A potential danger of contamination of the domestic hearth may be clearly detected here (Eur. *Or.* 46-8).

The bringing of new, pure fire to places tainted by pollution of death or by the invader was usual in Greece. Most of our information comes from later sources. Plutarch refers to an Argive ritual called *enkisma*, which involved a sacrifice to Apollo and then to Hermes immediately after the mourning of a dead person; the fire of this sacrifice had to be kindled anew at the hearth of a neighbouring household, because the flame of the home-hearth of the dead person was believed to be polluted (*Mor. Quaest. Graec.* xxiv, 297a).[10] An annual ceremony including the bringing of new, pure fire took place at Lemnos, in commemoration of the initial purification ritual inaugurated by Euneus (Hypsipyle's son by Jason), who had cleansed the island from the murders committed by the Lemnian women against their husbands (Philostr. *Her.* xix, 20). New fire was brought to Lemnos from Delphi once a year, and before this all fires on the island had to be extinguished for nine days.[11] A similar order to extinguish all the fires is reported to have been issued by the Greek commanders after the battle of Plataia in 479 (Plut. *Vit. Arist.* xx, 4). This order was the result of an oracular response from Delphi concerning the offering of a sacrifice by the Greeks. According to the oracle, the city had first to be purified by extinguishing the 'polluted' fire from its public hearth, which had come in contact with the barbarian invader. The importance and urgency attached to the act of bringing the new fire are clearly reflected in the story which immediately follows in Plutarch's account (*Arist.* xx, 5). A Greek, Eukhides, volunteered to fetch the fire from Delphi by running from Plataia to Delphi and by returning on the same day, an event which caused his own death shortly afterwards.[12]

2. Use of fire in prayer and divination

The use of torch-fire in the service of the gods is not restricted to sacrifice or purification rituals; it extends to everyday contacts with the gods in the form of prayer or offering, in order to ensure divine favour before any major undertaking. This is evident on at least three occasions in Aristophanes (*Thesm.* 36-7; *Vesp.* 860-2; *Ran.* 871-2), where light is required together with incense and a wreath (in two examples, a myrtle wreath is specified).

A more detailed – and, to my knowledge, the only – account of the use of light in a purification ritual before delivering a prophecy is offered by Euripides (*Hel.* 865-72). Theonoe the seer directs her maid-helpers to conduct the procedure of purging the earth and air before her with the aid of the light that they carry: 'Hold the lamp bright before me and lead on. Sanctify every corner of the air with pure ritual, that I may draw holy breath from heaven. If any man has polluted this place with unhallowed tread, purge my path with flame; wave the torch before me, that I may pass. Your sacred service done, carry back the fire to the central hearth' (trans. Vellacott 1972). The type of light held by the maids in lines 865 and 870 is specified first as *'lamptêres'*, and shortly after as *'peukê'*. The second refers clearly to a pine-torch, the pure flame of which was kindled at the hearth of the house, to where it is returned after the completion of the ritual (ll. 871-2). The torch-bearer performs a gesture with the torch before Theonoe under the instructions of the seer (*'krouson peukê'*), and this gesture with the torch apparently belongs to the narrower context of the purification of the earth after its contact with polluted foot. Lampteres, on the other hand, have been associated by both R. Kannicht and A.M. Dale with a *thumiaterion*, via which the air is filled with incense and purified for the seer.[13] In view of the special mention of the brightness of the lampteres (*'lamptêrôn selas'*), a vessel of combined use, both as lamp and incense-burner (thumiaterion), may be implied here; this would be possible if the oil-holder of the *lamptêr* contained oil mixed with aromatic substances.[14]

On some occasions at least, divination rituals appear to have been dependent upon fire. A particularly vivid description of the effects of ritual pollution upon an altar's fire which was used by Teiresias for divination is found in Sophocles (*Ant.* 1007-11). The absence of flame from the burnt sacrifice – despite the repeated attempts of the seer to ignite the altar at all points – alarms Teiresias who interprets it as the gods' refusal to reveal their will through his prophetic rites. Instead of blazing up, the long thighbones of the sacrificial victim are described as oozing with a dank slime, giving out smoke and sputter. Later on, Teiresias admits with despair that the public altars and sacred hearths are fouled as dogs and birds carry around decaying flesh from the unburied corpse of Polyneikes, which is the cause of the pollution. This pollution prevents the seer from exercising other methods of divination too, such as receiving omens from observation of the movement and voices of birds (*Ant.* 1021-2).

Later rituals combining divination and magic are recorded by Pseudo-Callisthenes and by Pausanias, and involve fire before and during the delivery of a prophecy. The sorcerer (*magos*) of the Macedonian court, Nektenavos, invokes the god Ammon by lighting lamps and by using magic plants and a wax female figurine prior to his prediction of the pregnancy of Olympias (*Historia Alexandri Magni* i, 10). The incident takes place during the evening. The role of the lamps is obvious in his instructions to Olympias; he advises her not to extinguish the lamps if the god comes to her disguised as a snake, in which case she should ask everyone to leave the room, while he would be engaged in further magical recipes (*Historia Alexandri Magni* i, 12). A more complex method of divination probably of Egyptian origin was conducted at the oracle of Hermes at Pharai in Akhaia and was still in use when Pausanias visited it (vii, 22.2). There, bronze lamps were attached to the stone-hearth, fastened with lead in front of the god's image. During the oracular procedure, which took place in the evening, lamps were lighted and incense burned on the altar, while the inquirer approached the god.

3. Pure fire and love-making

The purificatory effects of fire against some of the most severe forms of ritual pollution (e.g. homicide) – when even the rays of the sun had to be protected from the taint – are by no means immune to all forms of 'mortal' dirt. The pure home-hearth often becomes the ultimate refuge of blood-stained mortals, without itself running the risk of contamination. However, paradoxically, this same hearth may be extremely vulnerable to, and therefore have to be protected from, other forms of pollution, namely bodily emissions. Hesiod (*Op.* 733-4) explicitly refers to this form of pollution: 'Do not expose yourself befouled by the fireside in your house but avoid this' (trans. Evelyn-White 1929). A similar belief is reflected in a fragment of the sixth-century Ephesian poet Hipponax, where someone covers the fire before having sex.[15] It seems no coincidence that the goddess of the home-hearth, Hestia, is a virgin. Herodotus (i, 198) records a related custom of the Babylonians which involved the feeding of the hearth-fire with incense every time a married couple had intercourse; however, the actual timing of the act, before or after sexual intercourse, is not specified.

Night was the most suitable time of the day for erotic action for both gods and mortals. Zeus' burning desire for Io is expressed through night-time visions sent to Io which incite her to join in sexual union with him (Aesch. *PV* 649-57). On the other hand, lamps were the only 'intruders' in the secret, mainly night-life of lovers and married couples. Aristophanes devotes his prologue to the *Ecclesiazousai* to an address to a lamp, the secret witness of the female world inside the *oikos*. The presence of lamps during the act of love-making is separately mentioned (ll. 7-11). Lovers and lamp are associated again in a fragment by an anonymous comedian, where the lamp is treated as a comical parallel to a god (probably the sun-god as in the prologue of the *Ecclesiazousai*).[16] This gesture of lovers in addressing lamps in their private moments is attested in later literature on many occasions by poets such as Asklepiades and Meleagros.[17] A lamp was burning every night in Klytaimnestra's chamber (Aesch. *Ag.* 880-5) in anticipation of her lover, Aigisthos, while the unfaithful wife of Euphiletos one of Lysias' speeches (i, 14) allegedly used the lighting of a lamp as an excuse to meet lovers outside the house at night. In vase-painting, clay or metal lamps, often mounted on elaborate stands, illuminate symposia where a variety of erotic action takes place between heterosexual and homosexual couples. Lamps and lamp-stands may also turn into implements of punishment of the *hetairai*-participants in orgies; a good example is the scene on the exterior of a cup by the Pedieus Painter dated to *c.* 520-505, where a youth with a lamp-stand in his left hand and a lamp in his right approaches a naked hetaira threatening to punish her.[18] Another scene of erotic groups on a cup by the Brygos Painter shows a man with a lamp threatening to burn the bottom of a naked hetaira, who is engaged in erotic action with another man.[19]

Unlike lamps, torches are usually associated with legitimate unions such as pre-nuptial rites, as well as scenes of various stages of the wedding ritual. The leading of the couple to the bridal chamber on their first night is illuminated by torches held by a woman (usually the bridegroom's mother). On the basis of the surviving Attic vase-representations (discussed in Chapter III.4), torches do not cross the boundaries of the wedding chamber; their service ends at the bedroom door, from where lamps may have replaced them (though no visual evidence supports this assumption). Hetairai rarely hold torches. In the *Vespae* of Aristophanes, a series of comic connections are made between a slave-girl, Dardanis (possibly a hetaira), and a torch. In his conversation with Bdelykleon, Philokleon insists that Dardanis is a torch by pointing out the similarities between a torch and her body. Some of their shared features include that the female (Dardanis') body is 'split' between the legs (*eskhismenên*) just like a torch which is made of 'split' pieces of wood, as well as the black 'pitch' at the point where the body divides into two legs (meaning the public hair) and the 'knot' at the back of the girl (*Vesp.* 1370-7).[20] Such a daring parallel is not found elsewhere in comedy and provides an unusual – and therefore comical! – association between torches (so far seen as symbols of legitimate females) and less 'respectable' women.

Plate 1. Clay torch-holder from Ithaka (Museum Vathi 292).

Plate 2. Torch-racing silens with Dionysos. Berlin, Staatliche Museen 1962.33 (Cat. no. 1.28). Altamura Painter, *c.* 460.

Plate 3. Running torch-racer. St Petersburg, Hermitage 2215 (Cat. no. 1.13). Bulas Group, early fourth century.

Plate 4. Athletes preparing for a torch-race. Würzburg, Martin von Wagner Museum L 492 (Cat. no. 1.17). Jena Workshop, early fourth century.

Plate 5. Torch-lit procession of victorious tribe of torch-racers leading to the sacrifice of a bull. Mannheim, Reiss-Museum Cg 123 (Cat. no. 1.64). Painter of Athens 12255, early fourth century.

Plate 6. Relief from Miletos depicting a torch-bearing Kourotrophos with Apollo, Artemis and Leto. Dresden Museum inv. no. ZV 1050 (Cat. no. 2.9), first quarter of the fourth century.

Plate 7. Birth of Dionysos (?) attended by Zeus and Hera. Paris, Cabinet des Médailles 219 (Cat. no. 2.1). Diosphos Painter, *c.* 500.

Plate 8a&b. Seated, torch-bearing goddess (possibly Artemis) approached by worshippers. Mainz, University 116 (Cat. no. 3.6). Oppenheimer Group, *c.* 450.

Plate 9. A woman loosens or takes off her belt before a torch-bearing Artemis. Syracuse, Museo Archeologico Nazionale 21186 (Cat. no. 3.5). Achilles Painter, *c.* 450.

Plate 10. Pre-nuptial bath procession including torch-bearing assistants. Warsaw National Museum 142290 (Cat. no. 3.24). Leningrad Painter, c. 470.

Plate 11. Wedding procession including a *daidoukhousa* (possibly Artemis). Boston, Museum of Fine Arts 68.46 (Cat. no. 3.11). Circle of the Lysippides Painter, *c.* 530.

Plate 12. Arrival of wedding procession at the couple's new home. Berlin, Staatliche Museen F 2530 (Cat. no. 3.29). Amphitrite Painter, *c.* 460-450.

Plate 13. Scene at the altar of the home of a newly wed couple; possibly a ceremonial kindling of the altar. London, British Museum D 11 (Cat. no. 3.26). Splanchnopt Painter, *c.* 470-460.

Plate 14. Ascent of Persephone from the underworld, attended by Hekate, Hermes and Demeter (not shown). New York, Metropolitan Museum 28.57.23 (Cat. no. 4.11). Persephone Painter, *c.* 440.

Plate 15. A torch-bearing Hekate leads
Persephone to her mother. Bologna, Museo
Civico Archeologico P 236 (Cat. no. 4.4).
Alkimachos Painter, *c*. 470.

Plate 16. Ascent of Persephone attended by
Hekate who moves her torches up and down.
Athens, National Museum H 19605 (1414) (Cat.
no. 4.17). Late fifth century.

Plate 17. Nocturnal torchlit scene from the Eleusinian Mysteries; the 'Ninnion' tablet. Athens, National Museum 11036 (Cat. no. 4.25), *c.* 370.

Plate 18. Array of Eleusinian divinities including torch-bearing figures. St Petersburg, Hermitage St. 1792 (Cat. no. 4.34). Eleusinian Painter, *c.* 340-330.

Plate 19. Torch-bearing male figure
(possibly Eubouleus) between Persephone
(Thea) and Hades (Theos). Florence,
Museo Archeologico 75748 (Cat. no. 4.12).
Polygnotos, *c*. 450-425.

Plate 20. A torch-bearing Persephone
among Eleusinian divinities. Athens,
National Museum 1443 (Cat. no. 4.36),
c. 330.

Plate 21. Torch-bearing male figure (possibly Iakkhos) between Herakles and Iolaos; initiation of Herakles (?). Brussels, Musées Royaux A 10 (Cat. no. 4.5 = 5.1). Yale Lekythos Painter, *c.* 460.

Plate 22. Bronze statuette (probably of Artemis) from Lousoi, Arkadia. Karlsruhe, Badisches Landesmuseum F 1926 (Cat. no. 6.77), *c.* 450-400.

Plate 23. Cult-statue of Artemis as huntress holding a torch. Naples, Museo Archeologico Nazionale 81908 (H 3010) (Cat. no. 6.40), *c.* 440.

Plate 24. Torch-bearing Artemis or Hekate, followed by a dog. Paris, Louvre Ma 2849 (Cat. no. 6.123), late fourth century.

Plate 25. A possible representation of the abduction of Persephone by Hades including a torch-bearing Hekate. Würzburg, Martin von Wagner Museum L535 (H 4307) (Cat. no. 4.6). Painter of Tarquinia 707, *c.* 460-450.

Plate 26. The 'Great Eleusinian relief'; Demeter, Persephone and Triptolemos. Athens, National Museum 126 (Cat. no. 6.80), *c.* 430.

Plate 27. Torch-bearing, dancing Dionysos. Würzburg, Martin von Wagner Museum H 4906 (Cat. no. 6.32), *c.* 460.

Plate 28. Artemis walking swiftly to the right, dressed as a huntress and holding a burning torch. Tübingen, University Museum 1518 (Cat. no. 6.12), *c.* 500-450.

Plate 29. Torch-bearing unarmed goddess.
St Petersburg, Hermitage B 3368 (Cat. no.
6.2). Pan Painter, *c.* 480.

Plate 30. Female holding two torches (one higher
than the other) above an altar. St Petersburg,
Hermitage 673 (B1918) (Cat. no. 6.7). Bowdoin
Painter, *c.* 480-470.

Plate 31. Torchlit libation between Triptolemos and the Eleusinian deities. Basel, Antikenmuseum BS 1412 (Cat. no. 6.17). The Niobid Painter, *c.* 465.

Plate 32. Demeter or Persephone kindling a torch at an altar for the subsequent libation with Triptolemos. Copenhagen, Ny Carlsberg Glyptotek 2696 (Cat. no. 6.9). Berlin Painter, *c.* 480-470.

Plate 33. Torch-bearing Artemis receiving worshippers. Athens, National Museum 1950 (Cat. no. 6.78), *c.* 450-400.

Plate 34. Torch-bearing Artemis accompanied by a dog. Athens, National Museum 4540 (Cat. no. 6.103), fourth century.

Plate 35. Torch-bearing Artemis attending the punishment of Aktaion. Oxford, Ashmolean Museum 1980.31 (V 289) (Cat. no. 7.11). Lykaon Painter, *c.* 440.

Plate 36. Artemis in hunting action using an extinguished torch as weapon. London, British Museum E 432 (Cat. no. 7.24). Herakles Painter, *c.* 370.

Plate 37a&b. Herakles and Iolaos killing the Hydra at Lerna. Paris, Louvre CA 598 (Cat. no. 7.4). Diosphos Painter, *c.* 500-490.

Plate 38. Artemis and Zeus fight the Titans using fire as weapon; Artemis holds torches and Zeus the thunderbolt. Berlin, Staatliche Museen F 2531 (Cat. no. 7.18). Aristophanes, late fifth century.

Plate 39a. The worship of Dionysos by maenads. Naples, Museo Archeologico Nazionale H 2419 (Cat. no. 8.22). Dinos Painter, c. 420.

Plate 39b. The other side of 39a.

Plate 40. Enthroned goddess performing a ritual using a burning torch and grain. Athens, National Museum A 537 (5825) (Cat. no. 9.5), end of the fifth century.

Plate 41. Return of Hephaistos to Olympos accompanied by Dionysos and his thiasos. Naples, Museo Archeologico Nazionale 2412 (Cat. no. 9.19). Hephaistos Painter, *c.* 440.

Plate 42. Likely representation of a lamp fixed on a stick, designed for processions; it is held by one of the 'stool carriers' on the east frieze of the Parthenon (slab V31-35).

V

Light-Bearing Divine Images

1. Cult-statues and divine images involving light

a. Artemis

The lights of Artemis are often attested in literature via her cult-titles *Phôsphoros*, *Amphipuros* and *Purphoros*.[1] Two cult-statues of Artemis, each carrying two torches, are reported by Pausanias: a bronze of Artemis Hegemone in Arkadia which stood in front of the eastern entrance of the temenos of Despoina at Lykosoura (viii, 37.1)[2] and another at Aulis in Boiotia made of white stone (ix, 19.6).[3] A group of bronze statuettes from Lousoi in Arkadia dating from 470 to 400 (**6.75-6.77**; **Pl. 22**) bears strong affinities with the type of the cult statue of Artemis *Hêmerasia*, described by Pausanias (viii, 18.8).[4] These statuettes depict the goddess frontally with feet together, wearing a peplos with apoptugma. She holds a poppy[5] in her normally lowered left hand, and a short torch in her right, with its upper end tilting forward. Another well-known statue of Artemis in Lukosoura, closely related to one of Demeter, was the work of the sculptor Damophon (**Fig. 17**). The statue is described briefly by Pausanias (viii, 37.3-4) as holding a torch in one hand and two serpents in the other.

Recently, P. Themelis has identified a life-size statue of Artemis in marble fragments that he found in the fill around the temple of Artemis Ortheia at Messene. The statue is a work of an unknown sculptor and is dated by the excavator to the end of the fourth or the beginning of the third century. It depicts Artemis standing, wearing a short khiton with overfold, topped by an animal skin (*nebris*), high boots (*embades*) and a polos-like head-dress. Along her left side the goddess supports a long torch which reaches the ground. The type of this statue appears to have been widely reproduced in clay figurines of the goddess from the same site,[6] and also enjoyed popularity at other sites, such as the Athenian Agora, Volos, Veroia and Delos.[7] In the later Artemision at Messene (at the north end of the west wing of the Asklepeios sanctuary), Themelis identified the statue-base and fragments of the later cult statue of Artemis made by Damophon. This statue represented Artemis Phosphoros and was seen and recorded by Pausanias (iv, 31.10). One of the surviving fragments preserves part of the hand of the goddess holding a cylindrical object which resembles a

Fig. 17. Reconstruction of the sculptural group of Damophon at Lykosoura,
Arkadia. After Papachatzis.

torch; it, too, is comparable with contemporary clay statuettes of the
goddess from the site.[8] Very little is known of other cult-statues of Artemis.
I. Threpsiades suggested a combination of torch and bow for her cult statue
at Aulis.[9] Another ancient image of torch-bearing Artemis as huntress was
the work of Praxiteles for the sanctuary of the goddess outside Antikura
in Phokis (x, 37.1-2).[10] Here, the torch is held in her right hand and a quiver
hangs from her shoulder. It is likely that some at least glimpses of this lost
statue may be gained by representations of the goddess on two second-
century coins from Antikura. On these, Artemis advances to the right and
is accompanied by a dog. She wears a quiver on her back, and holds a torch
in her left hand and a bow in her right.[11] The influence of this iconographical type of Artemis of Antikura apparently exercised influence on further
hellenistic images of the torch-bearing goddess in similar hunting outfit,
such as a relief from Delos (A 3236). The latter depicts Artemis Soteira in
frontal view, accompanied by a dog. She holds two long torches on either
side of her body and wears a knee-long sleeveless girded khiton and boots,
with a quiver hanging from her right shoulder.[12] Numismatic evidence
suggests that comparable types of Artemis Soteira and Artemis Phosphoros existed at Megara, Buzantion and Odessos; these types depicted
the goddess as huntress, holding two torches.[13]
   The earliest Attic representations of torch-bearing statues of Artemis in

vase-painting are no earlier than the second half of the fifth century. A cult statue of Artemis is depicted on **6.40** (*c.* 440; **Pl. 23**) placed inside a temple of the goddess. Artemis stands in frontal view, wearing a long peplos with overfold and holding a bow in her left hand and a long torch in her right. The statue faces an altar, in front of which a male pyrrichist dances, dressed in military gear.[14] Further representations of the frontally standing goddess wearing a peplos and holding a bow in her left hand, a torch in her right and a quiver may be found on a relief of the second half of the fifth century (**6.79**). The bow may occasionally be omitted from this type, as on **6.90**, which is dated to the first quarter of the fourth century. Artemis or Hekate should be probably identified on another marble relief, now in the Louvre, dated to the late fourth century (**6.123, Pl. 24**), which depicts a goddess brandishing a torch in each hand and followed by a dog. A similar type of torch-bearing Artemis holding a torch in each hand may also be found on a series of statuettes of Artemis from her sanctuary in Metaponto.[15] Fourth-century clay busts of a goddess – possibly Artemis – who holds one long torch with both hands across her chest have been discovered in Epirus (**6.110-6.111**).[16] This type is not missing from Attic fourth century marble reliefs (**6.112**). In the fourth century the rich iconographical repertoire of the goddess includes further types, such as reliefs **6.113** and **6.114,** where Artemis carries a long torch in one hand while the other rests on her hip. Despite her lack of weapons, Artemis' nature as huntress is indicated by the rest of her outfit which includes a khlamys and boots, as well as by her wild animal companion, as in reliefs **6.114** and **6.133** (fourth century).

b. Hekate

The associations of Artemis with light are shared by Hekate, a fact reflected in Hekate's cult-epithets (*Amphipuros, Phaesphôriê, Phôsphoros, Dadoukhos, Daidophoros* and *Purphoros*)[17] and representations. The latter include torches on either side of the frontally standing goddess, who is often accompanied by a dog. This iconographical type of Hekate appears to have had a lasting impact upon sculptural representations of the goddess throughout the hellenistic period.[18] The strong iconographical affinities between Artemis and Hekate may be demonstrated on a marble relief now in Louvre (**6.123; Pl. 24**), where a goddess stands in frontal pose, dressed in a khiton and himation and followed by a dog;[19] her two long upright torches are placed on either side of her body. With regard to the identification of the goddess as Artemis or Hekate, one may rule out neither possibility in view of the attributes, dress and animal companion which are common to the iconography of both goddesses. Two likely representations of cult statues of torch-bearing Hekate are a work of the Painter of Tarquinia 707 (**4.6; Pl. 25**) in the third quarter of the fifth century and a fourth-century votive relief from Piraeus (**6.105**). Both depictions share common traits: the goddess, dressed in a long garment, stands frontally on a pedestal and carries two long torches in her extended hands which are positioned on either side of her body. The statue on the vase wears a peplos and a hair-band. The statue on the relief is visible at the back of a cave, in the foreground of which stand Kybele and Hermes *Kadmilos*. Although caves are not uncommon in the iconography of Artemis, there should be no doubt that here the goddess depicted is Hekate, judging from the presence of her usual divine companions, notably Hermes Kadmilos and Kybele. A closely related type of the goddess is observed in a Thasian votive relief of the end of the fifth century (**6.84**), with the exception that in this example the goddess holds short torches and is followed by a running dog.[20] Further possible representations of Hekate appear in vase-painting on fragmentary works by the Splanchnopt Painter (**6.22**, early fifth century), where a goddess is depicted in profile view with two long torches in front of her.

A very distinct statue of Hekate known as Hekate *Epipurgidia* was created in honour of the goddess by the sculptor Alkamenes in the last quarter of the fifth century. The statue depicted the goddess in frontal view with three bodies, joined at the back.[21] Pausanias (ii, 30.2) reported that Alkamenes was the sculptor who devised this type of the triple Hekate which became very popular thereafter under the name of *Hekataion*.[22] The statue of Alkamenes most probably stood on the bastion of the temple of Athena Nike on the Athenian Akropolis as guardian of the entrance to the citadel. One may indeed only speculate about the objects held by the goddess in her original statue by the temple of Athena Nike, on the basis of surviving fourth-century or later Hekataia. Some of them depict the goddess with torches, which are usually combined with other objects, such as phialai.[23] The only surviving original of a triple Hekate dated to the late fifth century (in the collection of the British School at Athens) cannot be reconstructed as holding torches, according to T. Kraus.[24] Among the possible images of the goddess which apparently derive from torch-bearing types of Hekataia is a mid-fourth-century relief (**6.98**) which depicts a goddess in frontal view, holding two long torches on either side of her body. Long torches have been preserved in the hands of two of the figures of a possibly late fourth-century marble Hekataion from Nikopolis, Epirus. A torch is held in the left hand of the goddess, while with her right she touches her khiton, which is girded below her chest and forms a low apoptugma. The difficulties in linking the statue with a possible local cult of Hekate in Nikopolis are emphasised by Ch. Tzouvara-Souli, who also notes the imprecise date of most of the Hekataia found in the area, which range from the fourth to the first centuries.[25]

c. En(n)odia

One or two torches appear to be among the commonest attributes of the Thessalian goddess En(n)odia, whose fear-inspiring nature is intimately related to that of Artemis and especially Hekate.[26] A plank-like clay figurine of a goddess, possibly En(n)odia, found in her major sanctuary at Pherai bears indications that torches were held by the goddess in each hand as early as the archaic period, most probably reflecting the type of her *xoanon* (**6.70**).[27] The frontal goddess has her arms bent at the elbows with the lost lower arms, which probably once held upright torches, extended forward. Another clay figurine of the goddess dated to the first half of the fourth century comes from the votive deposit of a smaller shrine of En(n)odia at Pherai (**6.92**).[28] The frontal stance is retained, but here her right arm rests along her body and her left is bent at the elbow; a long torch is attached along her left side.

A small marble funerary stele from Larissa (**6.126**, *c.* 350-300) depicts a bust of the goddess with one raised, oblique, short torch in her left hand, bound at intervals by four rings.[29] En(n)odia wears a peplos and is crowned with a myrtle wreath. This iconographical type (with minor variations), is often found on coins of Pherai dated to the fourth century and later.[30] The goddess may be accompanied by a dog and a horse as on the relief from Krannon in Thessaly (**6.95**).[31] Here, her sleeved peplos has two crossed straps at the chest recalling the iconography of the huntress Artemis. Her left arm is bent at the elbow, with the forearm extended forward, and a short burning torch is held in her hand. A late fourth-century marble amphiglyph in Louvre (**6.124**) presents two different iconographical versions of Eno(n)dia.[32] The obverse depicts the goddess carrying a sceptre and a phiale, while on the reverse she holds two short burning torches on either side in a slightly oblique position. A dog lies at her feet, recalling representations of Hekate and Artemis.

d. The Eleusinian deities

Pausanias refers to torch-bearing statues of Demeter on at least three occasions in the context of descriptions of Arkadian sanctuaries. A wooden image of Demeter-Erinys with a torch and a *kistê* in hand is reported from Arkadian Thelpousa (viii, 25.7).[33] Another statue came from the sanctuary of Despoina in Arkadian Lykosoura (viii, 37.3-4).[34] It stood next to the statue of Artemis which also bore a torch, and was also the work of the sculptor Damophon. The torch is combined with a phiale in Demeter's hand on a fourth-century relief from Tegea (**6.127**), where she was worshipped together with Persephone as *Karpophorai theai* (Paus. viii, 53.7).[35] A statue of Demeter with torches (made of Pentelic marble) is recorded by Pausanias at Stiria in Phokis, where there was a sanctuary of the goddess (x, 35.9-10).[36] A simple composition on a fifth-century Korinthian plate

(**6.39**) depicting a goddess's head in profile and a short burning torch in front of her may be interpreted as Demeter in view of the long Peloponnesian tradition of torch-bearing sculptural images of the goddess. In Thessaly, a possible connection between Demeter and the local goddess Pheraia, who was also known by the epithet *Phôsphoros*, has been discussed by A. Daffa-Nikonanou. However, the epithet Phosphoros does not occur in Thessalian inscriptions before the second century.[37] In Sicily, an 'ancient' bronze image of Demeter at Enna is described by Cicero (*Verr.* iv, 109-10; v, 187) as bearing torches in both hands. Bronze and silver coins from Enna and other places in Sicily often depict the goddess holding at least one torch which is often coupled with sheaves of corn held in her other hand.[38]

In Attic iconography, Demeter is also associated with torches. On two occasions, an isolated figure of a goddess (possibly Demeter) with torches in hand decorates the reverse side of vases by the Berlin Painter (**6.3** dated to *c.* 480, and **6.18** dated to *c.* 465). The main scene on the obverse side of both vases represents Triptolemos involved in libation with an Eleusinian deity. In both examples (**6.3, 6.18**), the torch-bearing goddess holds one torch out in an almost vertical position, parallel to the axis of the figure's body, while the other torch leans loosely backwards, on her shoulder. Persephone is the Eleusinian torch-bearing goddess *par excellence*, as is attested by the quantity of representations of the goddess with torches in hand. However, in cases of small or fragmentary compositions such as **6.85** (where a female holds a long torch obliquely), **6.83** or **6.109**, it is impossible to identify the goddess depicted.

Several simple compositions, of mainly Attic provenance, comprise the pair of seated, sceptre-bearing Mother (Demeter) and standing, torch-bearing Daughter (Persephone). Persephone may carry one (**4.46**, late fifth century, **4.47**, *c.* 350 and **4.52**, *c.* 350-300) or two, long upright torches (**4.24, 4.28**, first half of the fourth century and **4.54**, second half of the fourth century), as she stands by the sceptre-bearing, seated Demeter. In **4.24** and **4.28** Persephone stands in profile, facing the Mother (Demeter) and in **4.54** she is depicted frontally next to the Mother (Demeter). A visual interplay between the Mother's sceptre and the Daughter's torch may be observed in various sculptural works of the fifth and the fourth centuries. Starting with the Great Eleusinian relief (**6.80**, *c.* 430; **Pl. 26**), both the sceptre of Demeter and the long torch of Persephone extend to the figures' full height as they flank Triptolemos.[39] Comparable devices are employed in **4.45** (end of fifth century), **6.127** (last quarter of the fourth century), **6.64** and **6.68** (*c.* 350-300), where a more striking effect is achieved, via similarities in posture, drapery and height of the figures, and the similar way in which the goddesses hold the torch and sceptre against their left shoulders. It is tempting to 'read' their different (but so similar in shape) attributes as reflections of the different status of the deities. In this context, the sceptre of Demeter could be taken as an allusion to her

Fig. 18. Array of Eleusinian divinities including torch-bearing figures. St Petersburg, Hermitage St.1792 (Cat. no. 4.34). Eleusinian Painter, *c*. 340-330. See also Pl. 18.

seniority as the divine patron of the Eleusinian cult, which is wrapped around myths concerning the divine figure of her daughter, Persephone. The latter is therefore justifiably the principal figure in the Eleusinian iconography who carries the torch which probably serves here as an abbreviated 'code' of the Eleusinian ritual.

The pattern of the seated Demeter with a sceptre and the standing Persephone with one or two torches may also form part of larger compositions including other Eleusinian deities, such as Triptolemos (**6.43** by Polygnotos, third quarter of the fifth century), **6.59** (by the Painter of Naples H 3245, early fourth century) and **6.131**. In these examples, the sceptre of Demeter and the torches of Persephone flank the hero who is seated between the two standing goddesses. Two torches are carried by Persephone who stands facing Triptolemos in **6.24** by the Pan Painter (*c*. 460) and **6.54** (late fifth century). In **6.24** Demeter holds a sceptre and stands next to Persephone, while another sceptre-bearing female (possibly Eleusis) stands at the other end of the scene, behind Triptolemos. Broader fourth-century scenes from the Mysteries, such as arrays of gods associated with them (such as in **4.32** by the Pourtalès Painter (**Fig. 15**), **4.34** by the Eleusinian Painter (**Fig. 18**), **4.37** (**Fig. 19**), **6.59**, **6.67**, **6.60**, **4.53** and **6.122**), or scenes of worship (such as **6.128**), include further examples of this sceptre-torch interplay between Mother and Daughter. Finally,

Fig. 19. Array of Eleusinian divinities including torch-bearing figures. St Petersburg, Hermitage St. 525 (B 1657) (Cat. no. 4.37), *c.* 330-320.

among the male Eleusinian torch-bearing divinities, one may add a statue of Iakkhos which, according to Pausanias (i, 2.4), stood near the Pompeion in the Kerameikos, together with statues of Demeter and Persephone.

e. Dionysos

Brightness is one of the most distinct features of Dionysos and is expressed through a variety of forms in both art and literature. The basic components of Dionysos' light are celestial brightness and torchlight.[40] The former is a widely shared trait among the gods.[41] Because of his divine radiance, Dionysos is invoked as 'most radiant light' in Euripides' *Bacchae* (l. 608). His divine light is enhanced by his golden crown of oriental type from which the god receives the epithet '*khrusomitras*' in tragic drama (Soph., *OT* 209-14). In vase-painting, a rayed crown often adorns the head of Dionysos' xoanon which is placed among his female worshippers. The rays of his crown may take a pyramidal form or may merely be ivy branches springing from the back of his head in a circular arrangement, similar to solar forms.[42] In Sophocles' *Antigone* (ll. 1146-7), Dionysos is further associated with celestial brightness of the nocturnal starry sky. He is hailed as 'leader of the dance of the stars breathing fire' (trans. Lloyd-Jones 1994). More imposing bright images of the god are found in Euripides' *Bacchae* (ll. 1082-5), where an epiphanic appearance of Dionysos takes the form of a sudden lightning flash which unites heaven and earth. Sound (the voice of the god) and light are here combined to describe the extraordinary effects of the presence of the god among his female worshippers on the mountain. This experience of the divine renders nature and humans motionless![43] The domination of Dionysos over nature by means of thunder and lightning is clearly reminiscent of the 'blazing torch of thunder' of his father Zeus (Eur. *Bacch.* 592), from which it possibly derives.

The human aspect of the the persona of Zeus' anthropomorphised son is clearly reflected in the 'earthly' component of Dionysos' light, namely his torches. The double light of Dionysos (divine radiance and torchlight) is a direct reflection of his double nature, the divine and the human, as he admits himself in Euripides' *Bacchae* (l. 53). Whenever the god carries his pine torches (*peukai*), he participates in scenes that are set firmly in the world of the mortals, such as his dances on the rocky ridges of Parnassos among his female worshippers (Eur. *Bacch.* 145-6; 306-8).[44] Glimpses of the leaping dances of the god among his followers, the *Bacchae*, may be also found in Euripides' *Ion* 714-18: 'Listen, peaks and ridges of Parnassus, / Enfolding high rock and cloudy seat,/ Where Bacchus, with flaming torch held high in the night,/ Swiftly leaps onward among his frenzied followers' (trans. Vellacott 1972). A fragment from Euripides' *Hypsipyle* (*TGF*[2] 652) combines thyrsoi, animal skins and blazing pine-torches in the description of the god among his female followers. Further references to the bright light of Dionysos' pine-torches are found in Aeschylus' *Bassarae* (*TrGF* 12a2) as well as in the *Nubes* of Aristophanes (ll. 603-6). In contrast with the rich literary imagery of the 'earthly' light of Dionysos, there is a scarcity of depictions of the torch-bearing god in art. Two examples may be mentioned here of red-figure unattributed vases (**6.32, 6.44**), the earliest of which dates to around 460 (**6.32; Pl. 27**). In both representations, one short burning torch is held in the right hand of a dancing Dionysos. The god is bearded, long-haired, and clad in a long-sleeved khiton and himation. His short torch follows the movement of his body as he dances with one arm raised and the other lowered in front of a kantharos, which rests on the ground.

f. Zeus

The thunderbolt of Zeus is the main source of his divine aura as father of the gods (**Fig. 20**). The form of his thunderbolt deviated substantially from the forms of light used by the other gods, such as the lamp of Athena or the torches of the Eleusinian deities, Artemis, Hekate and Dionysos. However, the reason for its brief discussion here is that, despite the

Fig. 20. Bronze statuettes of Zeus from Olympia and Dodona, fifth century.

differences of the thunderbolt from conventional lighting devices, it often shares a similar function with them – and especially with torches – since the thunderbolt entails both fire and light. The flash of Zeus' thunderbolt is attested in literature as early as Homer (*Il.* ii, 353),[45] while in sculpture and vase-painting it is one of the most frequent attributes of Zeus.

A number of statues of Zeus with thunderbolt in hand are reported by Pausanias on several occasions during his visit to Olympia. Among these, a statue of the god wearing a floral wreath and holding a thunderbolt in his right hand is said to have stood between the Bouleuterion and the great temple at Olympia (v, 24.1-2). It was a dedication of the Thessalians after their victory over the Phokians, a battle that Pausanias dates before the Persian wars. The sculptor is said to have been the Theban Askaros, pupil of Kanakhos of Sikyon. On at least two further statues of the god, one of which was a work of the Aeginetan sculptor Aristonous (Paus. v, 22.5), a thunderbolt was combined with an eagle in Zeus' hands. The work of Aristonous was a votive of the Metapontians and stood close to the so-called Hippodameion in Olympia. The second statue of Zeus was dedicated to the god by the Leontinians (Paus. v, 22.7). An over life-size bronze image of Zeus, made by the Aiginetan Anaxagoras and dedicated by the Greeks to Zeus at Olympia after their victory at Plataea might have also held a thunderbolt, as may be inferred from the remnants of its base in the sanctuary (Paus. v, 23.1-3; vi, 10.6; Hdt. ix, 81).[46] Likewise the statue of Zeus Ithomatas at Leuktra in Laconia probably depicted the god as *Keraunios* with thunderbolt in hand (Paus. iii, 26.6). Two thunderbolts held in each hand of the god are connected by Pausanias with two more votive-statues in Olympia, the first dedicated to Zeus *Horkios* (Paus. v,

24.9-11) and the second to Zeus *Dipaltos-Horkios* (Paus. v, 22.1; viii, 19.1). Finally, a colossal bronze image of the god, a work of Myron, probably held a thunderbolt in its lowered left hand, as may be deduced from surviving Roman copies. The statue was part of a dedication at the Samian Heraion and stood close to images of Athena and Herakles (Strabo xiv, 637b).[47]

Yet the association of Zeus with a thunderbolt is much earlier[48] than the previously mentioned images of the god. The earliest, albeit disputable, representation of the god as a nude unbearded male figure, holding a bird in his left hand and a thunderbolt in his right may be seen on a pithos lid from the Fortetsa cemetery at Knossos, dated to around 700. Twenty years later, a similar figure, dressed in a short khiton and holding a thunderbolt and a sceptre, is depicted on a Protokorinthian aryballos by the Ajax Painter. By the middle of the century, a winged male wearing a short khiton and boots (*endromides*) is depicted with a thunderbolt in each hand on a 'Melian' amphora from the cemetery of the isle of Rheneia near Mykonos. Although the identification of the male as Zeus is highly debatable in all these cases, they all bear strong resemblances to later images of the god.[49] The latter range from types of Zeus standing, striding or seated, with a thunderbolt in his raised hand often combined with attributes such as a sceptre or an eagle held in the other hand, to images where the god carries two thunderbolts, one in each hand. Broadly speaking, the various iconographical types of Zeus with a thunderbolt are best connected with his cult-epithets as *Keraunios, Keraunophoros, Dipaltos-Horkios* and *Ouranios*. A considerable number of mainly bronze statuettes, especially from sanctuaries of Zeus such as those on Mount Lykaion in Arkadia, Olympia, Dodona and Pherai in Thessaly, show the god in all the above types. Representations of the god extend chronologically to the Hellenistic period (with a large number continuing into the Roman times), and may also be found on black- and red-figure vases, clay relief plaques (*pinakes*) and hammered metal sheets as well as coins.[50]

2. The swiftly walking goddess and the source of her light

A common category of divine representations depicts a goddess engaged in swift movement, with one or two torches in hand. Although the occasional presence of animal companions of the goddess tend to associate her with Artemis on certain occasions (such as in **6.1**), a definitive case regarding the identification of the goddess cannot yet be made. The earliest surviving example of the swiftly walking goddess is on a white-ground lekythos, work of a painter close to the Diosphos Painter (**6.1**, dated to 500). The goddess wears a long-sleeved khiton, topped by a dark himation and a pair of wings spring from her back. She is accompanied by two animals (possibly a dog and a doe) who run next to her. It is tempting to compare this scene with well known literary images of Artemis walking in the mountains among wild beasts (e.g. *Od.* vi, 104-5).[51]

More secure identifications of the torch-bearing goddess may derive from her well defined hunting outfit (including weapons such as a bow, arrows and quiver, as well as accompanying animals) on a small group of terracotta relief *pinakes* from Brauron (**6.72-6.74**) and a black-figure disc (**6.12**), dated to the first half of the fifth century (**Pl. 28**). In red-figure, a painter from the circle of Douris (**6.28**) and Hermonax (**6.29**) represent the huntress goddess alone. She holds her bow and arrows in her often lowered left hand, and her short burning torch, upright, in her right hand. A similarly held short torch appears in the left hand of Artemis on a fragment of a red-figure krater from Brauron (**6.34**, *c*. 460-450). Some further, comparable representations are **6.57**, **6.94**, **6.134**, where the goddess is accompanied by a rearing doe, and **6.103** (**Pl. 34**), where she is followed by a dog.

The theme of the torch-bearing but unarmed walking goddess is taken up by the Pan Painter as early as *c*. 480 (**6.2**; **Pl. 29**). She wears a long-sleeved khiton and himation and has long hair falling onto her shoulders. The goddess walks to the right, turning momentarily to look back. Her two short blazing torches in each hand are not held in a strictly upright position, but their upper ends tilt forward slightly. By 470-460, the Bowdoin Painter adds an altar to the above image of the goddess, thus providing some clues regarding the source of the divine flame (**6.7**, **6.30**, **6.31**).[52] Both torches are held above the altar on **6.7**, with the right torch clearly held almost upright and much higher than the left, which is lowered towards the altar in an almost horizontal position (**Pl. 30**). Judging from their different position – the left torch being closer to the altar than the right – and their flame, we may assume that the moment chosen for depiction is immediately after the lighting of the torches from the altar. The ceremonial character of the lighting of the torches of the goddess is enhanced by her long-sleeved khiton, the tainia on her loose hair and her imposing stride towards the altar. Literary references to the origins of divine flames are scarce. Callimachus described how the goddess Artemis kindled her first pine torch at the cinders of a lightning-struck tree on Mysian Olympos (*Hymn 3* 116-18; third century). However, it seems that artists adopted their own versions of the theme, preferring an altar-fire as the source of goddesses' torches.

A goddess, possibly Hekate, seems to be engaged in a similar activity on a late fourth-century vase (**6.69**). She holds a burning torch in each hand as she approaches an altar, which burns in front of a statue of a triple Hekate. The decision to depict this particular moment after the kindling of the torches from the sacred flame of the altar (an image clearly alluding to the purity of the goddess's light), appears to have exercised a long-lasting influence upon later art, since it is found again later on a third-century bronze relief from Delos (A 1719).[53] A variation on the theme of the kindling of divine torches from an altar is offered by the Painter of Vienna 202 (**6.58**, first half of the fourth century). The painter depicts a goddess mounted on an animal, on her way to light her torch from an altar. The addition of the altar by the Painter of Vienna 202 enriches (or even possibly imitates) an earlier scene on a clay relief pinax from Brauron, where Artemis sits on the back of a bull, holding a flower[54] and a torch (**6.71**, *c*. 500). On **6.58** a doe replaces the bull, and both goddess and animal move towards the altar for the ceremonial kindling of her torch.

3. Torch-lit libations

The basic theme of the swiftly walking goddess with torch in hand is often enriched by the pouring of a libation by the goddess depicted; the earliest such examples date to the first quarter of the fifth century and are Attic works of the Berlin Painter (**6.8**, of *c*. 480-470) and a painter close to the Gela Painter (**6.13**, of *c*. 500-475). A wreath embellishes the head of the goddess in a similar scene on a white-ground lekythos, which also includes a dog following the goddess (**6.14**, in the manner of the Bowdoin Painter). An altar for the lighting of the torch shortly before, or at, the moment of the libation is introduced around 460 (**6.23**, **6.53**), recalling similar practices from the cult of the Eleusinian deities, notably in the following scenes of the departure of Triptolemos. The Washing Painter (**6.53**) enriches the earlier type of the embellished torch-bearing goddess next to an altar by adding more figures; Apollo is the recipient of Artemis' libation, while behind him Leto attends the ritual. The representations of a torch-lit libation poured by Artemis in the presence of, and close by, her brother continue in fourth-century vase-painting. These compositions increase in size and sometimes occupy more than one register. On a red-figure pelike (**6.55**) probably by the Kadmos Painter, Artemis stands before the seated Apollo with a jug and a phiale in her hands, while a long torch rests lightly on her left shoulder. A fourth-century fragmentary marble relief now in Thessaloniki depicts the goddess standing frontally, holding a phiale and most probably a torch (**6.108**); here Artemis appears in her hunting outfit, consisting of a short khiton topped by an animal skin (nebris).

The objects of a torchlit libation (torch and phiale) are found in the hands of a frontally seated goddess depicted on two reliefs of the fourth century (**6.106**, **6.115**). Her iconographical affinities with the Phrygian goddess Kybele include the animal (probably a lion) which rests in her lap.[55]

Within an Eleusinian context, representations of torch-lit libations are not uncommon. These scenes normally involve the principal Eleusinian deities, namely Demeter (the Mother) and Persephone (the Daughter), such as in **6.27** by the Nikon Painter (*c*. 460), **6.37** (*c*. 450) and **6.41** by the Athens Group 1826 (*c*. 440-430). The two goddesses stand facing each other. Demeter holds a sceptre and a phiale, and in one example she also holds corn in her sceptre-bearing hand (**6.38** by the Aberdeen Painter; dated to *c*. 450). Persephone carries a torch in her left hand and pours the libation with her right.[56] Representations of the ritual objects required for a torchlit libation (without the ritual itself being depicted in the scene) are offered by the Painter of Tarquinia 707 (**4.6**, of *c*. 460-450) and by three late fourth-century marble reliefs (**6.110**, **6.128** and **6.129**). Torch and phiale are here held by the Eleusinian goddesses (Demeter and Persephone), who are portrayed in wider arrays including other deities (such as possibly Iakkhos holding baby Ploutos in **6.129** or Hades with a sceptre and a horn of plenty in **6.128**) as well as close to groups of worshippers (**6.110** and **6.128**). Demeter is seated and holds sceptre and phiale in **6.110** and **6.129** and Persephone stands next to her, holding one or two long torches (**6.110**, **6.128** and **6.129**). A rather hieratic type of Demeter is observed on **6.110**, where the goddess is portrayed in frontal pose (instead of the more common profile one) and wears a polos. In this same scene, the torches held by standing Persephone are joined together.

A particularly distinct category of Eleusinian scenes to which the ritual of a torchlit libation seems to be central are those inspired by the myth of the divine mission of Triptolemos.[57] Torches constantly shed light on the scene of the libation between Triptolemos and one of the Eleusinian goddesses. This libation may have happened sometime before the hero's departure to teach humans the cultivation of land, under Demeter's instruction. The general iconographical pattern of the scene places Triptolemos usually in the centre, seated in his winged car and holding a phiale for the libation. One of the Eleusinian goddesses – usually Demeter – stands facing him; she too is equipped with a torch and a jug for the pouring of the libation into the hero's phiale. In most examples, Triptolemos is surrounded by torch-bearing figures. These may be the pair of Mother (Demeter) and Daughter (Persephone) (for example, **6.5**, **6.11**, **6.17** and **6.35**; **Pl. 31**), or one of the two, coupled with another goddess, possibly Eleusis or Hekate (such as in **6.15**, **6.19**, **6.33**, **6.4**, **6.21** and **6.51**), who is usually positioned behind the hero. A torch-bearing Persephone usually stands next to her normally sceptre-bearing mother facing the hero (as in **6.15**, **6.19**, **6.21** and **6.46**; **Fig. 21**). Persephone may also stand with one or two burning torches behind the hero, as on **6.47**, **6.49**, **6.48**, **6.50**, **6.52**, **6.65** and **6.116**. On **6.5** by Makron, **6.25** by the Niobid Painter and **6.36** by an imitator of the Villa Giulia Painter, Persephone is about to perform a libation into the hero's phiale, while her sceptre-bearing mother stands behind her or behind the hero. Simpler compositions of the libation comprising no more than two figures (Triptolemos and one goddess) are not uncommon (e.g. **6.16**, **6.20**, **6.10**, **6.26** and **6.38**). The Marlay Painter adds Hermes to the scene, behind the hero (**6.42**, of *c*. 450-425). Hekate often assumes a position among Eleusinian divinities, including Demeter, Persephone and Triptolemos, as on a mid-fourth-century relief (**6.96**), or she may stand behind Demeter who is involved in libation with Triptolemos (**6.45**, the Painter of London E 183; third quarter of the fifth century).

The position in which the torch is carried by the divinities involved in the scene appears to depend largely on the stage of the libation ritual. The kindling of the torch is clearly depicted on **6.9** (by the Berlin Painter; c. 480-470; **Pl. 32**), where it is held almost horizontally with its upper end above the altar flame, the presence of which enhances the religious atmosphere of the scene.[58] The moment shortly before the libation should probably be recognised in the scenes of **6.33** and **6.35** by the Niobid Painter (c. 460-450); this is implied by the respective positions of the jug and the torch used. The jug is lowered in the goddess's right hand which hangs loosely by her side, while her torch in her left hand is already lit and held upright from a point towards its lower end. Her left arm bends at the elbow at a right angle, letting the torch extend parallel to the axis of her body. The next stage of the libation depicts the jug raised for pouring; with the blazing torch being held out towards the centre of action in the scene, as on a vase by Makron (**6.5**), two by the Berlin Painter of c. 480-460 (**6.9**; **Pl. 32, 6.15**) and a much later votive relief from the Athenian Agora, dated to the last quarter of the fourth century (**6.125**). Alternatively, the torch is held loosely at its lower end and leans lightly against the left shoulder of the goddess, such as on **6.16** by the Cleveland Painter, c. 470-460, as well as in **6.17** (**Pl. 31**) and **6.20** by the Niobid Painter, c. 465-460. Apart from the phiale, the hero also carries a sceptre (**6.11, 6.16, 6.17**; **Pl. 31** and **6.20**) or ears of corn (**6.5, 6.9, 6.19, 6.35** and **6.33**) in his left hand.

A comparison between the libation scenes within an Eleusinian context and other representations of farewell libations before the departure of a hero or warrior shows that the new element here is the presence of the torch. The sheaves of corn are a typical attribute of the Eleusinian deities, reflecting the agrarian nature of their cult, and are directly linked with the purpose of Triptolemos' mission. The precise order of events in these mythical representations of the libation and the handing of the grain to Triptolemos, prior to his departure, is difficult – if not impossible – to establish on the basis of the visual evidence of the rituals performed. The moment when the hero receives the corn from the goddess Demeter is depicted by the Niobid Painter (**6.20**) and takes place under torch-light shed by Persephone, who also lights a similar scene dated to the mid-fourth century by the Marsyas Painter (**6.65**). Possible indications of the use of torches in later stages, after the completion of the ritual of libation (e.g. when Triptolemos' mounts his chariot with the sheaves of corn in hand) are offered by the Hector Painter (**6.46**, c. 450-425; **Fig. 21**). On a series of fifth-century red-figure representations (such as **6.5, 6.9**; **Pl. 32, 6.19, 6.35** and **6.33**, by Makron, the Berlin Painter, the Altamura Painter and the Niobid Painter respectively), the sheaves of corn held by Triptolemos shortly before, or during, the libation, may possibly suggest that the hero had already received them prior to the libation. Accordingly, one

Fig. 21 Departure of Triptolemos attended by torch-bearing Eleusinian deities. Paris, Cabinet des Médailles 424 (Cat. no. 6.46). Hector Painter, *c*. 450-425.

may interpret these scenes as the final stage of the ritual before his departure, or in any case shortly before that. While one may not rule out these possibilities regarding the stages of the torchlit libation ritual between Triptolemos and one of the Eleusinian goddesses, it is equally likely that, to an extent, the precise stages of this libation were not of such vital importance to the ancient viewer, particularly when compared to the meaning that the libation scene carried as a whole. If this assumption is valid, one may then admit that some of the surviving representations of these torchlit libations may be labelled as 'generic' scenes, the main purpose of which would be to recall the specific myth, which bore close associations with the nocturnal and torchlit Eleusinian ritual.

The hour of the rituals performed by the divinities under the light of torches cannot be securely determined. Nothing precludes influence from the nocturnal activities of the Mysteries, where scenes from the divine myth, such as the last libation between Triptolemos and Demeter, might have been reenacted with the aid of torches.[59] It therefore seems highly probable that it was contemporary ritual practice that inspired vase-painters to include torches in their works.

4. Receiving worshippers and sacrifice

Sculptural representations of Artemis often show the goddess carrying two long torches while she receives worshippers or attends a sacrifice in her honour. The earliest surviving examples begin in the second half of the fifth century and continue throughout the fourth century. The goddess, dressed in a long garment (peplos or khiton and himation) normally stands, holding one upright long torch in each hand; the upper part of her torches tilt towards the procession of worshippers (e.g. **6.78**; **Pl. 33**, **6.88**, **6.99** and **6.100-6.102**). This procession includes men, women and children who are depicted on a smaller scale than that of the goddess, and hold offerings for the goddess or make a typical greeting gesture towards her. A different arrangement of the two long torches of the goddess is found on a votive relief of the second half of the fifth century (**6.78**; **Pl. 33**). They are depicted joined together, resembling a double torch which Artemis holds with both hands across her body. Next to her, an altar, mounted on a stepped base, separates the planes between the goddess and the worshippers. A doe is occasionally depicted next to the goddess, underlining, in conjunction with the torches, her domination of the realm of nature (e.g. in **6.88** and **6.101**).

The size of Artemis' torches in these scenes often exceeds the height of the goddess, and is almost twice as high as the worshippers. Their thickness is greater in comparison with that of the torches that Artemis holds in other representations, such as those depicting her as huntress or daidoukhousa. They are held in a way that immediately attracts the attention of the viewer, resembling, and perhaps meant to be the equivalent of, a sceptre. In this respect, the torches may be taken as symbols of the power of the goddess, since the sceptre in its traditional form is absent from many representations of Artemis. Furthermore, the presence of an altar implies the source of her torches' sacred flame, which seems to have been required during the sacrifice. In view of these considerations, it becomes clear that in scenes where Artemis receives worshippers, her torches should not be understood as primarily sources for illumination of a ritual that takes place in the dark; they rather stand as attributes of the goddess, underlining her nature and authority over the mortal participants in the scene.

The light of Artemis is sometimes reduced to one long torch within a similar context depicting the goddess receiving offerings and sacrifices from her worshippers. This torch may be held obliquely across the body, upright as a sceptre, or it may lean lightly upon the shoulder of the goddess. The other (free) hand of Artemis rests on a rearing doe (**6.86**) or a pillar (**6.87**), as is seen on two late fifth-century reliefs from Brauron and Delos respectively. In these representations, Artemis' dress is long (peplos or long khiton, sometimes combined with a himation), and her hair falls onto her shoulders or is gathered in a *sakkos*. On a relief from Brauron dated to the second half of the fourth century (**6.117**), the goddess holds a torch in an oblique position with both her hands while she (together with Leto and Apollo) attends the leading of a bull for sacrifice in her honour.

A representation of a goddess carrying two long burning torches on either side of her body and accompanied by a dog may possibly be recognised as Hekate on a relief of the first half of the fourth century. The goddess is seated on a rock and is approached by a male figure with a horse, possibly a worshipper (**6.90**). The fourth-century reliefs discussed above (**6.106**, **6.115**),[60] which possibly depict Kybele seated holding a phiale and a torch, include figures of worshippers crudely carved on the panel of the reliefs.

Torches appear in similar scenes from the Eleusinian iconography (comprising the two chief Eleusinian goddesses and their worshippers) during the second half of the fourth century. In most of the surviving examples, a seated goddess, usually identified as Demeter, is depicted. The goddess raises her hand in a conventional gesture of address (probably to the worshippers), on the Attic reliefs **4.55**, **6.97** and **4.50**. Behind Demeter, a goddess (probably Persephone) stands, bearing two long torches, which are either arranged on each side of the frontal goddess (**4.55**, **4.50**) or tilt towards seated Demeter (**6.95**). Persephone may also stand in front of the seated goddess with a pair of long torches (**6.81**, **4.54** and **6.104**) or a single torch, often carried obliquely with both hands (**6.128-6.129**). A sceptre-bearing Demeter stands, accompanied by a standing Persephone who holds one (**6.127**) or two long torches, sometimes joined together (**4.51**), while on **6.119**, the Daughter (Persephone) is depicted alone with a similar pair of torches and receives the worshippers. An altar is added on **4.51** between Persephone and the worshippers who lead sacrificial victims towards it. Triptolemos is added to the scene in a relief from Eleusis (**6.121**, *c.* 330), where a standing Demeter and Persephone receive their worshippers. The two deities (Persephone, in frontal view holding two long torches and Demeter with a sceptre) flank the seated Triptolemos, while the worshippers are arranged in a different plane, behind Demeter and next to the other divinities, without any apparent contact with the divinities. The worshippers are always depicted on a smaller scale than the gods (usually half the gods' height).

Apart from torches, lamps also appear to have been connected with sacrificial procedures, though perhaps less directly. Clay and marble hanging lamps decorated with protomes of sacrificial animals have been reported from the sanctuary of Demeter at Predio Sola in Gela and the sanctuary of Artemis at Brauron.[61] A more explicit, though later, reference to the involvement of lamps in sacrificial procedures is found in a sacred law (*IG* V², 514, ll. 13-17)[62] from the sanctuary of Despoina at Lykosoura[63] and is dated to the third century or later. The Lykosoura law prescribes the essential materials for a sacrifice to the goddess Despoina. Here, lamps are only one of the components for an appropriate sacrifice to Despoina, together with olive, myrtle, honeycomb, barley-groats cleared of darnel, a figurine, white poppies, incense, myrrh and aromatics. No further specifications are made regarding the use of these materials, a matter which was apparently cloaked in secrecy. Finally, one may mention the inventory lists of the Delian Artemision which include a few bronze lamps along with other ritual vessels.[64] However, whether these lamps (and other vessels) were actually used in sacrifices or in any other particular ritual is not possible to define, since, in any case, the role of lamps (along with the rest of the ritual vessels mentioned in the inventories) as valuables appears to have been more important.[65]

5. Divine assemblies

As with images of isolated light-bearing divinities, torches are often found in divine hands in representations of broader assemblies of gods. The divinities included in these arrays vary. The Dionysiac circle is a common context, comprising satyrs and maenads as well as divine participants such as Apollo, Hermes and a torch-bearing Artemis (**6.61**, early fourth century). A sanctuary setting, indicated by a tripod, is given by the Kadmos Painter on the upper register of a kalyx-krater by the Kadmos Painter (**6.56**, late fifth century), while in the lower, a peplos-wearing Artemis with a torch and bow stands among divinities, such as Leto and Apollo. A roughly contemporary representation by the Painter of London F 64 depicts a torch-bearing Artemis (with her torch lowered in her left hand) next to her brother, touching his shoulder (**6.62**). It is possible that the mythical reconciliation between Apollo and Herakles is depicted here, and is witnessed by two goddesses and Hermes. The torch held by Artemis in the above representations of divine arrays does not appear to be functioning as a practical device, to illuminate a nocturnal event. On the other hand, it does not appear to be used otherwise, in relation to the action that is taking place in these scenes. One may therefore interpret the presence of the torch as an attribute which highlights the nature and authority of Artemis in a way comparable to its role in representations of the goddess with worshippers.[66]

Further companions of torch-bearing Artemis (who here wears her quiver) include Herakles, placed in a *naiskos*-like structure, and Athena, in a vase by the Telos Painter (**6.63**, *c*. 390-380). Kourotrophic deities,[67] such as Apollo, Zeus, Leto, Kybele, Asklepeios, Hygeia and Hermes are among the popular divine contexts which include torch-bearing divinities, especially Artemis and Hekate (e.g. **6.91**, **6.98**, **6.106-6.107**, **6.115**, **6.118**, **6.120** and **6.130-6.132**). Groups of torch-bearing Eleusinian deities are commonly arranged in arrays, the best examples of which are dated to the fourth century (**4.7**, **4.21-4.22** and **4.31-4.38**; **Pls. 18, 20**; **Figs. 15, 18, 19**). Among the deities depicted one may single out Demeter, Persephone and young male figures, usually identified as Iakkhos and Eubouleus. Finally, smaller compositions including torch-bearing divinities are not uncommon, such as divine processions accompanying chariots on which another divinity is mounted. Such examples are found in a votive relief from Brauron (**6.82**, *c*. 420) and a fourth-century red-figure vase (**6.66**; *c*. 350-330). In both examples, the principal torch-bearing deity is Artemis, who in **6.66** is portrayed in her hunting outfit (quiver, peplos with crossed straps across her chest) and with a long torch in hand.

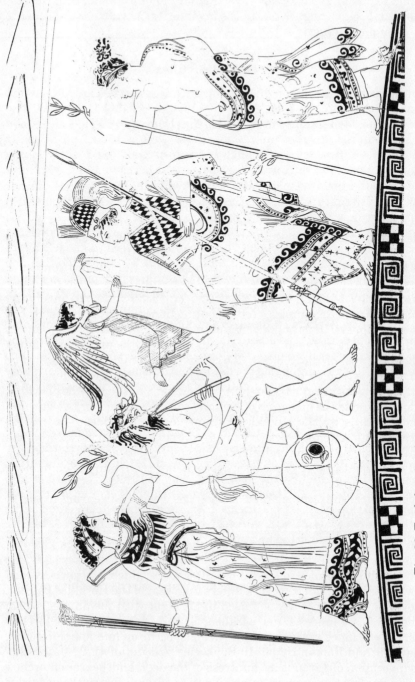

Fig. 22. Torch-bearing Artemis attending the music contest of Apollo and Marsyas. Athens, National Museum 1442 (Cat. no. 7.17). Semele Painter, c. late fifth century.

VI

Fire and Light in Divine Hunting
and Divine Retribution

1. Divine hunting and 'black' hunting

Torches are associated with Artemis in her capacity as huntress on a number of occasions. These range from simple representations of the goddess in hunting dress, standing or walking (**6.28-6.29, 6.71-6.73** and **6.90**), often accompanied by a dog (**6.12; Pl. 28, 6.103**) and a wild beast (**6.103; Pl. 34**), to larger mythological scenes (e.g. the musical contest of Marsyas and Apollo (**7.17; Fig. 22**) as well as the myths of Bellerophon and Aktaion; **7.13-7.14, 7.17, 7.19, 7.25, 7.10-7.11; Pl. 35** and **7.20**) and divine assemblies. On two examples a torch-bearing huntress Artemis is depicted with worshippers; the Achilles Painter places the goddess opposite a woman, probably engaged in a pre-nuptial ritual, who apparently unties her belt in front of the goddess (**3.5**, *c.* 450; **Pl. 9**). On a fourth-century relief, Artemis (peplos, quiver) is depicted in natural landscape denoted by the slope of a hill upon which a hare is running, chased by a dog (**6.103**). The hare attracts the attention of Artemis who tilts one of her two burning torches towards it. The Herakles Painter depicts a goddess – plausibly identified with Artemis – actively involved in hunting action (**7.24**, *c.* 380; **Pl. 36**), among two divine onlookers (Zeus and Apollo), and in the presence of a flying Nike. Here, Artemis does not carry her usual hunting equipment (bow, arrows and quiver), but an extinguished torch serves as her only weapon which she uses against a doe. The goddess (wearing a girded peplos and a white hair-band) restrains the wild animal by holding its ears and pulling its head backwards towards her. Her raised right hand is about to deliver the fatal blow to the animal, which is forced to kneel on its hindlegs. A late fifth-century Attic relief depicts the goddess in the same peplos outfit and stance in the act of killing a doe which is also restrained in a way similar to **7.24**; the work differs from that of the Herakles Painter, however, in the type of weapon used in her fight with the animal, which on the relief is a lance.[1] Later parallels for this scene, where the torch is replaced by a lance in the hands of Artemis, occur on late fourth-century, Hellenistic and Roman coins.[2] In Sophocles' *Trachiniae* (l. 214), the chorus's invocation of Artemis as 'huntress of the deer' and 'bearer of torches' possibly implies the supplementary function of torch-fire in the goddess's hunting activities. On another level, the presence of the torch in the hands of the goddess, combined with the act of killing, may possibly have alluded – in the eyes of the ancient viewer – to the sacred flame of sacrifice which purifies and destroys the victims in her honour.[3] Death-bringing fire was used particularly in the festivals of Artemis, where animals were thrown into the fire alive in holocaust sacrifices for the goddess, such as the Laphrian sacrifice at Patras.[4]

Several iconographical traits of the hunting outfit of Artemis are shared with other divine huntresses, whose victims are not animals, but humans. These are the Furies (Erinyes), whose hunting nature is referred to in literature on many occasions.[5] While chasing their victim to his death, the Erinyes hide in ambush, use torches, goads, nets and snares, and let out hunting cries.[6] Aeschines refers to the torches of the Erinyes as their means of punishing men who were disrespectful to the gods (*In Tim.* 190). A wealth of imagery showing Erinyes as huntresses with burning torches in hand may be found on fourth-century red-figure vases, mainly from South Italy, but also from Kertsch. Here, their hunting outfit primarily consists of a knee-length sleeveless khiton, often with crossed straps across the bust, and boots (*endromides*). This general image is enriched with weapons such as the serpents in their hair and around their arms, double spears and torches. Torches are sometimes the only weapon held or brandished by the goddesses, but they may also be carried along with double spears, snakes and phialae.[7] Alternatively, the presence of torches may be justified on more practical grounds, since the Erinyes, being the daughters of the Night, live underground.[8] A god who often hunts at nightfall and therefore is called *nukhios* by Aeschylus, is Hermes (*Cho.* 726-8). His ability to hide and disappear in the night, aided by his swift sandals, is specially mentioned in the *Homeric Hymn to Hermes* (ll. 80-3).[9] Torches are, however, absent from Hermes' iconographical repertory, apart from a reference to the fire-sticks of the god, the invention of which is credited to him in the Hymn (l. 111).

A hunting metaphor similar to that of the Erinyes may be observed in the case of Artemis, where the victim is a human, who experiences the forces of divine vengeance. Artemis' destructive power over a girl called Lakoreia is compared by Pindar to a raging fire, kindled by a small spark (*Pyth.* iii, 35-6). In Attic vase-representations depicting the punishment of Aktaion, Artemis is present, dressed in her hunting outfit, with an upright short burning torch in her right hand, a bow in her left and a quiver hanging from her shoulder (**7.10-7.11**; **Pl. 35** by the Lykaon Painter and **7.12** by the Dinos Painter or the Kleophon Painter). Zeus, Lyssa and Hekate are occasionally depicted in this scene,[10] the latter moving towards Aktaion. According to a version of the myth,[11] Aktaion was turned into a stag by Artemis and condemned to be devoured by his own hounds because of his love for his aunt, Semele. Death was Artemis' punishment for his sexuality, to which the goddess was opposed. It is tempting – though debatable – to link the torch-fire and hunting dress of Artemis with her vengeful nature which could, in many cases, bring about the death of those opposed to her will. In the case of Aktaion, the will of Artemis may be translated into a requirement of purity[12] and chastity from her servants, and may be best paralleled with the myths of Kallisto and Hippolytos, whose death was sent by the goddess as soon as they lost their virginity.[13]

A torch forms part of the hunting outfit of the goddess in further scenes alluding to, or depicting disrespectful acts by mortals (*hubris*). These include, for example, the audacity of Marsyas in comparing his musical skills with those of Apollo and in daring to compete with the god, or the act of Bellerophon who rode the divine horse, Pegasus.[14] A painter related to the Pronomos Painter inserts the bust of the goddess in a broader scene of Bellerophon riding Pegasus (**7.20**; early fourth century). Artemis holds a torch in her left hand and a bow in her right, with her quiver hanging from her right shoulder, and turns to Apollo on her left. The Kadmos Painter (**7.13-7.14**), the Semele Painter (**7.17**; **Fig. 22**), the Painter of Athens 1472 (**7.19**) and the Marsyas Painter (**7.25**) chose to depict the very expression of Marsyas' arrogance, namely the moment when the contestants play music: Apollo plays his lyre and Marsyas his flute. Artemis (wearing a long sleeveless khiton or a peplos) raises a burning torch in her left or right hand. The rest of her hunting equipment (quiver and bow) is either held by the goddess or hangs from a tree in the background.[15] Artemis normally stands among other divinities who also attend the contest, such as Athena, Aphrodite, Hermes and Rhea. According to a different iconographical version of the myth of Marsyas by the Kadmos Painter (**7.15**), Atremis holds two long burning torches, rather than just one, without any further alterations of the iconography of the scene.

Light is apparently used as a weapon by Dionysos in the *Bacchae*, when the god resists the arrogance of Pentheus which clearly derives from his limited mortal knowledge. The light of Dionysos, symbol of the divine power of the god, contrasts sharply with Pentheus' ignorance, best expressed as 'darkness'.[16] The climactic point of this opposition is the imprisonment of the god of light and his female followers in dark chambers (Eur. *Bacch.* 611) and their miraculous liberation by Dionysos (Eur. *Bacch.* 614-41). The 'darkness' imposed by Pentheus' confused ignorance and arrogance is triumphantly defeated by the light of Dionysos, which appears symbolically in the form of fire blazing up from Semele's tomb (Eur. *Bacch.* 623-4). The sacred fire of Dionysos, a recurrent epiphanic sign of the god in the *Bacchae*, functioned as a symbol of opposition to violently imposed rule which restricts freedom of thought and choice. On the opposite side stands Pentheus, who uses violence to impose his authority, for which he is criticised by Teiresias who advises him that force cannot govern human affairs (Eur. *Bacch.* 310-12).

Although the use of light by gods within a 'hunting' context – in the broader sense – does not necessarily appear to indicate a nocturnal ritual, the torch of mortal hunters served a practical function during night-hunt. Wild beasts avoid contact with artificial light, Xenophon explains, because it betrays human presence, and therefore night – the quietest time – is the best time to catch a deer in the plain (Xen. *Cyn.* xi, 3). However, if you chase the deer in the mountains, you may well also catch it during the day because of the peaceful nature of the wild landscape there, away from human threat (*Cyn.* ix, 17). More specific information about the use of torches in the capture of wild animals at night is furnished by Oppian in Roman times (*Cynegeticus* iv, 124-35). Speaking about the lion-hunt, he describes how the light of torches is used to surprise the beast – which is not accustomed to living near cultivated land and its inhabitants – in the darkness of the night. According to a nocturnal hunting strategy described by Oppian, three hunters lie in ambush by the nets, two of whom (those standing near the corners of the net) hold flaming torches in their right hands and a shield in their left. The key function of torches during the lion-hunt – perhaps the most dangerous of all hunts – was obviously the fact that they blind the animal and deprive it of the chance of a fair fight. Repelling a lion by throwing spears and burning faggots at it at night appears to have been a practice well-known to Homer, who uses it in two metaphors in the *Iliad* (xi, 552; xvii, 661); the beast is worn out after a night-long fight with men and dogs, and by early morning, despite its hunger, it no longer dares to attack the cows and cattle kept in the yard. A simile used by Agamemnon likens the Greek forces attacking Troy in the middle of the night to a rampant lion; the dependence of this image upon current nocturnal hunting practices appears very likely (Aesch. *Ag.* 825-6).

One of the earliest references to night-hunting (without separate mention of torches) may be found in Plato's *Leges* (vii, 822d-824e), where the *ethos* of the night-hunter (so-called '*nuktereutês*') is clearly coloured with negative connotations, because his hunting practices clearly contradict Plato's definition of a traditional hunt.[17] The latter takes place during daytime, and its practices involve the coursing of the animal and its killing with a lance, by a group of men; such an exemplary hunt in which many Greek heroes participated was the hunt of the Kalydonian boar. Plato's nuktereutes, however, uses nets and snares as well as the darkness of the night to catch his victims, and this enables him to gain clear advantages in his confrontation with the beasts by avoiding an open fight with them. By contrast, the notion of night-hunting as well as hunting with nets and setting ambushes for the victim are considered a natural part of hunting technique by Xenophon. His liberal attitude is best expressed in *Cyropedia*, where Kambyses finds that ambush is the right technique for fighting night-battles in rough areas (Xen. *Cyr.* i, 6.40).[18] Night-hunting – or 'black' hunting – which is based on tricks and not on open confrontation with beasts, is often associated in literature with youthfulness and more specifically with adolescence.[19] Oppian mentions Hippolytus as the youth with a clearly negative attitude to marriage, who invented the hunting net

(*Cynegetica* ii, 25), while another youth, Orion, is credited with the discovery of snaring by night and of guileful hunting (*Cynegetica* ii, 28-9). Xenophon agrees that night-hunting is a game for youngsters (Xen. *Cyn.* xii, 7).

Hunting was apparently not the only nocturnal – and therefore 'unconventional' – activity undertaken by male adolescents; nor was the use of tricks, which extended well beyond hunting activities. The duty of Athenian ephebes to serve their city as frontier-guards (*peripoloi*) on the margins of their polis (*eskhatiai*), away from cultivated land and often in mountainous areas, offered them an ideal opportunity to get involved in nocturnal military activities. For example, Thucydides records a night ambush near Nisaea in 425 set up by the Plataians and the lightly armed peripoloi (iv, 67-8). Comparable adolescent 'rituals' occurred in Sparta. Young Spartans, armed only with a dagger, left the city to roam in the mountains and the countryside, making use of the night for their involvement in various improper acts, such as the assassination of helots (Plut. *Vit. Lyc.* 28).[20]

Outside Athens and Sparta, Damon of Khaironeia is a later example (*c.* 88-87) of a young night-fighter of the frontier (peripolos).[21] Neither the limited literary sources available for night-hunting and night-wars nor relevant vase-representations make explicit mention of, or feature, any torches. However, considering the extent of these night-activities, it is hard to believe that all artificial illumination was absent. Furthermore, the negative connotations of torches, at least up to Plato's time, which may have recalled nocturnal 'unfair' hunting practices, may perhaps to some extent account for the lack of torch representations in the iconography of hunting scenes.[22]

2. Light and fire as divine weapons

The destructive effects of blinding light and burning fire are uniquely combined in the thunderbolt of Zeus, when he fights his monster-opponents, the Titans. Some of the earliest representations of the father of the gods involved in Gigantomachy may be found on an early seventh-century Protokorinthian aryballos by the Ajax Painter (*c.* 680). Although not epigraphically identified, the male god depicted wears a short khiton and holds a sceptre in his right hand and a flaming thunderbolt in his left, with a sword hanging from his waist.[23] A clearer representation of a bearded god with sceptre and thunderbolt in the act of attacking a giant is offered by the Copenhagen Painter (*c.* 470).[24] Terrifying images of both fire and light dominate the description of the fight between the Gods and the Titans in Hesiod's *Theogony*. Heat, flames and thunder form the essence of Zeus' thunderbolts, which are shot continuously against the Titans, as the father of the gods strides rapidly from Olympus to confront them (*Theog.* 689-90, 706-8). The cries of the burning earth together with the extraordinary heat deriving from Zeus' thunderbolts awaken and confuse the khthonic Titans who live underground (*Theog.* 690-700).[25] The image of destruction becomes more and more dramatic as burning earth encircles the sea (ll. 844-7), or as earth melts from the heat (ll. 861, 867). Among the Titans, the monstrous nature of the hundred-headed Typhoeus entails fire which flashes forth from the eyes and mouth of every one of his heads (*Theog.* 826-8; Apollod. i, 6.3).[26] During his fight with Typhoeus, Zeus strikes him with thunder, lightning and smouldering firebolt which burn off all of the heads of the monster (*Theog.* 853-6). Apollodorus' account of the fight mentions the thunderbolt as the weapon that Zeus uses from a distance, finally striking the monster down with an adamantine sickle (i, 6.3). Typhoeus spews out fire every time he receives a blow from Zeus (*Theog.* 857-9; Aesch. *PV* 359-63). A questionable black-figure representation of Typhoeus depicts a three-headed male monster with a burning torch in one hand, while the other carries a lightning bolt (Heidelberg Painter, *c.* 575-550).[27] The Titan Porphyrion also meets his death through Zeus' thunderbolt, according to Apollodorus (i, 6.2).

The effectiveness of torches as weapons against otherwise invincible monsters may be observed in the combined strategy followed by Herakles and Iolaos during their confrontation with, and killing of, the Lernean Hydra. Like Typhoeus, Hydra had many snaky heads – their number varies in the sources from eight or nine to fifty, a hundred or even ten thousand – one of which was immortal. Herakles attacks the Hydra and cuts off the monster's heads, assisted by Iolaos who holds one or two blazing torches to sear the roots of the heads and prevent the spurting of new ones from each spot. On **7.4** by the Diosphos Painter (*c.* 500-490), a fire burns behind Iolaos alluding to the source of his torch flame (**Pl. 37a-b**). Literary sources for this ingenious device are fairly late (Apollodorus ii, 5.2; Diodorus Siculus iv, 11.6), apart from a reference by Euripides to a representation on a metope of the temple of Apollo at Delphi (*Ion* 194-200). The scene of the metope, described by the chorus, depicted Herakles cutting off the heads of the monster and his assistant scorching the roots of the heads that had been cut. Athenian vase-painters include torches in their representations of the theme from as early as the middle of the sixth century until the beginning of the fourth (**7.1-7.7**). Apollodorus (ii, 5.4) and Diodorus Siculus (iv, 12.5) provide further evidence for the use of fire by Herakles as a weapon against the centaurs Agrius and Ancius, when they attacked him in the house of the centaur Pholus. Herakles threw fire-brands at them continuously, one after the other.

The thunderbolt of Zeus is mentioned on several occasions in literature as his essential weapon against mortals and gods. After a short description of how Zeus destroyed the sons of Amphareus (Castor and Pollux) by his fire-wrought consuming bolt, Pindar concludes that it is hard for men to strive against a mightier power (*Nem.* x, 71). The death of Kapaneus was delivered by Zeus in a similar way, as a punishment for his arrogance when he compared his mortal fire-weapon with the divine fire of Zeus' bolt (Soph. *Ant.* 134-7). In Aeschylus' *Septem* (ll. 453-4), the invocation of the chorus to Zeus reveals that the torch or thunderbolt of the father of the gods clearly functions as an agent for delivering justice. A similar role for Zeus' thunderbolt as a means of punishment for cheats and liars may also be found in Aristophanes (*Nub.* 397-9), while fire is again associated with justice in the *Aves* (ll. 1240-2). Torch-bearing Erinyes often occur in South Italian vase-painting in scenes depicting the punishment of mortal hubris, such as in the scene of the torture of Ixion on a wheel.[28]

Tragic drama offers several examples in which fire-bearing gods are invited to act as avengers of evil and brutal forces that threaten mortals. In Sophocles' *Oedipus Tyrannus* (ll. 188-215), fire and light assume various forms to function as divine weapons against the god of war who ravages the land of Thebes by bringing the plague with him. The chorus invokes a series of gods to avenge the destruction of Thebes caused by Ares. One clearly notes that every god invoked by the chorus has a distinct and unique association with light and fire which is different from that of the other gods. Athena is mentioned first as the 'golden daughter of god' and is asked to send 'radiant rescue' to the Thebans (*OT* 188-9). Zeus is invited to affront Ares with the fire of his thunderbolt (*OT* 200-2). Next comes Apollo whose association with light is highlighted by the chorus before they plead with the god to attack their city's enemies with his arrows (*OT* 203-5). The torches of Artemis and Dionysos are explicitly mentioned in their respective invocations by the Chorus. Artemis' torches (*purphorous aiglas*) are intimately connected with her capacity as huntress (*OT* 206-8),[29] while in the case of Dionysos, the pine-torches (*peukan*) constitute only part of his brightness. The latter is supplemented by his gleaming gold headdress (*khrusomitras*), his lightning and his 'aflame' face. He is invoked to burn this god of death, who is hated by all the gods. The notion that fire can only be fought with fire may be detected here with increasing clarity. This is effected through the emphatic opposition between the burning weapons of the gods on one hand (particularly the thunderbolt and the torches), and the burning caused by the the raging god of war and death (Ares) on the other (*OT* 190-2). Similar patterns are observed elsewhere in tragic drama, as in Aeschylus' *Septem* (l. 63) where the blast of Ares is explicitly mentioned. In Euripides' *Phoenissae*, ruthless Ares 'lights for Thebes the bloody torch' (*'aima daïon phlegei'*, *Phoen.* 241), while fire is used to describe violent images of battle in the following lines of the play (*Phoen.* 250-3). Here again, fire-goddesses – namely Demeter and Persephone – are invited by the chorus to fight on their side and to protect their land (*Phoen.* 683-8). On another level, the light of the pine torches of Dionysos is often treated in tragic drama as a symbol of peace, especially through the image of the god dancing with his followers on the rocky ridges of Parnassos, which shine under torchlight (Eur. *Bacch.* 226-38). This

scene is dramatically contrasted with 'burning' images of war found elsewhere in Euripides (e.g. *Phoen.* 239-49).

Fire and light combine again in the form of torches to serve as invincible
divine weapons against the Titans in vase-representations. Female deities
such as Artemis and Hekate often brandish burning torches against fallen
giants. The number of torches in the hands of gods varies between one and
two, according to artistic preference. On a cup by Aristophanes (**7.18**; late
fifth century; **Pl. 38**), Artemis (wearing a girded peplos with overfold) with
a torch in each hand burns a fallen giant who is dressed in a lion-skin.
Behind the goddess, and with his back turned towards her, a bearded Zeus
fights in a striding pose, hurling a thunderbolt in his raised right hand
towards a retreating giant. Larger compositions of the Gigantomachy
(**7.16**, **7.21-7.22**) include a torch-bearing Artemis (identified by her short
khiton, khlamys and boots on **7.16** and her bow and arrows on **7.21**)
engaged in fighting giants using as weapons two torches, or a torch and a
bow.[30] The motif of a torch-bearing goddess placed back-to-back with Zeus
who hurls the thunderbolt may be observed on **7.8**, a work in the manner
of the Niobid Painter (*c.* 450). Here the goddess is Hekate, engaged in a
fight with a giant whose helmet has fallen on the ground. Hekate uses
torches as weapons against Klytius in Apollodorus' account of the Gigantomachy (i, 6.2). The same composition (**7.8**) includes Artemis carrying her
hunting weapons (bow and arrows). Hekate may probably be identified on
6.21 and **7.9** (dating between the second quarter of the fifth century and
440), since Artemis joins in the battle using her bow. A peplos combined
with a rectangular billowing cloth on her shoulders (*epiblêma*) and a
diadem or a tainia in her hair form Hekate's regular outfit in this scene,
bearing obvious resemblances to Artemis in the type of her weapons, outfit
and fighting pose. On **6.21** a torch-bearing maenad takes part in the battle
on the side of Dionysos who also fights using a thyrsos and a vine branch.
Whether the torches may be taken to imply a night-fight is apparently of
little significance here, in view of the clear function of the torches as
weapons that burn the giants.

3. The torch of war

Brightness in the darkness of the night often implies hostilities or forthcoming disasters in the *Iliad*. In the poem, both torches and bonfires serve
as indispensable supplements to military action; the use of fire ranges
from fire-signals and watch-fires to torches for setting fire to the enemy's
camp and ships. The gleam of armour is likened to a forest fire (*Il.* ii, 455,
780), with the latter being a usual simile for fierce battles (*Il.* xi, 156; xvii,
736-41; xx, 492). In the eighth book of the *Iliad* (ll. 507-11), after a
victorious day for the Trojans, Hektor orders them to burn as many fires
as they could all night long until dawn, so as to prevent possible escape of
the defeated Akhaeans. Hektor's command applies to the Trojans' women-

folk, who must burn great fires in their homes, and at the same time keep watch, so that no Akhaean can get into their city while Trojan men are away (*Il.* viii, 520-1). Impressive and terrifying, a bright image of innumerable watch-fires burning between the ships and the stream of Xanthos ends that same book. This image is complemented by a calm gleaming sky, filled with the smaller fires of the stars and moon (*Il.* viii, 554-63). The threatening brightness of the Trojan watch-fires has an immediate effect on the psychology of their enemy, which is described as panic and sorrow (*Il.* ix, 1-3; x, 12-13). However, even more dramatic are the direct threats of the use of fire as part of war hostilities. The threat to torch the ships of the Greeks – their ultimate source of escape – is often used by the Trojans, clearly alluding to the massacre that would follow afterwards (*Il.* viii, 205-6; xiv, 46-7; xv, 600-2, 701-2, 718).

The disastrous effects of torches in captured towns are recalled by Pindar (*Pyth.* v, 84; *Pae.* ii, 30), while tragic drama paints a fuller picture of them (e.g. Eur. *Erechtheus* 23). Torches complete the works of the sword by consuming what is left after the slaughter. Teucer assures Helen that not even the walls of Troy can be traced anymore, after the burning of the city (Eur. *Hel.* 107-8). Fire is inextricably connected with the utter destruction of Troy on several occasions in literature. The chorus in *Helen* describes fire as the monument of Troy (Eur. *Hel.* 196-7), while both the heroine in Euripides' *Andromache* (l. 111) and a herald in Aeschylus' *Agamemnon* (l. 641) mention sword and flame as the main forces that turned Troy into a ruin. Smoke and ashes are also the predominant traits of the ruin of Troy in the memory of the leader of the victorious Akhaean forces, Agamemnon (Aesch. *Ag.* 818-20); earlier in the play, we learn that this fire was sent by Ares to cremate the Trojan dead (ll. 440-2). In Euripides' *Troades* (l. 814), fire is the weapon with which Herakles destroyed Troy. Talthybios' exhortation to his soldiers to let the torches consume the rubble that once was Ilion (Eur. *Tro.* 1260-3) is followed by a tragic image of the city burning in the night and by the laments of Hekuba and the chorus at the sight of their once glorious city (Eur. *Tro.* 1273, 1279, 1294, 1302, 1318). The Trojan women prefer to run to the flames of the enemies' torches instead of suffering a humiliating and shameful death (Eur. *Tro.* 1282-3): 'Come let us rush into the pyre. Best for me to die with this country of mine as it burns' (trans. Barlow 1986).

Torch-fire becomes the symbol of Troy's destruction in Aeschylus' *Agamemnon*; the watchman on the roof of the palace of Agamemnon awaits a fire-signal in the darkness of the night to 'enlighten' them concerning the news of the destruction of Troy (ll. 8-9). The fire-beacon arrives from Troy at Argos in the middle of a bright night, full of stars (ll. 6-7), very similar to the night of the Trojan watch-fires in the eighth book of the *Iliad* (viii, 554-63).[31] In an extended monologue, Klytaimnestra refers in remarkable detail to every single stop of the fire-beacons, which rushed the fire of captured Troy – the triumphant fire for the Greeks – to

Argos (Aesch. *Ag.* 281-316). T.N. Gantz and M.J. Anderson have rightly
emphasised the strong metaphorical connotations of this long chain of fire,
as reflections of the equally long chain of crime and retribution throughout
the *Oresteia.*[32] Taking into account the summary of the *Iliou Persis* by
Proklos, Anderson further suggests that the fire-chain in the *Oresteia* may
have been inspired by the torch raised by Sinon before the siege of Troy. In
Proklos' *Iliou Persis*, Sinon's torch signals the return of the Greek ships,
prefiguring the subsequent disaster for the Trojans.

The torch is part of an ingenious trick devised by the Greeks, which also
includes the wooden horse and the deliberate choice of night-time for their
final attack.[33] Both night and net are mentioned by the Argive chorus as
vital elements that brought about the Greek victory in Troy (Aesch. *Ag.*
358), while the nocturnal time of the Greek attack is recalled by both the
queen and the chorus on several occasions (Aesch. *Ag.* 279-80, 329, 355-6).
This combination of night-time and tricks that finally trap the enemy in
the tenth year of war clearly deviated from the fair code of honour of the
Greek warrior from Homer into classical times. The evidence of nocturnal
military operations and the use of torches in them is limited compared
with military activity which took place during daytime.[34] The repeated
reference to torches and fire in literary accounts of the destruction of Troy
may be taken as a symbol of excessive violence and unlimited revenge. In
Aeschylus, the theme of fire recurs in connection with descriptions of
war-scenes, such as in *Septem* 340-2, where slaughter and the carrying of
fire are mentioned side by side as inevitable aspects of the brutality of war.
Similar connotations – uncontrollable lust for violence – are found elsewhere in the play (*Sept.* 432-6).

Fighting in front of the Electran gate of Thebes, Kapaneus is portrayed
as an invincible warrior whose image assumes even more terrifying dimensions by the detailed description of the decoration of his shield. The
latter portrays a man with no arms other than a torch who cries out that
he will burn the town; this threat is inscribed with golden letters on the
shield. Earlier on (*Sept.* 423-32), Kapaneus himself vows that he will burn
the town, and his arrogance reaches the point of his comparing the fire
of his torch with the effect of Zeus' thunderbolt. In Sophocles' *Antigone*
(ll. 134-7), both Kapaneus' hubris and his fire-bearing outfit are recalled
in connection with his death via the thunderbolt of Zeus, whose fire he
had compared with his torch. A fourth-century Campanian red-figure
amphora depicts Kapaneus (bearded, wearing a khlamys and a helmet)
standing outside the wall of a besieged town. He brandishes an axe in
his left hand towards the defenders of the town and carries a torch in
his right.[35]

In another scene of the same play describing the storming of the Proetid
gate of Thebes by Tydeus, the hero carries a shield upon which an equally
terrifying scene of celestial brightness is depicted (Aesch. *Sept.* 387-90);
the sky is ablaze with stars and a full moon right in the centre of it. We

have seen how similar images of brightness in the *Iliad* and in Aeschylus' *Agamemnon* function as heralds of forthcoming disasters, and therefore one may envisage the terror that such a shield-sign would have conveyed to the enemy. A further example of a shield-emblem bearing the figure of Prometheus with a torch in hand comes from Euripides' *Phoenissae* (ll. 1120-2). The shield, upon which a lion-skin is thrown, belongs to Tydeus and its decoration bears an obvious resemblance to the Aeschylean pattern of Kapaneus' shield. The notion of fire as a weapon against fire becomes even clearer through the range of variations of fire-patterns which decorate the shields of heroes. An impressive pair of fire-patterns decorate the shields of a pair of opponents in *Septem* (ll. 488-94). The fire-breathing monster Typhon is depicted on the shield of Hippomedon, belching smoke from his mouth. A counter-image of the latter is found on the shield of Hippomedon's opponent, Hyberbius, which depicts Zeus with a thunder-bolt ablaze in his hand (*Sept.* 505-14).

4. Light and fire as symbols of destruction and justice among mortals

Outside war-activities, fire and light assume various forms to prefigure disasters on many occasions, especially in tragic drama. In Sophocles' *Antigone* (ll. 474-6), Kreon uses a metaphor of the terrifying effects of fire that can crack and melt the toughest iron, to threaten the heroine with the disastrous consequences of her disobedience of his orders.

Hekuba's dream that she gave birth to a blazing torch instead of to Paris (Eur. *Alexandros*, fr. 10) is alluded to in Euripides' *Troades* (l. 922) by Helen, who considers Paris to be one of the causes of the fall of Troy and of her own death. This unique metaphor, combining the contradictory elements of the birth of a child and the destructive fire of a torch[36] which becomes the cause of death of his mother, resembles aspects of the birth of Dionysos. In Aeschylus' *Choephoroe* (ll. 604-11), the life of Meleagros is envisaged as a metaphorical parallel to a fire-brand, the burning of which would bring about the death of the hero; in a deliberate attempt to cause her son's death, which was prescribed by the Fates at his birth, Meleagros' mother, Althaia, pushes the half-burnt brand into the hearth-fire.

Themes taken from traditional wedding imagery, such as the torches which lighted the procession leading the bride to her new home, are often employed in tragic drama to contrast sharply with other major transitions in life, such as the way to death. On two occasions the tragic protagonists are women who, more or less willingly, walk to their deaths which are caused by fire, dressed as brides. In Euripides' *Supplices* (ll. 990-1030), Evadne re-enacts her marriage with Kapaneus in the middle of the funeral of the Argive Seven. In her monologue, she paints a picture of her happy wedding, full of brightness (caused by the torch-light) and songs (*Supp.* 993-4).[37] However, she now wishes to share the fate of her dead husband by throwing herself onto his funeral pyre, dressed as a bride. Both transitions in Evadne's life (a happy one, leading her to her home as bride, and a tragic re-enactment of the first, leading her to her death) are surrounded by brightness. The funeral pyre is the light that she now pursues (*Supp.* 1002) which serves the function of, and is compared with, a tragic wedding torch by the heroine, in her attempt to renew her marriage in Hades (*Supp.* 1025: 'Kindle the wedding-torch, begin my nuptials!', trans. Davie 1998). Another bride who meets her tragic death in fire unwillingly is Glauke, the new bride of Iason, in Euripides' *Medea*.[38] Here, fire takes the form of a shining crown, a wedding gift to the bride from Medea. As soon as Glauke wears it, she catches fire and the brightness of the flame doubles every time she shakes her head to remove the crown (*Med.* 1194). The horrific image of the burning bride is enhanced by a unique metaphor of the mixture of blood and fire dripping from Glauke's head like resin from a pine-torch (*Med.* 1200-3). The implications of the pine-torch should clearly be sought in the dramatic reversal of the role of nuptial torches in Glauke's wedding, where, instead of bright symbols of a happy union, they become symbols of destruction. Furthermore, this metaphor of the dripping torch – the ultimate result of Medea's revenge – most probably relates to Medea's earlier lament that she would never experience the happiness of raising the nuptial torches of her own children (*Med.* 1026-7). In the endless chain of crime and retribution, Medea, having torched her own marriage (*Med.* 378), seeks to deprive her rival Glauke of her right to enjoy the brightness of nuptial torches at her wedding by delivering to her a 'bright' funeral instead.

Fire-and-light imagery as the herald of disaster is repeatedly used by Aeschylus in his *Oresteia*. The forms of fire conveying the message of destruction vary. The central message of the destruction of Troy in the trilogy is given at the very beginning of *Agamemnon* in a reduced, symbolic form of a beacon-torch (*Ag.* 2-9). Thereafter, large sections of the play are devoted to the powerful meaning of this fire-symbol which stands as a sign of both destruction and triumph. The emphasis on the nocturnal setting of the arrival of the beacon-fire – which no doubt connoted the tragic night of the killings at Troy – is shown by the words of the watchman who lies in wait for twelve months, night after night (*Ag.* 2), along with a detailed description of the stars of the night-sky and the comparison of their brightness with that of the beacon-torch (*Ag.* 4-8). The power of the beacon-torch to 'cheer the dark night with good news' and to 'kindle night to glorious day' (ll. 20-1) is clearly reflected in the watchman's reaction: he believes that the symbol should be accepted by the queen straight away with pious acts (*Ag.* 25). The fire-omen is received with bright nocturnal sacrifices (*Ag.* 89-96) ordered by Klytaimnestra, who later describes at length the way the beacon-torch followed to reach her (*Ag.* 283-311). In her narration, the starting point of the torch is Mount Ida, where it was kindled by a fire-god – the identity of whom is not given – and whence it reached Argos through a series of relays.

However, the Aeschylean figure of gleaming light in the middle of the night as an alarming sign does not stop with the beacon-fires.[39] The lamp by which Klytaimnestra confesses that she spent sleepless nights while weeping for her husband could be taken as her secret companion in her illicit nocturnal life with Aigisthos (*Ag*. 888-9). Another kindling of the lights in the palace is ordered by Klytaimnestra in the *Choephoroe* (ll. 536-7). She awakes in terror in the night after a prophetic dream revealing her later killing by her son. In the brightly gleaming palace, Klytaimnestra offers nocturnal sacrifices, just as she had done the night when she received the fire-beacon from Troy. As the time for Klytaimnestra's punishment approaches, the chorus express their horror through images such as the teeming of the earth and the swarming of the ocean with fear, as well as the glare of fire from mid-sky at noon (*Cho*. 590). Since the murderous plan of Orestes immediately precedes this scene, it is tempting to see this celestial fire as not only an omen of destruction, but also an allusion to the shining light of justice. Indeed, the function of torch-fire as a means of punishment – and therefore an agent of delivering justice – for Aigisthos and Klytaimnestra was implied by the chorus' earlier wish that they both die in spitting pitch-flames (*Cho*. 267-8). On the other hand, we see that brightness is at least one of the features of justice in *Agamemnon* (ll. 772-4), since 'Justice with her shining eyes/ Lights the smoke-begrimed and mean/ Dwelling;' (trans. Vellacott 1959). When Orestes asks his dead father whether he can bring some light to cheer the dark bed where Agamemnon lies, the chorus advises him that the murderer will be brought to light only after the murdered man is mourned and burnt (*Cho*. 319). Finally, blazing hearths sometimes seem to be an index of moral disorder calling for justice; an example is the kindling of Klytaimnestra's hearth by Aigisthos, at the sight of which she says she feels no fear (*Ag*. 1438).[40]

VII

The Fire and Light of the Senses

1. 'Bright' and 'burning' images of emotions

Burning emotions are well known in Greek literature and are mainly used as metaphors to describe excessive feelings and behaviour ranging from love, joy and triumph to anger, revenge and terror, as well as ecstatic feelings inspired by contact with the gods.[1] Blazing fire is reflected from the eyes of Agamemnon as a result of his wrath, when he hears Kalkhas' verdict that he should return Khryseis to her father (*Il.* i, 104). The wrath reflected in the eyes of Ares during his confrontation with Kyknus is compared to glowing fire in the *Scutum Herculis* (l. 390), where he is further likened to a tusked boar. This concept of fire-emitting eyes as a poetic metaphor of uncontrollable frenzy, encountered again in the case of Typhoeus,[2] may, at least partially, have been influenced by early theories of natural philosophers, such as Empedokles (*DK* fr. 84).[3] Empedokles' theory on vision, which maintained that eyes entail fire, was found inadequate by Aristotle (*Sens.* 437B-438A), since it could not explain the phenomenon of limited human vision in the dark. According to Aristotle, if eyes were made of fire, one should have unlimited visual ability with the aid of the fire-rays hidden in the eyes.

The quenching of Akhilles' anger is referred to in book nine of the *Iliad* 678, implying the fire-like fury of the hero (*'sbessai kholon'*). The fury of the same hero should be understood by the simile of his head blazing with fire, when he appears at the battlefield to rescue Patroklos' body (*Il.* xviii, 207-14). A similar reflection of Akhilles' fury while active on the battlefield is given in xxi, 522-5, where his inflamed head is said to resemble the smoke and flames rising from beacons in a besieged city. In Euripides' *Andromache* (ll. 488-90), the chorus describes the inflamed rage and jealousy of Hermione against the eponymous Trojan heroine of the play ('like fire she (Hermione) raged against her rival in love', trans. Davie 1998). This state of ultimate anger urges Hermione to extremes, such as her planning of the death of her rival Andromakhe. The burning of the soul or the heating of the entrails (*splakhna*) caused by scorning and anger is experienced by Aristophanic characters in the *Nubes* 992 (*'phlegesthai'*) and the *Ranae* 844 (*'thermênê kotô'*). The flame and heat of fire often takes the form of raving madness in both comedy (Ar. *Thesm.* 680: *'maniais phlegôn'*) and tragic drama; in the second example, the madness sent by Hera to Io through a gadfly burns her with a flameless fire (Aesch. *PV* 879-80: *'maniai thalpous', oistron ardis khriei m' apuros'*).

Further occurrences of inflamed feelings are to be found in Pindar. Medea's desire for Hellas sets her heart on fire in *Pythian* iv, 219: 'and a dear desire for Hellas light in her mind a flame' (trans. Conway & Stoneman 1997). In lyric poetry and tragic drama, erotic desire is connected with the warming up of the heart, as in the case of Zeus' desire for Io (Aesch. *PV* 590-1). Fire 'steals beneath the flesh' of lovers during their encounter in a fragment of Sappho (*LP* fr. 31); this burning feeling is combined with other 'symptoms' of erotic desire which disrupt the senses, such as speechlessness, humming in the ears, limited vision, sweating and change of the colour of the flesh to green. In another fragment of Sappho (*LP* fr. 48), the moment when the lovers meet coincides with the cooling of the heart which was burning with desire (*'epsuxas eman phrena kaiomenan pothô'*). On the other hand, beauty radiates brightly, like the face of Helen in a Sapphic fragment (*'lampron idein prosôpon'*, *LP* fr. 16). In Plato's *Charmides* 155D, Sokrates' sexual excitement, provoked by his looking inside the cloak of young Kharmides, resembles the feeling of catching fire (*'kai ephlegomên'*). In art, the cause of the burning feeling of love takes the form of torches held by a naked Eros. The latter may be flying carrying a torch in each hand, as on a red-figure amphora by the Charmides Painter around 460-450.[4] From the fourth century onwards, Erotes with torches become more popular and appear on bronze mirror-handles and gold earrings, as well as on vases.[5] The boiling of the heart, as the organ which mostly experiences human passion, is described in more detail in Plato's broader discussion of the functions of the heart in *Timaeus* 70B. In his *Moralia*, Aristotle asserts that passion produces heat (*Part. an.* 650b35: *'thermotêtos gar poiêtikou ho thumos'*), while in his *Rhetoric* 1406a, he recalls an earlier poetic expression by Alkidamas which associates the anger in the soul with a fire-coloured face.

The fire-metaphor is often used by dramatists to describe sadness, anxiety and fear. In Aristophanes' *Lysistrata*, the heroine burns in her heart because of her grief for Greek womenfolk (*Lys.* 9-10: *'kaiomai tên kardian'*). Sorrow scorches the heart of Ismene and Antigone when they receive the advice of the chorus that they should put an end to this unnecessary emotional burning (Soph. *OC* 1695). The chorus of the *Septem* reveal their dread, which is inflamed by anxiety in face of the forthcoming attack on their city (Aesch. *Sept.* 289-90). Similar burning feelings of anxiety warm Electra's soul with a fire unlike that of Hephaistos (Soph. *El.* 887-8: 'What do you look to, that you are warm with this fire not of Hephaistus?', trans. Lloyd-Jones 1994).

The actual practice of raising beacon-torches to celebrate victories in war apparently corresponds with the poetic use of the concepts of fire and light as symbols of hope, joy, enthusiasm and triumph. Aias of Telamon brought a light (*'phaos'*) of deliverance to his comrades in the Greek camp after he smote the Thracian Akamas in the *Iliad* (vi, 5-6). Pindar refers to the long-lasting flame of glory of the winners in panhellenic or local athletic contests on several occasions. In his *Olympian* iv (ll. 10-11), in honour of Psaumis of Kamarina who won a mule-cart race, Pindar asserts that the famous deeds of strength bring a light that will long endure among mortals ('Bringing a light will long endure / On famous deeds of strength', trans. Conway & Stoneman 1997). Both the joy and the glory of a victory shine like a flame in *Pythian* xi, 45 ('for the joy and glory of both flame like fire', trans. Conway & Stoneman 1997), while in *Nemean* x, 2, Argos, the mother-city of many winners in athletic games, is lit up by countless glorious flames of the deeds of its bold sons ('It [Argos] is ablaze with achievements beyond number because of its valiant deeds', trans. Conway & Stoneman 1997). The torch as a symbol of triumph and escape from death recurs in Medea's address to Iason. In her attempt to underline her contribution to his killing of the dragon-guardian of the Golden Fleece, she reminds him that she was the one who raised the light of fair-hope, the torch of salvation, for him and his companions (Eur. *Med.* 481-2: 'I raised aloft for you the fair light of escape from death', trans. Kovacs 1994). In tragic drama and comedy, the lifting aloft of torches is often combined with dances and songs praising the glory of individuals, such as the torchlit procession escorting the poet Aeschylus in Aristophanes' *Ranae* 1525-8, or that of the female participants in the Thesmophoria who also dance and sing (Ar. *Thesm.* 101-3). The former example bears a strong resemblance to the nocturnal torchlit escorts of the Eumenides in Aeschylus' *Eumenides* 1005. Both processions combine the light of torches with songs and dances amid a general feeling of euphoria, which also comes at the end (or near the end) of the plays.

Brightness reflects hope and joy in the scene of the welcoming of Menelaos by Helen, in which Menelaos lights Helen's dark despair (Eur. *Hel.* 629: 'He [Menelaus] comes like a flare of flame / Lighting my dark despair', trans. Vellacott 1972). Similar connotations may be sought in Telemakhos' invocation as 'sweet light' (*'glukeron phaos'*) by both Eumaios (*Od.* xvi, 23) and Penelope (*Od.* xvii, 41) when he arrives safely at Ithaka from his trip to Pylos. The 'brightness' of Telemakhos also reflects his role as guarantor of the safety of the members of the royal family on Ithaka and as protector of the just order in the palace. In Aeschylus' *Agamemnon* the warming properties of fire (*'thalpos men en kheimôni'*, *Ag.* 968-9) as well as its brightness (*'pheggos'*, *Ag.* 602) are used by Klytaimnestra to pretend happiness and relief upon the return of Agamemnon from Troy. Earlier in the same play (ll. 479-82), a broader contrast is brought up by the reaction of the elders to the arrival of the beacon-fire at Argos with the news of the destruction of Troy. The brightness of the beacon in the night kindles fires of hope in the hearts of the Argive elders, a feeling which they consider inappropriate for their age and status, since it is associated with youthfulness. False hope is said to have warming qualities in Sophocles' *Ajax* 478, while villainous behaviour apparently produces heat (for example, in Aesch. *Cho.* 1004 and in *Sept.* 603)! In the first example, reference is made to the warming of passion in the heart and mind (*phrena*) of Klytaimnestra, caused by her cunning snare which kills innocent men, and the second is a metaphor used by Eteokles to describe the effects of evil partnerships at war.

A different concept of brightness may be found in the *Persians* of Aeschylus (l. 150) where the Persian queen Atossa is seen by the chorus as 'light' (*phaos*). Within the context of the Persian court, where members of the royal family were regarded as equal to gods (*isotheoi*; *Pers.* 76-80), such an appellation undoubtedly alluded to the divine nature of Atossa by recalling the divine brightness so well known in Greek literature since the Homeric times.

Light is not only used in literature to describe an excited emotional state. There is a recurrent association between light and knowledge in tragic drama, as opposed to darkness, the latter being a common metaphor for ignorance. In Sophocles' *Oedipus Tyrannus*, the tragic ignorance of Oedipus about his origins is perceived by Teiresias as blindness despite Oedipus' physical ability to see the light! This contrast between physical and real vision is further exploited through the comparison of the 'eyes' of Oedipus with those of Teiresias (*OT* 413: '*su kai dedorkas kou vlepeis*').[6] Teiresias, though blind, *sees* not only the tragic reality in Oedipus' illusion but can also *see* into the future. Teiresias' ability to foretell the future obviously exceeds the limitations of human knowledge, since it is a divine gift from the god Apollo whom Teiresias serves. It is the light of Apollo (who sees and knows everything concerning humans) that 'shines' through the seer despite his physical blindness. Teiresias therefore functions as the humble vehicle of the bright, all-knowing god. Associations between brightness and knowledge are attested in the Homeric poems, where the brightest god, Helios, sees and hears everything from above ('*hos [Helios] pant' ephora kai pant' ephakouei*', *Il.* iii, 277; *Od.* xi, 109; xii, 323). The sun-god is a traditional informant in Greek literature and it is to him that Demeter and Hekate turn to enquire about the fate of Persephone in the *Homeric Hymn to Demeter* (l. 62: '*Helion d' ikonto theôn skopon hêde kai andrôn*'). The notion of an all-seeing Sun is commonly found in tragic drama.[7] In Aeschylus' *PV* 91, Prometheus calls upon the 'all-seeing circle of the Sun' to bear witness to his sufferings caused by the gods. Helios is called to perform a similar function by Orestes in the *Choephoroe* (ll. 985-7), where he is asked by Orestes to witness the crime of his mother, Klytaimnestra.

For mortals, dreams sent by the gods in the middle of the night often shed light on their knowledge of future events. A good example is the dream of the Persian queen Atossa which is terrifying but prophetic of the disaster of the Persian fleet at Salamis, led by her son Xerxes (Aesch. *Pers.*

176-208). As the queen later admits with grief, the vivid dream lit the darkness of her sleep (*Pers.* 517). That this prophetic 'light' of knowledge experienced by the queen is the work of the gods is unquestioningly admitted by everyone at the Persian court, and they advise Atossa to offer sacrifices to the gods. A similar enlightening dream in the middle of the night is found in the *Choephoroe* of Aeschylus (ll. 536-7). The dream is sent to Klytaimnestra revealing a horrible course of future events prefiguring her own murder by her son. The metaphorical 'light' of knowledge received by the queen is here visually reflected by a sudden lighting up of the palace in the middle of the night, according to her orders, which was followed by nocturnal sacrifices. On this occasion, Orestes asserts (*Cho.* 534) that the dream was a 'message' from her murdered husband, Agamemnon.

2. Divinely inspired emotions; the fire of the maenads

a. Scenes from the worship of Dionysos

Torches are introduced in Attic representations of the worship of Dionysos as early as the second quarter of the fifth century. The earliest surviving example depicts a bearded Dionysos, set on a pillar in profile view, in front of a silen, who holds out a kantharos to the god (**8.8**, *c.* 460-450). Two maenads, the staunch female worshippers of the god, dance on the reverse of the vase; one holds a short burning torch. More figures and tension are added to the same basic scene on **8.22** by the Dinos Painter (*c.* 420; **Pl. 39 a-b**); here, on either side of the god's image, a pair of maenads (wearing long sleeveless khitons, ivy wreaths on their heads and with their hair loose on their shoulders) are engaged in different activities of worship. The torch-bearing maenads dance to the music of a *tumpanon* next to other maenads who scoop wine out of a stamnos into a skyphos nearby. The torches held by the maenads are long and follow the movement of their bodies, usually with one hand raised to the head and the other lowered. On the reverse, a lowered torch is combined with an upright thyrsos in the hands of one of the four maenads depicted, who dances to the music of a double-flute and a tumpanon played by her maenad-companions.

In Euripides' *Bacchae* (ll. 485-6), the god himself specifies the time of his worship as primarily nocturnal: 'At night for the most part: darkness possesses solemnity' (trans. Seaford 1996). However, in the *Bacchae* most of the activities of the maenads seem to take place in daytime, after their night's sleep (e.g. in ll. 692-3 and 677-9 they wake up after sunrise). The most likely explanation for this contradiction has been offered by V. Leinieks, who argues that emphasis on daytime activities was intended to eliminate or minimise suspicions of drunkenness and sexual licence, both of which were associated with the night.[8] This is made clearer by Pentheus' characterisation of female night-time activities as devious and corrupt (Eur. *Bacch.* 487: '*dolion kai sathron*'), a view contradicted by Dionysos on two occasions (ll. 486 and 488: 'Even in the daytime one might discover the shameful', trans. Seaford 1996).

Frenzied nocturnal dances performed by the maenads are attested in the *Bacchae* (ll. 862-5): 'Shall I ever in the all-night dances set my white foot in bacchic revelry, tossing my throat to the dewy air of heaven' (trans. Seaford 1996). The dance included twisting movements of the body and tossing of the head and hair, which was normally allowed to hang loose on the shoulders, as shown in Attic red-figure representations.[9] The divine possession of the maenads by the god is often compared with the fire of their torches. This parallel was explicitly drawn by Sophocles, who connects the state of being *entheos* with the worship-inspired fire (Soph. *Ant.* 962-3): 'For he tried to check the inspired women and the Bacchic fire' (trans. Lloyd-Jones 1994). The state of being entheos is directly linked by Euripides with the power to foretell the future, as Teiresias asserts in the *Bacchae* (ll. 298-301): 'This god is also a prophet: for the bacchic and the manic have much mantic power; for when the god enters abundantly into the body, he makes the maddened speak the future' (trans. Seaford 1996). A clearly similar concept of the inflamed prophet possessed by the god when delivering a prophecy may be detected in Aeschylus'*Agamemnon* (ll. 1256-7). Kassandra feels Apollo's fire burning inside her as she arrives at the palace of Agamemnon and begins to predict the chain of killings that would take place there, including her own death. Some centuries later (first century CE), Plutarch (*De def. or.* 432F) uses fire as a metaphor for the state of divine empowerment, recalling Euripides' earlier attitude: 'For Bacchic rout and frenzied mind contain much prophecy, according to Euripides, when the soul becomes hot and fiery, and throws aside the caution that human intelligence lays upon it, and thus often diverts an extinguishes the inspiration' (trans. Babbit 1984). The words *'enthermos'* and *'purôdês'* describe the ultimate excitement of the human soul under the influence of the god. This is contrasted with the 'mortal reasoning' (*thnêtê phronêsis*), which 'extinguishes' the manic enthusiasm inspired by the god (*to bakkheusimon kai to maniôdes*). All-night dances and songs in honour of Bakkhos (Dionysos) in a Theban context[10] are vividly described by Sophocles in *Antigone*, where the chorus incites Dionysos to visit the temples of the gods with all-night dances, following the mighty god who shakes the land (ll. 152-4). The burning enthusiasm of the maenads is further reflected in images such as their fire-bearing hair (Eur. *Bacch.* 757-8): 'and on their locks they carried fire, and it did not burn them' (trans. Seaford 1996).

This latter image appears in the context of the tearing (*sparagmos*) and subsequent eating of a living animal, a common activity of the maenads in the myth, known as *ômophagia*.[11] It highlights the uncontrollable and destructive force of these women under the influence of Dionysos, a force which resembled fire. Torches are introduced in a scene of omophagia on another occasion, notably in the nocturnal ceremonies of the Kretan *kouretes* in a fragment of Euripides' *Kretes* (*TGF*² fr. 472, ll. 9-15). The burning enthusiasm and extreme activities of the maenads become a real threat to the traditional socio-political structure of the polis. In the *Bacchae*, Pentheus makes this point several times with particular reference to the sexual licence of the Theban women, who abandoned their homes and marriage-beds to devote themselves to Dionysos in a state of divinely inspired mania (Eur. *Bacch.* 220-3, 236). The literary description of their unbridled state as a blaze ('*to pur uphaptetai*') is given concrete form in art in the shape of torches. These 'inflamed' women, out of control, are thought to bring shame to a traditionally dominant male population, as is attested in the *Bacchae* 778-9: 'Already this indecent violence of the bacchants is blazing up close like a fire, a great reproach for the Greeks' (trans. Seaford 1996).

b. Scenes of the thiasos

Maenads are by far the most distinctive torch-bearing figures in Attic vase-painting. They are commonly found engaged in a variety of activities, such as ecstatic dances and processions of the thiasos often including Dionysos and his mythical male companions (silens and satyrs). They may also walk hurriedly across the surface of a vase or merely stand at the sides of a composition shedding light with their torches on the nocturnal activities of the scene.

The Altamura Painter opens the series of representations of torch-bearing maenads in a thiasos context around 460. On **8.2**, his maenad (long-haired, wearing a long-sleeved belted khiton with overfold) shakes a torch in each hand in front of a kneeling satyr. One of the most distinct images of the thiasos (which includes satyrs) is offered by the Achilles Painter (**8.11**, c. 440). The dancing maenads are involved in a range of activities, such as carrying torches and snakes, and tearing into two pieces (sparagmos) a deer which is swung in the lifted hands of a maenad. The Dinos Painter enriches the repertoire by increasing the number and variety of torch-bearing maenads in the thiasos-procession. On **8.25** the procession – which includes Dionysos – 'opens' with a pair of a maenad and satyr-musicians, and ends with a maenad holding two torches. On **8.23**, Dionysos, clad in Thracian dress with *ependutes* and boots, appears in a procession of satyrs and maenads with thyrsoi, torch and tumpanon. Calmer processions of the thiasos include torch-bearing maenads who lead the thiasos groups (such as in **6.21** by the Niobid Painter and **8.28** by the Pothos Painter), walk behind Dionysos ready to pour wine into his kantharos (such as in **8.17** by the Curti Painter), or assume different positions inside (as in **6.21**, **8.10**, **8.15** by the Duomo Painter, **8.20** by a painter in the manner of the Kleophon Painter, **8.33** and **8.39**) or at the ends of the group of the thiasos (**8.27**, **8.29**, **8.30** and **8.31** by the Pothos Painter).

Simpler groups of the thiasos, consisting of three figures, mainly repeat these iconographical patterns. Dionysos (long-haired, bearded, ivy-crowned, and clad in a long khiton and sometimes a himation) always occupies the centre of the composition. The most usual arrangement, such as on **8.5** by the Agrigento Painter, places a satyr or silen at the head of the group, with a torch-bearing maenad coming last. The combination of a torch and oinokhoe in the hands of maenads and the position of the latter behind Dionysos remain the most popular iconographical motifs, which have already been seen in larger compositions, such as **8.13**, **8.19** and **8.35**. The placing of Dionysos between two maenads appears in red-figure iconography at the same time as the arrangement of the god between a leading satyr and a maenad (which has been noted above); however, the popularity of the former grouping (Dionysos flanked by two maenads) was comparatively limited. The Blenheim Painter offers the earliest preserved example (**8.3**, *c*. 460), where the leading position is assumed by a maenad holding a torch and an oinokhoe. A leading torch-bearing maenad is also found on **8.18** by the Danae Painter. The alternative arrangement of Dionysos between a leading maenad and a satyr is not found until the third quarter of the fifth century. The Biscoe Painter (**8.14**) depicts Dionysos standing between a musician-satyr and a torch and oinokhoe-bearing maenad. A very similar ordering of the figures is observed on the unattributed vase **8.34** of the beginning of the fourth century.

Distant associations with maenads seem to bear the females depicted on **8.12** by the Phiale Painter (*c*. 440) on the basis of their attributes which comprise a horn of plenty, a torch and a stamnos as well as musical instruments (lyre and *aulos*). A different arrangement of a three-figure group may be seen on the reverse of **8.5**. A maenad stands frontally holding two short burning torches, one in each hand, repelling two silens who pursue her from each side.

From 450 Dionysos occasionally appears on a mule in the context of thiasos, which includes torch-bearing maenads. The broader iconographical type of a god mounted on an animal and flanked by standing torch-bearing women (often with maenadic traits) who face him is much earlier in Attic vase-painting. A good example may be found on a black-figure lekythos by the Edinburgh Painter, dated to 510-500.[12] It depicts Hermes riding a ram which is placed between a pair of women, possibly maenads, dressed in elaborate khiton and himation; each holds two short, upright torches (**Fig. 27**). The earliest representation of Dionysos on a mule among torch-bearing female participants is offered by the Painter of Bologna 228 (**8.9**); the god is accompanied by a silen, who pours wine into the god's kantharos from an oinokhoe, and by a torch and thyrsos-bearing maenad. The subject of a 'riding Dionysos' among torch-bearing figures in the thiasos survives at least until the middle of the fourth century. On **8.36** by the Black Thyrsus Painter, Dionysos is represented riding a panther between two standing maenads, one of whom carries a short burning torch and a tumpanon. By the middle of the fourth century, Dionysos is depicted mounted on a cart drawn by panthers (**8.37**), following a maenad with two short torches. A variation of Dionysos on the back of a flying panther is offered by a painter of Group G (**8.38**). The youthful god appears to a torch-and tumpanon-bearing maenad who steps back in fear.

Smaller compositions of pairs of Dionysos (with various attributes, such as thyrsos and kantharos) and a maenad with two burning torches (**8.1** by the Mykonos Painter, **8.4**) or with a torch and an oinokhoe (**8.21** by the Kleophon Painter) exist as early as 470. On the reverse of **8.21**, a scene of erotic pursuit between a satyr and a fleeing maenad with a torch recalls the three-figured example of the Vienna vase (**8.5**). A possible pursuit scene may also be seen on the reverse of **8.26** by the Pothos Painter, combined with a scene of an ecstatic dance of the thiasos on the obverse. A torch-bearing maenad (wearing a long khiton and with a nebris hanging from her left arm) stands next to a satyr who faces her. Finally, isolated standing maenads, or women in long khitons who stride across the scene of the vase carrying a torch, are not uncommon. The Dinos Painter represents such a maenad on the reverse of **8.24**, holding her unlit torch low.

These images of women with torches and oinokhoe in hand and often in the company of satyrs or silens[13] – for some of which it is hard to draw a clear distinction between myth and reality – must have been too liberal for the standards of many fifth-century Athenians. The god of light – who is regularly included in the thiasos – takes women away from their dark, confined chambers and introduces them into bakkhic company. The latter is visually defined by shaking torches, pouring wine, playing music and dancing for the god, and enjoying the company of the male participants of the thiasos.[14] Dionysos provides the opportunity for normally enclosed women to enjoy some of the benefits belonging to men, and so pose a threat to domestic patriarchy. These male benefits enjoyed by the maenads during their worship of Dionysos include night-time celebration with male company, following the male customs of the nocturnal *kômoi*.[15] Torches were traditionally held by male participants in revels,[16] along with an oinokhoe, cup or kantharos.[17] The image of the torch and the oinokhoe in the hands of maenads among males other than their husbands may have been unusual and provocative, even in its mythical dimension. Possible suspicions of corruption that may have arisen among the fifth- and fourth-century viewers of these representations appear to have been discarded by Teiresias, who asserts in the *Bacchae* (ll. 317-18): 'One should consider the facts. For even in bacchanals the really self-controlled woman will not be corrupted' (trans. Seaford 1996). According to him, women act in accordance with their own reasoning and character, with no restriction than their own *sôphrosunê* to determine their sexual behaviour. In the *Bacchae*, it is made clear, that Dionysos does not compel them to chastity, but offers them freedom of choice (ll. 314-16).

On the other hand, the role of the torch as a sacred object associated with marriage rites, the lawful aspect and ultimate purpose of every woman's life, is challenged in the hands of maenads. Maenads' torches are mentioned as a cynical parallel to wedding torches, because of the contradictory double meaning that they carry, referring to the status of a bride and a maenad at the same time.[18] In such a case, their function appears to be confused and, from peaceful symbols guaranteeing a legitimate union, they may become symbols of destruction and violence,[19] spreading panic and confusion. For example, Kassandra carries her supposed wedding torch in a manic and confused state (Eur. *Tro.* 307),[20] arousing the bitter interference of Hekuba, who remarks upon her inappropriate and ill-timed maenad-like performance. Her maenad torch prefigures her fate never to be a legitimate bride, and particularly her rape which would be the cause of her own destruction.[21]

VIII

Cultivation and Prosperity of
Land: Fire as a Creative Power

1. Fire and grain rituals

A considerable number of red-figure and sculptural representations of
rituals associated with the prosperity of land include torches carried by
different divinities. The largest group depicts the libation between one of
the Eleusinian goddesses (Demeter or Persephone) and Triptolemos before
his departure on his sacred mission to teach humans the blessings of
agriculture. Torches often shed light on this ritual, which is also attended
by other divinities. An account of the general arrangement of the torch-
bearing female figures in this scene has been given earlier in Chapter V.3;
here, a closer observation of possible gestures performed with torches will
be attempted in comparison with similar rituals performed by apparently
agrarian deities.

Torch and grain are involved in rituals of agrarian significance performed by goddesses on several occasions. These rituals centre around an
altar, above which the torch and the grain-stalks are held by a goddess
(often identified with Demeter). On a red-figure lekythos by the Berlin
Painter (**9.1** dated to 460), the altar depicted is burning; a goddess holds
out the grain with her right hand, and in her left lightly supports a short
torch which partly rests on her shoulder. A related black-figure representation on a Boiotian plate of the late fifth century depicts an elaborately
dressed, enthroned goddess who is about to perform a similar ritual at an
altar (**9.5**; **Pl. 40**). She has both arms extended towards the altar in front
of her, where a pomegranate is placed.[1] The goddess carries a short
burning torch in her right hand and the grain-stalks in her slightly
lowered left. Whether the ritual has anything to do with the burning of
grain – as a possible symbolic image of its purification – should remain an
open question.[2] A combination of torch and grain in the hands of an
Eleusinian deity (most probably Demeter) is found on a skyphos from
Tanagra by the Diomed Painter (**4.18** dated to the late fifth century), and
also on a stamnos by the Niobid Painter in the context of the libation of
Triptolemos (**6.17** dated to *c*. 460). In both examples, although the size of
the torch varies, it is held upright by the goddess with the stalks of corn
lowered to the ground.

In the above rituals, one may observe that both torch and grain assume fairly consistent positions, with the grain-stalks closer to the ground or the burning altar, and the torch held more or less upright. A possible reconstruction of this almost antithetical positioning of the torch and grain would reveal an alternating up-and-down gesture, with the aid of the two most prominent agrarian symbols of the Eleusinian cult. Although these are not the only occurrences of this gesture in Eleusinian scenes, it does not seem to have been exclusive to them. A mid-sixth-century black-figure dinos depicts a priestesses executing an identical gesture with three sprigs of olive in each hand above an altar before a sacrifice to Athena.[3] In these cases, the sacrificial procession following the priestess indicates that a preliminary ritual is performed. The nature of the ritual is confirmed by the type of vegetation chosen for it, since olive branches were known for their cleansing qualities.[4] A later representation is found within a Triptolemos scene,[5] where Demeter makes a similar gesture with three grain stalks in each hand. There is a marked preference for this particular gesture before certain rituals, such as libations and sacrifices. Torches borne in both hands replace the torch and grain combination in a number of scenes inspired by the myth of the mission of Triptolemos. Persephone often keeps one arm lowered with one torch directed downwards, while her other arm is bent at the elbow to support the other torch upright. Most examples come from scenes of the libation with Triptolemos (e.g. **6.15** by the Berlin Painter, **6.47** and **6.48** by the Duomo Painter), with Kaleos (**6.6** by the Triptolemos Painter) and the departure of Triptolemos (e.g. **6.46** by the Hector Painter and **9.3**). Hekate should be added as a fairly common torch-bearing figure in scenes of the libation of Triptolemos. On **6.51** by Polygnotos, she stands behind the hero carrying a short torch upright in her left hand and sheaves of corn in her right, which is lowered to the ground.[6] Hekate's involvement in the scene of the libation of Triptolemos should probably be explained in view of her divine dimension which entails powers over the earth's produce. This is attested as early as Hesiod (*Theog.* 411-52) who refers to her ability to bestow and withdraw fertility.[7]

Further scenes including torch-bearing females – mostly Persephone – within a context alluding to natural abundance are included in representations of Persephone as *Thea*, mistress of the underworld, together with Plouton (*Theos*), her husband. (**9.7**; **Fig. 23**) According to the usual iconographical pattern, Plouton carries a horn of plenty and Persephone, two long torches (e.g. **9.7**, **9.8**, **9.9**, **4.6**, **4.35**, **6.125**, **6.114** and **9.4**). Outside an Eleusinian context, a black-figure Kabiric krater of the end of the fifth century represents a female – possibly a goddess – walking with two short upright burning torches and accompanied by a water-bird (**9.6**). In each hand she holds a torch together with a twig (myrtle or laurel), while a similar branch grows from the ground to the left side of the goddess. The combination of the torches and twig of the goddess recalls the combination

Fig. 23. Hades (Theos) holding horn of abundance, and torch-bearing Persephone (Thea). Athens, National Museum 1519 (Cat. no. 9.7), c. 350-300.

of torch and grain held by the Eleusinian goddesses in scenes of the departure of Triptolemos, both promoting similar connotations relating to the fecundity of earth. Whether this 'coupling' of torch and grain (or some other sort of vegetable material) has anything to do with notions such as the symbolic warming of the earth as a natural 'fertiliser', should be left open – though it is a tempting suggestion.[8]

2. Thesmophoria and Haloa

In literature, the epithet 'sacred' (*hieros*) is repeatedly applied to torches in context of the festival of the Thesmophoria,[9] emphasising the torches' extensive involvement in the rituals of the festival. Aristophanes' *Thesmophoriazusae* (ll. 101-3) provides evidence of dances with torches performed by maidens, as well as of torchlit circular dances (ll. 955-68). The scenes must be associated with the 'hour of freedom'[10] enjoyed by the female participants in this festival, which also included licence for obscene language (*aiskhrologia*) and behaviour.[11] Women, torches and obscenity are again combined on series of clay figurines from a number of Thesmophoria sanctuaries. Those found in Priene (Asia Minor), mainly from the fourth century, best display all these three elements. In particular, a limited variety depicts headless females, whose faces figure on their bare bellies, with a long burning torch on each side. Their torches narrow toward the ends which are held close to the body.[12] A burning torch may be combined with other attributes held in the same hand, such as stalks of wheat,[13] or more frequently a pig, held in the other hand[14] (**Fig. 24**). Variations exist, such as a single torch held obliquely across the body,[15] or an upright torch

Fig. 24. Clay bust of a female figure holding a piglet and a torch from Sicilian sanctuary of Demeter.

attached to one side (**Fig. 25**).[16] Similar types of figurine are found in sanctuaries of Demeter in South Italy and Sicily, with the exception of the form of the torch. This has a crossed upper end,[17] corresponding to the representation of torches on red-figure vases from that area (**Fig. 26**).[18]

Torchlight is linked in literature to the mystic rites of women in a festival from which men are excluded (Ar. *Thesm.* 1149-53). Since women alone are acquainted with the mystery of the birth of life, they are the only participants in a ritual that brings them close to the great fertile powers of nature. Under the purifying light of torches, the women would descend down to the chasms of the earth (*megara*) on a symbolic night-time journey to the underworld to fetch the rotten remains of piglets which they had earlier sacrificed by throwing them into these pits alive.[19] Obscene language – probably echoing the episode of Iambe in the Hymn (*Hom. Hymn Dem.* 203)[20] – and torches remain standard elements during this ritual. The torches light this symbolic transition between the two worlds which involves a ritual descent (*kathodos*) and an ascent (*anodos*); common

Fig. 25. Torch-bearing female figurines from Sicilian sanctuaries of Demeter.

points of reference should be recalled here in connection with the use of torches in other nocturnal rites of passage of the Eleusinian cycle, notably the Mysteries.[21] The women would carry the pigs' bones back to the upper world, where their ritual purification would be effected along with a symbolic sacrifice. A likely candidate for the depiction of the throwing of the pigs into the megara appears on a red-figure Attic lekythos of the mid-fifth-century (**9.2**). A woman is portrayed standing with a basket in her left hand and an animal which she holds by its tail in her right hand.[22] Three burning torches are stuck in the ground next to her, possibly to light the 'passage' of the animal she is preparing to throw into a chasm. The position of the torches right at the boundaries of the two worlds may rarely be supported by archaeology. Holes cut in the rock have been reported from the so-called Nekuomanteion at Akheron in Epirus, and explained as torch-supports by S. Dakaris.[23]

Fourth-century Attic inscriptions[24] confirm the literary evidence of the range of activities in the Thesmophoria for which torches were needed. In the sacrificial regulations of the Attic deme of Holargos,[25] a list of materials required for the festival include a torch (*das*) of the bare variety (without a handle) made of multiple thin wooden stems.[26] The value of the torch is specified as not less than two oboloi. A similar document from the Eleusinion of the deme Phrearrhioi[27] requires a torch-holder (*lampadeion*) together with the torch that it held (*lampas*). The lampadeion suggests a

Fig. 26. Female figurine of worshipper
holding torch with crossed end.

more solid form of torch,[28] consisting of a few, or even a single, wooden
stem, which was more suitable for burning for longer periods with a
steadier, less flagrant flame. The holder is a necessary equipment for
ritual activities that required light for a prolonged period, such as during
the *pannukhis* at the Thesmophoria.[29] Purchase of firewood ('*xula epi ton
bômon*'),[30] in some cases together with oil and incense,[31] is specified for the
sacrifice at the Thesmophoria in Eleusis. Wood for the preparation of the
sacrificial dinner ('*xula epi ton khutron*') is prescribed in the cult regulations of the deme of Phrearrhioi.[32] Other fifth- and fourth-century
inscriptions from Eleusis and Athens[33] list firewood among other materials
for purificatory purposes ('*kai t' alla ta epi katharmati*'), which also have
to be associated with the preparations for the sacrifice at the festival.

The use of torches can be inferred during the pannukhis of Haloa[34] from
a fifth-century Eleusinian inscription[35] which records immense quantities

Fig. 27. Hermes riding a bull among torch-bearing female figures. Berlin,
Staatliche Museen F 1881. Black-figure lekythos, Edinburgh Painter, *c*. 510-500.

of wood (*xula*) purchased for the festival. The lack of information about the
possible use of this wood, combined with the specification '*klêmatidas*' in
line 127, speaks in favour of a function most likely as combustible material, at least for a part of it. A.C. Brumfield's suggestion[36] that it must have
been burned on the sacrificial fires of the pannukhis seems likely, but it is
again not adequate to explain such large quantities of wood. The absence
of the frequent indication '*xula epi ton bômon*' permits the assumption that
at least part of the wood mentioned in the inscriptions may have been used
as torches. More force is added to the argument if we consider the numerous similarities in ritual practice between the Haloa and other festivals of
Demeter, such as the Mysteries and the Thesmophoria. All of them shared
activities[37] like obscene language and behaviour, a night-long celebration,
and exclusively female participation, and therefore it is only reasonable to
assume that during the Haloa torchlight was required for which a substan-
tial quantity of wood would have been consumed.

3. Natural abundance in a Dionysiac context:
the wedding of Dionysos and Ariadne (*hieros gamos*)

An image of natural abundance with special reference to milk, wine[38] and
nectar of bees is closely associated with torchlight in the *Bacchae* 143-9.
The light emanating from the raised pine-torch of Dionysos, the smoke of

the incense burnt by his worshippers, along with their dances and cries, reach the sky providing an imaginary link between heaven and earth. The ripe clusters of vine-shoots form part of the image of the dancing god and his followers on the rocky ridge of Parnassos, which shines in the torchlight (Eur. *Phoen.* 226-35).

Allusions to this image of natural abundance may be found in representations of Dionysos' attachment to, and sacred marriage with, Ariadne (*hieros gamos*). Torches are combined with vine-branches (**9.10** by the Eucharides Painter, *c.* 490-480, and **9.23** by the Polygnotos Group), thyrsoi (**9.33** by the Codrus Painter, *c.* 430-420), phialai for libation (**9.10** and **9.11** by the Mykonos Painter, *c.* 470), kantharoi (**9.10**, **9.23** and **9.24**), musical instruments (**9.23**), wine-skins and *bakkhoi* (**9.14** by the Alkimachos Painter *c.* 450) in the hands of the participants in these scenes. Apart from the couple, these scenes often include other divinities such as Poseidon, Artemis and Apollo (**9.11**), Dionysos' mother Semele in her role as daidou-khousa (**9.10**), and members of the thiasos (**9.23**). A distinct natural setting for the hieros gamos is offered by the Pronomos Painter in the early fourth century (**9.49**; **Fig. 28**). A young long-haired Dionysos holding a lyre touches Ariadne on the shoulder, as she walks next to him holding a burning torch. Her long dress is richly embroidered with floral motifs, and they both wear floral wreaths on their heads. The rest of the participants include a flying Eros, silens (one playing the double-flute and another holding a thyrsos), while the lower register depicts frenzied, torchlit dances of the thiasos. Motifs such as the uncovering of the shoulder of a dancing maenad, or the move of a panther towards another maenad who

Fig. 28. Dionysos and a torch-bearing Ariadne surrounded by the thiasos. Naples, Museo Archeologico Nazionale H 3240 (Cat. no. 9.49). Pronomos Painter, early fourth century.

tries to repel the beast with her torch, are surely loaded with sexual implications.

The presence of torches may be explained partly as implying the legitimate side of the bridal rite – the central aim of which was fecundity, and it partly belongs to the typical Dionysian natural scenery, as that is known to us from Euripides' *Bacchae*. A similar context with possible fecundity connotations may be sought on the representation of the so-called Anthesteria-skyphos (**9.15**, attributed to the 'Lewis' Painter).[39] A bearded satyr holding a burning torch in each hand leads a bride whose head and right arm are covered with her himation. It is likely that the scene depicts an enactment of the marriage between the god and the wife of the Archon-Basileus at the annual festival of the Anthesteria.[40]

4. The fire of satyrs – creative fire

The tendency to narrative is more distinct in representations of torch-bearing satyrs than in those of torch-bearing maenads. Because of their confused and primitive animal nature,[41] satyrs take part in scenes where the comic element is particularly pronounced.[42] Torch-bearing satyrs dance, pursue females revealing their excessive sexual appetite, parody myths from the divine or the heroic world (with which the audience was probably familiar), and participate in events that usually arouse their astonishment, such as great achievements in human civilisation (e.g. in connection with the fire of Prometheus).[43]

The comic element in Attic representations of satyrs with torch in hand is introduced as early as 470-460 by the Painter of Bologna 228 (**9.12**). On the reverse of **9.12**, two satyrs – one of whom holds a torch – draw a cart on which another armed satyr is mounted. It is not possible to ascertain whether these activities parody specific scenes known to the audience probably from satyr-plays, or are just creations of the painter's imagination.[44] Long torches are carried by very short satyrs on **9.38** and **9.39** by a painter close to the Shuvalov Painter, while on **9.37** (*c.* 430-425), the torch is combined with a bag of food hanging from the shoulder of a satyr. Torch-bearing satyrs often take part in ecstatic processions including maenads and often Dionysos, such as on **9.16** (Achilles Painter, *c.* 440) and **9.36** by the Pothos Painter, while they are not absent from calmer scenes of the thiasos, such as **9.13** by the Eupolis Painter (*c.* 450) and **9.40** by the Pronomos Painter.

Representations of the return of Hephaistos to Olympos, accompanied by Dionysos with the thiasos, include torches. Sixth-century parallels on the theme of a male god riding an animal and surrounded by torch-bearing females may be sought in the iconography of Hermes as illustrated on a black-figure lekythos by the Edinburgh Painter (*c.* 510-500; **Fig. 27**).[45] In the scenes depicting the return of Hephaistos, here, the light is carried by both maenads and satyrs with the earliest surviving examples offered by the Group of Polygnotos, which prefers torch-bearing maenads in the procession (such as in **9.17-9.18** and **9.26**). Their short torch is borne upright in the left hand and is combined with a lyre or a jug held in the right, or alternatively, it rests on the hip. Variations are offered by the Hephaistos Painter (**9.19**, *c.* 440; **Pl. 41**) who represents the pair of Hephaistos and Dionysos, followed by a maenad with a burning torch in each hand and a satyr carrying an amphora topped by a wreath.[46] A decade later, the Kleophon Painter offers fuller versions of the thiasos, such as in **9.27**, where two processions are portrayed, namely the return of Hephaistos to Olympos including the thiasos, and a divine procession to the sanctuary of Apollo at Delphi.[47] The same painter also produced simpler compositions of the route of Hephaistos to Olympos (**9.28**), where a pair of satyrs – one of whom carries a torch – lead the way, together with a maenad who plays the tumpanon. Dionysos figures in the middle of the scene together with Hephaistos, who is supported by a satyr.[48] The presence of torches in these scenes should be seen in the context of the realms of both gods, apart from, and in addition to, possible allusions to a nocturnal event. In the realm of Hephaistos, fire is conceived as a basic creative power which gives birth to several different crafts beneficial to humans, such as metallurgy. Torches certainly play a central role in the cult of Hephaistos in Athens in classical times – if not earlier – an example being the famous torch-race held during the Hephaisteia.[49] On the other hand, the torches held by the participants of the thiasos in scenes of the return of Hephaistos to Olympos appear as pure symbols of Dionysiac worship, intimately linked with natural powers which may often be destructive and violent, but are also generous and protective to humans. In that respect, the torches held by satyrs and maenads in these representations may be taken as reflections of the uncontrollable element of fire which resembled the nature of Dionysos' staunch worshippers. One might indeed be tempted to contrast this uncontrollable fire of unspoilt nature represented via the torches of the thiasos to the tamed, civilising fire belonging to the realm of Hephaistos.

Further representations of this tamed fire occur in the broader context of the myth of Prometheus. The fire of civilisation is depicted mainly on Attic red-figure kraters of the last quarter of the fifth century and is transmitted to humans in the form of torches via the satyrs.[50] Although the figure usually identified as the Titan Prometheus is in most cases not epigraphically recognised, he retains certain standard features, namely a beard, long hair confined by a broad band, and a long garment, usually belted, which occasionally leaves one shoulder bare. He holds a long solid torch-like object, which may possibly be identified with the *narthêx*, the mythical carrier of the fire stolen from heaven for mankind. The scenes take place in natural landscape, as may be inferred from the uneven ground in most of the representations. Prometheus is identified epigraphically on the Oxford kalyx-krater (**9.41**) by the Dinos Painter, as are the satyrs, under the names *Kômos, Sikk[i]nnis* and *Simos*.[51] The Titan is placed among a group of satyrs almost in the centre of the composition. He holds the narthex obliquely with both hands and faces two dancing, torch-bearing satyrs on his left. Behind him, another satyr dances with a long torch in his left hand, and looks towards Prometheus. The torch of the satyr closer to Prometheus crosses with the torch of the Titan, perhaps suggesting the moment after the transmission of the divine flame received by the satyrs on behalf of the humans. A similar scene by a painter near the Dinos Painter depicts Prometheus holding his narthex vertically in the fashion of a sceptre (**9.42**).[52] The satyr immediately to his left – the most distinct figure of the whole group, supported by a crook and wearing a fawn skin – holds his short torch close to the narthex of 'Prometheus' (**Fig. 29b**). However, it is not possible to determine whether the moment depicted is before or after the lighting of his torch, owing to the bad preservation of the surface of the vase around the upper end of the torch.

A dancing group of three satyrs accompanies 'Prometheus' on a column-krater by the Orpheus Painter (**9.30**; **Fig. 29a**).[53] Prometheus holds what is most probably a narthex obliquely with both hands and looks to the left, towards a dancing satyr. Behind him, two more satyrs dance and stare in astonishment towards the centre of the composition. The satyr at the right end of the scene holds a stick or an extinguished torch in a horizontal position, following the movement of his body. The moment of kindling of the torch of the satyr is perhaps implied by the Painter of Munich 2335 in a two-figure composition (**9.32**),[54] as the upper ends of the Titan's narthex and the satyr's torch approach each other. The same theme may be found – with minor variations – on works of the Group of Polygnotos (**9.29**, *c.* 420),[55] the Painter of Louvre G 433 (**9.47**),[56] the Lykaon Painter (**9.21**, *c.* 440-430),[57] a painter close to Kleophon Painter (**9.31**, *c.* 430)[58] and an unattributed vase now in Mytilene (**9.34**, *c.* 430-420). A figure bearing the traits of Prometheus and holding two long upright torches is accompanied by torch-bearing satyrs on **9.44** (*c.* 425-420),[59] and **9.48** by the Bull Painter (*c.* 410-400). A combination of a narthex and a short torch are held by Prometheus (bearded, long hair with hairband, long embroidered garment) on **9.35** (*c.* 430-420) and **9.45** by the Group of Polygnotos (*c.* 420-410) as he stands flanked by satyrs. Finally, a related scene on an unattributed lekanis (**9.43**) omits the typical figure of 'Prometheus' and depicts two groups of torch-bearing satyrs instead, who play with the fire of their torches.[60]

The choice of the theme of Prometheus in the company of satyrs in the second half of the fifth century and more specifically from 440 onwards may betray possible influence from the lost satyr-play by Aeschylus, *Prometheus Pyrkaeus*.[61] The latter probably belonged to the trilogy which also included the extant *Persae*, both of which were staged in 472. This accords well with the date of most of the vases, thus explaining the sudden popularity of this subject. A.D. Trendall and T.B.L. Webster emphasised

Fig. 29a. Male bearded figure, possibly Prometheus, holding object resembling a narthex and surrounded by torch-bearing satyrs. Athens, National Museum 1167 (CC1339) (Cat. no. 9.30). Orpheus Painter, *c.* 430.

Fig. 29b. Male figure, possibly Prometheus, holds his narthex close to the torch of a satyr (Cat. no. 9.42). Paris Market; Ex Collection Hamilton, then Feuardent. Near the Dinos Painter, *c.* 425- 420.

the similarities in the posture of the satyr-companions of Prometheus in many more vases of this group. They singled out four different, recurrent satyr-postures, and plausibly suggested that these postures were inspired from the actual dances of satyrs in the satyr-play.[62]

IX

Use of Light in the Worship
of the Gods

A review of the archaeological contexts of Greek sanctuaries which yielded lighting material is essential for our better understanding of the multiple uses of light in religious ritual. Many of these uses are partially known to us from other sources, such as the offering of costly, elaborate lamps to the gods, the 'ever-burning' lights in temples or the storing of valuable lighting-devices in temple-treasuries. Furthermore, the study of the various types of lighting material found in excavated sanctuaries, their quantity, state of preservation, find-location and context offer valuable insights into often otherwise completely unknown aspects of Greek cult. The following discussion is a first broad presentation of the cults which employed wide ranges of lighting devices in their rituals, in such a distinct way, that the latter may sometimes serve as unmistakable indicators of the identity of these cults (for example, that of Demeter and Persephone). The role of light in the worship of each god will be treated separately, with respect to the particular nature of the cults involved, which was, after all, the chief determining factor for the amount, types and uses of lighting devices that were required.

1. The cult of Demeter and Persephone

a. Light as a gift to the gods

The wide variety of roles played by light and fire in Greek ritual practice is reflected with particular clarity in the finds from sanctuaries of the Eleusinian deities across the Greek world. Lighting devices, ranging from lamps to torches and pyres, have been employed in the rituals of these deities from as early as the late seventh century. The nocturnal rituals during the festivals of the two goddesses (including the Mysteries, the Thesmophoria and the Haloa)[1] were undoubtedly some of the primary occasions for the use of artificial light in their sanctuaries. Lamps and torches were included among the commonest type of votive offered to the goddesses, in addition to the practical role that they fulfilled, as sources of artificial light in nocturnal rites.

Fourth-century inventories of the Athenian Eleusinion record torches (*lampas*) as votive-offerings among other valuables, including objects used in sacrifices, such as *lebêtia, kana, hudria, oinokhoai, sphageion, labides, khutridia, khoes* and *kadoi*.[2] The term 'lampas' mentioned in the inscriptions must have described torches of a solid type, which would have been set into a form of stand, or more simply a torch-holder (*lampadeion*). It seems likely that the dedication of torches to the goddesses followed their prior use in the cult, as is suggested by an example from the deme of Phrearrhioi. A gilded torch of the simpler variety (*daïs*) was dedicated at the Eleusinion of the deme by the authorities, on the occasion of the celebration of the Thesmophoria at around 300.[3] Outside Athens, the sanctuary of Demeter at Troizen yielded clay torch-holders of shape and decoration similar to Bronze Age examples.[4] They are covered with a pale yellowish slip and decorated with painted black parallel bands, which contrast with the pale surface of the clay. Their presence among other votives found in the sanctuary should probably be linked with their earlier use in nocturnal rituals, as the lamps from the site suggest, most of which bear traces of use.[5] A few clay torch- or lamp-holders, dated to the seventh century, may be added from the sanctuary of Aetos on the island of Ithaka; these examples were intended to stand upon a wide hollow base but are also furnished with a vertical handle.[6] Each piece was individually designed and decorated, since none of them is similar to any other from that site in size and painted ornament. The latter included figurative decoration and a potter's signature (**Pl. 1**; **Fig. 3**). The practice of dedicating torches to the goddesses goes beyond mainland Greece, with some truly elaborate examples appearing in South Italy. A torch of the local type with a crossed end made of sheet bronze has come to light at the sanctuary of the goddess at Santa Maria d'Anglona.[7] The find should be dated to the second half of the fourth and no later than the early third century. Its front side bears a dedicatory inscription to Demeter in Doric dialect by a woman with a Greek name ('Philimêna').

Painted representations of torches of similar local type may be further found on vessels intended for dedication to sanctuaries of the goddesses in Sicily and South Italy, from as early as the late archaic period. This is the date of a hydria from the sanctuary at Monte Papalucio in Oria; a painted torch with a crossed end figures on the handle of the vessel.[8] Ten large hydriai, bearing dedicatory inscriptions to Demeter on their rim, are also marked on their necks with the symbol of a torch with a crossed end. This impressive find, dated to the late fourth century, comes from the sanctuary of Demeter at Herakleia. The hydriai were found in the area of a sacred spring, in the vicinity of sacrificial deposits which contained miniature jugs, open vessels filled with natural products, a bottomless krater probably for libations, and, possibly, a square stone altar.[9] A high concentration of votives was found around a spring within a sanctuary of Demeter at Contrada Ferrona, outside Timmaris. These included a cluster of black-

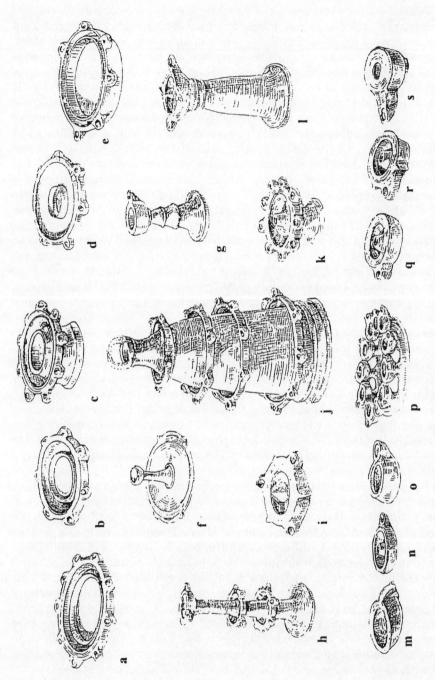

Fig. 30. Selection of lamp-types from the sanctuary of Malophoros at Selinous.

glazed skyphoi, bearing on their bellies incised decoration of torches of the crossed-end type, dated to the second half of the fourth century.[10] A similar representation is found on a late fourth-century tile from the sanctuary at Santa Maria d' Anglona[11] and on the handle of a large local vessel from Contrada Crucinia in Metaponto, which argues for a cult of Demeter at the site.[12] Three further fourth-century examples of torch-representations on artifacts should be mentioned from the area of temples A and C of Metaponto. Two are hydriai bearing a torch-symbol on their handles, and the third is a portable hearth marked with a relief representation of the same symbol. In the two last cases of the finds from Metaponto, the crossed torches may also be an allusion to a cult of Artemis who was worshipped at temple C.[13]

A further important category of finds which clearly reflect the function of torches as votive offerings from worshippers of the Eleusinian deities are the large quantities of torch-bearing figurines found in the sanctuaries of goddesses across the Greek world. These usually represent the dedicants themselves who offer their gifts to the goddesses.[14] The type and size of the torches held by the figures varies substantially as does the position in which they are held. One short torch is often carried obliquely across the body of the dedicant (who may often be reduced to a bust) while long torches tend to be held loosely parallel to the axis of the body. The torch may also be combined with other offerings, notably grain and piglets (**Figs. 24-6**).

Lamps, too, fulfilled a votive function in Greek sanctuaries of Demeter and Persephone. With the exception of a few fifth- and fourth-century temple-inventories from the Athenian Eleusinion and Eleusis,[15] all evidence for the use of lamps in the cult of Demeter comes from archaeology. Among the most distinct types of votive lamps are marble series, which often bear relief decoration comparable with those discovered on the Athenian Akropolis (**Fig. 2**). Some of the earliest examples dating to the late seventh century come from the sanctuary of Demeter Malophoros at Selinous in Sicily (**Fig. 30**). The strata of the first megaron yielded three semi-circular marble lamps, decorated with heads in the daedalic style,[16] while similar examples of circular shape continued to be produced in the early sixth century, as the lamp-finds from the second megaron of the goddess in the same sanctuary suggest. More specifically, the marble lamps were carefully deposited together with other valuables in the space between the wall of the megaron (which was built after 625) and its surrounding wall (*peribolos*), which was apparently built for that purpose. Seventh- and sixth-century marble and clay lamps of circular and semi-circular shape, furnished with central spike-holes and provision for hanging, have been reported from the sanctuaries of the goddesses at Bitalemi and Predio Sola in Gela.[17] A closer observation of these elaborate lighting devices shows that their size, and especially their weight (both of which were partly dependent on the number of nozzles and extent of decoration), cannot have made them easy to transport. However, their impressive forms and often valuable material, combined with elements such as provision for hanging, partitioned oil chambers, and their frequent discovery in, or close to, temple cellas, suggest their use as temple furniture. The diffusion of similar lamps in sanctuaries across the Greek world indicates that their use was not exclusive to the cult of the Eleusinian deities, or any other particular deity. One might assume that they were either commissioned by the sanctuary authorities to fulfil the need for illumination inside cult buildings or that they were gifts from individuals to the deities. The latter seems more likely, in view of the popular practice of dedicating lamps to the gods, as will be seen in the following discussion.

A further distinct category of clay lamps offered to the Eleusinian goddesses both on mainland Greece and in the colonies are the large multi-nozzled corona lamps furnished with a bowl- or funnel-shaped oil-chamber and a base of variable height. Their nozzles may be arranged in one or more tiers, while in other examples nozzles are replaced by whole small lamps attached to a flat base or ring. Limited traces of burning around the nozzles of the multiple lamps show that most of them were not intensively used.[18] These traces of burning are in most cases faint, and sometimes altogether lacking, yet their presence shows that the lamps undoubtedly served as sources of light. However, a purely practical purpose for them should probably be discounted, as this would have resulted in the blackening of their nozzles. The limited traces of burning suggest occasional and/or short-term use, and the possibility that such lamps were lit only once cannot be ruled out. A further argument against the practicality of these multiple lamps is that they make economical use of neither material and fuel nor display space. Similarly impractical are the flat-based miniature lamps, which were meant to rest on the rim of large shallow vessels, on clay discs or rings; these, too, bear only faint traces of fire around their nozzles, or occasionally their sides. Without rejecting or undermining the well established argument for pottery dedications to gods, it appears that in the case of lamps, it was the lighting effect that was dedicated to the deities and not its physical container. The lamps were probably dedicated alight to the goddess and were lit only once during some ceremonies.[19] This also explains the specially selected forms of multi-nozzled lamps, which shaped the light into consistently circular patterns,[20] and which enjoyed popularity from the classical period onwards. Whether the number of nozzles of these lamps was of any significance is hard to determine.

Clay multi-nozzled lamps have been found in all areas of Greek sanctuaries of Demeter and Persephone, ranging from the interior of temples or cult-buildings to areas around and inside altars (of both the 'traditional' built type and the 'pit-altars' which were particular to this cult). In the sanctuary of Demeter in S. Biagio of Akragas, particular accumulations of lamps (including miniatures as well as multi-nozzled specimens) were observed in the area around and inside the large circular 'well-altars' (especially altar 2) as well as in the so-called Temenos at the northernmost extremity of the peribolos of the sanctuary.[21] Multi-nozzled lamps together with miniature bowls, skyphoi and cups come from an open-air circular pit-altar (A8) at the Khthonian sanctuary of Akragas; the deposit covers the entire time-span of the use of the altar from the mid-sixth to the third century.[22] At Predio Sola, abundant and varied material was unearthed from the so-called 'upper stratum' in the reports, which dates from the middle of the sixth to the first quarter of the fifth century.[23] This included multi-nozzled lamps along with lamps of simpler types, numerous clay-masks of the goddess, hydriai, bowls, pitchers, kothons and a thymiaterion. Lamps with a central spike-hole are the predominant type in Gela, with variations in size and number of nozzles, while some are occasionally furnished with a clay cylindrical stick, attached to their bases. Multi-nozzled lamps were also found in votive deposits of open-air shrines of Demeter, notably at Santuzza, outside the town of Syracuse. They were buried in a single trench at the site, mixed with a large quantity and variety of terracottas.[24] The 'new' sanctuary of Demeter at Heloros yielded lamps of this type, dated to the third and second century, while the sanctuary of Demeter at Selinous produced further varieties of clay multi-nozzled examples; the latter are singled out by E. Gabrici as the most frequent offering to the goddess.[25] More examples of multi-nozzled lamps mounted on stands come from a votive deposit in area N of the (demolished) city walls of Megara Hyblaia in Sicily.[26] The deposit also contained bronze objects, glass beads and animal bones, all of which speak in favour of a cult of Demeter which might have once existed in the vicinity of the deposit. Finally, multi-nozzled lamps were not absent from the sacrificial deposits of the sanctuary of the goddesses at Monte Papalucio in Oria, where they were found together with large groups of terracottas and ring-vessels.[27]

A limited number of multi-nozzled lamps are known from sanctuaries of Demeter and Persephone in Attika. A few corona-types with an open, funnel-like oil-chamber, together with single-nozzled lamps of very small size which appear to have been attached on clay rings or discs to form larger lighting vessels, constitute our knowledge for this type of votive to the goddesses at their sanctuary in Eleusis. The main body of lighting material from this major site consists of open one-nozzled plain and black-glazed lamps and awaits publication.[28] In the fill of the retaining wall of the Athenian Thesmophorion, south of the Pnyx,[29] both single-nozzled and corona lamp types were discovered in limited quantities, dating between the fifth and the third centuries. Miniature vases, such as bowls, kalathoi, krateriskoi and figurines were among the most frequent finds in the contexts which also included lamps. Many pieces were seriously damaged by fire. The sanctuary of Demeter and Persephone at Akrokorinth yielded a large quantity of lighting material dating from the late seventh to the third century; its publication is still awaited.[30] The lamp-types from the sanctuary vary considerably, including corona lamps as well as flat-based, plain, single or multi-nozzled miniatures, sitting on either a clay ring, a stand, or a clay disc, as is sometimes suggested by the traces of attachment on their bases.

On Krete, corona lamps are found in wide variety and quantity in sanctuaries of Demeter and Kore such as Gortun (between the fifth and third centuries), Olous and Knossos (from deposits B-H).[31] In all these sites, simpler lamps co-existed with the large specimens, which, towards the end of the fourth and the beginning of the third century, increase dramatically in size and number of nozzles. As shown by the few complete examples, small single-nozzled lamps (hundreds of which were excavated in sanctuaries such as Gortun) were used in groups of dozens attached around the rim of large pedestalled vessels; alternatively, the small lamps might have rested on clay discs in order to produce an extraordinarily bright effect in a circular pattern. The multi-nozzled lamps could be very large, with hundreds of nozzles sometimes arranged in two or more tiers, as is the case with some Knossian examples. Apart from some miniature lamps from the latter site which do not exhibit traces of burning, the rest of the lighting material from the sanctuary appears to have been used. Fragments of used multi-nozzled lamps resembling the examples from Knossos were found on the west side of the cult-building of the sanctuary of Demeter, probably a Thesmophorion, at the Kretan site of Vruses Kudonias.[32] The associated find-contexts (the earliest of which dates to the sixth century) included kernoi, hydriai, votive vessels with attached clay offerings and a variety of pottery. Further impresssive series of multi-nozzled lamps and large 'lighting vessels' have been recently found on Kuthnos (Cyclades).[33] The nozzles of the corona lamps are arranged in a variety of ways (in tiers, around the periphery directed outside and inside the oil-container), while an unusual type of large lighting vessel from the site bears holes in its walls to accommodate a large number of wicks. The latter category may not be identified among the lighting material of any other sanctuary of Demeter and appears to be a development from the tiered-nozzle corona examples, which were also found at the site. The size of these plain lighting vessels may reach from 40 to 45 cm, thus accommodating hundreds of nozzles. Miniature unglazed lamps also existed at the same site during the fourth century, considerably later than the earliest, sixth-century, lighting material from the site.

Single-nozzled lamps, a find far more common in Greek sanctuaries of Demeter in Italy than their multi-nozzled counterparts, also fulfilled a votive function. The Geloan sanctuaries at Carrubazza and Predio Sola were rich sources of votive deposits containing single-nozzled lamps from the middle of the sixth to the late fourth or third century.[34] F. Boitani emphasised the good state of preservation of the lamps, which were found in compact layers in the fill of area C (or *oikos*) in the Greek sanctuary at

Gravisca, together with imported and local pottery, fragments of statuettes and unguentaria.[35] Considerable quantities of sixth-century lamps with nozzles blackened by burning are recorded, among which the one-nozzled flat-based types are predominant. These are often furnished with a central tube or a raised, conical base, while unglazed bowl-shaped lamps of the 'punic' type with a slightly pinched nozzle are also present and date between 580-570 to 490.

In mainland Greece, the Eleusinian sanctuary of Demeter yielded dozens of complete or near-complete mainly one-nozzled lamps, plus hundreds of fragments, dating from the seventh down to the fourth and third centuries.[36] The fragments consist mainly of handles and parts of nozzles, while the rest of the sherd material survives in fairly large pieces, in many cases easy to restore. No heavy traces of fire have been observed around the nozzles, while some lamps do not appear to have been used at all. The flat-based, unglazed, one-nozzled miniature lamps, mainly dated to the seventh and sixth centuries, bear traces of burning on different parts of their side walls and sometimes on their bases. Most of the black-glazed examples which also have low bases (dated from the fifth to the third century) lack heavy traces of burning around the nozzles. Both plain and glazed examples are furnished with handles. Decoration is confined to a few unglazed lamps and is incised free-hand by means of a sharp implement. The incised ornaments are mostly linear, consisting of crossed, wavy or zig-zag lines and dot patterns, while one lamp bears a very simplified representation of a branch with leaves. A couple of poorly preserved examples consist of flat clay rings surmounted by miniature lamps, while corona types with open, funnel-like oil-chambers appear to be extremely limited. One black-glazed lamp preserved a purpose-made cover.

A quantity of plain, mainly small lamps, attached to clay rings or resting in groups on clay discs, were unearthed from the votive fills of the sanctuary of Demeter at Troizen near Damala.[37] About twelve hundred examples (between 0.25 and 0.055 m in diameter) are reported by Ph. Legrand; they were found within a broader context of at least five hundred skyphoi, protokorinthian pottery, figurines and clay torch-holders with band decoration of the sixth and fifth centuries. Although the material has not received systematic publication, the lamp-types described mainly date to the fourth or even the third century. Another sanctuary of Demeter was discovered at the site of Haghios Sostes, Tegea, from where numerous lamps are reported, together with almost two thousand terracotta figurines of standing and enthroned goddesses, clay fruits and animals. The deposit dates to the first half of the fifth century and has not yet received full publication.[38] The votive deposit at the sanctuary of Demeter and Kore at Speliotaki in the Argolis also yielded lamps of sixth- and fifth-century date. The deposit also contained figurines, miniature vessels, phialai and hydriskai, as well as metal offerings of which only a very brief mention is given in the excavation report.[39] In Laconia, few or no lamps have been reported from two sites which yielded votive fills containing offerings which strongly resembled typical dedications to Demeter. The first, identified with an Eleusinion at the foot of Taygetos (Kalyvia tes Sokhas),[40] produced some wreaths made of lead, small plain vases and a few lamps and figurines of rough fabric. The second, located close to the road from Sparta to Megalopolis,[41] was a rich source of miniatures which numbered up to eight thousand pieces. Some fragments of lead figurines and vases, and a few terracottas were found, but no lighting material.

The Thesmophoria at Eutresis in Boeotia[42] and at Eretria[43] yielded comparable categories of finds, among which lamps are represented in considerable quantity; at the former site, lamps were found in a context containing miniature vases, such as kalathiskoi, cups, skyphidia, hydriskai, and terracottas including hydriaphoroi and piglets. The lamps from Eutresis date to the fifth and fourth century. The small number of lamps from Eretria is emphasised by I. Metzger, referring to the plain flat-based type current in Greek Thesmophoria. Corresponding simple types, covered with a poor quality greenish-black glaze, some of which are of small dimensions (diam. 0.020 m), are described by H. Goldman at Eutresis. At both sites, the votive deposits were scattered in different areas of the sanctuary, while at Eutresis a particular concentration is noted in the fills of retaining walls, together with other types of votive pottery and figurines. Very occasionally, lamps are completely absent from votive contexts of Thesmophoria sanctuaries, such as the sanctuary on Evraiokastro of Thasos and at Pella in Macedonia.[44] On Thasos, torch-bearing statuettes are also not found, in contrast with the presence of the usual ranges of miniature votives, including kernoi and other types of figurines. Similarly, no lamps have neen reported from Pella, where there is an additional absence of kalathoi and offering trays. A brief report of a votive deposit connected with a sanctuary of Demeter at Taxiarkhaki of Khios is known to have yielded numerous finds, such as ring-shaped kernoi and some small hand-made lamps.[45]

An impressive quantity of pottery lamps of uniform types and of generally small size has been found stacked in purpose-made votive chambers among other votive material in the large sanctuaries of Demeter at Halikarnassos and Knidos (Asia Minor).[46] In Halikarnassos, thick layers of lamps were deposited in underground built chambers, together with other offerings of mixed date, such as figurines and pottery. Vast deposits of lamps and other votives of similar nature were unearthed in Knidos. The deposits strongly recall the finds from Halikarnassos, since the same practice of votive storage is used, while the nature and quantity of offerings remains the same. Apart from those deposits, lamps appear to have been found in most strata of the excavation, in many different contexts, some containing statues once erected in the sanctuary. Similar ways of storing votives (including lamps) are found in the west, too, notably at the northernmost extremity of the peribolos of the sanctuary of Demeter at S.

Biagio of Akragas.[47] A rectangular roofless construction was found, divided into three compartments, which contained vases, lamps and statuettes close to a statue-base. Lamps of fairly uniform types and fabric, but of varying sizes and number of nozzles, were found mixed in the deposits. The finds of the deposits point to a date from the early fifth to the third century. The context includes typical categories of offerings to Demeter, such as kernoi, hydriai, a variety of pottery vessels including miniatures, unguentaria and female protomes or statuettes holding torches, hydriai, kalathoi and pigs. From mainland Greece, a comparable example of storing votives is found in the lower undisturbed layers of the cella of the classical temple of Demeter at Dion of Macedonia; many black-glazed lamps of the fifth and fourth centuries were deposited under a layer of tiles and close to the south wall of the room.[48] Their context included a fragment of a sizeable kernos, a female figurine holding a fruit and a piece from another circular ritual vase, plausibly interpreted as a lamp.[49]

The sanctuary at Priene also yielded lighting material, but it receives only a summary mention in the reports with a brief description of their types.[50] The Demeter sanctuary at Troas was another rich source of votive material, which contained lamps of diverse types, ranging in date from the seventh to the fourth century.[51] G. Welter reports many hundreds of lamps, some of which seem to have been used in groups, mounted on cylindrical stands. The great abundance of clay lamps and their presence in virtually every sector of the extramural sanctuary of Demeter and Persephone in Kyrene is underlined by D. White.[52] Extending chronologically from the seventh to the fourth century, the lamps are proof of continuous cult activities in the sanctuary throughout this period. A great quantity came from the votive dumps of the south archaic peribolos wall and its later replacement, where similar practices are noted for the disposal of used votive material, to those observed at Halikarnassos and Knidos. Fills of the west peribolos wall, the fill beneath the floor of the sacred building S12 and the votive dump west of the Fountain House F2 yielded mainly small plain lamps, most of which bore clear traces of previous use. A number of stone lamps of early date can be added to their list; the associated find-contexts consist of pottery, figurines and other artifacts, including glass.

b. Lamp-lit sacrifices

The burning of lamps was apparently required during sacrifices in honour of Demeter, which were often followed by the consumption of sacrificial meat by the worshippers at ritual meals. The repeated presence of lamps in sacrificial deposits inside and around altars, cult-buildings or in the open air within and also outside the boundaries of sanctuaries should probably be interpreted as an indication that most, or at least a great part of the sacrifices took place at night.[53] After their use to light sacrifices, the lamps were left at the sanctuary, as may be inferred from the finding of used lamps among remains of sacrifice. A good example is the sanctuary of Demeter Malophoros in Contrada Gaggera (Selinous).[54] Since architecture is missing from the site during its earliest phase (from the end of the seventh to the first quarter of the sixth century), one can explain the presence of small used lamps from the votive deposits around the altars (which are the first cult-feature of the site) as evidence for nocturnal sacrifices. The find-location of the lamps *in situ*, inside remains of sacrificial deposits in the area (many of which were scattered or dug into the earth), shows their subsequent dedication to the goddesses after their use in nocturnal rites. 'Well-altars' often contained lamps, such as the monumental example from the Khthonian sanctuary of Akragas which was located inside the west room (A1) of the northernmost building (R1) of the sanctuary.[55] Miniature vessels as well as lamps date the use of this altar until at least the fourth century. The same sanctuary as well as the sanctuary at S. Biagio in Akragas yielded further rich lamp-finds from 'pit-altars' located in the vicinity of cult-buildings.[56] A round well-altar (A3) east of the temple of the sanctuary at the 'Piazza della Vittoria' at Syracuse was found full of pottery lamps mixed with simple bowls and animal bones; the deposit dates from the late fifth to the middle of the fourth century.[57] Small unglazed open lamps, dated to the late fourth and third century, products of a nearby lamp-factory, were discovered in a small room at the southwest corner of the walled temenos of the central sanctuary at Morgantina; the function of this room (and its contents) must be linked to the 'pit-altar' in the middle of the open court of the temenos, which also contained lamps.[58] From mainland Greece, one may mention a further example from the sanctuary of Demeter at Vrysai Kydonias on Krete;[59] the area around the altar of sactuary A yielded a number of nozzle-fragments, all bearing traces of use, the earliest of which have been assigned a date in the sixth century. A few clay one- and two-nozzled lamps, together with a female protome, were found in black earth within the built *eskhara* at the sanctuary of Demeter at Iasos. D. Levi attributes them to the first sanctuary of the goddess, which was destroyed and abandoned in the sixth century.[60] He also believes that the lamps and the protome were left *in situ* at the moment of abandonment. The classical phase of the sanctuary yielded numerous finds, such as hydriai, small lamps, female figurines and protomes. The lamps stand out from the rest of the finds by their quantity and persistence throughout the life of the sanctuary.[61]

Sacrificial deposits in the form of stone-lined, ususally circular trenches (*bothroi*) which contained remains of sacrifices including animal bones, iron knives, some pottery and lamps, further support the argument for nocturnal sacrifices in the sanctuaries of Demeter and Kore. Distinct examples of such deposits have been unearthed at the sanctuary of S. Anna at Akragas, outside building G1;[62] here, the sacrificial offerings were arranged in groups or individually among the pebbles and were covered with tiles. The deposits contained iron knives, pottery, bronze fragments, some figurines and lamps. Similar deposits were unearthed from the interior of the main (and only) cult-room of the sanctuary of S. Maria d' Anglona.[63] A series of layers of sacrificial deposits was found inside the building, with each category of offerings placed together in small groups. Pottery vessels were found turned upside down, some still holding grain inside; lamps were the predominant find, but other finds including unguentaria, metal objects, miniature vessels and terracottas may be noted. The 'ancient' sanctuary of Helorus, south of Syracuse, yielded lamps in sacrificial deposits dug into the earth in stone-lined trenches in which the pottery was placed in a circular arrangement so as to create free space in the middle for depositing animal bones from sacrifices.[64] Sixty-two such deposits were found in total with finds dating from the late sixth to the end of the third century. In central Sicily, remains of nocturnal sacrifices including pottery lamps have been found in the sanctuary at Montagna di Marzo (between 500 and 300), Monte Adranone (from the early fourth century onwards) and Terravecchia di Culti (up to the end of the fifth century).[65] At Monte Adranone, the sacrificial deposits were scattered inside the temenos and particular concentration was observed in front of the bench at the southwest corner of room G1; among the finds, one may note iron sacrificial knives, lamps, a few terracottas and small vessels turned upside down. A further sacrificial deposit from Sicily containing lamps is also known from Taormina (from the mid-fourth century).[66]

Turning to mainland Greece, a votive deposit related to a hearth-altar (eskhara) was discovered in an extramural shrine of Demeter in Abdera in Thrace.[67] It contained about two thousand hydriskai which were found in black earth, mixed with ashes, animal bones and fragments of pottery, including lamp-bases, dating from the late fourth to the early third century. Further debris containing pottery, lamps, animal bones and ashes was reported from other parts of the sanctuary, where the number of plain hydriskai reached six thousand. The date of the deposits at Abdera, at the end of the fourth or the beginning of the third century, is also consistent with the dates of the lamp-types. Lamps are also recorded from the archaic deposits of the sanctuary of Demeter at Tokra in Kyrenaica,[68] together with similar categories of finds, such as ring-kernoi, hydriai, miniature vases and pig bones. Deposits II in level 8 and III in level 6/7, 7 yielded a number of open lamps, most of them in near-complete condition.

c. Lighting ritual meals

Remains of sacrificial meals from sanctuaries of Demeter are not uncommon. The sanctuary at Bitalemi in Gela yielded such deposits from as early as its first phase (stratum 5a) in the first quarter of the sixth century.[69] Among the finds of this phase, which included miniature vessels and other dining pottery as well as small clay tripods, lamps were also present, pointing to the time the ritual took place. Lamps continued to be found in the sanctuary during the next phase, dating to the fifth century (stratum 4). Some remains of sacrificial meals containing fragments of lamps have been reported from the sactuary at Helorus,[70] while a special ritual meal appears to have taken place inside building III3 in the fourth century at the sanctuary of the goddesses at S. Francesco Bisconti in Morgantina.[71] A small L-shaped bench in the corner of the room has been explained in connection with nocturnal meals; this interpretation is reinforced by the presence of iron knives as well as by the remains of meals (mostly bones) inside the room and the lamps that were found on and around the benches.

In mainland Greece, extensive evidence for nocturnal ritual meals comes from the dining rooms of the lower terraces of the sanctuary of Demeter and Kore on Akrokorinth.[72] The dining rooms (often furnished with benches) yielded a considerable quantity of lamps, among dining pottery and cooking vessels; the finds cover a wide time-span from the late seventh to the third century or later for the use of the dining rooms. More lamps have been reported from the so-called 'Rock-Cut Platform' (area D), the southwest corner of which seems to have been used for animal sacrifices from as early as the sixth century. Lamps were also found in votive stone-lined pits from the higher terraces of the sanctuary, among large quantities of other pottery such as kalathiskoi, hydriai and phialai as well as female statuettes carrying torches and piglets. A possible *hestiatorion* (dining room) has been reported from Kuthnos (Cyclades), the dining deposits of which included a large quantity of lamps.[73] Deposits containing dining pottery, lamps and often animal bones have also been found in the sanctuary of Demeter at Knossos[74] as well as Mytilene.[75] In the latter sanctuary, one is tempted to associate the large quantity of used lamps from a deposit to the west of the sanctuary-complex with the surviving architecture and dining pottery from the main site of the temenos, which is contemporary to the deposit (dating from the late fourth to the middle of the third century). Among the architectural features of this phase, dining halls, a hearth-altar and bothroi are reported, which, if linked with the lamps and the dining pottery, may constitute evidence for sacrificial meals at the site.

d. Lamps in sacrificial pyres

Limited but important is the surviving evidence of the placing or throwing of lamps into pyres during, or at the completion of, a sacrifice. Remains of sacrificial pyres containing fragments of lamps have been discovered outside the peribolos of the sanctuary of Demeter at Eleusis.[76] The fragments were of plain and black-glazed one-nozzled lamps, damaged by fire subsequent to their use. An almost complete black-glazed example which also bears traces of use (now in the museum), still rests in the ashes in which it was discovered, while a further fragment came from ash-layers. The date of the pieces ranges from the sixth to the fifth century. A limited number of fragments from the Eleusinian sanctuary seem to bear traces of burning on their broken sides, while some one-nozzled plain flat-based lamps from the site are burnt on their undersides, suggesting that they were placed on hot ashes, possibly after use. Another possible example of such a deposit, dated to the fifth and fourth centuries, comes from the sanctuary of Demeter at Krane on Kephallonia.[77] Small lamps together with hydriai, miniature vessels, figurines of various types, bronze and iron rings and ear-rings were found deposited in an ash-layer up to 50 cm thick.

e. Light in lustration rites

The discovery of lamps in connection with fountains and natural sources of water, cisterns or inside buildings with hydraulic installations may possibly be taken as an indication that lamps may have lighted some type of lustration rites, the details of which are unknown to us. An *aduton* or inner room, adjacent to a large altar-room was furnished with a small projecting shelf, which could well have accommodated a lamp, according to the excavator of the southern sanctuary of Demeter in Morgantina. This small room also contained a lustration area, similar to the shower-rooms found at the sanctuary of Akrokorinth.[78] An example of lamps being deposited close to where they had once been used, probably in some sort of lustration rites, is found at the so-called sanctuary 'rupestre' at Akragas.[79] Two artificially made caves, carved close to each other in the rock, contained an impressive number of lamps and terracottas (along with local pottery, miniature vessels, a kernos and a hydria), dated to the fourth and third centuries; the votives were placed along the walls of the caves, on ledges or in cavities. Both caves formed the northern boundary of a large fountain-house furnished with cisterns and hydraulic installations. Some of the votives, including small hydriai, lamps and bowls, were found scattered around the fountain-house. Although it is not possible securely to identify the practice of lustration rites in connection with the fountain, the cultic use of the area by the locals before the arrival of the Greeks and the establishment of a cult of a Demeter is well attested by the finds.

Further evidence regarding possible rituals around fountains is found at the sanctuary of Demeter at Herakleia in the late fourth century.[80] Painted torches with a crossed end, often accompanied by dedicatory inscriptions to Demeter, mark the neck of hydriai which were found around a spring on the north side of the sanctuary at Herakleia. Among the other finds, a bottomless krater is recorded for libations inside which a large number of miniature vessels was found. Miniature jugs and open vessels were found scattered around the spring. A related deposit (66B) from room 2 of the cult-building, situated to the southwest of the spring, yielded lamps, miniature vessels, unguentaria, clay imitations of hair-locks and human fingers. The possibility that lamps might have lighted nocturnal rites of symbolic ritual purifications with water should be left open.

Finally, one may note the frequent finding of lamps in the same contexts with water carriers (such as hydriai or perrirhanteria) in sanctuaries of Demeter. For example, about two thousand hydriai of very small size were found together with lamps as well as animal bones and ashes in the eskhara of the sanctuary of Demeter at Abdera in Thrace.[81] Another cult-building from the temenos of the goddess in Mesembria of Thrace contained fragments of lamps together with a fragment of a clay perrirhanterion and a number of gold and silver plaques with hammered decoration. Although both the lamps and the perrirhanterion shared a common find-location, a confined rectangular area within the main cult-building, it is not possible on the basis of the present evidence securely to determine whether any symbolic lustration rites took place there.[82]

f. Use of light in oath-taking

Plutarch (*Dion* lvi, 3) and Cornelius Nepos (*Dion* viii, 5) describe a ritual of the taking of an oath by an opponent to Dio, the tyrant of Syracuse, who was active in the area during the first half of the fourth century. The ritual took place in the sanctuary of Demeter and Kore in whose name the oath was sworn. According to the ritual procedure, the man who was taking the oath had to dress in a purple robe and hold a burning torch. This ritual procedure of oath-taking in sanctuaries of Demeter in Sicily must reflect a regular practice in view of the special political role of the cult on the island.[83]

g. 'Lighting' funerals

The involvement of torches in Greek funerals may be inferred by the timing attested for the ritual (Dem. xliii, 62; Plut. *Sol.* 21). According to Solon's famous legislation restricting excessive funerary rites in Athens, a lighted coach containing the bier would have been the centre of funeral processions which were attended by the close relatives of the deceased; the latter would have had to be over by sunrise. In southern Apulia, representations of torches with crossed ends are often found painted or incised on the walls of grave chambers from as early as the late fourth century.[84] These are accompanied by dedicatory inscriptions to Demeter. It is however not possible to reconstruct any of the rituals that might have taken place at the grave-site and might possibly have included torches.

2. The cult of Artemis

a. Light as a gift

Light, mainly in the form of lamps, is a common offering to Artemis. The contexts that contained lamps in sanctuaries of Artemis indicate their use in various aspects of her cult, though, perhaps, not as intensely as in the rituals of the Eleusinian deities. A marble hanging lamp, bearing relief decoration of lion heads, is perhaps the only published reference to a lamp from the Attic sanctuary of the goddess at Brauron.[85] A circular marble lamp with partitioned oil-chamber was found deposited in a hole inside the cella of the sixth-century Artemision in Ephesos of Ionia together with a smaller one of steatite.[86] Clay lamps bearing dedicatory *graffiti* to Artemis are known from both the Athenian Agora and the Kerameikos, and have been associated with a shrine of the goddess on the road to the Akademy (possibly Artemis Kalliste) or with another shrine near Ilissos (possibly Artemis Soteira).[87] At Mounukhia, L. Palaiokrassa asserts that lamps represent one of the most abundant categories among the pottery finds. However, because of the circumstances of the rescue excavation, no information about the find-locations and the contexts of the lamp-finds is recorded.[88] The lamps are very fragmentary and their black glaze is now poorly preserved. Most of them belong to the single-nozzled, Attic types, common during the classical period, with thick raised bases, a groove around filling holes, and handles or pierced lugs.[89] Sixth-century, single-nozzled black-glazed types form a smaller group, with flat rims decorated with concentric linear ornament. A late fourth-century single-nozzled lamp preserves part of a cylindrical stick fixed to its base, which would have made it ideal for carrying in processions, such as the great procession of the sixteenth of the month Mounukhion (**Pl. 42**).[90] Variations on this type have a tube into which a stick could be fitted for the same purpose, as well as for achieving a steady grip, necessary for transport, on occasions when the lifting of the light was not desired.[91]

Lamps are also recorded from the sanctuary of the goddess at Aulis in Boiotia among other categories of pottery and figurines, with a particular concentration to the south of the temple of Artemis. This area contained extensive workshop installations for supplying the sanctuary with votives, as well as buildings for the accommodation of worshippers.[92] In the Peloponnese, where the cult of Artemis enjoyed popularity, few votive assemblages are published from her sanctuaries, and even fewer are known to have contained lamps. The sanctuary of Artemis Ortheia at Sparta was well-known for its nocturnal cult-activities performed by female participants in honour of the goddess.[93] Apart from R.M. Dawkins' information that lamps were a common offering to the goddess (especially those with many nozzles), the material awaits publication. In fact, the lamps from Ortheia amount to many dozens, most of which are covered with a brownish-black matte glaze, applied over the orange-buff local clay.[94] Most of the material is fragmentary and presents considerable variety in types, suggesting a different manner of use. Multi-nozzled lamps with flat-based oil-chambers and more or less regularly disposed nozzles around their periphery, dating mainly to the Laconian III period with some examples from Laconian II, are commonly found in the sanctuary. Their diameters range between 0.153 m and 0.157 m; the narrow rim of the oil-chamber obviously did not permit the transportation of the vessel when filled with oil. One example still preserves part of the bronze attachment of the chain from which the lamp once hung. The flat bases of most lamps from Ortheia suggest that they rested on flat surfaces, while it remains possible that they were furnished with central tubes for setting them on vertical sticks (since most of the preserved fragments are nozzles or from the upper body of lamps, rather than bases). Traces of fire around the nozzles indicate their previous use, although this does not appear to have been intensive, or at least not as intensive as that of the single- or double-nozzled specimens. The use of the latter in processions may be suggested by the provision for lifting the light by means of a cylindrical hollow tube, which is preserved on a couple of examples. A few very small one- or two-nozzled lamps made of crudely hand-modelled clay were clearly intended to be used indoors, resting on flat surfaces, since they lack a handle and have lipless, bowl-shaped oil-chambers. Wheel-made lamps with handles are also well represented in the Ortheia material, and bear traces of heavier burning. In addition to the lamp types, one may mention one complete example and fragments of a few more possible oil-fillers; the best preserved examples have black painted decoration of parallel lines, dots and a row of water-birds. They date to the Laconian III phase, according to associated pottery. Finally, one should mention a number of base and body fragments of unglazed, perforated vessels with no traces of burning on their interior or exterior, and also fragments of lattice-work which came from the same contexts. The possibility that they belonged to vases containing lamps appears to me very likely in view of their common find-context with lamps, and the absence of heavy burning traces on them.

Excavations at the sanctuary of Artemis Ortheia at Messene have discovered rich deposits of pottery which remain unpublished.[95] No mention of lamps is made in the excavation reports from the sanctuary of Artemis at Kalapodi in Phokis, and a similar case may be made for the Arkadian sanctuary of the goddess at Lousoi, with the exception of two bronze one-nozzled specimens published in the first excavation reports.[96] Lion-shaped feet and provision for hanging were some of the features of these lamps, demonstrating a high quality of workmanship which is also apparent in the rest of the bronze-finds from the sanctuary. These lamps were found to the 'west of the propylon' according to the excavation report, together with jewellery and an iron ring.[97] Two sanctuaries of Artemis in the area of Arkadian Mantineia yielded lamps of sixth-, fifth- and fourth-century date. The first is situated on the west slope of Gortsouli hill and has been identified by the excavator with the sanctuary of Artemis at Mantineia, mentioned by Pausanias (viii, 12.5).[98] The lamps, though not in any great quantity or good state of preservation, came from rich votive deposits which contained fragments of clay figurines, bronze and silver rings, bronze ear-rings, bands with hammered decoration and vessels, a bronze early classical female statuette, bronze and iron pins and bone seals. The pottery is described in the reports as poor, including a few geometric sherds, lamp fragments and miniature vases of the archaic period as well as some sherds of black-figured kylikes and later black-glazed ware.

A large quantity of complete and fragmentary lamps of the archaic period is reported from the Thasian Artemision.[99] A simple, unslipped single- or double-nozzled type is most common, among which are handleless examples with central tubes. Lamps were only a part of the rich votive deposits of the temenos of Artemis *Polô*, which also included female seated and standing figurines, local and imported pottery (for example Attic and Korinthian) as well as fragments of bone and ivory small objects, dating from the seventh to the second quarter of the fifth century.

Lamps were found inside temple-cellas in the sanctuaries of Artemis on a number of occasions. Several sixth century of a so-called 'candlestick' type, according to the excavator, furnished with high stands, have been unearthed during the clearing out of the cella and other parts of the archaic temple of Artemis at Ephesos. Some of the earliest (seventh century) lamp-finds came from further deposits of the temple-cella; the latter include two elaborate stone lamps.[100] A few more clay lamps were reported by J.T. Wood from the cella of the later Artemision, dating not later than the middle of the fourth century.[101]

b. Amphiphôntes: bright gifts for Artemis

Our literary sources for amphiphontes are as late as the second century CE.[102] Amphiphontes were circular cakes bearing thin torches or candles: '*Amphiphôn plakous Artemidi anakeimenos, ekhei d' en kuklô kaomena daïdia*' (Ath. *Deipnosophistai* xiv, 645a). They were offered at the temples of Artemis and at crossroads (*triodoi*) on the sixteenth of every month,[103] when the sky was lit by both the sun and the moon from either side and thus became *amphiphôs* (Ath. *Deipnosophistai* xiv, 645a). The widely accepted lunar associations of amphiphontes rest primarily – if not exclusively – on the addition of torches or candles to the round-shaped sacrificial cakes which were common in the cult of other deities too.[104] The shape of these cakes, the circular arrangement of their lights, the special timing of their offering and the mention of crossroads as the place for their offering, recall Artemis' lunar associations. These are enhanced by her assimilation with Hekate, the primarily moon-goddess, who was also worshipped at crossroads; in certain localities in Greece (especially in Thessaly and Mace-

Fig. 31. Possible representation of an amphiphon on a Boiotian vase.

donia) she takes the name of En(n)odia.[105] Her two torches which 'shone from both sides' gave her the epithet *amphipuros* (Soph. *Trach.* 214) and are comparable with the 'shining from all sides' of the amphiphontes, possibly bearing associations with the pale light of the moon.[106]

Torches and amphiphontes co-exist in what may be the only secure depiction of these shining sacrificial cakes on an Attic/Boeotian red-figure skyphos, now in Laon Museum (**10.1**, *c.* 370-360). A goddess who should probably be identified with Artemis-Hekate is seated on a rock, with two long torches lying next to her. She receives Pan who offers her an amphiphon. On the reverse of the same skyphos, the same goddess is depicted in frontal view as amphipuros, moving hastily to the right with burning torches in both hands. Another possible depiction of a similar 'shining' cake may be found on a Boeotian vase (**Fig. 31**).[107] A goddess dressed in a sleeved khiton, with a sceptre in her left hand, is represented in profile seated on a rock. She receives a young female worshipper in a similar outfit who brings a tray bearing fruit offerings, a myrtle twig and a cake with a candle or thin torch stuck in it, the flame of which is clearly visible. Although the goddess has been interpreted by O. Kern as a healing female deity, in accordance with the reclining male figure on the other side of the vase, this appears very close to the iconography of Artemis and thus comparable to the Laon vase.[108] Clay imitations of amphiphontes may have also existed, parallel to the clay imitations of other sorts of cakes,[109] as offerings to female deities, such as Demeter, Hera or Artemis. A group of fragmentary clay rings with solid clay decoration attached to their upper surface, from the sanctuary of Artemis Ortheia at Sparta, may perhaps be interpreted in this way.

c. Lamps in sacrificial deposits

Lamps are not absent from the interior of cult buildings or temple-cellas where sacrifices took place, as may be inferred from the ashes and animal bones which are found in their contexts. A clay lamp of possible seventh-century date allegedly stood close to the cult images of Apollo and Artemis on the *keraton* altar inside the cult building at Dreros in Krete.[110] The rest of the finds from the cella mainly included plain pottery and bones. A sanctuary of a female deity, most probably Artemis, at Sane of Khalkidike, has yielded a considerable number of lamps which range chronologically between the seventh and the fourth centuries.[111] In the brief excavation report, a group of multi- and one-nozzled lamps is singled out as a special find from the sacrificial eskhara outdoors. The contexts of the latter contained bones, tiles, different types of pottery (including miniature kotyliskoi), relief plaques and figurines, mixed with ashes from sacrifices. I. Vokotopoulou emphasised that some of these lamps were deliberately thrown into the fire, judging from their extensive burnt surfaces.

A further particularly rich find, yet unpublished, comes from a sanctuary of a female deity (or deities), possibly Artemis, at Lathoureza in Attica.[112] Hundreds of offerings including lamps, terracotta figurines, plank-like idols, protomes, metal objects, jewellery, miniature one-handled vases, amphoriskoi, plates, animal bones and sea-shells mainly from the late geometric-archaic period, were found in a circular structure at the summit of the site. The poor preservation of the finds, including the lamps, suggests that they were deliberately smashed, according to A. Mazarakis-Ainian. Lamps of both the simple and the multi-nozzled type were present inside the circular structure, with a particular concentration in its western half. The building, the cult function of which appears evident from the finds it contained, is also furnished with a bench for votives, where some of the lamps might have been placed.

d. Lighting lustration rituals in aduta

In mainland Greece, lamp-finds from the aduton or inner room of the temple of Artemis at Aulis of Boiotia are recorded by the excavator of the site, I. Threpsiades, in connection with his dating of the temple. He considers that the lamps found in the temple of Artemis at Aulis and especially in the aduton give a *terminus ante quem* for the building of the end of the fourth century. Inside the aduton at Aulis, two statue bases, the larger of which is of triangular shape, and an offering table are reported.[113] Lamps are not uncommon in aduta, which, especially in the cults of Artemis and Demeter, may be supplied with water installations for the preliminary purification of the worshippers.[114] The finding of lamps in aduta shows that this ritual may have possibly taken place after the dark, aided by lamp- or torch-light.[115] At the sanctuary of Artemis at Lukokheia in Mantineia, which has been identified with that of Artemis *Kalliste* seen by Pausanias (viii, 55.5-8),[116] a limited number of lamps point to a nocturnal preliminary purification practice, according to the excavator, G. Steinhauer. A lamp, placed inside the lid of a pyxis, was found in the interior of the cult building at Lukokheia, which also contained four clay perirrhanteria. The latter were supplied with water from a nearby cistern. An isolated lamp-find came from the ashes of a circular stone-lined eskhara opposite the entrance of the cult building at Lukokheia of Mantineia, while in a layer of black earth in front of the cult-building, goats' horns, bronze sheets and sherds were found. The lamps from Lukokheia fall into two broad chronological categories, as is also the case with the rest of the finds; the earlier covers the end of the sixth and the first decades of the fifth century, and the later shows possible continuation of these rites in the third century.

3. The cult of Athena

a. Lamps from votive deposits

The use of lamps in rituals honouring Athena appears to have been dramatically limited in comparison with the requirement for artificial illumination in the rituals of the divinities discussed above. However, one notes the existence of similar types, namely the flat-based one-nozzled lamps with central tubes (or spike-holes) and occasionally stone hanging lamps which would have made suitable pieces of temple-furniture. A group of early examples dating to the seventh and sixth centuries have come to light from the destruction deposits of the temple of Athena in Smyrna.[117] Lamps were found in various layers of the so-called 'chip-stratum' which extended in the area around the cella of the destroyed temple III and on the floor of the so-called 'interim' temple IVa. The predominant type is of single-nozzled open clay lamps, with incurved or vertical rim and often a central tube or boss in the interior. Hundreds of similar type, dating from the sixth to the third centuries, were unearthed during the excavations of both A. Furtwängler and D. Ohly of the temple of Aphaia on Aigina.[118] A long series of single- and multi-nozzled lamps, the earliest dating to the sixth century (or possibly even earlier), come from well V (north slope) and other spots on the Athenian Akropolis.[119] Corona types co-exist with open plain ones, and many of these are attached to a flat base or a ring. Specimens of the latter have been published by O. Broneer from the sanctuary of Athena Khalinitis in Korinth.[120] More than two hundred classical lamps are reported from a large votive deposit on the Akropolis of Lindos on Rhodes together with series of figurines and small votives.[121] A considerable quantity of lamps of the archaic period are reported from the rich votive deposits of the sanctuary of Athena Polioukhos on Thasos.[122] These also included a variety of small bronze objects, such as fibulae, cups, arrow-heads and spears, ivory fragments as well as fragments of local and imported pottery, dating from the orientalising period to the beginning of the fifth century.

b. Lamps from temple-cellas

Apart from the famous dedication of an 'ever-burning' golden lamp to Athena which was housed in her temple on the Akropolis, the information that valuable lamps were stored in temple-treasuries on the Akropolis, and the possible association of two particularly elaborate lamps from the Athenian Akropolis with temple-interiors at that site (Chapter II), all other evidence for the use of lamps in temple-cellas in the cult of Athena comes from outside Athens. The temple of Athena at Emporio, Khios,[123] contained thirteen lamps, dating mainly from the middle of the fifth to the middle of the fourth century. A lamp (inv. no. 498) is associated with 'altar A' by the cult-statue base, while four more lamps also came from the cella (inv. nos. 497, 500-2). One of the latter group (inv. no. 500) which came from the northeast corner of the cella was furnished with a cover to facilitate its transport, most probably within the temple. The porch of the temple yielded a further lamp-fragment. Along with the open single-nozzled lamps from the site, some of which were provided with central tubes, two clay lamp-stands were discovered in the cella of the temple dating to the same period as the rest of the lighting material (period II in the report). The rest of the lamps from the temple were scattered inside the building, together with the rest of the votive material, some of which had been tidily stacked, possibly after use.

A large destruction deposit was discovered on the terrace beneath the temple of Athena at Koukounaries of Paros,[124] containing schist-stones from the destroyed cella of the temple, mixed with a quantity of pottery and other votives, among which lamps, pottery, clay plaques and figurines are singled out by the excavator D. Schilardi. Most of the lamps from the temple are dated to the fourth century, but fifth century examples are not missing. A marble three-nozzled lamp of the archaic period is also noted from the deposit. The latter testifies to the use of lamps during the early phases of the life of the temple (for which the given date is the late eighth or early seventh century); traces of burning around the nozzles of later clay lamps from the site confirms the possibility that they once illuminated rituals inside or outside the temple.

Finally, a semicircular lamp of soft stone furnished with provsions for hanging was unearthed from the cella of the so-called 'interim' temple (IVa) of Athena in Smyrna.[125] A few clay lamps of types common at the site (described above) also came from the cella, but their use in that context may not be ascertained. However, the type and material of the semicircular lamp would have undoubtedly made it suitable as temple furniture, similar to those found in temples of Athena in Athens and elsewhere.

4. Use of light in nocturnal feasts for the gods (*pannukhides*)

One of the commonest ritual occasions illuminated by lamps, torches and bonfires were the nocturnal feasts in honour of various gods of the Greek pantheon, known as pannukhides. A pannukhis was a vigil which lasted all night. Dances, songs, a sacrifice and a meal in which the participants consumed the sacrificial meat were some of the standard features of a pannukhis. The exact sequence of events in a pannukhis is difficult to ascertain as it might have been dependent on the nature and ritual requirements of each cult. There is however sufficient evidence to suggest that the dances and songs generally followed the sacrifice, the distribution of sacrificial meat (*kreanomia*) and the subsequent meal.[126] A distinct feature of a pannukhis was the participation of women, since pannukhides provided one of the limited opportunities for women to leave their oikos and enjoy participation in a public ritual.[127] Pannukhides normally took place in a sanctuary and their traces may be recognised among the surviving physical remains in Greek sanctuaries in contexts such as sacrificial deposits, dining rooms (*hestiatoria*), 'pit-altars' and other votive deposits. The great quantity of used lighting materials from sanctuaries probably indicates that they were largely associated with nocturnal feasts, the rituals of which they illuminated, before they were left permanently at the sanctuary as offerings to the gods. Fifth-century dramatists and a few mainly fourth-century inscriptions offer valuable insights into these nocturnal vigils. Pannukhides may have been organised by the authorities of the *polis* as part of state religious festivals or held privately in sanctuaries at the expense of individuals.[128]

A decree (dated to 335-334) regulating the financing of the Lesser Panathenaia refers to a pannukhis which was probably held the night after the sacrifice in honour of Athena and before the procession which took place at sunrise.[129] Some information concerning the events of the pannukhis of the Panathenaia may be found in Euripides' *Heraclidae* (ll. 777-83), a passage which is usually taken to refer to this particular feast. Songs of youths (*neôn t' aoidai*), dances of choruses (*khorôn te molpai*) and dances of virgins (*parthenôn iakhei podôn krotoisin*), accompanied by ritual cries (*ololugai*) are included in the description of the night of the Panathenaia. Apart from the Panathenaia, the inclusion of nocturnal feasts in other festivals honouring Athena may not be supported securely by the available evidence. It is not clear whether a nocturnal feast followed the sacrifice at the Khalkeia in honour of Athena and Hephaistos, where a procession of metalworkers appears also to have been included.[130] A further possibility of a pannukhis in honour of Alea Athena at Tegea depends on the restoration of a fragment of Euripides' *Auge*.[131]

Pannukhides were an important part of festivals in honour of Demeter, namely during the Eleusinian Mysteries, the Thesmophoria and the Haloa.

In the last two festivals, women seem to have been the only participants in the nocturnal feast and also played the leading role in the rituals involved. Aristophanes in his *Thesmophoriazousae* offers a vivid description of such a female gathering taking place in a Thesmophorion in Athens, which is however not known from any other literary source.[132] Evidence of the location of other Thesmophoria in the Attic demes is provided by the sources, such as the Thesmophorion of Peiraeus, Melite, Pithos, Halimous, Oe, Phrearrhioi, Holargos, and certainly Eleusis.[133] A sacrificial calendar from Eleusis (dated to the early third century) explicitly refers to a pannukhis among other arrangements for the Thesmophoria and other festivals of Demeter.[134] Special mention of the use of artificial light provided by torches and bonfires is sometimes made in official documents which prescribe the materials required for sacrifices and other rituals. For example, a decree of the deme of Holargos (dated to 334-333) specifies the supply of a torch along with various grains and foods which were to be provided by the women-leaders of the festival (*arkhousai*) for the priestesses in their performance of rituals at the Thesmophoria.[135] Similar arrangements for the provision of wood (*xula*), brushwood (*phrugana*) and torches (*daïs*, *lampas*) are often made in sacred regulations of both Thesmophoria and Haloa organised by other Attic demes.[136] For the pannukhis at Haloa, information about the participation of hetairai and indecent female behaviour is offered in the *Letters of Courtesans* by Alkiphron (iv, 6.3) and Lucian (*Dial. meret.* xiv, 1). A pannukhis was included in the Eleusinian Mysteries, probably following the procession of the mustai on the night of the twentieth of the month Boedromion (Ar. *Ran.* 447; Soph. *OC* 1048-50). The dancing during the pannukhis would have been undertaken by the women initiates, since it was the women who first attempted to appease the wrath of the goddess Demeter in the Homeric Hymn (*Hom. Hymn Dem.* ll. 292-5) by keeping an all-night vigil in honour of the goddess, 'trembling with fear'. A reference by Aristophanes to the '*kallikhorôtaton tropon*' (*Ran.* 450-1) of the initiates as they perform the dances of Iakkhos during the Mysteries may lead to speculation about the location of the dances during the pannukhides at Eleusis; these would have taken place around or near the Kallikhoron well, which is an important landmark of the Eleusinian sanctuary. When Pausanias saw this well during his visit at Eleusis, he was told that it was where the women first honoured Demeter with songs and dances (i, 38.6).[137]

In the cult of Dionysos nocturnal celebrations were also common, a fact reflected in his epithet *Nuktelios*.[138] In the *Bacchae* (ll. 485-8) the god himself admits his preference for darkness as the most suitable time for his worship, a comment received suspiciously by Pentheus, who sees inevitable associations between night-time and indecent behaviour.[139] All-night dances in honour of Dionysos, performed by his staunch mythical female followers, the maenads, are described by the chorus in the *Bacchae* (ll. 862-76). These are manic dances involving tossing of the head in

imitation of wild animals such as fawns, with which maenads are compared by the chorus in the same play. These wild dances in the *Bacchae*
took place in natural landscape. A pannukhis in honour of Dionysos from
which men were excluded is attested by a fourth-century inscription from
Methymna on Lesbos.[140] Another nocturnal public feast which involved eating
and drinking and in which men participated seems to have been included in
the Anthesteria in Athens, the festival of the new wine; more specifically, the
pannukhis took place on the second evening of the festival, the day of the
Khoes to which reference is made by Aristophanes (*Ran.* 216-19).[141]

A sacred law for the cult of the Thracian goddess Bendis in Athens,
dated to the second half of the fifth century, mentions a pannukhis[142] which
is also referred to in Plato's *Respublica* (328A). The second source sheds
light on the relative place of the nocturnal vigil in relation to the festival
which, along with a torch-race, appears to have preceded the pannukhis.
Artemis was honoured in nocturnal feasts such as the pannukhis described by Pausanias at Letrinoi of Elis (vi, 22.9) and possibly during the
Athenian Tauropolia.[143] Whether the cult at Brauron included any nocturnal celebations may not be securely shown despite the representations of
torch-bearing girls on vase-fragments and the numerous lamps found in
sanctuaries of Artemis.[144] Equally uncertain is the interpretation of the
fragmentary poem *Partheneion* by Alcman as a song of nocturnal celebration for Artemis Ortheia at Sparta.[145] A nocturnal banquet may have
followed a series of rituals including a sacrifice at the annual festival of
Artemis Ortheia at Messene, according to the reconstruction of the rituals
proposed by P. Themelis.[146]

Particularly famous for their orgiastic character were the pannukhides
in the cult of the Phrygian goddess Kybele. These resembled many aspects
of Dionysiac nocturnal vigils, such as the use of tambourines (*tumpana*)
and cymbals (*krotala*) as well as the orgiastic wild dances in natural
landscape (often mountainous areas) and the howling of the participants
(*ololugê*).[147] Such nocturnal feasts which included songs and dances of
maidens in honour of the Mother of the gods and Pan are known from
Thebes from as early as Pindar's time; the poet attests that these lively
nocturnal feasts took place before his own door (*Pyth.* iii, 77-9), while later
on, when Pausanias visited Pindar's house in the second century CE, he
saw an adjoining shrine of the goddess Kybele next to it containing a
notable statue (Paus. ix, 25.3).[148] Further evidence about the performance
of nocturnal rites for Kybele at Kyzikus is provided by Herodotus who
made a remark on the pomp of the feast in which cymbals were used and
adds information about a custom of hanging images of the goddess all
about the participants (iv, 76). In tragic drama, the nocturnal rites of the
Mother of the gods are often recalled with special reference to the loud
percussion of the tumpana and krotala (e.g. Eur. *Hel.* 1308, 1351, 1365;
Bacch. 130-4, 146-7; *Kretes* fr. 79)[149]

Pan was often worshipped alongside Kybele in an orgiastic fashion, as

attested in Pindar's *Pythian* (iii, 77-9). Strong cult-associations between
the two gods are found in the Parian marble, where they are said to have
shared a common mode of worship with Dionysos (the so-called 'Phrygian
mode'). The 'Phrygian mode' defined a form of group-worship which included songs and dances.[150] Later, Plutarch refers again to the cultic bonds
between Kybele, Dionysos and Pan by classing their rites (*orgia*) together
(*Amat.* xvi, 31).[151] Pan was worshipped in mixed feasts, as apparently was
Kybele; a large part of the pannukhides in honour of Pan were organised
privately in sanctuaries of the god. The most conspicuous example of such
a private feast is described in Menander's *Dyscolos*, which takes place at
the sanctuary of Pan at Phule on mount Parnes in the fifth century.[152] The
feast comprises a sacrifice (*thusia*), a meal consumed at the hestiatorion
of the sanctuary, music, dances by women and drinking by men. Participation in the dances seems to have been an exclusively female activity,
while the drinking (*sumposion*) was restricted to male participants of the
pannukhis. Excavations at the cave of Pan at Phule brought to light a large
quantity of pottery lamps which undoubtedly served to light nocturnal
ceremonies at the sanctuary; some of the lamps were found deposited in
layers of ash, pointing to their use in sacrifices.[153] The use of torches to
light the activities of the pannukhis in Menander's *Dyscolos* is also specified in the poem (ll. 963-4). Further evidence for mixed nocturnal feasts
inside a cave of Pan and the Nymphs that were privately organised is
provided by Alkiphron (iv, 13).[154] Although the basic rituals of a sacrifice,
a wineless libation, a meal and dances are performed, the religious nature
of the feast is spoiled by the liberal sexual attitudes of the female participants (many of whom are courtesans) and their lovers. Allusions to the
bibulous propensity of women are made in Menander's *Dyscolos* too (ll.
855-9). The earliest hints of such conduct of women are found in Attic
comedy (e.g. Ar. *Nub.* 1069), with further relevant references made by
Lucian (*Dial. meret.* xiv, 1) and later authors. Private pannukhides which
included a sumposion in which men participated alongside women have
been identified in fragmentary works of Kritias (fifth century),[155] Anak-
reon[156] (sixth century), Callimachos[157] and a dithyramb (*PBerol.* 13270).[158]
The surviving evidence for pannukhides mentioned above seems to be only
a fraction of a much more extensive practice of nocturnal celebrations in
Greek sanctuaries in the archaic and classical periods. Further evidence
for pannukhides in the Hellenistic period adds, among others, Asklepios
to the list of recepient deities of such nocturnal celebrations,[159] while
references to the pannukhides of the ancient Greeks are still remembered,
loaded with strong negative connotations for their corrupting influence, by
Christian authors (e.g. Dion. Hal. *Ant. Rom.* ii, 19.2).

Conclusion

From all the evidence available, it is clear that the level of involvement of light (both as a concept and as a device) in ancient Greek religious ritual was much deeper and more diverse than its practical function to illuminate nocturnal rituals. Brightness was linked with divine epiphanies in the Homeric poems, and often assumed concrete forms, such as the lamp of Athena, to express divine power in human terms. Light encloses and reflects what is extraordinary about the gods, and in this form this symbolism survives throughout the archaic period and into classical times. A reconsideration of archaeological data in conjunction with literature indicates the use of lamps in sanctuaries probably earlier than the seventh century, when the hitherto first accepted lamp types appear. Open clay vessels of variable shape, with or without handles, seem to have served as lamps with floating wicks at several early cult sites, including the Heraia at Argos, Tiryns and Perakhora, the so-called Agamemnoneion at Mycenae, and the sanctuary of Athena Alea at Tegea. Torches were surely used alongside lamps in those early cult activities, as may be inferred from their repeated mention in the Homeric poems. As yet, however, no torch-holder of whatever kind, securely datable before the seventh century, has been found in a Greek sanctuary (excluding a number of well-known examples of Mycenaean date).

The seventh century saw a remarkable change in the use of lighting devices in cult practice. Apart from the appearance of the first nozzled lamps, elaborate series of marble lamps with carved decoration and bronze *lukhnoukhoi* are known from different sanctuary sites across the Aegean. The size, material, workmanship, find-locations and distribution of the marble lamps, together with their decorative motifs (e.g. human heads of the daedalic style and heads of sacrificial animals), associate them directly with important cult activities. These may have included lights which burned day and night in temple-cellas, a practice attested in literature by Pausanias when he refers to the golden lamp of Athena in the Erekhtheion. This argument is supported by some marble lamps found in temple cellas, such as those from the sanctuary of Demeter Malophoros at Selinous, the Ephesian Artemision and the Hephaisteion on Lemnos. In addition to marble lamps, isolated finds, such as the lamp said to have been found on the *keraton*-altar of the shrine of Apollo and Artemis at

Dreros, further suggest the practice of burning of lights in temple-cellas or in the main cult-room of a shrine where sacrifices took place. The Samian Heraion has furnished us with seventh-century lamp- or torch-stands, as has also the Athenian Akropolis, although in the latter the find-locations are not precisely known. Torch-holders with painted decoration and handles are reported from the sanctuary at Aetos on Ithaka during the same period (**Fig. 3**; **Pl. 1**). In the seventh century, the earliest painted representations of certain forms of light appear on Greek vases; a male figure (probably a god, often interpreted as Zeus) holding a thunderbolt as a weapon against a giant-opponent figures on a Protokorinthian aryballos by the Ajax Painter and is dated to the first half of the seventh century.

From the middle of the sixth century, Attic black-figure and sculptural representations of torches begin to be associated with divinities such as Artemis, Hermes and Hekate. Attic black-figure representations of divine weddings, which enjoyed popularity during the second half of the sixth century, include Artemis as torch-bearer (daidoukhousa) in wedding processions (**Pl. 11**). A work of the Diosphos Painter furnishes us with the earliest known Attic representation of torches in the context of the birth of Dionysos (**2.1**, dated to around 500; **Pl. 7**), while a roughly contemporary work of the Edinburgh Painter depicts Hermes on a ram, flanked by torch-bearing women (possibly maenads) (**Fig. 27**). At the turn of the century, however, torch-bearing divinities are introduced into a variety of scenes in many divine circles. For example, the Ascent of Persephone (Eleusinian circle) is often attended by Hekate with torches in hand (**Pl. 14**), while the torch-bearing leader of the initiates (Daidoukhos) is included in one of the earliest cult scenes from the Mysteries (**4.2**; **Fig. 14**). The iconographical types of Artemis daidophoros (without arms) with one torch, as well as Artemis as huntress with a torch, are also formed during the early fifth century; the earliest such examples in vase-painting are found on a white-ground lekythos by a painter close to the Diosphos Painter and a clay relief pinax from Brauron. Thereafter, types of torch-bearing deities increase in number and variety in vase-painting and sculpture throughout the fifth century.

The picture of torch-bearing gods becomes fuller during the fifth and fourth centuries, when illumination devices appear repeatedly in divine hands in both vase-painting and sculpture, and they are also a regular find in sanctuaries. There is adequate evidence for the use of lamps in rituals that took place in temple aduta, such as that at Lykokheia in Mantineia. Lamps appear to have been included in sacrificial rites, as is extensively indicated by the archaeological evidence as well as by the sacrificial regulations of Despoina at Lykosoura (which are of a later date). Lamp-processions may be inferred from as early as the middle of the fifth century, mainly by the presence of lamp types with provision to fit a stick into the underside of the base, such as those from the sanctuary of Artemis Mounukhia at Piraeus or a possible lamp-bearer from the eastern side of the Parthenon frieze (**Pl. 42**). In addition to lamps, torches were also used in rituals in the sanctuaries of Artemis, as is shown by the surviving representations on black-figure krateriskoi from Brauron; they depict girls running with torches in hand. Cleansing rituals using torches are attested in literature and may be related to rituals of similar nature which used lamps in the aduta of temples. Circular cakes with candles, or thin torches, are also found in the symbolism pertaining to special occasions in the cult of Artemis, especially in the form in which she was assimilated with Hekate.

Close reading of the iconography of different divine circles allows us to observe in greater detail several stages of important rituals in which light was extensively used from at least as early as the fifth century. In some cases, one may suggest reconstructions of well-known stages of rituals which then, in turn, offer further possibilities for interpretation of their significance within specific festivals. For example, the up-and-down gestures of Iakkhos with his torches when he is depicted leading the *mustai* possibly reflect the actual movements of the daidoukhos procession, which was familiar only to those who had been initiated (**Fig. 14**). Similarly, depictions of the torch and grain held by an agrarian goddess before an altar, or in the context of the libation before the departure of Triptolemos, may reflect the actual procedure of fertility rituals performed by priests at the sanctuaries of Demeter or other agrarian deities (**Pl. 40**). The pure fire of torches is emphasised repeatedly by the standard motif of their ceremonial lighting from an altar by a goddess (**Pl. 30**). Their use as purifiers may be inferred from a range of literary references, from Iphigenia's mock-cleansing ritual in the land of the Taurians to the purification of Herakles from homicide. The recurring depiction of fire (in the form of torches or thunderbolt) as a weapon in the hands of gods (Zeus, Artemis and Hekate) and heroes (notably Herakles), either in divine wars or in connection with their treatment of disrespectful mortals, reinforces its symbolism, alluding to utter destruction. From here, the destructive forces of fire extend to the mortal world in connection with war or even metaphorically, to mortal 'burning' feelings, which are so extreme that they may destroy those possessed by them.

Transition rituals made extensive use of torches such as in the procession of Iakkhos, when a nocturnal passage through the dark underworld was symbolically enacted. Similarly, Hekate's torches often appear in connection with the passage of Persephone to and from the underworld. Both transitions, the first during her abduction and the second during her ascent, needed to be accompanied by torches. Both Hekate and Hermes, as transition gods, are present at Persephone's symbolic passage from one world to another. The connection between brightness and the fulfilment of an aim, namely the successful passage through the underworld, reflects the initiates' reward by the promise of a happy afterlife. This image of happiness-brightness after the symbolic experience of death-darkness is found not only in the Eleusinian Mysteries in honour of Demeter and Kore, but also in those of Dionysos and Orpheus.

Apart from those transition rituals enacted within sanctuaries, a number of others, more secular in context, but surely embodying religious values, make use of torches. For example, the custom of daidoukhia in human or divine weddings probably symbolised the brief social 'death' of the bride during her passage from her father's to her husband's oikos with its own domestic gods. The torches lit at the hearth of the oikos of the father of the bride symbolically guaranteed a successful social transition, her 'death' as parthenos and her 'rebirth' as a future mother. The purity reflected by her hearth-lit torches underlines her yet untamed virginity, required for all girls who abandoned the wild and pure realm of Artemis for that of Aphrodite. The wider association of brightness with the concept of birth and death is revealed in literature, particularly in the context of Semele's miscarriage of Dionysos which brought about her death. Both birth and death were a result of the thunderbolt of Zeus, and took place amidst extraordinary light produced by the father of the gods. Dionysos' later birth from the thigh of his father, Zeus, is again associated with torches. The myth is represented by the Diosphos Painter around 500 (**Pl. 7**). A young Dionysos holds two short torches as he leaps out of Zeus's thigh, while an inscription identifies the child as the light of Zeus (*Dios phôs*). Birth-goddesses such as Artemis Lokhia or Eileithyia are represented in art holding torches, a fact explained in antiquity (by, for example, Homer, Pindar and Pausanias), as a symbolic expression of their bringing of children to light.

Another important aspect of the torch, as a primarily male attribute connected with the world outside the oikos, is its incorporation in the athletic events of many major state-festivals, such as the Panathenaia, Prometheia, Hephaisteia, Bendideia in Athens, festivals of Attic demes like Rhamnous as well as festivals outside Attika, notably in Amphipolis and elsewhere. The preservation of the flame, which was the ultimate goal in torch-races, seems to have been loaded with connotations of the preservation of political stability and traditional values of a polis. Here, one might metaphorically see the handing over of a race-torch (diadokhe) as an image of transition between generations. Particular reference is made by Aristophanes to the younger generations who have to be physically and mentally fit to take over the 'torch' of state affairs. It would probably not be too extreme – if we are right to identify the scenes of **1.1-1.19** in Catalogue 1 with torch-races at the Panathenaia – to ascribe significance to their relatively late date, after the Peloponnesian war, when the need for reorganisation of Athenian state affairs was particularly urgent.

On another level, it is clear that lamps played an important role as a source of light for nocturnal religious feasts (pannukhides), public or private, which were regular features of many cults (e.g. those of Demeter,

Artemis, Dionysos, Bendis, Pan, Kybele and others). Yet several indications suggest that certain types of lamp types performed functions beyond that of mere illumination. For example, lamps of almost miniature size, despite frequently observed burn-marks around their nozzles, can hardly have provided adequate illumination; yet at the same time most of the large multi-nozzled lamps from Greek sanctuaries do not appear to have been heavily used. These extreme categories apparently point to practices less directly associated with the practical need for illumination, and at the same time manifest an involvement of light in cult of a different nature. Here, one may mention the symbolic burning of a lamp in order to offer light as a votive gift to the goddess, rather than the lighting vessel itself being the offering. Such lamps cannot really have fulfilled the needs of artificial illumination of a sanctuary, which was instead probably lit by torches or the ordinary lamp-types, brought to the sanctuary by worshippers. Rituals, such as the deliberate smashing and subsequent burning of lamps in bonfires are attested from places like Eleusis as early as the sixth century. Lamp-processions may be inferred from the common types of lamp with fixed stick-handle and cover. The plethora and diversity of evidence for various forms of illumination device in Greek cult reveal significant aspects of the inadequately known, though apparently widespread, nocturnal rituals of the archaic and the classical periods. But these also point to a number of rituals which should not be associated exclusively with night, such as the ever-burning light placed next to the cult-image in many Greek temples, the ritual integration of the bride to her new household, the purification of a new-born child at the hearth of the house, torch-races, or the dedication of light to the gods usually in the form of lamps.

It is probably not a coincidence that on a considerable number of occasions the light offering to the gods is shaped into circular patterns, through circular multi-nozzled lamps or smaller specimens, sitting on a clay disc. Herodotus' attestation of a feast of lamps in Egypt offers additional evidence of the importance of this circular pattern, according to which lamps were placed around houses and were left alight throughout the night. Aristophanes uses the lamp as a comic parallel for the sun, while 'brighter' offerings to gods, such as amphiphontes, consistently assumed a circular shape. Solar parallels cannot be excluded, while from the fourth century onwards further possible interpretations are suggested by the concept of the circle in philosophy, a link especially evident in Orphism. In this last connection, it should be no surprise that large circular multi-nozzled lamps from sanctuaries increase even more markedly in variety and quantity from the end of the classical period, and this increase continues uninterrupted throughout hellenistic and Roman times.

Light, as a concept, has been regularly employed in Greek literature to express a variety of oppositions, one of which is its contrast with darkness. Light marks the experiences of the living, who exclusively enjoy the natural light of the sun, while darkness covers the eyes of the dead. This belief is repeatedly found in Homer and apparently forms the basis of several equally widespread concepts reflected in literature. These include the eternal brightness of the gods, who do not face the threat of death, and the firm association of the birth-goddess Eileithyia and other kourotrophic goddesses (such as Artemis Lokhia or Artemis Euonumos) with brightness, since they assist the newly-born in their first passage to the natural light of life. Further examples are the promise of a bright, and therefore happy, afterlife for the initiates of the Eleusinian and Dionysiac mysteries, as well as the conflation between knowledge and brightness which is associated with the aim of the mysteries and is also employed in literature to describe the peculiar ability of certain mortals to foretell the future. The latter finds an ideal parallel in the persona of seers, for example, who experience some of the 'brightness' of the gods in their capacity as vehicles of divine will. A good example of the latter is Teiresias who, though blind, can *see* the light! These positive, abstract connotations of light extend to a range of psychological states such as hope, joy, love and triumph, as well as reflections of physical beauty.

On the other hand, the dangerous aspect of extraordinary light is often perceived as blazing fire, which burns out of control, in the hands of gods or men. The blazing thunderbolt of Zeus punishes the hubris of the Titans and kills Semele causing the premature birth of Dionysos. Hekate and Artemis are represented with torches in hand during their fight against the giants, whose fearful nature, like that of Typhoeus, entails fire. A variety of torch-bearing images of gods are regularly introduced in visual representations of excessive behaviour of mortals (hubris), such as the flute competition between Apollo and Marsyas or the myths of Bellerophon and Aktaion. In the mortal world, the concept of an extraordinary blaze which causes destruction is intimately associated with images of battles and takes the concrete form of a torch. The threatening implications of the latter, often voiced by mortals, is a dominant concept in literary descriptions of battles, notably in those taking place in Troy or Thebes. The god of war, Ares, is often associated with destructive fire which can only be repelled by fire, as may be inferred from the chorus' invocation to a series of gods in *Oedipus Tyrannus* (ll. 188-215) and elsewhere. The association of women with fire may often have destructive results. 'Inflamed' maenads, for example, when under divine inspiration, carry torches which reflect the threatening dimensions of their unbridled state. 'Bright' deaths are delivered by women like Medea who chose to kill Glauke, the bride of Jason, by means of 'inflamed' crowns. Finally, the justice of mortals, just like divine justice which punishes hubris, is commonly expressed through images of fire, which 'burns' away moral corruption and dishonesty.

To conclude, one may locate the beginning of regular involvement of light in Greek religious belief in the time of Homer. The first clear signs of the use of light as a cult component in rituals cannot be placed later than the seventh century from the material evidence available. A clear, gradual expansion of the use and significance of light, both in terms of cults with which it came to be associated and of functions that it fulfilled, may be observed during the archaic and classical periods. During the classical period light became an important component in the practice and system of beliefs of many cults, such as those of Demeter and Kore, Dionysos and others, and this laid a firm foundation for the deeper involvement of light in the cult of subsequent periods, notably those of hellenistic times. The study of the role of light as both a concept and a practical device in Greek cult therefore has considerable implications for our better understanding of the 'birth' and gradual development of Greek religious belief and ritual, and is a clear reminder of how much is still to be learned about many aspects of Greek cult.

Notes

I. Light in Early Greek Religious Thought and Practice

1. According to Odysseus' initial plan (*Od.* xvi, 281-98), two sets of weapons (sword, spear and shield) were to be left out for the two heroes, as necessary equipment for the coming fight against the suitors. However later (*Od.* xix, 1-46), the action taken by Odysseus and Telemakhos does not follow the plan closely, since all weapons were hidden without exception until the fight, when the two heroes hastily armed themselves almost at the same time as the suitors. The difficulties that arose during the fight with the suitors as a result of the change of plan led scholars to assume that the passage was a later interpolation. E. Cook has shown how the slaying of the suitors (book xxii) was conceived and carefully organised as *aristeia* in such a way as to glorify the exploits of the two heroes by giving their enemies a fair chance to defend themselves too. From this viewpoint, the decision of Odysseus in book xix seems justifiable and fits well into the wider plot of the story. In addition, Athena's advice and co-operation in establishing moral order in the house of Odysseus had been continuous since the arrival of the hero on Ithaka (*Od.* xiii, 221-439; xvii, 363-4; xix, 2). Odysseus' change of mind at xix, 1-46 can be fully explained by the repeated interference of the goddess, and is indispensable to the structure of the poem because it leads finally to the *aristeia* and the heroes' triumph over the suitors. For recent discussion: Cook (1995), 163-4 nn. 112-13.

2. Monro (1901), 149 n. 34: 'lukhnos is post-homeric, both word and thing.' Lorimer (1950), 509-10. As an important further argument for the later addition of the passage in book xix, Lorimer called attention to the constant allusions to *sidêros*, which is considered (in terms of historical background) an apparent breach in epic convention. The point had been made earlier by Monro (1901), 339, who noticed the greater proportion of iron rather than *khalkos* in the *Odyssey* compared to the *Iliad*.

3. Pfeiffer (1960), 2-3; Dindorff (1855), 670.

4. Pfeiffer (1960), 6-7: 'sollte nicht die goldene Lampe schon der "mykenischen" Athene angehört haben, deren Existenz kaum bezweifelt werden kann? Manche vereinzelten mykenischen Züge sind ja den epischen Dichtern wohl bekannt gewesen, wenn wir auch noch nicht sagen können, wie sie zu jener Kenntnis kamen.'

5. Müller (1966), 125-6.

6. Rose (1951), 1-2; according to Rose, Homer wrote around 900, at which time Mycenaean practices could not have been forgotten. The aegis is used as a parallel example of the survival of Mycenaean elements in the 'Dark Ages'.

7. The earliest architectural remains on the Athenian Akropolis – other than tombs – date to the Late Helladic IIIA I and are not primarily associated with cult, but perhaps with a ruler's residence: Mountjoy (1995), 69-70. Nor do the F-shaped figurines provide secure evidence for cult of any particular deity: Pantelidou (1975), 199. The earliest roof on the Akropolis – not necessarily a temple – is dated by N. Winter to the first quarter of the sixth century, while M. Korres places the date of the first temple of Athena on the Akropolis in the first decades of the fifth century. Winter (1993), 213-14; Korres (1997), 224-5. For discussion of the Mycenaean and Early Iron Age evidence from the Athenian Akropolis: Glowacki (1998), 78-82; Parker (1996), 17-20, esp. 19 n. 37; Crielaard (1995), 253-5; Mountjoy (1995), esp. 13, 24, 27, 41-2, 50-1; Pantelidou (1975), 200-1, 203. In favour of a Mycenaean cult of Athena on the Akropolis: Simms (1980), 120; Cook (1995), 166 n. 124.

8. Heubeck (1992), 76.

9. Bennet (1997), 532-3.

10. Persson (1942), 109; Jantzen & Tölle (1968), 84, 87.

11. Whitman (1958), 121-2; Richardson (1974), 208; Heubeck (1992), loc. cit. (n. 8), ll. 36-40. Scholars agree on the symbolic role of the goddess's light, which foreshadows the forthcoming victory of Odysseus. Also see Dindorff (1855), 671, l. 43.

12. For example: *Il.* xviii, 205-14: a golden cloud lit by Athena crowned the head of Akhilles on his way to rescue Patroklos' body from sacrilege: 'but Achilles dear to Zeus roused him, and round about his mighty shoulders Athene flung her tasselled aegis, and around his head the fair goddess set thick a golden cloud, and forth from the man made blaze a gleaming fire' (trans. Murray 1995); *Il.* xx, 95: Athena made a light, going before Akhilles as he was chasing Aeneas on Mount Ida; *Il.* v, 3-6: the same goddess kindled unwearing flame on the head and shoulders of Tydeus' son, Diomedes, so as to shine bright among all the Argives, preparing him for his *aristeia* in the battle. Common patterns in Athena's help in Homeric texts may be discerned, such as the light in which the goddess envelops her favourite heroes, just before their aristeia, or the fact that she goes before the humans whom she wants to help providing light for them, and thus arming them for a forthcoming victorious fight. For a discussion of similar scenes: Constantinidou (1993).

13. Whitman (1958), loc. cit. (n. 11); Cook (1995), 145-6.

14. Woodhouse (1930), 176; Whitman (1958), 122.

15. For discussions: Whitman (1958), 122; Müller (1966), loc. cit. (n. 5); Woodhouse (1930), loc. cit. (n. 14); Dimock (1989), 246-7.

16. Dindorff (1855), 671.

17. See nn. 11-12 above.

18. Cook (1995), 165; he rightly observed that Homer felt no need to gloss his word for lamp with a description. B. Powell also admitted that lamps, though a rarity in Homer, may have been used in exceptional circumstances, for example by a god. Powell (1991), 202.

19. For a discussion including earlier literature: Parisinou (1998), 327-8.

20. Jantzen & Tölle (1968), 83-8.

21. Persson (1942), 109-10: 'One can point of course to the fact that the immigrants from the North were accustomed to use fire-sticks and chips for lighting, but since it is impossible to believe that a complete extermination of the older population occurred, this does not suffice in explaining the disappearance of the previous use of oil-lamps ... The explanation most readily acceptable is that the old olive plantations were so badly devastated and the general cultivation of the olive had declined to such an extent that oil became too expensive for use as a combustible'; Jantzen & Tölle (1968), 96-7.

22. Even in these catastrophic cases, one might perhaps be able to justify a limited production of lighting objects, a dramatic altering of types towards cheaper and simpler forms, or even a change in the combustible material used to something more easily available, such as animal fat. A total disappearance of lamps cannot be thus explained.

23. Latest discussions: Donlan (1997), 650-1; Foxhall (1995), 244-5, n. 28, 246; Cook (1995), 165-6 and n. 123. Also: Wright (1972), 195-9; Luckerman & Moody (1978).

24. Recent references to Mycenaean evidence: Foxhall (1995), 241-2, nn. 9-11.

25. Foxhall (1995), 244 n. 30, 248.

26. Hdt. ii, 62: 'the lamps they use are flat dishes filled with oil and salt, with a floating wick which keeps burning throughout the night' (trans. de Sélincourt 1972).

27. Ure & Burrows (1911), 88-99, figs. 16-17; their theory was based on the idea that the provision of a leaning wick to a nozzled vessel is not a decisive factor in identifying it as lamp. Using stylistic similarities and functionality as main criteria, they suggested that *kothon*-vases may have served as lamps, if furnished with one or more floating wicks. A number of features that are shared between both lamps and kothons were cited in support of this theory, such as incurved rims to avoid oil spilling, horizontal handles for transportation, similar size, find-places, and signs of burning in the interior. For successful 'applications' of this theory to excavation-finds: Frickenhaus (1912), 100; Nilsson (1950), 100 n. 4.

28. Benton (1953), 359; in her discussion of spouted ring vases with feet, she considered the possibility of them functioning as lamps, since she found them inconvenient for oil or perfume. She did not, however, mention any traces of use (signs of burning, for example).

29. Such examples have been published from a considerable number of sanctuary sites: Schliemann (1886), 142-3, 366, pl. xxvii figs. b-c (Mycenae); Furtwängler (1906), 467, pl. 130 (Aigina); Blinkenberg (1931), 100, no. 196, figs. 33-6 (Rhodes); Waldstein (1905), 96-8, fig. 32a (Argos); Legrand (1905), 310-12 (Troizen); Caskey & Amandry (1952), 194 n. 38 (Perakhora); Frickenhaus (1912), 95-9, figs. 29-32 (Tiryns); Cook (1950), 48-9 n. 32, pl. 20, nos. 11-19 (Mycenae); Dunbabin (1962), 302-3, pls. 52-3, nos. MP11-14 (Perakhora); Metzger (1985), 15, pl. 15, fig. 2 (Eretria); Pemberton (1989), 81 no. 15, pl. 4, 84, 95 no. 101 pl. 13, 100 no. 149 pl. 17, 103 no. 170 pl. 18, 169 no. 508 pl. 50, 170 nos. 520, 522, 174 no. 560 (Korinth); Voyatzis (1990), 79-82, 87, 298-301, pls. 42, 43, 44, 49 (Tegea).

30. For clear signs of burning on small kalathiskoi, krateriskoi and kotylai, see Pemberton (1989), loc. cit. (n. 29). Also, my own observations on similar vases from the sanctuary of Demeter at Knossos and Hera at Tiryns accord with Pemberton's information. For a modern experiment on these cup-lamps and a discussion of their burn-marks: Parisinou (1998), 332-5.

31. Robins (1939), 185; Robins made it clear that this kind of lamp grew out of ordinary pottery household vessels, thus stressing their likely multiple function.

32. For recent discussions based on the finds at Lefkandi and Knossos: Crielaard (1995), 224-31; Morris (1997), 609-16 (focusing on references to such trade-contacts in the Homeric texts).

33. Jantzen & Tölle (1968), 96; Bailey (1975), 12-13: 'no break of continuity in the use of open lamps'; Heres (1969), 15-17; Kassab & Sezer (1995), 33-45.

34. Bailey (1975), 212-14 Q478 pls. 90-1; 217-18 Q483 pls. 92-3; 219-21 Q485 pl. 95. For simple bowl-shaped lamps with pinched nozzles: Bailey (1975), 215, Q280 pls. 92-3, 216 Q481 pls. 92-3.

35. Desborough (1956), 129-30, pls. 33b, 34a, no. 4.

36. Information provided by the excavator, Dr A. Mazarakis-Ainian. The material is still unpublished.

37. Marinatos (1936), 259-60, fig. 23; Marinatos refused to accept a date in the eighth century as suggested by D. Levi for either site, mainly on the grounds that there is no evidence of lamps from that period.

38. Furtwängler (1906), loc. cit. (171 n. 29).

39. Frickenhaus (1912), loc. cit. (171 n. 29).

40. Persson (1942), 103-7, 108, fig. 113: category A: 'Hand' Lamps.

41. The conical bowls were found in wells of Mycenaean date on the south slope of the Akropolis. The burning on the rim and around the spout led Mountjoy to identify them as lamps: Mountjoy (1981), 57 nos. 93-7, 249. Mountjoy (1993), 58, 124. Similar Attic examples were published earlier by Pantelidou (1975), 85, 96, 117, 187-9, pls. 31g, 35g, 36a, 55b.

42. The kylikes interpreted as lamps with floating wicks come from the Fountain House on the North Slope of the Akropolis: Mountjoy (1995), 44, fig. 57.

43. Howland (1958), 20-1; Bailey (1975), 29.

44. Beazley (1940), 22-49.

45. For Bronze Age examples from shines and tombs: Warren (1969), 53, 54, 55, 58; Rutkowski (1986), 21, 23, 28, 29, 32-3, 37, 57, 85, 115, 117, 151, 165, 179, 184, 247.

46. Recent treatment of the subject: Sherratt (1990), 807-24; Crielaard (1995), 201-88.

47. See 17, 173 n. 80.

48. Now in Palermo Museum. Beazley (1940), 32-3.

49. Orlandini (1963), 34-5, 37-8 figs. 14-16, pls. 8-9; Holloway (1991), 57 fig. 68.

50. This lamp-type with sculptural decoration of human or/and animal heads finds many parallels. For example: Sabbione (1984), 274-5, n. 61; Croissant (1992), 548, 551, 557; Rolley (1981), 191-3.

51. Orlandini (1963), 34-8, 43-50 pls. 12-13.

52. Marconi (1926), 142; Marconi (1933), 23, 66-7, 69; White (1964), 66-74.

53. Kron (1992), 629-30, 646-7, 625; White (1964), 39. Also see Chapter IX.1c.

54. Beazley (1940), 38-40 figs. 17-20.

55. Papadimitriou (1949), 86 fig. 15.

56. Howland (1958), esp. 18-19; for seventh-century lamps see 19-20, type 8 no. 58 and type 9 and 23-4, type 11.

57. These observations are based on my own examination of the lighting material from Eleusis and discussions that I have had with Dr K. Kokkou-Viridi on the pyres from the site. Also see Chapter IX.1a.

58. The rough dating and comment on the types come from my own examination of a limited part of the material in the storerooms of the museum, with the permission of Dr N. Bookidis. For this early deposit: Bookidis & Stroud (1997), 32 n. 24.

59. Frickenhaus (1912), 100-2.

60. Dunbabin (1962), 389.

61. Broneer (1977), 4-5 nos. 1-2.

62. Bailey (1991), 57, 65; Margreiter (1988), 48 pl. 46.

63. Beazley (1940), 28.

64. Daux (1958), 808, 814, figs. 16-17; Daux (1967), 162, 163 fig. 103.

65. Vokotopoulou (1993), 180, 181, 182, 184.

66. Marinatos (1936), 259 fig. 23.

67. Rolley (1994), 112-13; he assigns an eighth-century date to the statuettes in accordance with the construction of the temple. For a late eighth-century date: Boardman (1993), fig. 16.

68. Marinatos (1936), 257, 259 fig. 23. For other finds around the *keraton* altar: 258-60.

69. Marinatos (1936), 260.

70. Furtwängler (1980), 166-8; Walter (1957), 50; Technau (1929), 53; Beazley (1940), 30-2, 34 figs. 12-13.

71. Beazley (1940), 28, 30, 32, 35 fig. 14, 36.

72. Welter (1941), 21-4.

73. For description of the so-called 'Croesus' structure: Hogarth (1908), 247-64. See also Chapter IX, 200 n. 101.

74. Hogarth (1908), 320-1; Beazley (1940), 30, 44.

75. Bailey (1975), 93-5 Q146-9 pls. 28-9; the lamps Q147 and Q148 share an almost identical shape but are dated to the first quarter of the sixth century. Also Kassab & Sezer (1995), 50-1.

76. Akurgal (1983), pl. 123, D.

77. White (1984), 21, 30, 59-60, 80, 84-5, 92; White (1993), 11, 14, 16-18, 25, 30, 33, 35.

78. Boardman & Hayes (1966), 140; Boardman & Hayes (1973), 64 n. 2.

79. From Olympia: Herrmann (1966), 162, pl. 65.1 (U1: found in front of the west side of the temple of Zeus); From Samos: Jantzen (1972), 43-6, esp. 46 (various find-locations within the Heraion); From Rhodes: Blinkenberg (1931), 207 (sanctuary of Lindia Athena); Bailey (1996), 85 (Q 3851); From Isthmia: Raubitschek (1998), 110 pl. 62, 115 (no 393: found in the north temenos area trench I 1956 NB10).

80. Robertson (1948), 88-9; Benton (1953), 328.

81. Bosanquet (1904-5), 307.

82. For a comparison of the Ithakan and Palaikastro examples: Robertson (1948), 88.

83. The piece is said to be from Asia Minor, with the closest comparable material from Cyprus. Bailey (1975), 218-19 Q484 pl. 94.

84. For evidence of seventh-century cult-statues and their place in the development of cult-space and activity in early Greek shrines: Crielaard (1995), 262-5.

85. For discussion of the earliest evidence of the cult-image of Athena on the Athenian Akropolis (not before the later seventh century): Alroth (1989), 48-54.

II. Keeping a Flame 'Alive'

1. For discussions of the ancient image of Athena, including earlier literature: Nick (1997); Alroth (1989), 48-54.

2. Strabo, *Geographica* ix, 1.16: 'On the rock is the sacred precinct of Athena, comprising both the old temple of Athena Polias, in which the lamp that is never quenched, and the Parthenon' (trans. Jones 1927).

3. Plut. *Sull.* xiii, 3-4: 'while he suffered the sacred lamp of the goddess to go out for lack of oil' (trans. Perrin 1916); Plut. *Num.* ix, 5: 'Since wherever in Greece a perpetual fire is kept, as at Delphi and Athens' (trans. Perrin 1948).

4. Hitzig-Bluemner (1896), 291, 62.2; Frazer (1898), 341-2; Papachatzis (1974), 360 n. 1.

5. Schol. to Dem. *Contra Androtion* 13, 597 (ed. Reiske). Also see Alroth (1989), 48 n. 252. For the cult image of Athena Polias see nn. 85, 1 above.

6. Herodotus places the olive tree of Athena in the temple of Erekhtheus, together with the sea-water (Hdt. viii, 55). Philochorus (third century) attests that the olive tree stood in the precinct of Pandrosos above the altar of Zeus (*FGrH* 328 F67), a view which is also found in Apollodorus' *Bibl.* iii, 178. Pausanias refers to the tree at the end of his description of the contents of the temple of Athena Polias and immediately before his discussion of the Pandroseion (Paus. i, 27.1-2). However, it may not be ruled out that a conventional name was sometimes given by ancient authors to all the parts of the shrine of Erekhtheus, after the most dominant cult housed in it, namely that of Athena Polias. If this holds true, one may then seek the olive tree in the Pandroseion, in accordance with the more detailed ancient accounts preserved, such as those of Philochorus, Apollodorus and possibly, Pausanias. It seems likely that Herodotus' description in viii, 55 might well have meant the Pandroseion, just to the west of the Erekhtheion. The plausibility of such an interpretation has been pointed out by Papachatzis (1974), 361-2 n. 5.

7. For example: Papachatzis (1974), 361; Burkert (1983), 157; Palagia (1984), 516 n. 7 (with earlier literature); Robertson (1996), 43.

8. These have been collected and discussed by Robertson (1996), 43, 68-9 nn. 44-5. A recently discussed important detail of the building depicted on the 'olive tree pediment' is its antefix, the pentagonal form of which resembles the antefix of the earliest roof preserved from the Akropolis; this has been dated to *c*. 580-570 and may probably be associated with an early temple of Athena Polias at the site. For further discussion of this piece: Glowacki (1998), 83-4 and see 170 n.7; 177-8 n. 61.

9. The inadequate evidence for the support of Dörpfeld's theory has been pointed out by Hoepfner: Dörpfeld (1904); Hoepfner (1997), 159. J.A. Bundgaard explained a number of architectural irregularities of the Erekhtheion as necessary adjustments imposed by the existence of an overgrown olive-tree directly outside the western wall of the building. Among these irregularities, I note the lack of foundations in some parts of the building, a lacuna under its south door, the thinning of the threshold of the south door in comparison to the thickness of the wall above it, traces of adjustment with a pointed chisel on the orthostate connecting the south wall with the west door and traces of the negative image of the east side of the bole of the olive tree on the marble temple. For detailed discussion: Bundgaard (1976), 85-102.

10. For example: Borrmann (1881), 390; Julius (1878), 26; Frazer (1898), 335-6; Gardner (1902), 362, 364; Paton (1927), 488-92; Dinsmoor (1950), 188 fig. 70, 189, 191 fig. 71; Robertson (1954), 128 fig. 54; Overbeck (1972), 128; Papachatzis (1974), 352-3 n. 4; Brommer (1985), 64 fig. 55; Mansfield (1985), 135, 150 n. 1, 205-6. Most recently: Hoepfner (1997), 152-9, esp. 159 fig. 3. Other scholarly arguments relied on later accounts, such as a peculiar incident recorded by Dio Cassius (*Lives* vii), when a statue of Athena on the Akropolis turned its face to the west and spat blood. Another anecdote recorded by Philochorus (Dion. Hal. *De Dinarcho* 3) described the route that a dog followed to Athena's olive tree, through the Polias temple and then to the Pandroseion; this incident has been employed for an argument concerning the interior arrangement of the Erekhtheion with the eastern part dedicated to Athena. Dyer (1873), 418; Frazer (1898), 335-6; Weller (1913), 331-2; Travlos (1971a), 213; Wycherley (1978), 152-3.

11. Travlos (1971a), 213, 218 fig. 281; Travlos (1971b), 79-80 fig. 1. Travlos alleged that Pausanias must have entered the eastern part of the building then to move westwards, into the room where the cult-statue and the lamp stood, and from there, to the adjoining temple of Pandrosos.

12. Wycherley (1978), 150-3.

13. Robertson (1996), 32. The main irregular elements of the western part of the

Erekhtheion are the two side porches, the almost blind front, the elevated colonnade, the considerably low level of the floor as well as the more extensive floor area and height that it occupies. N. Robertson regarded the eastern part as an appendage with the main function of holding offerings.

14. Bötticher (1862).

15. Jeppesen (1979), 393.

16. Earlier interpretations are summarised by Palagia (1984), 516 nn. 7-8.

17. Palagia (1984), 518, n. 11. The Hellenistic houses on Delos offer good parallels, but are much later than the period of our concern.

18. Palagia (1984), 518: 'It is probable that Pausanias' passage on the lamp is not part of his regular tour of the temple but a digression connected with the statue of Athena Polias.'

19. Palagia (1984), 517; Palagia does not make quite clear where the xoanon stood in relation to the lamp, apart from a suggestion that it rested close to floor level. According to Palagia, the lamp and statue did not necessarily have to share either a common display room or a supplementary function.

20. However, Palagia seems convinced that the two (cult-image and lamp) are related when she says that the mention of the lamp in Pausanias' account is connected with the discussion of the statue: Palagia (1984), 518.

21. Palagia (1984), 517 fig. 2, 518 fig. 3, 519.

22. For discussion of the architectural form of the southwest corner of the Erekhtheion: Palagia (1984), 518.

23. Michaelis (1877), pl. 1, fig. 8; Hitzig-Bluemner (1896), 291; Rangabé (1882), 325; Fergusson (1880), pl. 1; Dell (1934), pl. 4; Sotiriades (1913), 32 fig. 18; Tsountas (1928), 309, 311; Brouskari (1974), 96 pl. 9.

24. Travlos (1971b), 80 fig. 1; Travlos (1971a), 218 fig. 281.

25. Robertson (1996) 30, 31.

26. Lamp on stand: Jahn & Michaelis (1901), pl. 26; Sotiriades (1913), loc. cit. (n. 23); Tsountas (1928), 311, fig. 286; Beulé (1862), 353. Hanging from the ceiling: Dell (1934), 21-2, pls. 12-13. For the broader concept of the lamp in front of the cult statue: Fergusson (1880), loc. cit. (n. 23); Rangabé (1882), 324-5; Weller (1913), 331; Travlos (1971a), loc. cit. (174 n. 11); Brouskari (1974), 96-7.

27. Of those, only the most important are selected for reporting, notably, the tokens of the victories of the Athenians over the Persians.

28. For recent discussions of the inscription: Lipka (1997), 37-44; Robertson (1996), 34-5; Németh (1993). The date of the Hekatompedon inscription is disputable, and should probably be placed in the period after Kleisthenes (*c.* 508) but not later than 480. The *terminus post quem* may however be shifted earlier than 508 as shown by the following discussions: Németh, op. cit., 78-9; Lipka, op. cit., 41. For the area of the Hekatompedon: Tölle-Kastenbein (1993). Also see Parker (1996), 70 n. 10. In any case, the sacred fire mentioned predates the lamp of Kallimakhos, thus serving as its possible, more primitive predecessor, carrier of the 'eternal' flame.

29. Papachatzis (1974), 360 n. 2; Dell (1934), pls. 12, 15.

30. Jahn & Michaelis (1901), pl. 26; Tsountas (1928), 311, fig. 286; Beulé (1862), 353; Sotiriades (1913), 32 fig. 18; Loicq-Berger (1970), 150. The difficulty with these reconstructions would be that the palm could have not served as a chimney since it was under the lamp.

31. Dell (1934), 12, 13; Julius (1878), 31; Jacobsthal (1927), 96-8. In this case, one would have to estimate the height of the candelabrum up to the ceiling as well as make provisions for the opening for the extraction of the smoke.

32. Harrison (1977), 155 n. 75, 157; Palagia (1984), 519. Harrison's interpretation is closely connected with the reconstruction of the chimney that drew off the smoke from the altars of Athena and Hephaistos in the Hephaisteion.

33. Palagia (1984), 518. Although it apparently solves the problem of the awkwardness of an extremely high candelabrum, it is not clear at all how the smoke was extracted from the building.

34. Miller (1979), 40-1; Palagia (1984), 520-1; Sourvinou-Inwood (1991), 123 n. 1.

35. The idea of a hollow tree trunk which can serve as a chimney was first proposed by Benndorf (1879), 40.

36. This idea of extracting smoke can be found in small scale version on incense burners from South Italy Sicily (a clay flower from the centre of which smoke comes out). For example: Lattanzi (1996), 29; Carratelli (1988), 134 fig. 201.

37. This might be the reason why the lamp and the palm were not included in the inventory lists of the Erekhtheion. If the smoke was always visible, their presence was taken for granted, unlike the cult statue and its accessories, as well as the rest of the treasures, which were invisible.

38. Brouskari (1974), pls. 120-1 nos. 3869 and 190. Also see Chapters I.2b, IX.1a.

39. For a general discussion of Kallimakhos' works and their copies: Stewart (1990), 271-2, 39.

40. On the symbolism and use of Gorgoneion-decoration: Karagiorga (1970), esp. 103-11.

41. For discussion of seventh-century Gorgoneia: Touloupa (1969), 876-7. For the decorative possibilities of Gorgoneion: Leipen (1970), 10-11.

42. Touloupa (1969); Glowacki (1998), 82.

43. Perlzweig (1961), 118; Bovon (1966), 42; Bailey (1988), 37-8, fig. 42.

44. Brendel (1995), 288-90, 289 fig. 205; Haynes (1985), 109 no. 122 pl. 193.

45. *IG* II-III^2 1424a, Add. p. 802 l. 364. Also Plut. *Them.* x, 7; Eur. *Erechtheus TGF* fr. 360, ll. 46-9; Isoc. *Contra Callimacho* xviii, 57 (402). A full account of the sources recording the gold Gorgoneion may be found in Mansfield (1985), 139, 144, 49, 185-8 (c140-4). Also: Ridgway (1992), 120, 210 n. 7.

46. All relevant literature pertaining to the association of Apollo with the palm has been collected and discussed by Palagia (1984), 520.

47. The fact that palm and lamp had a complementary function does not necessarily prove that they were commissioned by the same person. In favour of the association of the commission of the lamp and palm with Nikias: Furtwängler (1895), 437; Miller (1979), 41. Against that view: Palagia (1984), 520-1.

48. Another chronological indication for the activity of Kallimakhos is offered by Pausanias (ix, 2.7) who records a statue of Hera made by Kallimakhos for the new temple of the goddess in Plataia, after the city was razed in 427. For Kallimakhos also see Stewart (1990), 36-7 and see n. 39 above. The golden lamp of Athena for her temple on the Athenian Akropolis cannot be dated before the completion of the building that housed it, around 406. The Erekhtheion building accounts (*IG* I^3 474, ll. 29-30) show that the building was still unfinished in 409-408, by which time construction resumed, to be completed a couple of years later.

49. For discussion of the historial circumstances surrounding the last years and fall of the Athenian empire: Kagan (1988), esp. 259-61, 10-11.

50. A perpetual fire was kept inside the temple of Apollo at Delphi: Paus. x, 24.4; Plut. *Num.* ix, 12; *Arist.* xx, 4; *De E apud Delphos* 385c; *SIG*^{3} 826 C14 (the Amphictionic oath was taken in the name of the 'immortal fire' as well as the names of gods such as Themis, Apollo Pythios, Leto, Artemis and Hestia); *Homeric Hymn to Apollo* 24; Aesch. *Cho.* 1037; Callim. *Hymn 2*, 83. For the old temple of Hera at Argos: Thuc. iv, 133; Paus. ii, 17.7. The Argive temple of Apollo Lykeios also contained a fire (the so-called 'fire of Phoroneus'): Paus. ii, 19.5. In Arkadia, such fires are reported from the temple of Demeter and Kore in Mantineia (Paus. viii, 9.2), the temple of Pan (Paus. viii, 37.11) and that of Artemis Pyronia on mount Krathis (Paus. viii, 15.9). In Koroneia, the fire in the temple of Athena Itonia was renewed every day: Paus. ix, 34.2. For 'perpetual' fires in the *prutaneia* of Greek cities: Pind. *Nem.* xi.1; Theoc. xxi, 34-7; Ath. xv.700d. Also see the regulations concerned with ritual purity which mention a public hearth, such as an example from Kos dated to the first half of the third century on Kos: *LSCG* no. 154B, pp. 263-9. For discussion: Malkin (1987), 114-43 (ch. 3), esp. 115 n. 4. Most evidence for 'eternal' flames is collected in general works, for example: Delcourt (1981), 32-3, 150-7; Brulé (1987), 92; Burkert (1985), 60-1, 370 n. 54; Simons (1949), esp. ch. iv; Malkin, op. cit., 125-9. See also 179 n. 73.

51. For evidence of the use of elaborate lamps on the Athenian Akropolis before Kallimakhos, see Chapters I.1b, IX.1a.

52. It is worth noting here that no earlier extinguishing of the lamp in the Erekhtheion is recorded in the sources. A striking case is the Persian invasion in 480/479, during which many monuments on the Akropolis were destroyed and Athena's olive tree was burnt down (Hdt. viii, 55; Paus. i, 27.2). This could not have left the lamp unaffected. However, the alleged extinguishing of the lamp during the siege of Sulla implies that it needed refilling from time to time, and also that the olive tree was not its only source of fuel, as Palagia observed: Palagia (1984), 519.

53. Deubner (1932), 20. For his followers: Mansfield (1985), 387 n. 23. For discussion and references: Mansfield (1985), 370-1; Burkert (1983), 151; Cook (1995), 166 n. 125.

54. Various views have been voiced regarding the possibility of an earlier 'history' for the lamp of Athena on the Athenian Akropolis, before its elaborate replacement by Kallimakhos: Benndorf (1879), 40; Pffeiffer (1949), 6; Lorimer (1950), 511; Beazley (1940), 48 n. 33; Scheibler (1976), 174.

55. Roussopoulos (1862), 39 no. 9; Pittakis (1862), 91, 93; Paton (1927), 572 nn. 2-3, fig. 229.

56. Mansfield (1985), 68, 101 n. 61; Barber (1992), 114, 122-3, 209 n. 27. For the Panathenaic procession: Löhr (1997).

57. de Ridder (1896), 139, no. 425, 140 fig. 95.

58. Göttlicher (1978), 68 no. 362. The features of the oarship from the Erekhtheion included a ram, an aperture in front of the stem post (for the wick of the lamp), four incised lines across the hull from stem to stern (possibly representing wales), a row of compass-drawn circles above the 'wales' (probably representing ports) and an engraved eye on the stern, recalling similar decoration of sixth-century black-figure representations of ships.

59. Morrison & Williams (1968), 179 pl. 27b. The date of the inscription is based on R.P. Austin's observations which rely on the understanding that the ship-shaped lamp was an original offering to the goddess (not a chance find) and should therefore be dated after the completion of the Erekhtheion which housed it.

60. Brouskari (1974), nos. 190, 3869 pls. 120-1; Beazley (1940), 38-9, fig. 17. For more marble lamps from the Akropolis of slightly later date: op. cit., 39-40.

61. Travlos (1971a), 213 pointed to two passages from Homer (*Il.* ii, 546-51 and *Od.* vii, 80-1) which refer to the *oikos* of Erekhtheus, suggesting therefore an early date for the building. The rest of the suggestions for an early cult-building on the

Athenian Akropolis have been based on archaeological evidence from the site. C. Nylander (1962) and S. Iakovides (1962), 63-5 singled out two stone column-bases which may have once supported wooden columns of an early building on the Akropolis, which, according to the latest dating suggestion, may be placed in the late eighth or the seventh century. For recent discussions including earlier literature: Glowacki (1998), 82, 87 n. 39; Parker (1996), 19 n. 37. E. Touloupa (1969) argued for a seventh-century temple on the Akropolis on the basis of a fragmentary bronze Gorgoneion set into a large bronze disc and fashioned in the cut-out technique, which she interpreted as an akroterion. For further discussion, see also Glowacki, op. cit., 82, 87 n. 43. Another possible fragment of early architectural decoration of a building on the Akropolis is a painted terracotta plaque (Athens Agora A.P. 1085), attributed to the late seventh-century Nettos Painter. See Glowacki, op. cit., 82. However, the date of the earliest architectural terracottas from the site seems to make the date of the earliest structure on the Akropolis considerably later. In particular, a pentagonal antefix (Athens, Akropolis Museum 10124 and Bper 327) once believed to be of late seventh-century date (based on comparisons with other antefixes from Korinth) has been re-dated to around 590-580 by N. Winter (1993), 213-14. She gave a date of around 570 for the sima K11/13, 80 (op. cit., 215-16 n. 30) which, together with the antefix, had been used as the basis for the hypothetical late seventh-century temple of Athena, as suggested by J. Travlos (1971a), 53. For a recent discussion of the architectural terracottas from the site: Glowacki, op. cit., 82-4, 88 nn. 51, 53, 55. M. Korres has recently supported the view that the old temple of Athena Polias was destroyed no later than the first decade of the fifth century: Korres (1997), 220-5, esp. 224-5.

62. See 175 n. 28.

63. Parke (1977), 158; Lorimer (1950), 511.

64. For the date and authenticity of the poem: Wölke (1978), 1-70. Wölke does not believe that the scene takes place in the old temple of Athena on the Akropolis, taking it (the mention of a lamp) more as a comic element of everyday life that in this case applies also to a goddess. Wölke (1978), 235 n. 4, 236 n. 7.

65. For discussion: Parker (1996), 19-20; Crielaard (1995), 253-5.

66. See also Nonnus *Dion.* xiii, 173-4 and xxvii, 320-31. Callimachus refers again to the lamp of the goddess in his *Marathon*.

67. For discussion: Hollis (1990), 227-8.

68. For discussion of Callimachus' influence upon the passage of Euphorion: Hollis, op. cit., 228, 230. Also see Brulé (1987), 121.

69. Burkert (1983), 151-2; Burkert (1985), 229. Accepted by Cook (1995), 166 n. 125. There is still considerable debate about the month in which the Arrhephoria took place. A plausible suggestion for the month Skirophorion (at about the end of the Attic year) has been made by Brulé (1987), 83-4; Burkert (1985), 228; Mansfield (1985), 274, 314 n. 36; Mikalson (1975), 166-7; Papachatzis (1974), 362 n. 2; Simon (1985), 39. In favour of Mounukhion is Parke (1977), 142. The summer month Thargelion was proposed by Deubner (1932), 20. Latest discussions with references: Wesenberg (1995), 158-9 n. 55; Robertson (1996), 60-2; Brulé (1987), 79-84.

70. For the contents of the box: Elderkin (1941), 120-1; Papachatzis (1974), 363; Simon (1985), 42.

71. Burkert (1985), 229; he saw in the lamp of Athena a direct reflection of the myth of the conception of Erikhthonios by the goddess: the woollen wick is paralleled with the wool with which the goddess wiped off the discharge of Hephaistos on her thigh. The oil was the gift of the goddess which kept the wick 'alive'. Latest discussion: Deacy (1997), 48-57, where Athena is presented as vulnerable *parthenos*.

72. Mansfield (1985), 277, 322 n. 52.

73. Plut. *Num.* ix, 5-6: 'Since whenever in Greece a perpetual fire is kept, as at Delphi and Athens, it is committed to the charge, not of virgins, but of widows past the age of marriage' (trans. Perrin 1948). For sexual/biological restrictions which often determined eligibility to undertake certain religious tasks: Malkin (1987), 126 n. 58; Parker (1983), 92; Brulé (1987), 121.

74. The surviving pre-nuptial representations of women and marriage ritual are particularly good examples. See the discussion in Chapter III.3. For the common association of torches with public aspects of the lives of 'respectable' women in Greek art and literature in contrast to the use of lamps to light the private, enclosed life of married women and the sexual activities of *hetairai*: Parisinou (2000).

75. Brulé (1987), 121.

76. See 176-7 n. 50.

77. Williamson (1995), 9, 16-17, 28-9.

78. For discussion: Williamson (1993), 28-31, n. 13; Held (1990), 56-7.

79. Williamson (1996), 27, 26 fig. 8c.

80. Rangabé (1882), loc. cit. (n. 23); Hitzig & Blümner (1896), 291.

81. Harris (1995), 25-6, 65, 77.

82. de Ridder (1896), 141, cat. no. 426, fig. 96.

83. de Ridder (1896), 39, 131, 250, 303.

84. This is rightly suggested by Harris (1995), 28: 'In the fifth century private dedications are not included and only items for cultic needs were inventoried.'

85. For information on reorganisation and melting down of the Parthenon treasures: Harris (1995), 28, 77.

86. For sources and earlier literature: Kyle (1987), 36, 190-1 nn. 95-7.

87. Probably the evening before the procession that happened the next morning: Kyle (1992), 15; Robertson (1996), 63.

88. Kyle (1987), 191 n. 99; on the basis of Aristotle's information in *Ath. Pol.* 57.1 that the Arkhon Basileus was responsible for all torch-races (implying both the antiquity and the religious nature of the races) in Athens, D.G. Kyle has proposed a date of 566 for the institution of this type of race.

88a. For full discussion of the ancient authorities on this matter: Robertson (1992), 105-8.

89. For example, *IG* II^2 3019, dated to *c.* 346-345, which records a victory won by tribe Akamantis at the Great Panathenaia; *IG* II^2 2311, ll. 76-7 (early fourth century) which includes lists of special tribal events; *IG* II^2 3023 (*c.* 338-337) which was dedicated by the gymnasiarch of the winning tribe Kekropis. Also *IG* II^2 1250 (=*SEG* XL, 124; dated to 350s or 340s by Sekunda). The victory of the tribe Aiantis in the last inscription has been linked by Sekunda with the torch-race of the Hephaisteia rather than the Panathenaia. For discussion of the Panathenaic torch-races: Kyle (1987), 69, 192 n. 113; Sekunda (1990), esp. 159-76.

90. For example, *IG* II^2 2311, l. 77. For discussion of the participation of ephebes in the Panathenaic procession and games: Robertson (1992), 108-14. However, possible evidence for men's participation in torch-races may be found in *IG* II^2 3022.

91. For prizes in Panathenaic torch races: *IG* I^2 84, l. 33 (=*SEG* X; 93; *SEG* XXV, 35; *c.* 421); *IG* II^2 2311, ll. 76-7 (early fourth century). The second inscription specifies the prize of thirty drachmas and a hydria for individual athletes, while the winning tribe would receive the prize of a bull and thirty drachmas. For discussion of prizes at the Panathenaia torch-race: Kefalidou (1996), 120; more generally for prizes of lampadedromiai: op. cit. 31 nn. 11-13.

92. *IG* I² 84, l. 33 (=*SEG* X; 93; *SEG* XXV, 35 of *c.* 421). Sekunda interprets *IG* II² 1250 (=*SEG* XL, 124 of *c.* 350s or 340s) as a document related with the Hephaisteia; Sekunda, op. cit. (n. 82). For discussion including earlier literature: Kyle (1987), 192-3 nn. 113-16; Davies (1967), 35-6.

93. Sekunda (1990), 154-6.

94. For the festival and tribal organisation of the Prometheia: Davies (1967), 36. For the torch race: Parke (1977), 171-3; Kyle (1987), 192. The late fifth-century inscription *IG* I² 84, ll. 34-5 (=*SEG* X 93; *SEG* XXV, 35) explicitly mentions the organisation of the Prometheia by *lampadarkhoi*. Fifth-century evidence of the race is provided by Ps. Xen. *Ath. Pol.* iii, 4; Isaeus vii, 36.

95. For literary sources and references: Kyle (1987), 36, 60, 75, 132, 190-2; Parke (1977), 45-6; Kyle (1992), 96; Kefalidou (1996), 30-1, 155-6.

96. Recent discussion of the foundation date of the cult of Bendis in Athens (including sources and earlier literature) may be found in Parker (1996), 171-2.

97. The inscription (*SEG* XXXIX, 210) is discussed by Themelis (1989), esp. 25-6.

98. For discussion including earlier literature: Parker (1996), 163-4 nn. 36-7; Kyle (1987), 193 n. 117.

99. For discussion: Simon (1976).

100. *IG* II² 3105 (=*SEG* XXXI, 162, dated to 333-332). Two more adjoining fragments were found in Rhamnous and published by Petrakos (1981), 68-9. For discussion: Themelis (1989), 27 n. 19; Palagia & Lewis (1989), 333-8; Parker (1996), 254 n. 126.

101. For discussion of the reliefs including earlier literature: Palagia & Lewis (1989), esp. 339-44.

102. For the most recent discussion: Palagia & Lewis (1989), 341-4, esp. 343. For an earlier interpretation of the goddesses as Demeter and Persephone: Ashmole (1962), esp. 234.

103. *SEG* XXI, 680 (dated to *c.* 333-332). For discussion: Themelis (1989), 26-7 n. 18.

104. For a commentary on this passage: Rhodes (1981), 638-9. For discussion of the evidence of torch-races in the cult of Dionysos: Kyle (1987), 45-6, 192 n. 105 (for Anthesteria); Hamilton (1992), 68 n. 19, 173.

105. On Korinthian torch-races: Herbert (1986). However, the author accepts that other divinities such as Artemis may be associated with this torch-race, in view of the meagre evidence available.

106. Herbert (1986), 32 n. 8, 30, 31; Williams (1978), 44 n. 55, 155. For the new pottery evidence: Herbert (1986), 30-1, figs. 1-5. According to S. Herbert, another possible deity-recipient of the Korinthian torch-race may have been Artemis, in one of her Bakchic aspects: Herbert, op. cit., 35. On the cult at the Sacred Spring see also Steiner (1992), esp. 402-6, who argues in favour of a cult of the local nymph Kotyto.

107. On the basis of a representation on a Korinthian oinokhoe discussed by Broneer (1942b), 152-3, n. 71, fig. 8 and a scholion on Pindar *Ol.* xiii, 56, O. Broneer less plausibly suggested an annual torch-race honouring Athena *Hellôtia*. The unusual type of torch-race depicted on the vase is clear from the shape of the torch without a hand-shield, and the fact that the racers hold a pitcher in the other hand. Despite the Dionysiac connotations hinted at by the shape of the vessel, Broneer linked it with Athena and the Aiginetan *amphiphoritês agon*. However, no shrine of Athena has been found, probably because the Greek Agora in Korinth has not yet been excavated. As there is no definitive evidence for any cult in that area, it is possible that the cult of Athena Hellotia remains to be discovered. Broneer (1942), 128-61. For the cult of Athena Hellotia: Steiner (1992), 405; Furley (1981), 163-72.

108. Launey (1944), 96 no. 17; 93-4 no. 8 (first half of the third century).

109. Pouilloux (1948), esp. 856-7; Pouilloux (1954), 368 n. 3. The epigraphical evidence for the inclusion of contests in the Herakleia is discussed by Bergquist (1973), 37.

110. For the coin-series from Amphipolis: Lorber (1990), 118-19; Grose (1926), 26, 27.

111. For discussion of evidence for the attribution of the Amphipolitan torch-races to the cult of Artemis *Tauropolos*: Lorber (1990), 81; Kraay (1976), 151; Babelon (1932), 694.

112. Wroth (1894), 45 (Kebren of Troas), 49 (Dardanus of Troas), 53 (Gargara); Head (1889), 36, 54 (Korinth); Grose (1926), 128, 129 (Thracian Khersonesos), 341 (Hestiaea), 464 (Hermione).

113. For Aptera: Grose (1926), 486.

114. *SEG* II, 579 l. 3 (the decree prescribes immunity from taxation to several groups of citizens, among which are the lampadarkhai). Also see *SEG* XXVII, 1114 and 1305.

115. *CIG* 2034 and *SEG* XIII, 539. Both inscriptions record dedication to Hermes by a victor at the children's torch-race at Buzantion.

116. Pingiatoglou (1981), 140 nos. 7-8. Pingiatoglou found the presence of the race torch doubtful.

117. For short appraisals of the race-torch: Rudolph (1967), 84-6; Kefalidou (1996), 87 fig. 3; Valavanis (1991), 108 n. 242.

118. For the spiked headdresses of torch-racers and their possible symbolism: Kefalidou (1996), 30 fig. 1; For the age of the athletes: Kefalidou, op. cit., 130. For nudity in Greek athletics: Kefalidou, op. cit. 39 n. 73.

119. On the iconography, find-locations and style of the amphorae: Valavanis (1991), 20-4, 99-107, 102, 108, 223-4, 226-8.

120. For the iconography of victory in torch-races: Kefalidou, op. cit., 155-6, esp. n. 20. However, representations of torch-bearing young athletes leading a bull to sacrifice, or in procession for a revel do not always indicate the feast that followed lampadedromiai. For discussion of relevant iconographical evidence: Kefalidou, op. cit., 87-8.

121. See n. 118. For a general discussion on ephebic traits in red-figure iconography: Sourvinou-Inwood (1991), 40-1, 83.

122. For further discussion including epigraphical and literary evidence: Sekunda (1990); Pelekides (1962), 254-5; Gardiner (1955), 142; Harris (1964), 75; Miller (1991), 132-8, 140-8, 217; Pritchett (1987), 183. For discussion of *ephêboi* parading with torches: Parke (1977), 65, 153-4.

123. Kyle (1987), 40-1.

124. *IG* II² 2311. See 179 n. 89.

125. For the symbolism of 'perpetual' fires in ancient Greece see Chapter II.1-2 and 176-7 n. 50.

126. For the ritual character of torch-races: Gardiner (1955), 142; Valavanis (1991), loc. cit. (n. 117); Kyle (1987), 103 n. 6, 190-1; Kyle (1992), 96. For their gradual conversion into a spectacle in Hellenistic times: Graf (1985), 234-5. For Hellenistic torch-races: Golden (1998), 20 (Eumeneia at Delphi), 105 (Theseia in Athens); Gauthier (1995) (torch-races on Kos in honour of Hermes Enagônios and

Zeus Alseios). The latter also updates the evidence available for torch-races in Hellenistic times.

127. A criticism of clerks and demagogues who are everywhere in the city deluding the people, precedes the ridicule of unfit Athenians for the torch-race. For a discussion: Kyle (1987), 132 nn. 36-41.

128. Sekunda (1990), esp. 154-5. The passage by Aristophanes is supported by evidence from Xenophon *Poroi* 51-2, which refers to ephebes who are ordered to train in the *gumnasia*; both texts have very plausibly been interpreted by Sekunda as indicative of temporary setbacks to the system of training the ephebes possibly caused by financial difficulties during the last stages of the Peloponnesian war. For a different interpretation of the incident in *Ran.* 1086-7: Golden (1998), 167-9.

129. Malkin (1987), ch. 3 esp. 114-29. See also transition rituals in Chapter III.

130. A similar concept is found in Lucretius ii, 79.

III. Light in Rites of Passage

1. For the darkness of women's bodies: Padel (1992), 99-102, esp. 100 n. 7 (for the darkness of the womb).

2. *LIMC* III, Eileithyia 695 no. 94b. Papachatzis (1980), 140-1.

3. For discussion of the identification of Eileithyia on these coin-series: Pingiatoglou (1981), 81-4, esp. 84; *LIMC* III, Eileithyia 695 nos. 95-100.

4. Papachatzis (1974), 430.

5. van Straten (1995), 85.

6. van Straten (1995), 82.

7. For full discussion: Pingiatoglou (1981), 113-14 pl. 17.1, 116-18; van Straten (1995), 86.

8. For the dedications of women's clothes to Artemis: Cole (1998), 36-42.

9. For the kourotrophic associations of Hermes and Apollo: Hadzisteliou-Price (1978), 153, 201.

10. For discussion: Pingiatoglou (1981), 109-11 n. 297.

11. See nn. 4-8 and discussion of the iconography of torch-bearing Artemis as kourotrophos in Chapter III.1a.

12. For discussion of the identification of the building: Pingiatoglou (1981), 116-17, 115 no. 5 pl. 16.2.

13. Pingiatoglou (1981), 115 no. 4 pl. 16.1, 117.

14. Hadzisteliou-Price (1978), 157-8 no. 657, 201, 211 n. 50; Hadzisteliou-Price (1971), 59 II.Ia; Clinton (1992), 33 n. 100.

15. See Chapter VI.1.

16. The torch is an element that testifies to the assimilation of the cult and iconography of Artemis and Eileithyia before the second century: Pingiatoglou (1981), 86 n. 235. For local assimilations and/or shared cults, Pingiatoglou, op. cit., 104-5, 116 n. 306.

17. For the custom of *daidoukhia* see discussion in Chapter III.2b.

18. For the miasma of giving birth: Parker (1983), 48-73; Blundell (1995), 111 n. 26; Furley (1981), 48-52.

19. Pingiatoglou (1981), 84-5 nn. 225-9; Pingiatoglou also denies that the torches reflect any associations between Eileithyia and Selene.

20. Furley (1981), 94. On the birth of Dionysos: Arafat (1990), 41-50.

21. The motif of the snatching of the baby by Zeus amidst light is also seen in Eur. *Bacch.* 522-5.

22. Daraki (1985), 21-4; Boardman (1974), 272.

23. On the iconography of the birth of Dionysos: Beaumont (1992), 35-79; Arafat (1990), loc. cit. (182 n. 20).

24. Furley (1981), 67 n. 2.

25. Kontoleon (1961-2). Recent references to these representations (previously discussed by N.M. Kontoleon) may be found in *CVA* II, 68-9 pl. 105 (black-figure lekythos of the Haimon Group, dated to *c.* 490-480; Leiden, Rijksmuseum van Oudheden PC 32). For a recent discussion of scenes of magical methods of rejuvenation practised by Medea: Halm-Tisserant (1993), 26-48; Reeder (1995), 408-9 (discussion by C. Benson).

26. For the ritual (with earlier bibliography): Furley (1981), 65-70; Parker (1983), 51 n. 71; Oakley & Sinos (1993), 138 n. 93.

27. For discussion of both myths: Halm-Tisserant (1993), 50-7; Furley (1981), 72-8. Also (for Damophon): Clinton (1992), 13, 30-4. On practices of immortalisation by fire (or baptism in fire) and hearth-initiates: Halm-Tisserant (1993), 50-87; Richardson (1974), 231-4; Furley (1981), 81-5; Brulé (1987), 64-8; Parry (1992), 243; Clinton (1992), 137-8 no. 6, 98-199; Clinton (1974), 98-199. For the purificatory qualities of torches: Richardson (1974), 166-7; Parry (1992), 75 n. 39; Parker (1983), 227-8.

28. See Chapter II.2.

29. Later literature is collected by Clinton (1992), 32 n. 91.

30. Vienna, Kunsthistorisches Museum I 1095. Bianchi (1976), 23 no. (fig.) 28; *LIMC* IV, Demeter 867 no. 272, pl. 580.

31. For a discussion of relevant scholarly attitudes: Clinton (1992), 91 n. 147.

32. For the birth of Dionysos-Zagreus, son of Persephone and Zeus: Arafat (1990), 42-4. On the myth of Dionysos-Zagreus: Fol (1993). For the Orphic version of the myth: West (1983), 140-3, 152-4.

33. For discussion of the scene: Arafat (1990), 42; Beaumont (1992), 60-2.

34. Arafat (1990), 42-3; Beaumont (1992), 66-7.

35. Beaumont (1992), 103.

36. Beaumont (1992), 103-4.

37. For the types and decoration of the krateriskoi: Kahil (1965), 20-2; Palaiokrassa (1991), 75-7; Brulé (1987), 250-1. For the use of the krateriskoi as incense-burners (*thumiateria*) in the cult of Artemis: Kahil (1965), 24-5; Kahil (1977), 88 n. 27; Palaiokrassa (1991), 79-80 nn. 207-10; Brulé (1987), 251.

38. On the animality of the arktoi: Sourvinou-Inwood (1991), 65-6, 75-7; Dowden (1989), 34-5; Brulé (1987), 214-18; Bonnechère (1994), 28. For the age of the arktoi on the basis of the evidence from Aristophanes' *Lysistrata*, and of surviving pictorial representations of the arktoi on the krateriskoi: Sourvinou-Inwood (1988), 21-30, 31-66, 119, 120; Palaiokrassa (1991), 79 nn. 203-6; Bonnechère (1994), 27-9 nn. 21, 22; Demand (1994), 110-11 nn. 3-9; Dowden (1989), 28-31. For the association between virginity and female athletics: Lee (1988), 104-8; Kefalidou (1996), 39 n. 72.

39. Brauron Museum 915 (found near the small heroon of Iphigeneia); Kahil (1965), 21, pl. 8.4.

40. Athens, Agora inv. no. 934 (from the sanctuary of Artemis *Aristoboulê* in the Athenian Agora); Kahil (1965), 24, pl. 9.10.

41. Palaiokrassa (1991), 152 Kk16, MP5429, pl. 41, 162 Kk 56 MP 5429, pl. 41; also possibly 153 Kk21, pl. 40b.

42. Brauron Museum 546 (A26); Kahil (1963), 13-14, pl. 6.2; Kahil (1965), 21 pl. 7.3.

43. See references to the pieces in nn. 40 and 39.

44. Sourvinou-Inwood (1988), 120, 123, 124.

45. The suggestions made by Ch. Sourvinou-Inwood (see 183 n. 44) concerning the relative age-groups of the arktoi in the Attic sanctuaries of Artemis remain basic. Recent debate on the relevance of the outfit of the arktoi as a possible age indication is summarised by Golden (1998), 126 and Scanlon (1990), 80-1.

46. For the type of men's race-torch, see Chapter II.3a and n. 117.

47. For a general discussion on men's torch-races in Attica, see Chapter II.3.

48. See 183 n. 42.

49. On nudity in Greek female athletics: Lee (1988) 107-8; Kahil (1965), 30-1 n. 80; Golden (1998), 68-9. For the nudity of the arktoi: Scanlon (1990) in n. 45. For ritual nudity in general: Lada-Richards (1999), 75-8.

50. A possible representation of an altar serving as starting point of a female run without torches is found on a black-figure lekythos from Brauron by the Beldam Painter: Kahil (1965), 30, pl. 10.6-7. Can it then be assumed that the girls ran around the sanctuary of the goddess, starting from, and terminating at, the altar of Artemis? Alternatively, one may envisage the girls running around an altar, which would be totally incompatible with the identification of this run as a torch-race. However, there is a strong possibility that the altar, often combined with a palm-tree, is merely a symbol of the sanctuary of the goddess, thus offering the viewer an indication of the location of the athletic event: Kahil (1965), 30-1; Scanlon (1990), 83-4.

51. These images of running girls do not necessarily reflect races. For discussion: Lee (1988), 106-7; Golden (1998), 123-32; Scanlon (1990), 74 n. 4, 100-1. For further discussion of these 'races': Kahil (1965), 20, 22-4, 30 n. 76; Kahil (1977), 85; Palaiokrassa (1991), 80-1; Dowden (1989), 31, 33.

52. See 183 n. 39.

53. Scanlon (1990), 81-2 n. 20.

54. For the associations of Artemis with torch-light see Chapter V.1.

55. Sourvinou-Inwood (1991), 107-8, n. 79; Oakley & Sinos (1993), 34-5; Sourvinou-Inwood (1985), 129, 140 nn. 76-7. It is not impossible that there is here an allusion to the actual custom of sacrificing to Artemis just before the passage through marriage to the realm of Aphrodite: Oakley & Sinos (1993), 12.

56. For discussion: Cole (1998), 34, 37-9; Oakley & Sinos (1993), 14-15 nn. 26-8; King (1993), 120-1; Hadzisteliou-Price (1978), 121-2, 211.

57. For the torch as destructive symbol see Chapter VI.3-4. Demand (1994), 88, 211 n. 5; Oakley & Sinos (1993), 12 n. 7; Blundell (1995), 29; Brulé (1987), 233-6; Kahil (1963), 14.

58. Oakley & Sinos (1993), 25, 26, 27 n. 28; Avagianou (1991), 11 n. 52, 57; Furley (1981), 187. L. Kahil in *LIMC* II, Artemis, 744 uses the term *numpheutria* to denote the same function of the goddess. However, the term numpheutria describes a female attendant of the bride, who was responsible for the bride's appearance.

59. On weddings without torches (*adaidoukhêtoi gamoi*) as opposed to the socially 'correct' legitimate sexual unions: Oakley & Sinos (1993), 26, 136 n. 24; Furley (1981), 186 n. 7; Blundell (1995), 113-27; Just (1989), esp. 40-75. For the apotropaic role of music and noise in weddings: Oakley & Sinos (1993), 26, 136 n. 23; Avagianou (1991), 11 n. 53.

60. Barlow (1986), 175-6. In her commentary she interprets the word *ortha* as either 'straight' or 'correct'. Whichever of the two is chosen, the significance of the way the torches are held is obvious.

61. For discussion of text: Kannicht (1969), 188-90, 207-8. For a parody of Helen's bridal procession with torches held by two phlyakes: Trendall & Webster (1971), 138-9 (Apulian phlyax bell-krater: Matera 9579).

62. For the time of the year and time of day of Athenian weddings: Oakley & Sinos (1993), 10.

63. For the *epithalamia*: Oakley & Sinos (1993), 42, 138 n. 107, 141; Griffiths (1972), 18, 20-1.

64. The identification of the ceremony has been a matter of controversy, with interpretations ranging from a nocturnal ceremony (*thôsteria*) at the sanctuary of Artemis *Ortheia* at Sparta put forward by Page (1951), 71, 79-80 to a *diegertikon* song proposed by Griffiths (1972), esp. 29-30. See also Borgeaud (1988), 32. A different reading of the word *'pharos* for *phaFos'* led J.B. Carter to argue that the *Partheneion* was sung during the ritual of the sacred marriage (*hieros gamos*) in the sanctuary of Artemis Ortheia: Carter (1988), esp. 91-2. A contrary view was voiced by P. Themelis (Carter, op. cit., 98), who prefers a ritual of initiation for young girls to a sacred wedding of a virgin goddess like Artemis.

65. For a commentary on Catullus 62: Thomsen (1992), esp. 184; Fordyce (1990), 254-5. For the possibility that the mention of Hesperos in the Sapphic fragment has nothing to do with a wedding, see Thomsen, op. cit., n. 119.

66. See 184 nn. 59-60.

67. Similarly, the couple is not always possible to identify. The nuptials of Zeus and Hera have been recognised by A. Avagianou on 3.1 and 3.9; Avagianou (1991), 86 no. 17, 90-1 no. 27.

68. For more fragmentary representations: *CVA* i Sarajevo, 38-9 pl. 32.3-6.

69. Full discussion of the ritual with literary references: Oakley & Sinos (1993), 34-5; Furley (1981), 186-8.

70. For the feast of Epaulia: Palaiokrassa (1991), 68 nn. 156-7; Oakley & Sinos (1993), 38-42; Redfield (1982), 188.

71. Palaiokrassa (1991), 67-9, nn. 156-61.

72. Palaiokrassa (1991), 135 Ka30 MP 5411, pl. 30a; 137 Ka36 MP 5411, pl. 30b; 137 Ka37 MP 5411, pl. 36.

73. Separate mention is made of the torches twice in the Hymn: ll. 31, 48.

74. For further discussion on the 'Sicilian' tradition: Sfameni-Gasparo (1986), 144-55.

75. For discussion: Clinton (1992), 119, n. 26. General discussions of representations of the ascent of Kore: Peschlow-Bindokat (1972), 92-7; Clinton (1992), 84.

76. For the meaning and synonyms: Richardson (1974), 294-5.

77. Representations of this theme on South Italian vases often include a torch-bearing Hekate; however, her torch there has a crossed end with flames emanating from it: Richardson (1974), 155.

78. For Hekate as goddess of boundaries: Kraus (1960), 56, 59, 87, 104, 128; Richardson (1974), 156; Johnston (1990), 24-5, 27-8, 34-5 n. 15; Parry (1992), 74, 75 n. 40. For Hermes Khthonios and the journey to death: Sourvinou-Inwood (1995), 104-5, 304-7. On Hermes' associations with magic: Parry (1992), 78; Richardson (1974), 264.

79. For the 'master-servant' iconographical pattern: Peschlow-Bindokat (1972), 102-3, 116.

80. Mylonas (1961), 192.

81. Clinton (1992), 69, 73-4, fig. 34. For the complex problem of the identification of Iakkhos in Eleusinian iconography: Clinton (1992), 64-71, esp. 68-9.

82. All epigraphical and literary evidence for the office of Daidoukhos has been collected by Clinton (1974), 47-50, 67-8 (for the fifth and fourth century). See also Kourouniotis (1937), 240-1, 245-6, figs. 12-14, 17-18; Bianchi (1976), 25, no. 37, fig. 37.

83. Richardson (1974), 165-6; Burkert (1983), 275-6.

84. For a detailed account of the procession of the initiates from the Dipylon Gate to Eleusis, which passed by the grave monuments of the Sacred Way: Mylonas (1961), 252-6; Parke (1977), 66; Clinton (1992), 73 and n. 54.

85. For discussion including references: Clinton (1992), 84-90.

86. For the links of Hekate and Persephone with the underworld see 185 n. 78; 60-2. For the home of Iakkhos in the underworld: Ar. *Ran.* 323-4. For the pollution of death: Parker (1983), 33-46. For the function of funeral fires as purifiers: Parker, op. cit., 227 n. 111.

87. According to Mylonas (1961), 256, the purpose of the gephurismoi was the humbling of certain people by insults, which would render them immune to the jealousy of evil spirits; Parke (1977), 66, sees the custom as repelling ill-luck; Burkert (1983), 278, links it with the broader aggressive behaviour shown by the brandishing of branches (*bakkhoi?*) in threatening gestures to 'strengthen' one's position.

88. Bérard (1974), 91-5; Clinton (1992), 72. For the interpretation of the chief figures of the scene as Pandora and Epimetheus and their connection with a lost satyr-play called *Pandora*: Trendall & Webster (1971), 33. For the iconographical traits of Eubouleus in art: Clinton (1992), 56-63.

89. Although the exact role of Eubouleus in Eleusinian myth is not clear, his particular associations with both the Anodos and Kathodos of Kore are recorded in the Orphic version of the *Hymn to Demeter*. Orphic fragments 50 and 51, referred to by Clemens Alexandrinus and Pausanias, present him as a swineherd and the informant of Demeter about the fate of her daughter. His pigs disappeared in a chasm in the earth, by which Persephone was most probably led to the underworld. His involvement in the Ascent of Persephone is attested in an Orphic Hymn (41.5-8), according to which he guided Demeter on her trip to Hades to recover Persephone. For discussion: Richardson (1974), 81, 84; Sfameni-Gasparo (1986), 102-10; Clinton (1992), 72.

90. Clinton (1992), 84, figs. 26-8; Richardson (1974), 84; he discusses the involvement of Hekate and Hermes in the return of Persephone as attested in the *Homeric Hymn* in relation to the Orphic version which associates Eubouleus with this activity.

91. Clinton (1992), 81-2, fig. 21.

92. Clinton (1992), 83, figs. 24, 25.

93. Clinton (1992), 71-2, figs. 36, 37, 38-41.

94. Clinton (1992), 78-80, fig. 9.

95. For discussion: Peschlow-Bindokat (1972), 105-7; Clinton (1992), 73-5.

96. Recent commentaries: Dover (1997), 129-30; Sommerstein (1996), 184-5. For the procession of the Mysteries: Graf (1996), 61-4. For its associations with the procession described in the parodos of Aristophanes' *Ranae*: Graf (1974), 40-50; Lada-Richards (1999), esp. 81-4.

97. For the image of happiness in the afterlife: Dover (1993), 60, 228; Clinton (1992), 85 n. 120; Lada-Richards (1999), 98-102. For similar symbolism in Orphic eschatological beliefs: Graf (1974), 79-94; Bowie (1993), 230-4. For the association of Orpheus and Eleusis: Parker (1996), 100-1; Foley (1994), 151-3. For the cult of Orpheus in Athens: West (1983), 20-4.

98. Papachatzis (1974), 154-5.

99. Clinton (1992), 69, 83, figs. 24, 30.

100. Burkert (1983), 279-80. Also see discussion on similar gesture of Eubouleus with torches in hand in the representations of vases 4.22 and 4.34.

101. For the order of ritual events in the Mysteries: Clinton (1993), 116-19; Brumfield (1981), 195; Mylonas (1961), 256-80; Parke (1977), 66-7.

102. For more literary occurrences and the meaning of the word 'pheggos': Stanford (1958), 112.

103. For the experiences of the initiates during the procession: Clinton (1992), 84-90; Graf (1974), 126-39.

104. Dover (1997), 111; Sommerstein (1996), 171. Similar practices of beating the ground with the hands were employed in order to recall dead spirits, such as that of the Persian King Dareius in Aeschylus *Pers.* 683. For discussion: Hall (1996) 157. S. Dakaris argued that such rituals were most probably acted at the oracle of the Nekuomanteion at the river Akheron during the preparation of the initiates for calling up the dead spirits. Dakaris (1964), 118.

105. Sommerstein (1996), 196-7.

106. See discussion in Chapter III.6a.

107. Obscenity has traditionally been seen as an agent which encouraged fertility; it is also found in the Thesmophoria and the Haloa. For discussion: Brumfield (1981), 80-1, 113; Brumfield (1996), 67-74. For a reconsideration of these 'fertility associations' of the two latter festivals: Lowe (1998).

108. This particular episode also bears clear associations with the festival of the Thesmophoria. For discussion, see Chapter VIII.2.

109. More discussion and references to circular dances in other festivals of Demeter: Stanford (1958), 112. Also see discussion in Chapter IX.4.

110. For discussion: Owen (1939), 140.

111. For the rituals involved in the showing of the *Hiera:* Burkert (1983), 276-91; Clinton (1992), 89-90. For the office of Hierophant: Clinton (1974), 10-47.

112. For the literary references to this great light at the conclusion of the Mysteries: Burkert (1983), 276 n. 7, 277 n. 11; Clinton (1974), 46 n. 273; Clinton (1988), 71 n. 25; Richardson (1974), 26, 28, 208-9, 316.

113. Rubensohn (1955), 44-7 n. 263.

114. For discussion of the *opaion*: Mylonas (1961), 114-15; Burkert (1983), 276-7 n. 12.

115. In K. Clinton's view, the practical difficulties of sacrificing in the Telesterion are: (a) the excess of smoke and smell which could have not been let out by an opaion (if we assume that there was one), (b) the Telesterion's inaccessible position for viewing by the initiates, and (c) the lack of secrecy behind the light in the Telesterion, since the smell and smoke of the burned meat would have betrayed the activities to the initiates before the opening of its doors. Clinton (1988), 71-2. Also Clinton (1993), 118.

116. This information derives from discussion with Dr Kokkou-Viridi, whose study is in course of publication by the Greek Archaeological Society. Philios (1885), 76; Mylonas & Kourouniotis (1933), 80-282; Mylonas (1961), 57-8; Kérenyi (1967), 93.

117. For the kinds, quantity and purchase of firewood for sacrifices: Pritchett (1956), 296.

118. *SEG* XXI 527, l. 91; *SEG* XXV 41, ll. 6-7.

119. *SEG* XXX 61, l. 11. However, the broader context in which the torch is mentioned is rather obscure.

120. The *Historia plantarum* by Theophrastus furnishes us with information about the kinds and qualities of wood suitable for torches. Wood from fir and silver-fir seems to be most suitable, because of the considerable quantity of resin they contained. For example: Theophr. *Hist. pl.* iii, 9.7.2; ix, 2.2.6; iii, 9.7.8; iii, 9.3.13 and iv, 5.3.13.

121. Vanderpool (1970), 49.

122. The most conspicuous early epigraphical records are the inscribed golden

Notes to pages 71-81

leaves from Pelinna, the vocabulary and imagery of which correspond closely to further series from Krete and Thessaly. For discussion: Cole (1993), 276-8; Cole (1980), 233.

123. For the Orphic elements in the Dionysiac Mysteries: Graf (1993); Bowie (1993), 230-8.

124. For the rites of Dionysos at Lerna: Lada-Richards (1999), 79, 89; Casadio (1994), 223-5; Piérart (1996).

125. Papachatzis (1976), 292-4.

126. Furley (1981), 192. For discussion of rites of passage which involved such a symbolic 'descent' to the underworld: Lada-Richards (1999), esp. 78-90.

IV. Pollution-Repelling Fire

1. For discussion including earlier literature: Heubeck, Russo & Fernandez-Galiano (1992), 306-7.

2. For the preliminaries to Greek sacrifices in the archaic and classical periods: van Straten (1995), 13-102.

3. For discussion: Parker (1983), 370-4.

4. The vase is in San Antonio, Texas, Museum of Art (*c.* 440-430; the Naples Painter). Knoepfler (1993), 82 no. (fig.) 65. For the purificatory role of certain plants: Parker (1983), 229.

5. Clinton (1992), 69-70, fig. 33. For discussion of the purification of Herakles and relevant representations: Kerényi (1967), 52-9.

6. For discussion: Clinton (1992), 69.

7. For the Torre Nova sarkophagos: Bianchi (1976), 27-8 no. 47; Parker (1983), 285. For the Naples fragment: Bianchi, op. cit., 28 no. 49.

8. For Roman representations: Jucker (1998), 128-9, 130-1, 132.

9. Parker (1983), 309-10

10. Parker (1983), 35.

11. For discussion of the ritual and possible nature of this fire: Burkert (1970); Burkert (1983), 192-3.

12. For further examples mainly of later date: Parker (1983), 23-6.

13. Kannicht (1969), 230-1; Dale (1967), 124.

14. For such examples: Hornbostel (1980), 23 no. 17, 250-1 no. 143.

15. For discussion: Parker (1983), 76-7; West (1978), 337; Parisinou (2000), forthcoming.

16. Edmonds (1961), 384-5 no. 15.1-2.

17. Parisinou (2000), forthcoming.

18. Paris, Louvre G 13. Add^2 170. Kilmer (1993), R156 (ill).

19. Florence, Museo Archeologico Etrusco 3921. Add^2 225. Boardman & La Rocca (1978), 91 (ill).

20. The reading of '*eskhismenên*' rather than '*estigmenên*' should be preferred here, since the second would have barely made sense in this context. This reading has been proposed by MacDowell (1988), 310 and Sommerstein (1983), 239, while Starkie (1968), 366 devotes a brief discussion to the other available options.

V. Light-Bearing Divine Images

1. Kahil (1984), 619; Graf (1985), 228-36.

2. Papachatzis (1980), 335-7. For the statue of Artemis *Hêgemonê*: Themelis (1993), 104-5.

3. Papachatzis (1981), 132.

4. For the cult-statue of Artemis of Lousoi: Mitsopoulos-Leon (1993), 34, 35, 36.

5. White poppies were particularly significant in the sacrificial rituals of Artemis in Arkadia, as the *lex sacra* from Lukosoura indicates: *IG* V^2, l. 16.

6. Themelis (1991), 92-3; Themelis (1994), 105-6, 107 fig. 7; Themelis (1993), 106.

7. Themelis (1994), 106 n. 6.

8. Themelis (1994), 111-12 n. 12, fig. 13.

9. Threpsiades (1961-2), 141. Literary evidence supports this reconstruction: Eur. *IT* 21.

10. Papachatzis (1981), 446-7.

11. Kahil (1984), 656-7 no. 434.

12. Siebert (1966), 454-5.

13. All primary material is discussed in Graf (1985), 228-36, esp. 228 nn. 91 and 94.

14. For dances and competitions of pyrrhichists which took place in Artemis festivals: Kahil (1984), 634.

15. Carter (1994), 187.

16. Tzouvara-Souli (1979), 20-1, 34.

17. For literary references to this aspect of Hekate: Sarian (1992), 619, 985; Kraus (1960), 11, 28, 45, 49, 53, 78, 85, 88.

18. For example, a hellenistic relief now in the Athens National Museum inv. 1416. For discussion: Siebert (1966), 454 fig. 7; Graf (1985), 229-32, 257-9; Oakley & Sinos (1993), 137 n. 58.

19. For the significance of the dog in the cult of Artemis: Kahil (1984), 619, 748-9.

20. For the significance of the dog in the cult of Hekate: Kraus (1960), 25, 60, 89; Simon (1985b), 273.

21. Kraus (1960), 84-5, 95-101.

22. Sarian (1992), 998-1000 nos. 112-42, 1014-16, 1018.

23. For fourth-century Hekataia: Kraus (1960), 119-28. For later representations of Hekate with torches: Kraus, op. cit., 29, 30, 41, 49, 52, 79, 148.

24. For the Hekataion of the British School no. S21: Kraus (1960), 98-101 n. 483, pl. 3.2.

25. Tzouvara-Souli (1979), 81.

26. For discussion of the nature of En(n)odia: Chrysostomou (1998), esp. 118, 131-2, 202. For the torches as attribute: Chrysostomou, op. cit., 131, 157 n. 556, 265.

27. Chrysostomou (1998), 156-7.

28. Chrysostomou (1998), 157.

29. Chrysostomou (1998), 154.

30. On representations of torch-bearing En(n)odia on coins from Pherai as well as from other regions: Chrysostomou (1998), 141-4 (representing mainly the bust of the goddess with a torch in the field), 145-50 (depicting a torch-bearing En(n)odia riding a horse).

31. Chrysostomou (1998), 152-3.

32. Chrysostomou (1998), 160-2.

33. For the cult and statue of Demeter-Erinys in Thelpousa: Jost (1985), 63-4, 302-9; Dietrich (1962).

34. Papachatzis (1980), 334-8.

35. For the kourotrophic associations of Demeter and Persephone: Hadzisteliou-Price (1978), 133, 134, 153-4, 159-60, 182, 190-1, 200, 201, 204. For their cult as *Karpophorai theai* at Tegea: Jost (1985), 349-51; Stiglitz (1967), 81-97.

36. Papachatzis (1981), 440-1.

37. Daffa-Nikonanou (1973), 29. Also see *IG* IX^2 1060-1 (dedications to Phosphoros dated to the second and first centuries).

38. For discussion of such coin-types: Hinz (1998), 122-3 n. 743.

39. According to the recent study by K. Clinton he is Damophon. Full discussion: Clinton (1992), 39-41.

40. On the light of Dionysos: Seaford (1997); Daraki (1985), 21-4, 25-8.

41. See Chapter I.1, esp. nn. 11-12.

42. For discussion of such representations on red-figure vases: Frontisi-Ducroux (1991), 23-4, 73 figs. 3, 5, 7, 76 figs. 9-10, 79 figs. 14, 16, 80 fig. 17.

43. For discussion of such lightning effects relating to Dionysos' epiphanies: Seaford (1997).

44. It should be stressed that the necessity of torches in the Theban rites of Dionysos as seen in the *Bacchae* are not observed in an Attic context, as may be seen in Pindar's *Dithyramb for the Athenians*. From the latter rites, apart from torches, tambourines, thyrsoi, wild-landscape, beasts and serpents are also missing. For discussion: Leinieks (1996), 137-8.

45. For discussion of the literary material: Voutiras (1997), 310; Graf (1985), 22-4.

46. Papachatzis (1979), 311-12 n. 4.

47. For discussion of literary descriptions of Zeus' images with thunderbolt: Tiverios (1997), 322 nos. 60-1, 330-1 no. 127, 336-7 nos. 152, 153, 155, 180, 343 no. 237.

48. W. Burkert sought the predecessors of the type of Zeus with thunderbolt in hand in the Syro-Hittite region, where bronze statuettes have been found, depicting a warrior god brandishing his weapon in his right hand: Burkert (1992), 19-20.

49. Tiverios (1997), 316-17 nos. 12, 13, 16.

50. For these types: Tiverios (1997), 319 nos. 27-9; 320 nos. 35-7; 321 no. 42; 322 no. 52; 324 nos. 62-4; 325 nos. 73, 75, 76; 326 no. 79; 328 no. 95, 98, 101, 105; 329 nos. 111, 112; 330 no. 118, 121, 123. For hellenistic examples: Leventi (1997), 339 no. 187; 339-40 nos. 195-7.

51. For discussion of these literary images of Artemis: Burkert (1985), 149-50; Blundell (1995), 29.

52. The Bowdoin Painter's particular preference for this theme is notable, since it recurs repeatedly in his repertoire: *ARV*^{2} 678.2-678.9.

53. Kahil (1984), 699-700 no. 1027.

54. Sourvinou-Inwood (1991), 65 n. 34, 98 n. 139, 108-10.

55. See Chapter IX.4.

56. For discussion of the scene: Peschlow-Bindokat (1972), 91-2.

57. For the myth of Triptolemos: Allen (1936), 146-7; Richardson (1974), 194-6; Parker (1996), 99.

58. Another depiction of an altar in the scene with the torch already lit and the corn held by Triptolemos appears on 6.9.

59. See Chapter III.3a.

60. See Chapter V.3.

61. Papadimitriou (1949), 86 fig. 15, 90. For the lamp from Predio Sola, see Chapter I, n. 49.

62. *IG* V^2 514, ll. 13-17.

63. Loucas (1994), 98-9.

64. The evidence from the Artemision of Delos begins between 372/367 and 354/3 and continues with interruptions until 342/340: *luknoukhoi II* (*IDélos* 7, 103, l. 71); *luknoukhoi IIII IDélos* 7, 104, l. 127; 104 (11), l. 21; 104 (12), l. 101; *lukneion* and *luknoukhos khalkous hugiês*; *IDélos* 7, 104(28), face B, fr. b, l. 7 and 23; *IDélos* 7, 104 (29), l. 8 and ll. 35-6.

65. For metal lamps (and other valuables) listed in the Erekhtheion inventories, see Chapter II.2.

66. See Chapter V.4.

67. Hadzisteliou-Price (1978), 127-8, 133, 141, 150, 151-2, 157, 192-5, 201, 211 n. 50.

VI. Fire and Light in Divine Hunting and Divine Retribution

1. Kahil (1984), 653 no. 397 pl. 478.

2. Kahil (1984), 654 nos. 400-2 pl. 478.

3. For the notion of sacred hunting in connection with Artemis: Kahil (1977), 93 n. 33; Brulé (1987), 224 n. 211, 181. For the relationship between hunting and sacrifice: Vidal-Naquet (1988b), 143-7.

4. For the cult of Artemis Laphria at Patras: Papachatzis (1980), 92-3; Furley (1981), 116-28, esp. 118, 129-51, esp. 131-2. Although the holocaust rites at Patras in honour of Artemis are not attested earlier than Pausanias (vii, 18.8-19.1), W.D. Furley suggested a much earlier date for them in the fifth century, on the basis of the literary and numismatic evidence. Based on the same evidence, A.D. Rizakis has also accepted a pre-Roman date for this cult, though not as early as the fifth century: Rizakis (1995), 144-5, 170-1.

5. Aesch. *Eum.* 130, 138-40, 147, 210, 421; *Ag.* 1579; Soph., *El.* 490; Eur., *IT* 280-2, 935.

6. Aesch., *Ag.* 1056, 1115-17. For discussion: Padel (1992), 177 n. 40; Vidal-Naquet (1988), 150, 157.

7. For torches held alone: Sarian (1986), 828 no. 9 (side B), 829 no. 19, 832 no. 45, 833 nos. 57-8, 61, 834 no. 66. For torches and spears: op. cit., 828 nos. 10-11, 833 no. 55, 835-6 no. 85. For torches and snakes: op. cit., 833 no. 58. For torch and phiale: op. cit., 827 no. 4.

8. Aesch. *Eum.* 892, 928, 951-3, 990-1, 1005, 1007, 1023, 1033, 1036; Aesch. *Cho.* 321, 745, 791, 844, 1034. For discussion: Padel (1992), 80-1, 104.

9. Detienne & Vernant (1991), 30, 32, 38.

10. For the association of the scene on the Boston bell-krater (7.10) by the Lykaon Painter with drama, and in particular with Aeschylus' *Toxotides*: Trendall & Webster (1971), 62 III.1.28. The presence of Zeus and especially Lyssa, the mask-like animal face of Aktaion together with his labelling on the vase as 'Euaion' (name of the son of Aeschylus), form the basis of this argument.

11. For the different versions of and literary references to the myth of Aktaion: Bonnechère (1994), 139-41; Burkert (1983), 111-14; Fontenrose (1981), 33-40.

12. For purification practices in hunting and the sanctification of the act of killing: Meuli (1946), 224-6; Simon (1985), 156-8; Burkert (1983), 11, 15. On the other hand, an analogy between hunting and sexual coupling has been pointed out by Sourvinou-Inwood (1991), 65-6; Borgeaud (1988), 33-4.

13. For the myth of Kallisto: Borgeaud (1988), 32-3; Sourvinou-Inwood (1991), 49, 56 n. 76; Fontenrose (1981), 69-74. For the myth of Hippolytos: Halleran (1995), 39-42; Lawall (1986), 14-16, 85-6; Fontenrose (1981), 160-7.

14. For the myth of Bellerophon: Collard, Cropp & Lee (1995), 98-101.

15. The bow and the quiver do not always appear. However, their presence in most early examples supports the supposition that the torch-bearing Artemis was first introduced into the scene in her capacity as huntress.

16. On the opposition between light (Dionysos) and darkness (Pentheus) in the *Bacchae*: Seaford (1981), 255-8, esp. 256; Winnington-Ingram (1980), 113-14.

17. On the differences between 'ancient' and 'modern' hunting: Schnapp (1997), 123-71, esp. 157-62, 167-8. While planning their escape from the land of the Taurians, Orestes' view that 'night is for thieves and daylight for the truth' (Eur. *IT* 1026) is comparable to Plato's view about nocturnal hunting.

18. On new type of hunting and war: Schnapp (1997), 163-71; Hunt (1998), 195.

19. For discussion: Vidal-Naquet (1981), 159-62; Vidal-Naquet (1986), 117-19 esp. 118.

20. Vidal-Naquet (1986), 181; Vidal-Naquet (1981), 153-5; Whitby (1994), 105; Kennell (1995), 131-2.

21. For references and discussion: Ma (1994a-c); esp. (1994a), 51; (1994c), 72.

22. For hunting scenes in Attic black- and red-figure vase-painting: Schnapp (1997), 172-267, 318-452.

23. Tiverios (1997), 317 no. 16.

24. Tiverios (1997), 328-9 no. 105.

25. Detienne & Vernant (1991), 75-9, 101 n. 95.

26. For similar a fire-breathing monster: *Il.* vi, 182 (Khimaera).

27. Touchefeu-Mayhier (1997), 150 no. 25.

28. Sarian (1986), 829 no. 19.

29. For discussion: Faraone (1992), 65, 61.

30. For Artemis as war-goddess: Borgeaud (1988), 157.

31. Gantz (1977), 30 n. 18.

32. Anderson (1997), 127-9; Gantz (1977), 28-9, 31-2.

33. For similar nocturnal tricks: Faraone (1992), 96-7.

34. Night usually puts an end to military action in the *Iliad* (vii, 282, 290, 370-1, 377; viii, 485-8, 500-1, 502-4, 529-30; x, 82-5, 141-2, 159-61; xvii, 454-5; xviii, 241-2, 354-5; xix, 162-3). For discussion of ancient attitudes to time, place and methods of war in parallel with hunting: Schnapp (1997), 150-63.

35. Krauskopf (1990), 954 no. 12a (the Caivano Painter).

36. For discussion: Scodel (1980), 76-8; Craik (1990), 6: E. Craik finds phallic connotations – apart from the symbolism of destruction – in the replacement of the baby boy by a torch in the dream of Hekuba; I do not believe that we have sufficient evidence to justify that interpretation.

37. Rehm (1994), 112.

38. Rehm (1994), 103-4.

39. For discussion: Gantz (1977).

40. For discussion: Gantz (1977), 32-3.

VII. The Fire and Light of the Senses

1. For a short general discussion: Padel (1992), 116-17.

2. See Chapter VI.2.

3. More specifically, Empedokles compares the lighting effect of a lamp within a lantern on a wintry night with that of the eye, through rays emanating from it.

4. London, British Museum 96.7-23.1; *ARV*² 654.12; *CVA* V, pl. 49.3; *LIMC* III, 881 no. 366 (pl.).

5. For representations of the Eros as torch-bearer see *LIMC* III Eros, 881 nos. 366 (pl.) 367, 882 nos. 368-70, nos. 372-9, 890 no. 475.

6. In Homer's *Odyssey*, light is often synonymous to sight, with the word '*phaos*' being used to denote eyes at least on three occasions: *Od.* xvi, 15; xvii, 39; xix, 417.

7. For more examples: Richardson (1974), 171.

8. Leinieks (1996), 85.

9. On dances in the mad fashion: Leinieks (1996), 61-2.

10. For the differences between the Theban and the Attic rite, see 190 n. 44.

11. On maenadic *ōmophagia*: Bierl (1991), 66 n. 64; Daraki (1985), 62-8; Obbink (1993), 68-72.

12. Berlin, Antikenmuseum F 1881; *ABV* 478.2; *Add.*[2] 120; *CVA* V, pl. 45.

13. On maenads and wine: Frontisi-Ducroux (1991), 81-5; des Bouvrie (1993), 94-9.

14. On Dionysos as 'Destroyer of the Household': Seaford (1993), 133-8; Seaford (1994), 257-62; Seaford (1990), 163; Seaford (1988), 87-8; Daraki (1985), 74-8. For more general discussion on Dionysos' female followers and the polis: Seaford (1994), 235-80; Just (1989), 217-19; des Bouvrie (1993) 99-103; Lada-Richards (1999), 190, 192, 232-3.

15. On maenads as models for male behaviour: Schlesier (1993), 98 n. 40. For male attributes used by maenads: Bazant (1984), 43.

16. For discussion: Ussher (1986), 175.

17. For such examples on fifth- and fourth-century red-figure cups: Kassel, Staatliche Kunstsammlungen T 490, *ARV*[2] 1520.31, *Add*[2] 384, *CVA* I, pl. 38.3-4; Frankfurt, Museum für Vor- und Frühgeschichte b 407, *Para* 473, *CVA* II, pl. 67.3-4; Altenburg, Staatliches Lindenau-Museum 230, *ARV*[2] 1283.14, *CVA* II, pl. 72.1,2,4; Vienna, Kunsthistorisches Museum 2223, *ARV*[2] 1518.2, *CVA* I, pl. 27.2-3; Vienna, Kunsthistorisches Museum 203, *ARV*[2] 1518.3, *CVA* I, pl. 28.5; Vienna, Kunsthistorisches Museum 207, *ARV*[2] 1519.15, *CVA* I, pl. 26.2; Ferrara, Museo Archeologico Nazionale T 893 (3141), *ARV*[2] 1518.1, *Add*[2] 384; Rome, Museo del Palazzo dei Conservatori 365, *ARV*[2] 946.38, *Para* 432, *CVA* II, pl. 26.1-2; Oxford, Ashmolean Museum 308, *ARV*[2] 1139.5.

18. On maenadism and the wedding-ritual: Seaford (1993), 121-5. On violently destructive maenads: Seaford, op. cit., 127; Seaford (1987), 109-10, 122.

19. For the association of maenads and death: Schlesier (1993), 97-103, esp. 97 n. 36.

20. For Kassandra as a tragic bride: Seaford (1993), 128-9; Craik (1990), 6; Seaford (1987), 128.

21. For torches as symbols of destruction, see Chapter VI.4.

VIII. Cultivation and Prosperity of Land: Fire as a Creative Power

1. For the fertility associations of pomegranates: Richardson (1974), 276; Hadzisteliou-Price (1978), 210; Sourvinou-Inwood (1991), 160, 162.

2. For the replacement of animal sacrifices by fruits burnt on the altar: Detienne (1989), 6.

3. Black-figure representations of the ritual: Berlin, Staatliche Museen F 1686, *ABV* 296.4, van Straten (1995), 197 V21 fig. 4; Athens, Akropolis Museum 2298, van Straten (1995), 197 V19 fig. 3; Art Market, van Straten (1995), 202 V52, fig. 24.

4. The role of olive branches as purifiers is stressed by Parker (1983), 229 n. 124.

5. Red-figure footed dinos no. 89.AE.73 from Malibu: Clinton (1992), figs. 43, 46.

6. Schwarz (1987), 131; she misinterprets Hekate by identifying her with Demeter, which is not likely since Demeter clearly carries her standard attribute, the sceptre, and follows Persephone.

7. Kraus (1960), 46, 59, 86, 163, 169; Hadzisteliou-Price (1978), 153, 159, 192; Parry (1992), 75-6.

8. Later evidence such as Pausanias attests rituals in Demeter's sanctuaries that may be taken as local reflections of the concept of the warming of earth. Pausanias describes a custom of throwing torches into a chasm of earth (*bothros*) in honour of Persephone in Argos (ii, 22.4); Papachatzis (1976), 170-1. Pausanias refers to the sanctuaries of Demeter Thermasia in Troizen and Hermione (ii, 34.7-8); Papachatzis, op. cit., 267, 275. For discussion with further literary references: Allen, Halliday & Sikes (1936), 136-7; Richardson (1974), 167.

9. For example: Ar., *Thesm.* 101, 1525.

10. Translation of '*xun eleuthera*' of line 102 by Sommerstein (1994).

11. Clinton (1992), 30-2; Brumfield (1981), 80-1, 88, 93-4, 113; Demand (1994), 116-18.

12. Wiegand & Schrader (1904), 161, fig. 153.

13. Pemberton (1989), 135-6 no. 295, pl. 32, fig. 35.

14. For example: Cole (1994), 207 n. 38; Bookidis & Stroud (1987), 13, 15 fig. 13c; Bookidis & Fisher (1972), 316, pl. 62d; Stroud (1965), 22, pl. 11a; Higgins (1967), 82, 87, pl. 37b. For discussion of the iconography of Greek female figurines holding a pig and a torch: Sguaitamatti (1984), 32-3. For figurines from Sicilian sanctuaries of Demeter: Hinz (1998), 41, 46, 90 (from S. Nicola in Akragas), 159 (from Leontini), 185 (from Taranto), 190 (from Herakleia), 201 (Rivello in southern Lucania). For early torch-bearing female figurines from Mytilene: Cronkite (1997), 66 n. 110.

15. Coldstream (1973), 75 no. 126, pl. 49; Hinz (1998), 201 (near Timmaris in eastern Lucania).

16. Higgins (1967), 62; Levi (1967-8), 573 fig. 44c.

17. For example: Edlund (1987), 112 n. 140; Neutsch & Rolley (1981), 162 nn. 42-3; Rüdiger (1969), 192 fig. 32; Voza (1976-7), 558, pl. 98; Rüdiger (1967), 349; Lo Porto (1967), 188, 190-1 fig. 45; Marconi (1933), 66-7 fig. 38 nos. 1-3e, pl. 15 no. 7.

18. For full treatment of the subject: Leonhard (1974).

19. Full discussions of the ritual: Clinton (1988), 76-7; Detienne (1989), 129-47, esp. 134; Clinton (1993), 13. The broader concept of the ritual descent to the underworld as part of initiatory rites is discussed by Lada-Richards (1999), esp. 84-6. For a review of the often assumed fertility connotations of the rituals of the festival: Lowe (1998). Remains of pigs' bones in pits, which reflect this particular ritual activity at the Thesmophoria, are discussed by Cole (1994), 203-4 n. 18; Kron (1992), 617.

20. The episode of Iambe may also be reflected in the *gephurismoi* ritual of the Mysteries. However, Clinton links it primarily with the Thesmophoria, Clinton (1992), 30.

21. See Chapter III.3a-b.

22. I see no reason why the animal could not be recognised as a pig in this context. The shape of the body and the head resemble other red-figure representations of pigs. For example: Durand (1986), 135 figs. 58-9, 136 figs. 60-1. For debate about the kind of the animal to be sacrificed in this scene, and the religious occasion: Kron (1992), 616-17 (she accepts the Thesmophoria as the religious occasion for the sacrifice, but does not recognise the animal as a pig); Simon (1985b), 273 n. 12 (she dissociates the scene from Demeter's cult and attributes it to the Hekataia). For recent discussion: Hinz (1998), 45 n. 282.

23. Dakaris (1964), 113-14, pl. 69b.

24. A review of the epigraphical evidence concerning the Thesmophoria in Attika is offered by Clinton (1996), 111-25.

25. *IG* II² 1184, ll. 14-15.

26. The etymology of the word reflects its multiple bound wooden stems: Frisk (1960), 342-3; Chantraîne (1968), 270, 248-9.

27. *SEG* XXXV, 113 and more recently *SEG* XXXVI, 206, ll. 4, 24, 25. Sokolowski (1971), 217-20.

28. On the etymology of the word: Frisk (1970), 79; Chantraîne (1968), 617.

29. Similar formulas (*lampas* and *lampadeion*) are used in the case of torch-races, where the torches are recorded in connection with their holders, which are their essential accessories.

30. *SEG* XXIII, 80, col. I, fr. b, ll. 27; *SEG* XXV, 168, l. 27.

31. *SEG* XXV, 168, l. 27.

32. *SEG* XXXV, 113 and *SEG* XXXVI, 206, ll. 21-2.

33. *IG* I³ 129 face A, l. 5-6; *SEG* XVIII, 4, ll. 4-5; *SEG* XXIII, 80, col. I, fr. b, l. 27.

34. Evidence of the pannukhis and discussion of the rituals of Haloa: Brumfield (1981), 106-18; Simon (1966), 90-1: she interprets the scene on the pediment of the 'Ninnion' pinax as the second phase of the celebration of the Haloa, which was orgiastic in nature and included men; Pritchett (1987), 184. For a reconsideration of the traditionally accepted fertility connotations of the festival: Lowe (1998).

35. *IG* II², 1672 col. I, fr. b, ll. 124-5.

36. Brumfield (1981), 114-15.

37. Brumfield (1981), 195, 80-1; Brumfield (1996), 69 (for the aiskhrologia); 80, 115, 195 (for the pannukhis); 87, 115 (for exclusive women's rites).

38. On the role of wine in the cult of Dionysos: Daraki (1985), 48-50.

39. For discussion: Simon (1963).

40. For discussion with references: Jameson (1993), 54-7; Guazzelli (1992), 33-8; Seaford (1994), 262-75.

41. On the appearance of satyrs: Lissarrague (1993), 208-13.

42. On the comic drama of Dionysos: des Bouvrie (1993), 103-6. On the association of satyrs with dithyramb, the birth-song of drama: Arist. *Poet.* iv 1449a9-14. Trendall & Webster (1971), 15; Brommer (1937), 34-7; Hedreen (1992), 165-70. For the themes of silens' performances and vases which possibly depict satyr-plays: Hedreen (1992), 125-53, 105-24.

43. Lissarrague (1993), 214.

44. For a comparable scene on a khous by the Nikias Painter, inspired by a satyr-play: Trendall & Webster (1971), 117-18 VI.2: Herakles stands in a chariot driven by four centaurs, who are led by a man with two torches. The mask-like faces are reminiscent of characters from Late Middle Comedy. For the images of silens in black-figure vase-painting as reflections of satyr-plays, unknown to us: Hedreen (1992), 155-7. The problems with recognising specific theatre plays in vase representations have been pointed out by F. Lissarrague (1990), 230-6.

45. Berlin Staatliche Museen F1881, *ABV* 478.2; *Add*² 120; *CVA* 5, pl. 45; Stark (1868), pl. 9. See also **Fig. 27**.

46. Schöne (1987), 37.

47. Schöne (1987), 40.

48. Schöne (1987), 38.

49. On the fire of Hephaistos: Delcourt (1982), esp. 200-24.

50. For discussion: Edmundson (1977), 160-4; Brommer (1959), 48-9; Beazley (1939).

51. Trendall & Webster (1971), 31 II.4; Beazley (1939), 618-20.

52. Beazley (1939), 620-2.

53. Beazley (1939), 636.

54. Beazley (1939), 636-8.

55. Beazley (1939), 622-4.
56. Beazley (1939), 626-8.
57. Beazley (1939), 631-2.
58. Beazley (1939), 635.
59. Beazley (1939), 633.
60. Beazley (1939), 638-9; Brommer (1959), 49.
61. For discussion: Trendall & Webster (1971), 31; Beazley (1939), 624-6; Edmundson (1977), esp. 164.
62. For a list and description of these postures: Trendall & Webster (1971), 31.

IX. Use of Light in the Worship of the Gods

1. See Chapters III.3a; VIII.2; IX.4.
2. *IG* II², 1541, l. 15; *IG* II², 1543, col. III, l. 16.
3. *SEG* XXXV, 113 = *SEG* XXXVI, 206, ll. 23-5. Also see Sokolowski (1971), 220.
4. For torch-holders of prehistoric date see, most recently, Karageorgis (1999).
5. Legrand (1905), 302.
6. See Chapter II.2b.
7. Neutsch & Rolley (1981), 162-4. For a recent discussion: Hinz (1998), 32 n. 134, 198 n. 1178 fig. 55.
8. Hinz (1998), 197 n. 1164 (with earlier literature).
9. *SEG* XXX, 1150-61. For latest discussion: Hinz (1998), 32 n. 133, 190, 192 fig. 52.
10. Hinz (1998), 201.
11. Hinz (1998), 198 n. 1177 (with earlier literature). Also see n. 63.
12. Hinz (1998), 217 n. 1279.
13. Hinz (1998), 217 nn. 1280-1.
14. See Chapter VIII n. 14.
15. For the inscriptions from the Athenian Eleusinion: *IG* I³, 386 col. III, l. 142; *IG* I³ 387, col. III, l. 167, dated to 408-407 and 407-406 respectively, recording an iron *lukhneion*. For a recent discussion: Cavanaugh (1996), 185. For the inscription from Eleusis: *IG* II² 1541, l. 18. It is dated to 357-356, and records iron *lukhneia* (restored as two). Earlier in the document, a torch-holder is recorded, within a similar context.
16. See Chapter I.2b, 172 n. 48. Also Hinz (1998), 147.
17. See Chapter I.2b, 172 n. 49.
18. This observation has occasionally been pointed out by Rutkowski (1983), 323.
19. For a similar view: Williams (1994), 38.
20. It is tempting to link the preference for circular patterns in the design of multi-nozzled lamps from sanctuary contexts with intentions to imitate solar symbols. Although it would be too bold to speak directly of sun-symbolism, there must have been strong solar connotations associated with such circular radiant lamps. For a collection of early Bronze and Iron Age solar symbols and their imitation in art: Goodison (1989), 82-4, 126-31. Herodotus' testimony (ii, 62) of the festival of Neith in Sais, records a circular arrangement of clay lamps that burned all night around the houses ('*peri ta dômata kuklô*'). The notion of a circle of light is clearly combined with the imperative that the flames be maintained throughout the night. The circle as a symbol has been variously interpreted. It is the conventional solar form which has been observed in a series of different artifacts since the Bronze Age. In Aristophanes' *Eccl.* 1-5, the brightness emanating from the nozzles

of a lamp finds a comic parallel in the sunlight; it is the eye-witness of secret night-time activities, just as the sun is always present at the events of the day. For discussion see: Ussher (1986), 70-3; Taaffe (1993), 106-7; Bowie (1993), 255-6. In the case of Demeter, in whose sanctuaries a particular accumulation of such large corona lamps has been observed, there is limited evidence for the goddess's moon associations; these have been securely detected at the Dorian colony of Taukheira, in Kyrenaika, as early as the sixth century, where her cult was assimilated to that of Isis. Gold lunules from that date reflect the adoption of relevant symbols in artifacts in Kyrenaika: Boardman & Hayes (1966), 156 no. 3. A Knossian votive ring with an applied moon probably echoes a similar cult. Although the date of the ring could be as early as the end of the fourth or the beginning of the third century, J.N. Coldstream places the cult association between the two goddesses at Knossos in late hellenistic times. See Coldstream (1973), 185, 133-4 no. 23, fig. 29. All of these associations may have influenced the appearance of forms of lighting objects made specially for sanctuary use. A good example is the *kernoi* which most probably served also as lamps, as well as the *amphiphôntes*; see Chapter IX.2b.

21. Marconi (1926), 142-4; Marconi (1933), 23, 66-7, 69; White (1964), 66-74. Also, see recently Hinz (1998), 76.

22. Hinz (1998), esp. 84 (including earlier literature) and 49 nn. 320-1 (for the particular type of multi-nozzled lamp at Akragas).

23. Orlandini (1963), 10, 26, pls. 1-7, 12, 13, 34-8, 43, 46-50, 47 fig. 17; Holloway (1991), 57-8, 59 fig. 75; Hinz (1998), 68.

24. Hinz (1998), 108.

25. Hinz (1998), 118. For Selinous: Gabrici (1927), 369-70; White (1964), 90. For the marble examples from Selinous, see Chapter I, n. 48.

26. Hinz (1998), 139 n. 818.

27. Hinz (1998), 197.

28. Most of the information comes from my own examination of the unpublished lighting material from Eleusis and my discussion with Dr Kokkou-Viridi.

29. Thompson (1936), 179-80, fig. 23; Broneer (1942a), 256.

30. For brief discussions of the lighting material from the site: Bookidis & Stroud (1997), 32 n. 24, 37 n. 35, 49, 77, 79, 81, 109 n. 49, 50, 122, 124, 131 n. 90, 134, 161, 178, 189, 193 n. 42, 211 n. 93, 234, 242-3, 251; Cole (1994), 207. Some of the statuettes with polos represented Demeter or Kore, for example *LIMC* IV, Demeter 856 no. 102. However, the same type with pig and torch may also represent female worshippers.

31. For Gortun: Karo (1909), 102. A discussion of the large pedestalled lamps from Gortun is made by Rutkowski (1983). Also see Herakleion Museum no. 3239: the provenance is not given (probably Gortun). For Knossos: Coldstream (1973), 24-5, 27, 31, 33-5 fig. 16, 37, 44, 181 n. 9, 183. He refers to unpublished material of multi-nozzled lamps on stands at the museum of Aghios Nikolaos, Krete.

32. Mortzos (1985), 31-2, pls. 21b, 21d.

33. Mazarakis-Ainian (1998), 160, 164, 166, 169 figs. 24-5, 170 fig. 26, 171 fig. 27, 172-5.

34. For discussion with earlier literature: Hinz (1998), 66, 68.

35. Boitani (1971), 262-83. For the votives from building b which was dedicated to the cult of Demeter: Comella (1978), 89-95, esp. 92. For the sanctuary at Gravisca: Torelli (1977); Edlund (1987), 76-7.

36. This information derives from my examination of the lighting material from Eleusis.

37. Legrand (1905), 302, 310-12. The exact location of the shrine has not been re-identified, but the finds clearly suggest the nature of the worshipped deity.

38. Karo (1911), 132-3.
39. Verdelis (1964), 122, pl. 122.
40. Dawkins (1909), 12-14.
41. Dickins (1906), 173.The excavator identified the shrine as one of Akhilles.
42. Goldman (1931), 245, 262-3.
43. Metzger (1985), 19-20, 49.
44. Rolley (1990), 405-6; Rolley (1965); Rolley (1990), 406. He argues for a chronological fluctuation in the quantity of the torch- or hydria-carrying statuettes, ranging from great numbers to none at all. Athens, Korinth and Eretria are cited as places where this kind of statuette is absent. However, torch-bearing figurines have been found at least in Akrokorinth, although only a few examples appear in excavation reports. For the sanctuary at Pella: Lilibaki-Akamati (1996), 91. Only one lamp fragment is catalogued: op. cit., 295.
45. Stephanou (1958), 63.
46. For Halikarnassos: Newton (1862), 327, 331; Bailey (1975), 113-16; For Knidos: Newton (1863), 383, 390-1, 394, 402; Bailey (1975), 124-6.
47. See 197 n. 21.
48. Pingiatoglou (1991), 147, 149.
49. Pingiatoglou (1991), ill. 4, n. 17, pl. 5 n. 19, no. MD577, n. 20, no. MD3966.
50. Wiegand & Schrader (1904), 449-59.
51. Welter (1941), 21-4.
52. White (1984), 21, 30, 59-60, 80, 84-5, 92; White (1993), 11, 14, 16-18, 25, 30, 33, 35.
53. Hinz (1998), 76 suggested that the finding of lamps near and inside 'pit-altars' may be reflecting a ritual described by Pausanias (ii, 22.4) in which lighted torches or lamps were thrown into a chasm of earth in honour of Persephone, at a sanctuary of Demeter at Argos. One needs however to be cautious with regard to the antiquity of this ritual, which, according to Pausanias, was instituted by a local man, Nikostratos, and was still being practised during Pausanias' time. On the other hand, the repeated presence of lamps among sacrificial remains (in connection with knives and dining pottery), many of which reflect rituals that took place in the open air (and are not associated with any architecture), speak more directly in favour of nocturnal sacrifices. After these nocturnal visits, the central event of which seems to have been the sacrifice to the goddess, the lamps that had earlier served to illuminate the ceremony were left on the spot of the ritual (at the sanctuaries or at any other 'sacrificial ground'), together with the rest of the sacrificial remains.
54. Hinz (1998), 147 (with earlier literature).
55. Hinz (1998), 81.
56. See 197 n. 21.
57. Hinz (1998), 106.
58. Stillwell (1963), 164-5; Sjöquist (1964), 141-3; Edlund-Berry (1990), 333, 336-8. For the lamp-factory: Stillwell & Sjövist (1957), 156; Hinz (1998), 133.
59. See 197 n. 32.
60. Levi (1968), 569, fig. 39, 572, fig. 40.
61. Levi (1968), 573 fig. 47: 'Ma accanto alle i idrie gli oggeti votivi piu numerosi sono le lucernine.'
62. Hinz (1998), 72 (including earlier literature).
63. Rüdinger (1967), 340-1, fig. 15, 348, 352; Rüdinger (1969), 189, 192 fig. 32; Hinz (1998), 198.
64. Hinz (1998), 112.
65. Hinz (1998), 135, 136, 138 (including earlier literature).

66. Hinz (1998), 156.

67. Koukouli-Chrysanthaki (1987), 411-12, ill. 10; Koukouli-Chrysanthaki (1989), 84-5.

68. Boardman & Hayes (1966), 139-41, pl. 90; Boardman & Hayes (1973), 64-5.

69. Hinz (1998), 61-2; Kron (1992), 629-30, 646-7, 625; White (1964), 39, 42-3, 47-8. Apart from the sanctuaries discussed here, similar material was unearthed at other Geloan sanctuaries of Demeter, such as Scalo Ferroriano, Feudo Nobile, Villa Lacona and Molino al Vento.

70. See 197 n. 25.

71. Hinz (1998), 127, 125.

72. Bookidis & Stroud (1997), 77, 153, 158. Also see 197 n. 30.

73. For the proposed function of rectangular building 3 in the sanctuary on Kuthnos: Mazarakis-Ainian (1998), esp. 175.

74. For discussion of deposits B-D of the sanctuary at Knossos: Coldstream (1973), 22-31; Cronkite (1997), 150-2.

75. Cronkite (1997), 67-8, 55-6; Williams (1994), 37-40; Williams (1990), 179, 191.

76. Information based on discussion with Dr Kokkou-Viridi, whose publication of the pyres of the Telesterion is forthcoming. According to Kokkou-Viridi, it was pyres A and B which yielded lamp-fragments.

77. For a brief report of the excavation: Kalligas (1978), 144.

78. Stillwell (1959), 171; Hinz (1998), 130. For the link of the find with Akrokorinth: Hinz, op. cit., 130 n. 770.

79. Marconi (1977), 43 fig. 9, 45; Hinz (1998), 76-9.

80. Hinz (1998), 190-1 (with earlier literature).

81. See n. 67 (IX.1b).

82. Varvitsas (1973), 77, 79, 80. For a discussion of the role of water in Greek sanctuaries: Cole (1988).

83. Hinz (1998), 97-8.

84. Hinz (1998), 197 (including earlier literature).

85. See Chapter I.2b, 172 n. 55.

86. See Chapters I.2b, 173 n. 73 and IX, 200 n. 101.

87. Howland (1958), 160 no. 626; Scheibler (1976), 150, 46 no. 246.

88. Palaiokrassa (1991), 71. For the problems surrounding the excavation: Palaiokrassa, op. cit., 16-19, 42-6.

89. The information about the lamps from Mounukhia sanctuary comes from my own examination of the material at the Museum of Piraeus.

90. For this lamp-type: Palaiokrassa (1991), 146 Ka77, pl. 35b, MP 5417. Similar lamps have been identified by B. Wesenberg in the scene of the offering of the peplos on the east frieze of the Parthenon. For the procession in Mounukhion: Parke (1977), 137-8; Palaiokrassa (1991), 34-5 n. 7, 28-9. A second procession of young girls also took place on the sixth of Mounukhion, starting from the shrine of the goddess on the bank of Ilissos river, to the Delphinion.

91. Palaiokrassa (1991), 146 Ka76, pl. 35b, MP 5417.

92. Threpsiades (1961-2), 143. For lamps from the building M (possibly for the accommodation of worshippers): Threpsiades (1965), 31-2. No further details are given about the material from the Aulis sanctuary in this short excavation report, nor has it ever received publication.

93. For discussion of nocturnal celebrations at the sanctuary of Ortheia at Sparta based on Alcman's *Partheneion* and archaeological evidence (mainly clay-masks) from the site: Carter (1988).

94. The information is based on my own examination of the material at the

Sparta Museum. Apart from the types summarised here, a considerable number of lamps are dated to the hellenistic and Roman periods and are beyond the scope of this study.

95. For a synopsis of the published finds: Brulotte (1994), 240-1.

96. Reichel & Wilhelm (1901), 58 figs. 120-1, 59. For a recent treatment of the offerings from the temple at Lousoi: Brulotte (1994), 48-57.

97. Brulotte (1994), 57 n. 227.

98. Karagiorga (1963), 89. For the cult of Artemis at Mantineia: Jost (1985), 136-7; Stiglitz (1967), 72-81.

99. Daux (1958), 808, 814, figs. 16-17; Daux (1967), 162, 163 fig. 103.

100. For discussion of the contexts of the so-called 'candlestick' lamps: Hogarth (1908), 39; Bailey (1975), 88-9. For the stone lamps see Chapter I.2b, 173 n. 73.

101. Most lamps from J.T. Wood's excavations in his search for the Artemision are in the British Museum: Bailey (1975), 88-9, 272. The so called 'primitive' area is associated with the pre-sixth-century temples of Artemis at the site (temples A, B, and C). Remains of these temples were discovered within the cella of the the sixth-century 'Croesus' temple. Hogarth (1908), 52-73. For updated information of the architectural layout of the area: Bammer & Muss (1996), 33-8, 44. Also see Chapter I.2b, 173 n. 73.

102. Literary references have been collected by Palaiokrassa (1991), 32-3.

103. For the debate about the date of the offering of amphiphontes: Palaiokrassa (1991), 39 nn. 39-41.

104. For an account of sacrificial cakes: Kearns (1994).

105. For the lunar character of Hekate: Parry (1992), 74-9; Johnston (1990), 30-1. For the suppers in honour of Hekate which took place on nights of full moon: Johnston (1990), 60-1. On En(n)odoia: Chrysostomou (1998), esp. 118 n. 402; Kraus (1960), 63, 77-83.

106. On the lunar associations of amphiphontes: Palaiokrassa (1991), 38-9 n. 38.

107. Kern (1890), 138.

108. Another possible example of a representation of an amphiphon of hellenistic date is a relief from Ialysos on Rhodes: Rhodes, Archaeological Museum 10448; Kahil (1984), 699 no. 1024. The goddess is depicted as huntress and holds in her raised hand a round object with three torches apparently stuck in it, while receiving worshippers in front of a burning altar.

109. For example: Bookidis (1993), 55, 56 fig. 3.6 (for Demeter and Kore); Daux (1959), 607 fig. 9 (for Hera?); Waldstein (1905), 15, 42 fig. 77 no. 267 (for Hera); Payne (1940), 67 (for Hera).

110. S. Marinatos explicitly mentions that the lamp was said by the locals to have been found on the *keraton* altar. For details on the context see Chapter I.2b, 172-3 nn. 66-9.

111. Vokotopoulou (1993), 180, 181, 182, 184.

112. Mazarakis-Ainian (1995), 146, 148, 149, 154-155.

113. Threpsiades (1961), 100. For the finds inside the aduton: Travlos (1976), 203. For architectural details of the aduton at Aulis: Hollinshead (1985), 430-2. The full publication of the finds from the sanctuary of Aulis is awaited.

114. For aduta in temples of Artemis: Travlos (1976), 200-1 fig. 2 (Aulis), 204 (Tauropolos), 205 (Brauron): Travlos connects the existence of aduta in these temples of Artemis with her cult as Artemis-Iphigenia. Also, see below, 167-8 (Lukokheia, Mantineia). In favour of a more secular function for the aduta of the temples at Brauron, Aulis and Halai: Hollinshead (1985), esp. 439. Lamps were also found in the small chamber at the southern end of the Anaktoron at

Samothrace. The chamber was not connected with the central chamber and was entered only from the outside. K. Lehmann suggested its use for the preparations of the initiates, which probably included changing of their clothing and receiving a lamp, prior to their oath by torchlight and their lustral bath: Cole (1984), 28, 114 n. 226. An additional example of lustration rites inferred from the bathing installations in the cella of the Samothracian Sanctuary has been reconstructed by K. Lehmann: Cole (1984), 32-3 n. 263, 116 n. 266. For possible nocturnal lustration rituals in sanctuaries of Demeter, see Chapter IX.1e.

115. The use of torches in preliminary purification rituals has been suggested by K. Lehmann for the Mysteries at Samothrace: Cole (1984), 31.

116. Steinhauer (1975), 77, 79; Brulotte (1994), 275.

117. Cook & Nicholls (1998), 22-3, 24, 25, 26, 29; Akurgal (1983), 110, pl. 123, D, E1.

118. The lamps have been published by Bailey (1991), 31-68.

119. Broneer (1938), 198-9.

120. Broneer (1930), 34.

121. Blinkenberg (1931), 31-3.

122. Daux (1960), 866. This information does not apply to the entire votive material of the sanctuary, which has not yet been fully published, but to an extensive area at the north-west of the fifth-century temple-terrace.

123. Boardman (1967), 233-4, 174.

124. Schilardi (1988), 45-6.

125. Cook & Nicholls (1998), 26 (inv. no. SF 787).

126. A further late reference to the pannukhis at the Panathenaia is given by Heliodorus (*Aeth*. i,10). For discussion of the order of events in Greek pannukhides with special reference to the Panathenaia: Pritchett (1987).

127. For example: Ar. *Ran*. 371, 409; Eur. *Hel*. 1365; Men. *Dys*. 857; Men. *Sam*. 46.

128. This broad distinction is discussed by Bravo (1997), 12-13.

129. *IG* II² 334, l. 30; ll. 31-2. An early fourth-century inscription (*IG* II² 2311) which includes lists of prizes at the Panathenaia has often been used to clarify the programme of the feast. On this basis, the night on the twenty-eighth of Hekatombaion was proposed by Pritchett (1987), 187-8 as the night of the pannukhis. It followed a series of day activities, which included a procession, torch-race and sacrifice with a subsequent distribution of meat (*kreanomia*). Neils (1992), 15, Shapiro (1992), 56 and Lefkowitz (1996), 79 prefer the previous night (the twenty-seventh of Hekatombaion) for the celebration of the pannukhis.

130. For discussion including literary references: Mansfield (1985), 282, 331 n. 75; Parke (1977), 93.

131. Robertson (1996), 50.

132. Clinton (1996), esp. 112.

133. All primary material with discussion is collected by Clinton (1996), 112-15.

134. *IG* II² 1363, l. 17, 22 (dated to the early third century). For discussion of the inscription: Clinton (1996), 113, 115; Brumfield (1981), 81-2.

135. *IG* II² 1184 (=*SEG* XXXV 239). For discussion: Clinton (1996), 113 no. 2.

136. All material is collected in Chapter VIII.2a.

137. Most recent discussion: Lada-Richards (1999), 100 n. 213. Also: Borgeaud (1988), 168-72.

138. Most literary references of nocturnal festivals of Dionysos are collected by Seaford (1996), 189.

139. For illicit sex in festivals of Dionysos: Seaford (n. 138), loc. cit.

140. *IG* XII 2, 499 (= *LCSG* no. 127, p. 223).

141. Most recent discussion including earlier literature: Lada-Richards (1999), 126-8 n. 6.

142. *IG* I^3 136, l. 27. For discussion: Parker (1996), 172 n. 68; Pritchett (1987), 186.

143. See discussion in Pritchett (1987), 185; Dowden (1989), 33, 34, 210 n. 44. For the nocturnal ritual at Letrinoi: Dowden, op. cit., 103-4.

144. A circular dance around an altar should be identified on a red-figure fragment of a pyxis lid from the sanctuary at Brauron and is dated to the third quarter of the fifth century. Four young women (dressed in long khiton and himation) with raised short torches in each hand appear to be performing a dance to the music of a flute-player who is seated among them. Two different dance movements, each performed by a pair of females, may be distinguished: the first is executed with the torso in frontal view, the head in profile and the arms extended on either side of the body, holding (or trying to hold) the torches almost upright. The other pair of figures are in profile view and hold the torches at different levels, the left raised and the right lowered. The age of the females may possibly be determined partly by their long dress, indicative of the older *arktoi*, and partly by their similarity to older age-groups on the krateriskoi. Although the presence of torches is not necessarily indicative of night-time activity, the torch-lit dances probably reflect the literary evidence for pannukhides in Artemis' cult. For discussion of the vase: Kahil (1963), 24, A50, pl. 13.6. For the possible age-group of the girls depicted (wearing long khitons): Sourvinou-Inwood (1988), 123, 119. For dances in the cult of Artemis: Kahil (1965), 27, 28 n. 51, 31 n. 82; Kahil (1963), 28; Palaiokrassa (1991), 77-8 n. 201; Borgeaud (1988), 156. Evidence for pannukhides in honour of Artemis is found in: Page (1951), 80 n. 3; Dowden (1989), 33, 103; Pritchett (1987), 184-5. See also Chapter III.3.

145. See Carter (1988), esp. 91; Page (1951), esp. 71, 80.

146. Themelis (1994). According to Themelis, the preceding rituals would have included the following order: a mystic ceremony inside the cella of the goddess where the revelation of the *xoanon* would have been enacted, a procession carrying the xoanon, an exposition of the xoanon in the open next to an altar, dramatic performances, athletic contests ending with torch-races at night and setting light to the altar for the sacrifice and the subsequent banquet.

147. For the features of feasts in honour of Kybele: Robertson (1996), esp. 281; Pachis (1996), 218-19, 225 n. 99. For the cult of Kybele in general: Sfameni-Gasparro (1996).

148. For discussion: Robertson (1996), 263-7.

149. For the Euripidean fragment, see Austin (1968).

150. *IG* XII 5, 444; see also Borgeaud (1988), 170.

151. For discussion: Borgeaud (1988), 170, 259 n. 77.

152. For discussion: Bravo (1997), 15-24; Borgeaud (1988), 164-8.

153. Skias (1918), esp. 11, 13, 14.

154. For discussion: Borgeaud (1988), 164.

155. Fr. 88B1 DK. Also mentioned in Ath. *Deipnosophistai* xiii, 600D-E. For discussion: Bravo (1997), 25-9.

156. *PMG* 346/1, fr. 11+3+6, 13-22 and *PMG* 346/1, fr. 11+3+6, 1-12. For discussion: Bravo (1997), 29-42.

157. Pfeiffer (1949), fr. 227. For discussion: Bravo (1997), 101-17.

158. See Bravo (1997), 43-99.

159. For example: *IG* II^2 974, ll. 11-13; *IG* II^2 975, l. 8; *IG* II^2 1033, l. 11. For discussion: Clinton (1994), esp. 27-8.

Catalogues

CATALOGUE 1: Torch-races

Panathenaia

Vases

1.1 Cambridge Mass., Harvard University, Fogg Art Museum 1960.344. ARV^2 1041.10; *Para* 443; *Add.*^{2} 319. Kefalidou (1996), 218 no. 1 pl. 10. Manner of the Peleus Painter. *c.* 430-420

1.2 New York, Metropolitan Museum 56.171.49. ARV^2 1347.3. Kefalidou (1996), 224 no. 18 pl. 59-60. van Straten (1995), 209 V91, fig. 54. The Kekrops Painter. *c.* 425-400

1.3 Athens, Agora P 10542. ARV^2 1190 ad 32. Kefalidou (1996), 224 no. 17 pl. 57-8. van Straten (1995), 204 V60. The Pothos Painter. *c.* 420

1.4 World Heritage Museum, University of Illinois, Urbana-Champaign 77.1.1684. Neils (1992), 96, no. (fig.) 49, 177. The Painter of Louvre G 539. *c.* 420-400

1.5 Leipzig, Karl-Marx Universität, Antikenmuseum T 958. Kefalidou (1996), 224-5 no. 19. van Straten (1995), 208 V86. *c.* 400-375

1.6 Vienna, Kunsthistorisches Museum 1050 (706). *CVA* iii, 35 pl. 136; van Straten (1995), 210-11. Kefalidou (1996), 225 no. 20. The Black-Thyrsus Painter. *c.* 400-350

1.7 Munich, Staatliche Antikensammlungen. *ABV* 661.1. The Bulas Group. Early fourth century

1.8 Athens, National Museum 12397. *ABV* 661.2. The Bulas Group. Early fourth century

1.9 New York, Metropolitan Museum 41.162.53. *ABV* 661.3. The Bulas Group. Early fourth century

1.10 Paris, Louvre MNB 3224. *ABV* 661.7. The Bulas Group. Early fourth century

1.11 Cracow, Czartoryski Museum 1263. *ABV* 661.9. The Bulas Group. Early fourth century

1.12 Kassel, Staatliche Kunstsammlungen T 445. *ABV* 661.13; *Add.*^{2} 147. The Bulas Group. Early fourth century

1.13 St Petersburg, Hermitage 2215. *ABV* 661.14; *Add.*^{2} 147. Vankove (1993), 60.3. The Bulas Group. Early fourth century **Pl. 3**

1.14 London, British Museum 1894.7-18.4. *ABV* 662.23; *Add.*^{2} 147. The Bulas Group. Early fourth century

1.15 Once Deepdene. *ABV* 662.26. The Bulas Group. Early fourth century

1.16 Bonn, Akademisches Kunstmuseum. *ABV* 662.29b. The Bulas Group. Early fourth century

1.17 Würzburg, Martin von Wagner Museum L 492. ARV^2 1512.18; *Para* 499;

Add.[2] 384; Sinn (1996), 80-1, no. 26, fig. 56. The Jena Workshop. Early fourth century **Pl. 4**

1.18 Athens, National Museum 14902. Kefalidou (1996), 223 no. 14 pl. 61. *c.* 380-370

1.19 St Petersburg, Hermitage St 2070. van Straten (1995), 210 V96. Fourth century

Panathenaia?

Vases

1.20 Athens, National Museum 14902. Kefalidou (1996), 223 no. 14 pl. 61. *c.* 380-370

Hephaisteia

Vases

1.21 Ferrara, Museo Archeologico Nazionale di Spina 3033 (T 127 VT). *ARV*[2] 1171.1; *Para* 459; *Add.*[2] 338. Alfieri (1979) 81-2 figs. 182-5. Kefalidou (1996), 218 no. 2. Polion. *c.* 420

Prometheia?

Vases

1.22 London, British Museum 98.7-16.6. *ARV*[2] 1333.1; *Para* 480; *Add.*[2] 365. Kefalidou (1996), 219 no. 4 pl. 56. The Nikias Painter. *c.* 410

Bendideia

Sculpture

1.23 London, British Museum inv. no. 2155 (1895.10-28.1). *LIMC* III, Bendis 96 no. 3 (ill). Early fourth century

In Honour of Pan

Vases

1.24 Athens, National Museum 356 (CC1107). *ABV* 560.523; *Add*[2] 136. Simon (1976), 4.1. Manner of the Haimon Painter. *c.* 475

Nemesia at Rhamnous

Sculpture

1.25 Rhamnous Archaeological Museum 531 (ex Athens National Museum R 332). Palagia & Lewis (1989), 340 pl. 48c. *c.* 330

1.26 London, British Museum 1953.5-30.1 & Rhamnous Archaeological Museum 530. Palagia & Lewis (1989), 340 pl. 49. *c.* 330

In Honour of Dionysos

Vases

1.27 Bologna, Museo Civico Archeologico VF 354(208). *ARV*[2] 688.255(208); van Hoorn (1951), no. 360. The Bowdoin Painter. *c.* 470

1.28 Berlin, Staatliche Museen 1962.33. *ARV*² 1660.71bis; *Para* 394; *Add.*² 265. *LIMC* III, Dionysos 493 no. 831, pl. 399. The Altamura Painter. *c.* 460 **Pl. 2**

1.29 Rome, Villa Giulia. *ARV*² 1166.105. van Hoorn (1951), fig. 120. The Painter of Munich 2335. *c.* 430

1.30 Amsterdam, Allard Pierson Museum, coll. Roussopoulos and Scheurleer, Pierson. Gids no. 1422. van Hoorn (1951), pl. 121, no. 1. *c.* 430

1.31 Athens, Agora P 5223bis. van Hoorn (1951), no. 172 bis.

1.32 Korinth C-31-329. Herbert (1986), 30 fig. 1. Late fifth century

1.33 Korinth C-37-254. Herbert (1986), 30 fig. 2. Late fifth century

1.34 Korinth C-37-250. Herbert (1986), 30 fig. 3. Late fifth century

1.35 Athens, National Museum 1405. Herbert (1986), 31 figs. 4-5. The Student Sketch Painter. Late fifth century

1.36 Athens, Agora P 10675. van Hoorn (1951), pl. 118, no. 197.

1.37 Athens, Agora P 10949. van Hoorn (1951), pl. 122, no. 204.

1.38 London, British Museum E 111. *ARV*² 1514.44. The Jena Workshop. Early fourth century

1.39 Once Munich market (Helbig), Dr A. Preyss Collection, Athenian Agora. Kefalidou (1996), 223 no. 16; van Hoorn (1951), pl. 119, no. 719. The Pourtalès Painter or his Circle. *c.* 370-360

Other

Vases

1.40 Kition, Inv. 1509 (Area II, 1969). Karageorgis et al. (1981), 52-3 pl. 39.13. 450-400 Near the Haimon Group

1.41 Athens, National Museum. Metzger (1951), 351 no. 7 pl. xlv.3. *c.* 425

1.42 London, British Museum E 389. *ARV*² 1214.5(2). The Kraipale Painter

1.43 Florence, Museo Archeologico Etrusco. *ARV*² 1272.6. Manner of the Codrus Painter

1.44 Cologne, University. *ARV*² 1272.8. Manner of the Codrus Painter. *c.* 430-420

1.45 San Simeon. *ARV*² 1273.10; Cat. Soth., July 1929, pl. 8.44. Manner of the Codrus Painter

1.46 Istanbul, Archaeological Museum. *ARV*² 1333.2. Blegen et al. (1958), 278 VIII.168, pl. 303.24. The Nikias Painter. *c.* 410

1.47 Florence, Museo Nazionale PD 509. *ARV*² 1345.10. Kefalidou (1996), 220 no. 5 pl. 56. The Suessula Painter. *c.* 410-400

1.48 Aachen, Sürmondt-Ludwig Collection. *ARV*² 1345. 11; *Add.*² 368. Kefalidou (1996), 220 no. 6. The Suessula Painter. *c.* 410-400 **Fig. 10**

1.49 Vienna, Kunsthistorisches Museum 3734. *CVA* iii, 36 pl. 138. 1-2. *c.* 400

1.50 Ferrara, Museo Archeologico Nazionale di Spina T 1045. *ARV*² 1352.4. The Brown Egg Painter

1.51 Ferrara, Museo Archeologico Nazionale di Spina 2492 (T 782). *ARV*² 1356.1-2; *Add.*² 369. Alfieri (1979), 105 fig. 261.The Painter of Ferrara T 782

1.52 Amphipolis. Mandala (1990), 276 fig. 3. Late fifth century

1.53 Dion, Archaeological Museum inv. 2138. Tiverios (1990), 119-20 pl. 29.1. Probably the Suessula Painter. Late fifth century

1.54 Vienna, Kunsthistorisches Museum IV 935. *ARV*² 1441; *Add.*² 377. Near the Budapest Group. *c.* 400-375

1.55 St Petersburg, Hermitage St 2010. Kefalidou (1996), 220-1 no. 7. Kertsch. *c.* 400-390

1.56 Ferrara, Museo Archeologico Nazionale di Spina inv. T 2 (3038). *ARV*²

1517.1; *Para* 500; *Add.*² 384. Kefalidou (1996), 222 no. 12; Schiller Sammlung (1996), 56 fig. 48. Manner of the Jena Painter. *c.* 390-380

1.57 Braunschweig, Dr R. Loebbecke Collection. *CVA* Braunschweig, pl. 27. 6-7 (173). Kefalidou (1996), 222 no. 13. *c.* 390-380

1.58 Paris, Louvre N 3357. Metzger (1951), 352 no. 12. Early fourth century

1.59 Once Paris market, once Waterkyn and Hope Collection. *ARV*² 1439.2. Kefalidou (1996), 221 no. 10. The Hare Hunt Painter. *c.* 390-380

1.60 Once S. Agata de Goti, Collection of Professor Dom. Mustil. *ARV*² 1419.1. Kefalidou (1996), 221 no. 8. The Erbach Painter. Early fourth century

1.61 Once Hamilton Collection. Kefalidou (1996), 221 no. 9. Early fourth century

1.62 Rome, Musei Vaticani inv. 17934. Schiller Sammlung (1996), 58 fig. 50

1.63 Jena SAK Inv. 0485. *ARV*² 1513.27. Schiller Sammlung (1996), 82 pl. 2.2. The Jena Painter. Early fourth century

1.64 Mannheim, Reiss-Museum Cg 123. *ARV*² 1435; *Add.*² 377. Metzger (1951), 354 pl. 46.3. The Painter of Athens 12255. Early fourth century **Pl. 5**

1.65 Rome, Museo Gregoriano Etrusco Vaticano 35034. *ARV*² 1447.4. 1694. Kefalidou (1996), 222 no. 11. The Reverse Group of Ferrara T 463. *c.* 380-370

1.66 Paris, Louvre CA 1850. Kefalidou (1996), 223 no. 15. Unpublished. *c.* 370

1.67 Athens, National Museum inv. 20048. Valavanis (1991), 20-4 X1 pl. 32, 34. *c.* 363-362

1.68 Eleusis, Archaeological Museum inv. 2703. Valavanis (1991), 223 pl. 63a. *c.* 363-362

1.69 Eleusis, Archaeological Museum. Valavanis (1991), 226 pl. 68, 69. *c.* 363-362

1.70 Eretria, Archaeological Museum. Valavanis (1991), 227 (unpublished). *c.* 363-362

1.71 Eretria, Archaeological Museum. Valavanis (1991), 227-228 (unpublished). *c.* 363-362

Sculpture

1.72 New York, Metropolitan Museum 24.97.92. Mitropoulou (1977), 45 no. 66 fig. 104. Late fifth century

1.73 Delos, Archaeological Museum MA 3193. Mitropoulou (1977), 64 no. 127 fig. 184. Late fifth century

1.74 Once Kavala, M. Boulgarides Collection. Pouilloux (1948), 847 fig. 1. Late fourth – early third century

CATALOGUE 2: Use of fire in childbirth and in nursing

Vases

2.1 Paris, Cabinet des Médailles 219. *ABV* 509; *Add.*² 127. Boardman (1974), pl. 272. Schefold (1981), 29 fig. 20. The Diosphos Painter. *c.* 500 **Pl. 7**

2.2 Warsaw, National Museum 142465. *ARV*² 1019.82; *Para* 441; *Add.*² 315. Daraki (1985), 37 fig. 6. The Phiale Painter. *c.* 440

2.3 Once Paris, Hotel Lambert 42. *LIMC* III, Dionysos 482 no. 707. Frickenhaus (1912b), 39 no. (fig.) 28. *c.* 440

2.4 Once Roman market (Bassagio). Beaumont (1992), 469. The Phiale Painter or his circle. *c.* 440

2.5 Oxford, Ashmolean Museum 1956.355. *LIMC* IV, Demeter 876 no. 389, pl. 590. *c.* 380

2.6 St Petersburg, Hermitage St. 1792. *ARV*² 1476.1; *Para* 496; *Add.*² 381;

LIMC IV, Demeter 877-8 no. 404. Bianchi (1976), 17 pl. 2. The Eleusinian Painter. *c.* 340-330

2.7 Tübingen, University Museum S/10 1666 (E 183). *ARV²* 1477.7; *Para* 496; *Add.²* 381. *CVA* IV, pls. 50.1, 51.1-6. The Painter of Athens 1472. *c.* 340

2.8 Once Sandford-Graham Collection. *LIMC* IV, Demeter 878 no. 409; Clinton (1992), 133 no. 4, fig. 25. Bianchi (1976), 17 pl. 4. *c.* 340-330

Sculpture

2.9 Dresden Museum inv. Z.V.1050. Hadzisteliou-Price (1971), 59 no. II.Ia, pl. IV.8. First quarter of fourth century **Pl. 6**

2.10 Delphi, Archaeological Museum 1101, 3815, 8874. van Straten (1995), 294 R 77. Zagdoun (1977), figs. 8-9. Fourth century

2.11 Delos, Archaeological Museum A 3157. Pingiatoglou (1981), 115, pl. 16.1. End of fourth century

2.12 Delos, Archaeological Museum A 3158. Pingiatoglou (1981), 115, pl. 16.2. End of fourth century

2.13 Volos, Archaeological Museum 274. Pingiatoglou (1981), 109-10. Late fourth – early third century

2.14 Delos, Archaeological Museum A 3153. van Straten (1995), 294 R 78, fig. 89. Fourth or third century

2.15 Lamia, Archaeological Museum AE 1041. van Straten (1995), 293 R 75bis, fig. 88. *c.* 300 **Fig. 11**

CATALOGUE 3: Torches in nuptial rites

Pre-nuptial images

Vases

3.1 Dunedin (N.Z.), Otago Museum F 54.48. *ARV²* 264.63. Anderson (1955), no. 84 pl. XII. The Syriskos Group. *c.* 480-470

3.2 New York, Metropolitan Museum 41.162.117. *ARV²* 642.104; *Add.²* 274. Papoutsaki-Serbeti (1983), 205 no. 143 pl. 38. The Providence Painter. *c.* 470

3.3 Boston, Museum of Fine Arts 33.56. *ARV²* 600.12; *Para* 395; *Add.²* 266. The Niobid Painter. *c.* 460

3.4 Basle, Market Formerly. *ARV²* 720.23. Manner of the Aischines Painter

3.5 Syracuse, Museo Archeologico Nazionale 21186. *ARV²* 993.80. *Add.²* 312. *LIMC* II, Artemis 676 no. 721a, pl. 504. The Achilles Painter. *c.* 450 **Pl. 9**

3.6 Mainz, University 116. *ARV²* 1224.2; *Add.²* 350. *CVA* II, pl. 26.3-5. Oakley & Sinos (1993), 14 figs. 6-8. The Oppenheimer Group. *c.* 450 **Pl. 8a-b**

3.7 Münster, University Museum 586. Stähler (1980), no. (fig.) 20.

3.8 Cambridge, Fitzwilliam Museum 1.02. *Para* 465.2. *CVA* I, 35 pl. 34.2. The Class of Cambridge 1.02. Late fifth century

Weddings

Vases

3.9 London, British Museum B 197. *ABV* 296.1; *Para* 128; *Add.²* 77. Oakley & Sinos (1993), 86 fig. 66. The Painter of Berlin 1686. *c.* 550

3.10 New York, Metropolitan Museum 56.11.1. *Para* 66; *Add.²* 45. Oakley & Sinos (1993), 29-30, figs. 68-70. The Amasis Painter. *c.* 540

3.11 Boston, Museum of Fine Arts 68.46. *LIMC* II, Artemis 718 no. 1245, pl. 548. *CVA* Boston I, pl. 13 (635). Circle of the Lysippides Painter. *c.* 530 **Pl. 11**

3.12 Toronto, Royal Ontario Museum of Archaeology C 317. *LIMC* II, Artemis 718 no. 1248. *CVA* Toronto I, pl. 25.4; Robinson & Harcum (1930), pl. 32. *c.* 530-525

3.13 Athens, National Museum 19363. *Para* 122; *LIMC* II, Artemis 718 no. 1252. Schauenburg (1964), 69 pl. 11.3; 12.1-2. Manner of the Antimenes Painter. *c.* 525-500

3.14 Basle, Antikenmuseum, Ludwig Collection. *ABV* 287.13; *Para* 125; *Add.*² 75. *LIMC* II, Artemis 718 no. 1249, pl. 548. The Antimenes Painter: IX. The Eye-siren Group. *c.* 520-510

3.15 Munich, Staatliche Antikensammlungen J 692. *LIMC* II, Artemis 718 no. 1253, pl. 549. *CVA* VIII, pl. 380.3, 384.1. The Painter of Tarquinia RC 6847. *c.* 520-510

3.16 Los Angeles, private collection. *Para* 149.28bis; *LIMC* II, Artemis 718 no. 1250. Sotheby 1965, pl. 37 no. 93. The Rycroft Painter. *c.* 510

3.17 Munich, Staatliche Antikensammlungen 1406 (J 592). *ABV* 368.108; *Para* 162. 171.1; *Add.*² 98. *CVA* I, pl. 36.2, 38.1-3. Avagianou (1991), no. (fig.) 27. The Leagros Group. *c.* 510

3.18 Munich, Staatliche Antikensammlungen 1413. *ABV* 366.85; *Add.*² 97. *LIMC* II, Artemis 718 no. 1251, pl. 549. The Leagros Group. *c.* 510-500

3.19 Rome, Villa Giulia; ex Castellani Collection 22. Mingazzini (1971), 218 pl. 52.3 no. 450. Avagianou (1991), 91 no. 28. *c.* 510-500

3.20 London, British Museum B 298. *LIMC* II, Artemis 718 no. 1254. Oakley & Sinos (1993), fig. 67. *c.* 500

3.21 Warsaw, National Museum 142319. *LIMC* II, Artemis 721 no. 1284. Oakley & Sinos (1993), 106-8 figs. 100-4. *c.* 500

3.22 New York, Levy Collection. Oakley & Sinos (1993), 36 n.104 figs. 108-10. The Copenhagen Painter. *c.* 470

3.23 Reading, Public Museum 32-772-1. Neils (1997), 233 figs. 3-4. The Mykonos Painter. *c.* 470

3.24 Warsaw, National Museum 142290. *ARV*² 571.76; *Para* 390. Oakley & Sinos (1993), 15 figs. 10-13. The Leningrad Painter. *c.* 470 **Fig. 12** and **Pl. 10**

3.25 Houston, Museum of Fine Arts, Annette Finnigan Collection inv. 37.10. *ARV*² 554.79. Oakley (1995), 161-3 no. (pl.) 22. The Pan Painter. *c.* 470

3.26 London, British Museum D 11. *ARV*² 899.146; *Add.*² 303. Oakley & Sinos (1993), 34-5 figs. 96-8. The Splanchnopt Painter. *c.* 470-460 **Pl. 13**

3.27 Sarajevo, National Museum 425. *CVA* I, 38 pl. 32.1. Hermonax. *c.* 470-460

3.28 Copenhagen, National Museum 9080. *ARV*² 841.75; *Para* 423; *Add.*² 296. Oakley & Sinos (1993), 102-3 fig. 92-5. The Sabouroff Painter. *c.* 460

3.29 Berlin, Staatliche Museen F 2530. *ARV*² 831.20. 1702; *Add.*² 295. *LIMC* VI, Hekate 993 no. 45, pl. 657. The Amphitrite Painter. *c.* 460-450 **Pl. 12**

3.30 Athens, once Fetiche Djami NA 1957-Aa757 and 757a. *ARV*² 632.1. *LIMC* II, Artemis 735 no. 1440. The Methyse Painter. *c.* 450

3.31 Bonn, University Museum 994. Oakley & Sinos (1993), 31 fig. 79. *c.* 450-400

3.32 Cambridge, Fitzwilliam Museum 13/23. *CVA* I, pl. 36.3a-d. The Painter of the Naples Centauromachy. *c.* 440

3.33 Munich, Staatliche Antikensammlungen inv. NI 9493. Oakley (1995), 332-4 no. (pl.) 102. The Naples Painter. *c.* 440-430

3.34 Berlin, Staatliche Museen inv. F 2372. Oakley & Sinos (1993), 30-1 n. 52 figs. 72-3; Oakley (1995), 171-2 no. (pl.) 27. *c.* 430

3.35 Ferrara, Museo Archeologico Nazionale di Spina inv. 2893 (VT T 617). *ARV*² 1038.1.1679; *Para* 443; *Add.*² 319. Alfieri (1979), 64 fig. 148. Oakley (1995), 349-51 no. (pl.) 110. The Peleus Painter. *c.* 430

3.36 Toronto, Royal Ontario Museum 929.22.3. *ARV*² 1031.51; *Add.*² 317. Oakley & Sinos (1993), 32 figs. 82-4. Polygnotos *c.* 430

3.37 Karlsruhe, Badisches Landesmuseum 69/78, *ARV*² 1102.2; *Para* 451; *Add.*² 329. Oakley & Sinos (1993), 60-1 figs. 16-19. Near the Naples Painter. *c.* 430-420

3.38 London, British Museum 1920.12-21.1. *ARV*² 1277.23.1282 and 1686; *Add.*² 357. Oakley & Sinos (1993), 31 figs. 75-7. The Marlay Painter. *c.* 430

3.39 Athens, National Museum inv. 1453. *ARV*² 1127.18; *Para* 453; *Add.*² 332. Oakley & Sinos (1993), 58-9 figs. 14-15. The Washing Painter. *c.* 430-420

3.40 Baltimore, Robinson Collection. *CVA* II, pl. 49.1a-d. The Washing Painter. *c.* 430-420

3.41 New York, Metropolitan Museum 16.73. *ARV*² 1126.6; *Add.*² 332. Oakley & Sinos (1993), 20 fig. 37. The Washing Painter. *c.* 430

3.42 Vienna, Kunsthistorisches Museum inv. 2027. *ARV*² 1127.11; *Add.*² 332. The Washing Painter. *c.* 430

3.43 Athens, National Museum 1174. *ARV*² 1127.15; *Para* 453. Oakley & Sinos (1993), 32-3 fig. 85. The Washing Painter. *c.* 430

3.44 Boston, Museum of Fine Arts, Francis Bartlett Collection 03.802. Oakley (1995), 165-8; Oakley & Sinos (1993), 9 n.4 fig. 1, 105-7. *c.* 425

3.45 Houston, Museum of Fine Arts, Annette Finnigan Collection inv. 37.12. *ARV*² 1127.13; *Add.*² 332. Oakley (1995), 163-5 no. (pl.) 23. The Washing Painter. *c.* 425-420

3.46 Athens, National Museum 1388. *ARV*² 1317.1; *Para* 478; *Add.*² 363. Oakley & Sinos (1993), 33 figs. 87-9. The Painter of the Athens Wedding. *c.* 410

3.47 Brussels, Musées Royaux d'Art et d'Histoire A 3049. *CVA* III, 10 pl. 17.1b. Late fifth century

3.48 Athens, National Museum 1630. Oakley & Sinos (1993), 32 n.65 figs. 80-1. *c.* 370-360

Post-nuptial images

Vases

3.49 Copenhagen, National Museum 9165. *Para* 382 no. 2. *CVA* VIII, pl. 343. 3a-b, 344. The Mykonos Painter. *c.* 470-460

3.50 Brussels, Musées Royaux d'Art et d'Histoire A 1380. *ARV*² 841.74. *CVA* III, pl. 12.9a-c, 14.2. The Sabouroff Painter. *c.* 460

3.51 Geneva, Musée d'Art et d'Histoire H 239. *CVA* I, pl. 17.5-6, 19.1. The Painter of London E 489. *c.* 450

3.52 Tübingen, inv. 5646. *CVA* IV, 24-25 pl. 6.6. The Washing Painter. *c.* 420

3.53 Oxford, Ashmolean Museum 1927.4067. *ARV*² 1179. Oakley & Sinos (1993), 39 fig. 120. Near the Painter of Athens 1454. *c.* 420

3.54 Buffalo, Museum of Science C 23262. Oakley & Sinos (1993), 39 fig. 122. *c.* 420

3.55 Berlin, Staatliche Museen inv. 3373. Oakley & Sinos (1993), 38 figs. 115-19. *c.* 360-350

CATALOGUE 4: Light in the myth and ritual of the Eleusinian Mysteries

Vases

4.1 Athens, Akropolis Museum 1222. *LIMC* VI, Hekate 990 no. 10. Sixth century

4.2 Eleusis, Archaeological Museum 1215. Bianchi (1976), 25 pl. 37. Sixth century **Fig. 14**

4.3 Athens, Akropolis Museum 732. *ARV*^{2} 205.119. *Add.*^{2} 193. Kurtz (1983), 90 no. 45 pl. 52a. The Berlin Painter. *c.* 490

4.4 Bologna, Museo Civico Archeologico P 236. *ARV*^{2} 532.44. *Add.*^{2} 254. Berard (1974), 17 fig. 59. The Alkimachos Painter. *c.* 470 **Pl. 15**

4.5 Brussels, Musées Royaux A 10. *ARV*^{2} 661.86; *Para* 403; *Add.*^{2} 277; *LIMC* IV, Demeter 874 no. 357. Bianchi (1976), 24 pl. 34. The Yale Lekythos Painter. *c.* 460 **Pl. 21**

4.6 Würzburg, Martin von Wagner Museum L 535 (H 4307). *ARV*^{2} 1112.3, 1684, 1703; *Add.*^{2} 330. *CVA* II, pls. 23.1-5, 24.1-3. The Painter of Tarquinia 707. 460-450 **Pl. 25**

4.7 Munich, Staatliche Antikensammlungen 2685 (J 336). *ARV*^{2} 837.9; *Add.*^{2} 295; *LIMC* IV, Demeter 874 no. 358, pl. 587. The Sabouroff Painter. *c.* 450

4.8 Berlin, private collection. *LIMC* IV, Demeter 872 no. 329. Peschlow-Bindokat (1972), 95 fig. 32. *c.* 450

4.9 London, Leventis Collection. Clinton (1992), 135 no. 13, figs. 38-41. The Sabouroff Painter. *c.* 450-425

4.10 Ferrara, Museo Archeologico Nazionale di Spina T 579. *ARV*^{2} 612.1; *Para* 397; *Add.*^{2} 268. Alfieri (1979), 38-40 figs. 87-91. The Painter of Bologna 279. *c.* 450-440

4.11 New York, Metropolitan Museum 28.57.23. *ARV*^{2} 1012.1; *Para* 440; *Add.*^{2} 314. Peschlow-Bindokat (1972), 95 pl. 31. The Persephone Painter. *c.* 440 **Pl. 14**

4.12 Florence, Museo Archeologico 75748. *ARV*^{2} 1028.8; *Add.*^{2} 317; *LIMC* IV, Demeter 874 no. 361. Clinton (1992), fig. 36. Polygnotos. *c.* 450-425 **Pl. 19**

4.13 Stanford University 70.12. *LIMC* IV, Demeter 874 no. 364. Clinton (1992), figs. 11-14. The Kleophon Painter. 420-400

4.14 Eleusis, Archaeological Museum 636. *ARV*^{2} 1052.23; *Add.*^{2} 321. Bianchi (1976), 25 pl. 36. Group of Polygnotos. *c.* 440

4.15 Eleusis, Archaeological Museum 1244. *ARV*^{2} 647.21; *Add.*^{2} 275. Bianchi (1976), fig. 10; Kanta (1979) 137 fig. 73. Schefold (1981), 260 fig. 372. The Oionokles Painter. *c.* 440

4.16 Naples, Museo Archeologico Nazionale H 2642. *ARV*^{2} 1261.58. *LIMC* IV, Demeter 864 no. 226 pl. 577. The Calliope Painter. 440-420

4.17 Athens, National Museum H 19605 (1414). Berard (1974), 101 pl. 9.32. Late fifth century **Pl. 16**

4.18 Athens, National Museum 1341. *ARV*^{2} 1517.10; *Add.*^{2} 384. *LIMC* IV, Demeter 876 no. 388, pl. 587. The Diomed Painter. Late fifth century

4.19 Berlin, Staatliche Museen 2634. *ARV*^{2} 1187.33; *Add.*^{2} 341. Real (1973), pl. 10. The Kadmos Painter. Late fifth century **Fig. 13**

4.20 Boston, Museum of Fine Arts 03.842. *ARV*^{2} 1315.2(a); *Para* 477; *Add.*^{2} 362. *LIMC* IV, Demeter 874 no. 370. Clinton (1992), fig. 31. Painter of Carlsruhe Paris. Late fifth century

4.21 Kos, Archaeological Museum. *LIMC* IV, Demeter 876 no. 390, pl. 590. Schwarz (1987), 52 V125 pl. 28. *c.* 400-350

4.22 Sofia, Archaeological Museum. Clinton (1992), figs. 26-8. *c.* 400-350

4.23 Oxford, Ashmolean Museum 1956-355. *LIMC* IV, Demeter 876 no. 389, pl. 590. Bianchi (1976), 18 pl. 8. Early fourth century

4.24 Paris, Cabinet des Médailles 451. *LIMC* IV, Demeter 867 no. 262, pl. 578. Early fourth century

4.25 Athens, National Museum 11036. *LIMC* IV, Demeter 876 no. 392, pl. 591. Clinton (1992), fig. 136, 67-8, 73-5, 136. Bianchi (1976), 24-5 pl. 35. *c.* 370 **Pl. 17**

4.26 Tübingen, University Museum S/10 1610. *CVA* IV, pl. 39.1-3. c. 360

4.27 Istanbul, Archaeological Museum. *LIMC* IV, Demeter 877 no. 403. Bianchi (1976), 17 pl. 3. *c.* 360-350

4.28 Eleusis, Archaeological Museum 2666. *LIMC* IV, Demeter 867 no. 264, pl. 579. *c.* 360-350

4.29 Kiel, Dr Konrad Schauenburg B 268. *CVA* I, pl. 38.1-2. *c.* 360-350

4.30 Athens, National Museum 17297. *LIMC* IV, Demeter 877 no. 398, pl. 592. *c.* 350

4.31 Tübingen, University Museum S/10 1666 (E 183). *Para* 496; *Add.*[2] 381; *LIMC* IV, Demeter 878 no. 407. *CVA* IV, pl. 50.1, 51.1-6. The Painter of Athens 1472. *c.* 350

4.32 London, British Museum F 68. *Para* 492; *Add.*[2] 378. Bianchi (1976), 24 pl. 33. The Pourtalès Painter. *c.* 350 **Fig. 15**

4.33 Once Sandford-Graham Collection. *LIMC* IV, Demeter 878 no. 409; Clinton (1992), 133 no. 4, fig. 25. Bianchi (1976), 17 pl. 4. *c.* 340-330

4.34 St Petersburg, Hermitage St.1792. *ARV*[2] 1476.1; *Para* 496; *Add.*[2] 381; *LIMC* IV, Demeter 877-8 no. 404. Bianchi (1976), 16 pl. 1. The Eleusinian Painter. *c.* 340-330 **Fig. 18** and **Pl. 18**

4.35 Bern, Abbeg-Stiftung. *LIMC* IV, Demeter 878 no. 408, pl. 593. Clinton (1992), 133 no. 7 figs. 22-3. *c.* 330

4.36 Athens, National Museum 1443. *LIMC* IV, Demeter 877 no. 396, pl. 591. Bianchi (1976), 18 pl. 7. *c.* 330 **Pl. 20**

4.37 St Petersburg, Hermitage St. 525 (B 1657). Clinton (1992), 134 no. 5 figs. 17-19. Bianchi (1976), 17-18 pls. 5.1-5.3. *c.* 330-320 **Fig. 19**

4.38 Lyon, Musée des Beaux Arts 689. Clinton (1992), 138 no. 4, figs. 58-9. Bianchi (1976), 18 pl. 6. The Tyszkiewicz Painter. *c.* 330-320

Sculpture

4.39 Eleusis, Archaeological Museum 5235. *LIMC* VI, Hekate 991 no. 16, pl. 654. *c.* 485-480

4.40 Eleusis, Archaeological Museum 5085. *LIMC* IV, Demeter 867 no. 269, pl. 579. *c.* 460

4.41 Reggio, Calabria, National Museum. *LIMC* IV, Demeter 882 no. (fig.) 458. *LIMC* VI, Hekate 992 no. 26. *c.* 475

4.42 London, British Museum. Parthenon frieze. *LIMC* IV, Demeter 879 no. 423, pl. 595. *c.* 447-432

4.43 Eleusis, Archaeological Museum 5093. Clinton (1992), 140 no. 2 pl. 60. Bianchi (1976), 23, no. 30, fig. 30. *c.* 421-420

4.44 Catania, Museo Communale. Peschlow-Bindokat (1972), 150, no. 5, pl. 35. *c.* 425-400

4.45 Munich Glyptothek 198. *LIMC* IV, Demeter 865 no. 232, pl. 577. Peschlow-Bindokat (1972), 151, fig. 37. Late fifth century

4.46 St Petersburg, Hermitage Pan. 160. *LIMC* IV, Demeter 867 no. 270, pl. 579. Peschlow-Bindokat (1972), 151, no. 12, pl. 39. Late fifth century

4.47 Myrina, Archaeological Museum. *LIMC* IV, Demeter 868 no. 283. *c.* 350

4.48 Athens, British School at Athens S 10. *LIMC* IV, Demeter 868 no. 274. Waywell (1970), 272 pl. 73b. *c.* 350

4.49 Eleusis, Archaeological Museum 5114. *LIMC* IV, Demeter 868 no. 282, pl. 580. *c.* 350

4.50 Eleusis, Archaeological Museum. *LIMC* IV, Demeter 868 no. 279, pl. 580. *c.* 350-300

4.51 Paris, Louvre 752. *LIMC* IV, Demeter 865 no. 234, pl. 578. van Straten (1995), 291 R 67, fig. 81. *c.* 350-300

4.52 Kyrene, Archaeological Museum 74.931. *LIMC* IV, Demeter 868 no. 284. White (1976), 175 pl. 28, fig. 37. *c.* 350-300

4.53 Eleusis, Archaeological Museum 5068. *LIMC* IV, Demeter 878 no. 411. Bianchi (1976), 20 fig. 9. *c.* 350-300

4.54 Athens, National Museum 2376. *LIMC* IV, Demeter 868 no. 278. Svoronos (1908-1937), 639 pl. 145. *c.* 350-300

4.55 Eleusis, Archaeological Museum. Unpublished. Peschlow-Bindokat (1972), 153, pl. 49. Fourth century

CATALOGUE 5: Pollution-repelling fire

Vases

5.1 Brussels, Musées Royaux A 10. *ARV²* 661.86; *Para* 403; *Add.²* 277; *LIMC* IV, Demeter 874 no. 357. Bianchi (1976), 24 pl. 34. The Yale Lekythos Painter. *c.* 460 **Pl. 21**

5.2 Tübingen, University Museum S/10 1666 (E 183). *Para* 496; *Add.²* 381; *LIMC* IV, Demeter 878 no. 407. *CVA* IV, pl. 50.1, 51.1-6. The Painter of Athens 1472. *c.* 350

CATALOGUE 6: Representations of light-bearing gods

Vases

6.1 Paris, Louvre L 32 (MNC 650). *ARV²* 301.6; *Para* 356; *Add.²* 212. *LIMC* II, Artemis 65 no. 708, pl. 502. Side Palmette Lekythoi – Close to the Diosphos Painter. *c.* 500

6.2 St Petersburg, Hermitage B 3368. *ARV²* 556.111; *Add.²* 259. *LIMC* II, Artemis 658 no. 454, pl. 482. The Pan Painter. *c.* 480 **Pl. 29**

6.3 Vienna, Kunsthistorisches Museum 3726. *ARV²* 205.113; *Add.²* 193. *LIMC* IV, Demeter 872 no. 339, pl. 585. The Berlin Painter. *c.* 480

6.4 Frankfurt, Liebighaus St. V7. *ARV²* 386.387.1649; *Add.²* 229. Kron (1976), pl. 6; Schefold (1981), 50, 252, figs. 57-60, 357. The Castelgiorgio Painter. *c.* 480

6.5 London, British Museum E 140. *ARV²* 459.3; *Para* 377; *Add.²* 243. *LIMC* IV, Demeter 873 no. 344, pl. 56. Schwarz (1987), 39 V58 pl. 12. Makron. *c.* 480

6.6 Paris, Louvre G 187. *ARV²* 361.2; *Para* 364; *Add.²* 222. Metzger (1951), pl. 5. Schefold (1981), 59 figs. 72-3. The Triptolemos Painter. *c.* 480

6.7 St Petersburg, Hermitage 673 (B1918). *ARV²* 678.4; *Add.²* 279. *LIMC* II, Artemis 655 no. 408, pl. 479. The Bowdoin Painter. *c.* 480-470 **Pl. 30**

6.8 New York, Metropolitan Museum 21.88.163. *ARV²* 211.203. *Add.²* 196. *LIMC* II, Artemis 697 no. 990, pl. 520. The Berlin Painter. *c.* 480-470

6.9 Copenhagen, Ny Carlsberg Glyptotek 2696. *ARV²* 210.181; Schwarz (1987), 36 V42, pl. 4. The Berlin Painter. *c.* 480-470 **Pl. 32**

6.10 Graz, University G 30. *ARV²* (210.183bis). 1634; *Add.²* 196. Schwarz (1972-5), figs. 1-4, 6-7. The Berlin Painter. *c.* 470

6.11 Lyon, Musée des Beaux Arts E 120. *ARV²* 591.24; Dugas (1960), pl. 35.1-2, 36. The Altamura Painter. *c.* 470

6.12 Tübingen, University Museum 1518. *LIMC* II, Artemis 655 no. 407, pl. 479. *c.* 500-450 **Pl. 28**

6.13 Marienmont, Musée Ac. de Terranova 568. *LIMC* II, Artemis 697 no. 1003, pl. 522. Close to the Gela Painter. *c.* 500-475

6.14 Paris, Louvre CA 599. *ARV*² 691.27. *Add.*² 280. Manner of the Bowdoin Painter. *c.* 470-460

6.15 Paris, Louvre G 371. *ARV*² 208.158; *Add.*² 195. Schwarz (1972-5), 130 fig. 5. The Berlin Painter. *c.* 470-465

6.16 Copenhagen, Ny Carlsberg Glyptotek 2697. *ARV*² 517.11. Dugas (1960), pl. 28.1. The Cleveland Painter. *c.* 470-460

6.17 Basel, Antikenmuseum BS 1412. *Para* 395.41; *LIMC* IV, Demeter 873-4 no. 355, pl. 587. The Niobid Painter. *c.* 465 **Pl. 31**

6.18 Mississippi University, Museum of Classical Archaeology P.86. *ARV*² 203.97. *CVA* Robinson II, pl. 27. The Berlin Painter. *c.* 465

6.19 London, British Museum E 469. *ARV*² 589.1; *Add.*² 264. Schefold (1981), 96 fig. 124. The Altamura Painter. *c.* 460

6.20 London, British Museum E 274. *ARV*² 604.53; *LIMC* IV, Demeter 873 no. 353. Schwarz (1987), 43 V79 pl. 19. The Niobid Painter. *c.* 460

6.21 Ferrara, Museo Archeologico Nazionale di Spina inv. 2891 (T 313VT). *ARV*² 602.24; *Para* 395; *Add.*² 266. *LIMC* VI, Hekate 991 no. 20, pl. 655. *CVA* I, pls. 17-18. The Niobid Painter. *c.* 460-450

6.22 Basle, H.A. Cahn Collection HC 18. *LIMC* VI, Hekate 995 no. 74, pl. 660. The Splanchnopt Painter. Early fifth century

6.23 Berlin, Staatliche Museen 3312. *LIMC* Artemis 699 no. 1022. Fairbanks (1912), 44 no. 11. *c.* 460

6.24 Ferrara, Museo Archeologico Nazionale di Spina inv. 1499. *ARV*² 554.83; *Para* 386; *Add.*² 258. Alfieri (1979), 29 figs. 69-70. The Pan Painter. *c.* 460

6.25 Perugia, Museo Civico. *ARV*² 603.34; *Add.*² 267. Peschlow-Bindokat (1972), 85 fig. 18. The Niobid Painter. *c.* 460

6.26 Leiden, Rijksmuseum van Oudheden PC 76. *ARV*² 605.59; *Add.*² 267. *CVA* III, pls. 129.1-4, 131. 1-2, 132. 1-3. The Niobid Painter. *c.* 460

6.27 Copenhagen, Nationalmuseet 13789. *ARV*² 652.33; *Para* 402.33. *LIMC* IV, Demeter 864 no. 221, pl. 576. The Nikon Painter. *c.* 460

6.28 Once Zurich, Collection Hirschmann G 36. *LIMC* II, Artemis 655 no. 409, pl. 480. Circle of Douris. *c.* 460

6.29 Paris, Louvre G 573 (Cp 807). *ARV*² 489.106; *Add.*² 248. *LIMC* II, Artemis 639 no. 178, pl. 459. Hermonax. *c.* 460

6.30 Athens, National Museum 1313 (CC 1425). *ARV*² 678.11; *Add.*² 279. *LIMC* II, Artemis 699 no. 1021, pl. 524. The Bowdoin Painter. *c.* 460

6.31 Athens, National Museum 18590. *Para* 405. *LIMC* II, Artemis 699 no. 408. The Bowdoin Painter. *c.* 460

6.32 Würzburg, Martin von Wagner Museum H 4906. *LIMC* III, Dionysos 440 no. 149 pl. 312. *c.* 460 **Pl. 27**

6.33 Paris, Louvre G 343. *ARV*² 600.17; *Add.*² 266. *LIMC* VI, Hekate 991 no. 19, pl. 655. The Niobid Painter. *c.* 455

6.34 Brauron, Archaeological Museum 514. *LIMC* II, Artemis 658 no. 455. 460-450

6.35 New York, Metropolitan Museum 41.162.98. *ARV*² 606.80. *LIMC* IV, Demeter 864 no. 220, pl. 576. The Niobid Painter. *c.* 460-450

6.36 Vienna, Kunsthistorisches Museum 580. *CVA* III, pl. 144.1-3. Imitator of the Villa Giulia Painter. *c.* 450

6.37 Athens, National Museum 1754. *LIMC* IV, Demeter 864 no. 222, pl. 576. Simon (1985), pl. 301; Peschlow-Bindokat (1972), 147, no. 75, pls. 29-30. *c.* 450

6.38 Paris, Louvre G 452. *ARV*² 921.33; Schwarz (1987), 46 V94, pl. 22. The Aberdeen Painter. *c.* 450

6.39 Korinth, Archaeological Museum. *LIMC* IV, Demeter 860 no. 158, pl. 573. Fifth century

6.40 Naples, Museo Archeologico Nazionale 81908 (H 3010). *LIMC* II, Artemis 634 no. 113, pl. 452. *c.* 440 **Pl. 23**

6.41 Berlin, Staatliche Museen 3175. *ARV*² 747.28; *LIMC* IV, Demeter 865 no. 228, pl. 577. Metzger (1965), 22, no. 49, pl. xi.2. The Athens Group 1826. *c.* 440-430

6.42 Saint Louis, Missouri 2.29. *ARV*² 1276.4; Schwarz (1987), 51 V122, pl. 27a.b. The Marlay Painter. *c.* 450-425

6.43 Cannes, private collection. *ARV*² 1031.37; *Para* 442; *LIMC* IV, Demeter 874 no. 360. Polygnotos. *c.* 450-425

6.44 Agrigento, Museo Archeologico Regionale. *LIMC* III, Dionysos, 440 no. 150. Beazley (1939), 628 fig. 7. *c.* 450-425

6.45 London, British Museum E 183. *ARV*² 1191.1; *Add.*² 342. *LIMC* VI, Hekate 991 no. 21, pl. 655; *CVA* VI, pl. 84.2. The Painter of London E 183. *c.* 450-425

6.46 Paris, Cabinet des Médailles 424. *ARV*² 1036.12. Cook (1914), pl. 20. The Hector Painter. *c.* 450-425 **Fig. 21**

6.47 San Francisco, M.H. de Young Memorial Museum 230/24872. *CVA* I, pl. 22, 44-5. *c.* 450

6.48 Saint Louis, Missouri 40.21. *ARV*² 1117.6; *Add.*² 331. Peschlow-Bindokat (1972), 86 fig. 19. The Duomo Painter. *c.* 450-425

6.49 Würzburg, Martin von Wagner Museum L 529. *ARV*² 1117.5. *LIMC* VI, Hekate 991 no. 22, pl. 656. The Duomo Painter. *c.* 450-425

6.50 Brindisi, Museo Archeologico Provinciale. Sciarra (1976), 30 figs. 184-5. Circle of the Duomo Painter. *c.* 450-425

6.51 Durham, N. Carolina, Duke University Museum of Art DCC 64-27. *Para* 442.29bis; *LIMC* IV, Demeter 874 no. 362. Schwarz (1987), 48 V104 pl. 24. Polygnotos. *c.* 450-425

6.52 Vienna, Kunsthistorisches Museum 641. *ARV*² 1120.8. *CVA* I, pl. 91.3-5. Late Mannierist. *c.* 450-425

6.53 Taranto, Museo Archeologico Nazionale 52225. *ARV*² 1132.180. Neutsch (1956), 231 figs. 24-5. The Washing Painter. *c.* 430-420

6.54 Berlin, Staatliche Museen. *LIMC* IV, Demeter 874 no. 372. Cook (1914), 224 fig. 165. Late fifth century

6.55 San Francisco, California, Palace of the Legion of Honour 1811. *CVA* I, pls. 20-1. The Kadmos Painter? Late fifth century

6.56 Bologna, Museo Civico Archeologico 301. *ARV*² 1184.5; *Add.*² 341. *LIMC* II, Artemis 712 no. 1176, pl. 541. The Kadmos Painter. Late fifth century

6.57 Lid of pyxis. *LIMC* II, Artemis 655 no. 410. *c.* 400-390

6.58 Vienna, Lamberg Collection 204. *ARV*² 1523.1; *CVA* I, pl. 30. Painter of Vienna 202. *c.* 400-350

6.59 Naples, Museo Archeologico Nazionale H 3245. *ARV*² 1438.1; *Add.*² 377. *LIMC* II, Apollon 296 no. 933, pl. 264. The Painter of Naples 3245. Early fourth century

6.60 Eleusis, Archaeological Museum 1627. *LIMC* IV, Demeter 876 no. 391, pl. 579. Early fourth century

6.61 Berlin, Staatliche Museen F 2645. *LIMC* II, Artemis 713 no. 1188. Metzger (1951), 177 no. 34 pl. 225. Cook (1914), pl. 203. Early fourth century

6.62 London, British Museum 1924.7-16.1. *ARV*² 1420.6; *Add.*² 375. *LIMC* II, Apollon 308 no. 1040, pl. 272. The Painter of London F 64. Early fourth century

6.63 Würzburg, Martin von Wagner Museum L 645. *ARV*² 1427.39. *LIMC* II, Artemis 700 no. 1035. Metzger (1951), 226 no. 63. The Telos Painter. *c.* 390-380

6.64 Naples, Museo Archeologico Nazionale 146717. *LIMC* IV, Demeter 877 no. 395. Zervoudaki (1968), pl. 18.2. *c.* 350

6.65 Athens, National Museum 11037. *ARV²* 1475.8; *LIMC* IV, Demeter 877 no. 397, pl. 592. The Marsyas Painter. *c.* 350

6.66 Oxford, Ashmolean Museum 1939.599. *LIMC* II, Artemis 717 no. 1236, pl. 547. *c.* 350-330

6.67 Paris, Louvre CA 2190. *LIMC* IV, Demeter 878 no. 406. Kerényi (1967), 168 fig. 54. *c.* 350-330

6.68 Once New York, Hirsch collection. *LIMC* IV, Demeter 877 no. 394. Zervoudaki (1968), pl. 17.3. *c.* 350-300

6.69 London, British Museum 71.7-22.1. *LIMC* VI, Hekate 993 no. 48, pl. 658. *c.* 325-300

Sculpture

6.70 Volos, Archaeological Museum M 1274. Chrysostomou (1998), 156 pl. 15b. Archaic period

6.71 Brauron, Archaeological Museum K2077a,b+2503+3242. Kahil (1984), 674 no. 700, pl. 501. *c.* 500

6.72 Brauron, Archaeological Museum K 2614. *LIMC* II, Artemis 658 no. 470, pl. 483. *c.* 500-480

6.73 Brauron, Archaeological Museum K 2615. *LIMC* II, Artemis 659 no. 471, pl. 484. *c.* 500-480

6.74 Brauron, Archaeological Museum K 3352, 3265. *LIMC* II, Artemis 659 no. 472, pl. 484. *c.* 500-480

6.75 Berlin, Staatliche Museen Misc 7644. Kahil (1984), 633 no. 106, pl. 450. *c.* 470

6.76 Athens, National Museum 7565. Kahil (1984), 633 no. 108, pl. 451. *c.* 450-400

6.77 Karlsruhe, Badisches Landesmuseum F 1926. Kahil (1984), 633 no. 109, pl. 451. *c.* 450-400 **Pl. 22**

6.78 Athens, National Museum 1950. *LIMC* II, Artemis 658 no. 461, pl. 483. *c.* 450-400 **Pl. 33**

6.79 Berlin, Staatliche Museen K 78. *LIMC* II, Artemis 655 no. 411, pl. 480. *c.* 430-420

6.80 Athens, National Museum 126. *LIMC* IV, Demeter 875 no. 375, pl. 588. Clinton (1992), 134 fig. 1. Bianchi (1976), 22-3, pl. 27. Schwarz (1987), 65 R1 pl. 40. *c.* 430 **Pl. 26**

6.81 Eleusis, Archaeological Museum 5233. *LIMC* IV, Demeter 868 no. 280. Kanta (1979), 46. *c.* 420

6.82 Brauron, Archaeological Museum 1180. *LIMC* II, Artemis 716 no. 1225, pl. 545. *c.* 420

6.83 Eleusis, Archaeological Museum 5059. Schwarz (1987) 66 R7. *c.* 400

6.84 Thasos, Archaeological Museum. *LIMC* VI, Hekate 995 no. 68. Farnell (1896a), pl. 39a. Late fifth century

6.85 Würzburg, Martin von Wagner Museum HA 1754. *LIMC* IV, Demeter 865 no. 233, pl. 577. Late fifth century

6.86 Brauron, Archaeological Museum 1171(77). *LIMC* II, Artemis 658 no. 459, pl. 482. Late fifth century

6.87 Delos, Archaeological Museum A3193. *LIMC* II, Artemis 658 no. 456, pl. 482. Late fifth century

6.88 Athens, Akropolis Museum 2674. *LIMC* II, Artemis 658 no. 462. Walter (1923), 63-4 no. 110. Late fifth – early fourth century

6.89 Athens, Agora S 100. *LIMC* II, Artemis 655 no. 412. *c.* 400-375

6.90 Athens, National Museum 1475. *LIMC* VI, Hekate 993 no. 51, pl. 658. *c.* 400-350

6.91 Berlin, Staatliche Museen 1467 (K 106). *LIMC* VI, Hekate 1008 no. 273. Picard (1948), 25 fig. 4. *c.* 400-350

6.92 Volos, Archaeological Museum BE 1628. Chrysostomou (1998), 157 pl. 4b, 16a. *c.* 400-350

6.93 Athens, National Museum 3865. Peschlow-Bindokat (1972), 152, no. 39. Svoronos (1908-1937), 664 pl. 205. *c.* 394-393

6.94 Athens, National Museum 1380. *LIMC* II, Artemis 708 no. 1129. *c.* 375-350

6.95 London, British Museum 816. *LIMC* II, Artemis 687 no. 882, pl. 512. Chrysostomou (1998), 152-3. *c.* 360-350

6.96 Naples, Museo Archeologico Nazionale. *LIMC* IV, Demeter 878 no. 412, pl. 594. *c.* 350

6.97 Athens, National Museum 1332. *LIMC* IV, Demeter 881 no. 444. Svoronos (1908-1937), 247 pl. 36.2. *c.* 350

6.98 Athens, National Museum 1377. *LIMC* VI, Hekate 993 no. 50. Svoronos (1908-1937), 294-6 pl. 48A. *c.* 350

6.99 Athens, National Museum 1892. *LIMC* II, Artemis 708 no. 1128. Svoronos (1908-1937), 573 no. 225 pl. 95. *c.* 350

6.100 Brauron, Archaeological Museum 1182 (1). *LIMC* II, Artemis 658 no. 463, pl. 483. Fourth century

6.101 Athens, National Museum 2376. *LIMC* II, Artemis 660 no. 505. Svoronos (1908-1937), 639 no. 36 pl. 145. Fourth century

6.102 Athens, National Museum 2445. *LIMC* II, Artemis 655 no. 418; Svoronos (1908-1937), 643 pl. 152. Fourth century

6.103 Athens, National Museum 4540. *LIMC* II, Artemis 655 no. 417, pl. 480. Fourth century **Pl. 34**

6.104 Athens, National Museum 1016. *LIMC* IV, Demeter 868 no. 275. van Straten (1995), 291 R 68 fig. 82. Fourth century

6.105 Piraeus, Archaeological Museum. *LIMC* VI, Hekate 995 no. 70. Picard (1944), 129 fig. 8. Fourth century

6.106 Athens, National Museum 1556. *LIMC* VI, Hekate 1008 no. 276. Svoronos (1908-1937), 623 no. 287 pl. 120. Fourth century

6.107 Berlin, Staatliche Museen 690. *LIMC* VI, Hekate 1008 no. 274. Conze (1880), pl. 4.4. Fourth century

6.108 Thessaloniki, Archaeological Museum 30r. *LIMC* II, Artemis 696 no. 975, pl. 518. Fourth century

6.109 Eleusis, Archaeological Museum. Peschlow-Bindokat (1972), 153, fig. 51. Fourth century

6.110 Arta, Archaeological Museum 621. *LIMC* II, Artemis 660 no. 500. Tzouvara-Souli (1979), 20 fig. 10 a-b. Fourth century

6.111 Arta, Archaeological Museum 523. *LIMC* II, Artemis 660 no. 501. Tzouvara-Souli (1979), 34 fig. 14 b. Fourth century

6.112 Athens, National Museum 102. *LIMC* II, Artemis 658 no. 460. Svoronos (1908-1937), 681 no. 482.5 pl. 255. Fourth century

6.113 Athens, National Museum 208. *LIMC* II, Artemis 655 no. 413. Fourth century

6.114 Athens, National Museum 10145. *LIMC* II, Artemis 660 no. 495. Fourth century

6.115 Komotini, Archaeological Museum 1589. *LIMC* VI, Hekate 1008 no. 269. Reeder (1987), 430 fig. 6. *c.* 350-300

6.116 Paris, Louvre Ma 759. Peschlow-Bindokat (1972), 155, fig. 54. *c.* 350-300

6.117 Brauron, Archaeological Museum 1152(83). *LIMC* II, Artemis 708 no. 1127, pl. 536. van Straten (1995), 292-3 R 74 fig. 86. *c.* 350-300

6.118 Berlin, Staatliche Museen 692 (K107). *LIMC* VI, Hekate 1008 no. 278. Blümel (1966), no. 94 fig. 128. *c.* 350-300

6.119 Athens, National Museum 1461. *LIMC* IV, Demeter 868 no. 277. Svoronos (1908-1937), 463 pl. 77. *c.* 350-300

6.120 Thessaloniki, Archaeological Museum 783. *LIMC* II, Artemis 660 no. 507. Stephanidou (1973), 113 pl. 3. *c.* 350-300

6.121 Eleusis, Archaeological Museum 71. *LIMC* IV, Demeter 875 no. 379, pl. 589. Schwarz (1987), 67, R9, pl. 32. Bianchi (1976), 22 pl. 26. *c.* 330

6.122 Naples, Museo Archeologico Nazionale. *LIMC* IV, Demeter 878 no. 412, pl. 594. Bianchi (1976), 22 pl. 25. *c.* 330

6.123 Paris, Louvre Ma 2849. *LIMC* II, Artemis 660 no. 506, pl. 486. Late fourth century **Pl. 24**

6.124 Paris, Louvre 2723. Chrysostomou (1998), 160-2. *c.* 325-300

6.125 Athens, Agora S 1045. Peschlow-Bindokat (1972), 118 fig. 40. *c.* 325-300

6.126 Larisa, Archaeological Museum 1990/40. Chrysostomou (1998), 154 pl. 15g. *c.* 350-300

6.127 Athens, National Museum 1422. *LIMC* IV, Demeter 870 no. 307, pl. 582. *c.* 325-300

6.128 Athens, Agora S 1646. *LIMC* IV, Demeter 879 no. 414, pl. 594. Clinton (1992), 134 fig. 10. Late fourth century

6.129 Athens, Agora S 1251. *LIMC* IV, Demeter 878 no. 413, pl. 594. Clinton (1992), 135, no. 1, fig. 9. Late fourth century

6.130 Athens, National Museum 1554. *LIMC* VI, Hekate 1008 no. 277. Svoronos (1908-1937), 623 no. 284 pl. 119. Late fourth century

6.131 Athens, National Museum 1654. *LIMC* VI, Hekate 995 no. 79. no date

6.132 Athens, National Museum 3917. *LIMC* II, Artemis 708 no. 1130, pl. 536. Late fourth century

6.133 Volos, Archaeological Museum L 389. *LIMC* II, Artemis 658 no. 458. Helly (1973), pl. 167. *c.* 300

6.134 Volos, Archaeological Museum 274. Pingiatoglou (1981), 109-10. Late fourth – early third century

CATALOGUE 7: Representations of divine hunting and divine wars

Vases

7.1 Paris, Louvre E 851. *ABV* 97.24; *Add.*[2] 26. *LIMC* V, Herakles 36 no. 1998, pl. 53. The Prometheus Painter (Tyrrenian amphora). *c.* 565-550

7.2 Rome, Fond. Lerici. *Para* 157.11bis. *LIMC* V, Herakles 37 no. 2014. Moretti (1966). The Michigan Painter. *c.* 520-500

7.3 Agrigento, Museo Regionale. *ABV* 521. *LIMC* V, Herakles 36 no. 2002. Brommer (1949), pl. 1.2. Manner of the Theseus Painter. *c.* 500

7.4 Paris, Louvre CA 598. *LIMC* V, Herakles 36 no. 2004, pl. 54. The Diosphos Painter. *c.* 500-490 **Pl. 37a-b**

7.5 Berlin, Staatliche Museen F 1854. *LIMC* V, Herakles 37 no. 2015, pl. 56. The Leagros Group. *c.* 500-490

7.6 Palermo, Museo Regionale V 763(275). *ARV*[2] 251.34. *CVA* i, pl. 31(688), 4. *LIMC* V, Herakles 37 no. 2018. The Syleus Painter. *c.* 490

7.7 Ferrara, Museo Archeologico Nazionale di Spina 2891 (T 313VT). *ARV*[2]

602.24; *Para* 395; *Add.*[2] 266. *LIMC* VI, Gigantes 229 no. 311, pl. 655. The Niobid Painter. *c.* 460-450

7.8 Basle, Antikenmuseum, Ludwig Collection 51. *ARV*[2] 609.7bis.1661; *Para* 396; *Add.*[2] 268. Brommer (1978), pl. 18.1. *LIMC* IV, Gigantes 229 no. 312, pl. 140. Manner of the Niobid Painter. *c.* 450

7.9 Ferrara, Museo Archeologico Nazionale di Spina 44893. *ARV*[2] 1680; *Para* 446; *Add.*[2] 158. Alfieri & Arias (1958), pls. 68-73. *LIMC* IV, Gigantes 229 no. 313, pl. 141. Group of Polygnotos. *c.* 440

7.10 Boston, Museum of Fine Arts 00.346. *ARV*[2] 1045.7; *Para* 444; *Add.*[2] 320. *LIMC* I, Aktaion 462 no. 81, pl. 357. The Lykaon Painter. *c.* 440

7.11 Oxford, Ashmolean Museum 1980.31 (V 289). *ARV*[2] 1046.11; *Add.*[2] 320. *LIMC* II, Artemis 732 no. 1401, pl. 562. The Lykaon Painter. *c.* 440 **Pl. 35**

7.12 Borowski Collection V74-415. *LIMC* II, Artemis 732 no. 1398, pl. 561. The Kleophon or the Dinos Painter. *c.* 440-430

7.13 Bologna, Museo Civico Archeologico 303. *ARV*[2] 1184.6; *Para* 460. *Add.*[2] 341. *LIMC* II, Artemis 724 no. 1317, pl. 553. The Kadmos Painter. *c.* 420

7.14 Syracuse, Museo Archeologico Nazionale 17427. *ARV*[2] 1184.4; *Para* 460; *Add.*[2] 341. Froning (1971), pl. 8.2. The Kadmos Painter. Late fifth century

7.15 Ruvo, Museo Jatta 1093. *ARV*[2] 1184.1; *Para* 460; *Add.*[2] 340. Schefold (1981), 174 fig. 232. The Kadmos Painter. Late fifth century

7.16 London, British Museum E 701. *ARV*[2] 1326.64; *LIMC* II, Artemis 725 no. 1331. Vian (1951), 87 no. 396 pl. 45. Manner of the Meidias Painter. Late fifth century

7.17 Athens, National Museum 1442. *ARV*[2] 1343.2; *Add.*[2] 367. *LIMC* II, Athena 1014 no. 619 pl. 764. The Semele Painter. Late fifth century **Fig. 22**

7.18 Berlin, Staatliche Museen F 2531. *Para* 478; *Add.*[2] 363. *LIMC* IV, Gigantes 230 no. 318, pl. 143. Aristophanes. Late fifth century **Pl. 38**

7.19 Once Jadis, San Simeon Hearst Corporation 9941. *ARV*[2] 1477.5; *LIMC* II, Artemis 734 no. 1424. Metzger (1951), 162 no. 19. The Painter of Athens 1472. *c.* 390

7.20 Genoa, Museo Civico 1911.163. *ARV*[2] 1337.6; *Add.*[2] 366. Moret (1982), 127 fig. 8. Near the Pronomos Painter. Early fourth century

7.21 Paris, Louvre S 1677. *ARV*[2] 1344.1; *Para* 482; *Add.*[2] 367. *LIMC* II, Athena 991 no. 391, pl. 749. The Suessula Painter. Early fourth century

7.22 Würzburg, Martin von Wagner Museum H 4729. *ARV*[2] 1346.1691; *Add.*[2] 368. *LIMC* II, Artemis 725 no. 1330, pl. 555. Comparable style to the Suessula Painter.

7.23 St Petersburg, Hermitage B 4257. *LIMC* V, Herakles 36 no. 2009, pl. 55. *c.* 370-360

7.24 London, British Museum E 432. *ARV*[2] 1472.2. *LIMC* II, Artemis 653 no. 396, pl. 478. The Herakles Painter. *c.* 370 **Pl. 36**

7.25 St Petersburg, Hermitage St 1795. *ARV*[2] 1475.3; *Add.*[2] 381. Metzger (1951), pl. 21.3. The Marsyas Painter. *c.* 340-330

Sculpture

7.26 Delphi, Temple of Apollo (now lost). *LIMC* V, Herakles 37 no. 2022. Late Archaic period

7.27 Olympia, Temple of Zeus. *LIMC* V, Herakles 38-9 no. 2040, pl. 11. *c.* 460

CATALOGUE 8: Representations of light in images of divine empowerment

Vases

8.1 Harvard University, Art Museum 1916.264. Neils (1997), 237 fig. 13. The Mykonos Painter. *c.* 470

8.2 Vienna, Kunsthistorisches Museum 985. *ARV*² 591.20; *Para* 394; *Add.*² 264. *CVA* III, pl. 101.2. The Altamura Painter. *c.* 460

8.3 Florence, Museo Archeologico 4016. *ARV*² 598.5; *LIMC* III, Dionysos 455 no. 349. *CVA* II, pl. 66.2. The Blenheim Painter. *c.* 460

8.4 Cambridge, Mass., Fogg Museum 1916.264. *CVA* I, pl. 19. *c.* 460

8.5 Vienna, Kunsthistorisches Museum 3738. *ARV*² 575.17; *CVA* II, pl. 92. The Agrigento Painter. *c.* 460

8.6 Ferrara, Museo Archeologico Nazionale di Spina 20457. *ARV*² 575.18. Lezzi-Zindel (1991), 47, 46 no. 14. The Agrigento Painter. *c.* 460

8.7 Baltimore, Walters Art Gallery 48.2712. Reeder (1995), no. 44, 206-8. The Niobid Painter. *c.* 460-450

8.8 Paris, Louvre G 532. *LIMC* III, Dionysos 427 no. 40. *CVA* II, pl. 21. *c.* 460-450

8.9 Taranto, Museo Archeologico Nazionale 6990. *ARV*² 512.8; *Add.*² 252. *LIMC* III, Dionysos 458 no. (fig.) 398. The Painter of Bologna 228. *c.* 450

8.10 Vienna, Kunsthistorisches Museum 723. *ARV*² 584.20; *Add.*² 263. *LIMC* III, Dionysos 461 no. 443, pl. 351. Earlier Mannierists

8.11 Paris, Cabinet des Médailles 357. *ARV*² 987.2; *Para* 437; *Add.*² 311. Robertson (1975), pl. 106b. The Achilles Painter. *c.* 440

8.12 Naples, Museo Archeologico Nazionale 164332. *ARV*² 1019.83; Frontisi-Ducroux (1991), 239-40 L22. The Phiale Painter. *c.* 440

8.13 Baltimore, The Walters Art Gallery 48.74. *CVA* I, pl. 23. The Christie Painter. *c.* 440

8.14 Los Angeles, County Museum of Art 50.8.7. *ARV*² 1063.2; *Add.*² 324. *CVA* I, pl. 27.3-4. The Biscoe Painter. *c.* 440

8.15 Ferrara, Museo Archeologico Nazionale di Spina 3891. *ARV*² 1117.8; Lezzi-Hafter (1991), 69 no. (fig.) 31. The Duomo Painter. *c.* 440-430

8.16 Vienna, Kunsthistorisches Museum 782. *ARV*² 1047.10; *Add.*² 320. *CVA* III, pl. 113.1-2. The Christie Painter. *c.* 430

8.17 Cambridge, Mass., Fogg Museum 1925.30.40. *ARV*² 1042.1; *Add.*² 320. *LIMC* III, Dionysos 455 no. 350, pl. 336. The Curti Painter. *c.* 450-425

8.18 Copenhagen, Nationalmuseet Chrv. iii 794. *ARV*² 1075.1; *Add.*² 326. *LIMC* III, Dionysos 455 no. 351, pl. 337. The Danae Painter. *c.* 450-425

8.19 Vienna, Kunsthistorisches Museum 785. *CVA* II, pl. 65.4; *ARV*² 1194.5. The Leningrad Painter 702. *c.* 450-425

8.20 Vienna, Kunsthistorisches Museum 855. *ARV*² 1151.1; *Add.*² 335. *CVA* III, pl. 117.1-2. Manner of the Kleophon Painter. *c.* 430-420

8.21 Laon Museum 37.1026. *ARV*² 1148.6; *CVA* I, pl. 31.6. The Kleophon Painter. *c.* 425

8.22 Naples, Museo Archeologico Nazionale H 2419. *ARV*² 1151-1152.2; *Para* 457; *Add.*² 165. Bianchi (1976), 35 pl. 81. The Dinos Painter. *c.* 420 **Pl. 39 a-b**

8.23 Athens, National Museum 1488 (CC1598). *ARV*² 1152.5. Carpenter (1997), 102. Unpublished. The Dinos Painter. *c.* 425-400

8.24 Vienna, Kunsthistorisches Museum 1024. *ARV*² 1152.8; *Add.*² 336. *CVA* III, pl. 105.1-4. The Dinos Painter. *c.* 425-400

8.25 Naples, Museo Archeologico Nazionale 938. *ARV*² 1154.30. Carpenter (1997), 99. The Dinos Painter. *c.* 425-400

8.26 Providence, Rhode Island, School of Design 23.324. *ARV*² 1188.1. 1686; *Add.*² 341. Queyrel (1984), 128 fig. 7. The Pothos Painter. Late fifth century

8.27 Vienna, Kunsthistorisches Museum 1065. *ARV*² 1188.3; *Add.*² 341. Queyrel (1984), 133 fig. 15. *CVA* III, pl. 119.3, 6. The Pothos Painter. Late fifth century

8.28 Geneva, Musée d'Art et d'Histoire 14983. *ARV*² 1189.6; *Para* 461; *Add.*² 341. Queyrel (1984), 129 fig. 10. The Pothos Painter. Late fifth century

8.29 Rome, Vatican 17 893. *ARV*² 1189.8; *Add.*² 342. Queyrel (1984), 133 fig. 17. The Pothos Painter. Late fifth century

8.30 Madrid, Archaeological Museum 11075. *ARV*² 1189.10; *Add.*² 342. Queyrel (1984), 131 fig. 13. The Pothos Painter. Late fifth century

8.31 Naples, Museo Archeologico Nazionale 81438. *ARV*² 1189.11; *Add.*² 342. Queyrel (1984), 133 fig. 16. The Pothos Painter. Late fifth century

8.32 Paris, Louvre G 486 (N3385). *ARV*² 1163.34(25). The Painter of Munich 2335. *CVA* V, pl. 32.7. Late fifth century

8.33 Ephesos, Artemision A 50. Gasser (1990), pl. 40, 96-97. Circle of the Pronomos Painter? Late fifth century

8.34 Boston, Museum of Fine Arts 98.934. *LIMC* III, Dionysos 455 no. 352. Vermeule (1970), 99 fig. 3. Early fourth century

8.35 New York Metropolitan Museum 06.1021.183. *LIMC* III, Dionysos 457 no. 373. Early fourth century

8.36 Paris, Louvre G 511. *ARV*² 1431.2; *Add.*² 376. *LIMC* III, Dionysos 461 no. 433, pl. 349. The Black-Thyrsus Painter. *c.* 400-350

8.37 London, British Museum E 546. *LIMC* III, Dionysos 463 no. 458, pl. 353. *c.* 350

8.38 Mainz, University Museum 178. *CVA* II, pl. 9.178. Group G. *c.* 350

Sculpture

8.39 Athens, National Museum 1421. *LIMC* III, Dionysos 494 no. 852. Svoronos (1908-1937), 363-7 no. 119 pl. 45 fig. 182. Late fifth century

CATALOGUE 9: Representations of light in images of agrarian deities and satyrs

Fire and grain rituals

Vases

9.1 Munich, Staatliche Antikensammlungen 7515. *ARV*² 211.202; *Add.*² 196. *LIMC* IV, Demeter 850 no. 23, pl. 563. Peschlow-Bindokat (1972), 99 fig. 33. The Berlin Painter. *c.* 460

9.2 Athens, National Museum 1695. *ARV*² 1204.2. Deubner (1932), pl. 2. *c.* 450

9.3 Berlin, Staatliche Museen 3412. Rubensohn (1899), 67 pl. 7. Boiotian (?). *c.* 450-400

9.4 Piraeus, Archaeological Museum (formerly Geroulanos collection 343). *ARV*² 1154.38bis; *LIMC* IV, Demeter 870 no. 306. Clinton (1992), 67-70. *c.* 430

9.5 Athens, National Museum A 537 (5825). *LIMC* IV, Demeter 858 no. 121, pl. 571. Metzger (1965), 27 no. 63, pl. 9.1. End of fifth century **Pl. 40**

9.6 Bonn, Akademisches Kunstmuseum 363. *LIMC* IV, Demeter 857 no. 110, pl. 570. Bianchi (1976), 30 pl. 57. Late fifth century

Catalogues 221

Sculpture

9.7 Athens, National Museum 1519. *LIMC* IV, Demeter 876 no. 385, pl. 589. Clinton (1992), fig. 8. Bianchi (1976), 22 pl. 24. *c.* 350-300 **Fig. 23**

9.8 Berlin, Staatliche Museen SK 679. *LIMC* IV, Demeter 880 no. 435, pl. 596. *c.* 350-300

9.9 Edinburgh, Royal Museums of Scotland 1956.364. *LIMC* IV, Demeter 870 no. 308, pl. 582. *c.* 300

Fire in the context of Dionysos

Vases

9.10 London, British Museum E 279. *ARV²* 226.1. 1634; *Add.²* 199. *LIMC* III, Dionysos 464 no. 478, pl. 355. The Eucharides Painter. *c.* 490-480

9.11 Reading, Public Museum 32-772-1. Neils (1997), 233 figs. 3-4. The Mykonos Painter. *c.* 470

9.12 Brussels, Bibliothèque Royale 11. *ARV²* 513; *Add.²* 252. Schefold (1981), 98 figs. 128-129. Close to the Painter of Bologna 228. *c.* 470-460

9.13 Vienna, Kunsthistorisches Museum 1772. *ARV²* 1072.1; *Add.²* 325. *CVA* III, pl. 113.5-6. The Eupolis Painter. *c.* 450

9.14 Naples, Museo Archeologico Nazionale. *ARV²* 532.53; *Para* 384; *LIMC* III, Dionysos 491-2 no. 822. Simon (1961), pl. 6.2. The Alkimachos Painter. *c.* 450

9.15 Private Collection. Simon (1963), pl. 2. 1-3. The 'Lewis' Painter. *c.* 450

9.16 Paris, Cabinet des Médailles 357. *ARV²* 987.2; *Para* 437; *Add.²* 311. Robertson (1975), pl. 106b. The Achilles Painter. *c.* 440

9.17 Rome, Villa Giulia. *ARV²* 1051.8(A). Group of Polygnotos. *c.* 440

9.18 Once Naples. *ARV²* 1061.157; *Add.²* 323. Halm-Tisserant (1986), pl. 1, 2 figs. 1, 3, 5, 7. Group of Polygnotos. *c.* 440

9.19 Naples, Museo Archeologico Nazionale 2412. *ARV²* 1114.1; *Para* 452; Schöne (1987), 263 no. 103. *EAA* iii, 235 (fig.). The Hephaistos Painter. *c.* 440 **Pl. 41**

9.20.1 Germany, Private Collection. *LIMC* VII Prometheus 534 no. 5. Attributed to Peleus Painter. *c.* 440

9.21 Oxford, Ashmolean Museum 1927.4. *ARV²* 1046.10. Beazley (1939), 634 fig. 9. *LIMC* VII Prometheus 534 no. 4. The Lykaon Painter. *c.* 440-430

9.22 Ferrara, Museo Archeologico Nazionale di Spina 2809. *ARV²* 1098.31; Lezzi-Hafter & Zindel (1991), 60-1, 76, no. 59. The Naples Painter. *c.* 440-430

9.23 Tokyo, Museum Yamato Bunkanan, Collection Oka 31. *CVA* II, pl. 29.1-4. Group of Polygnotos. *c.* 440-430

9.24 Tarquinia, Museo Archeologico Nazionale RC 4197. *ARV²* 1057.96; *Para* 445; *Add.²* 157. Simon (1961), pl. 5.3; Kerényi (1967), fig. 100. Group of Polygnotos. *c.* 440-430

9.25 London, British Museum E 465. Simon (1963), pl. 7.4. Group of Polygnotos. *c.* 440-430

9.26 Rome, Villa Giulia 50 445. *ARV²* 1051.8(B); *Add.²* 321. Brommer (1978), pl. 6.4. Group of Polygnotos. *c.* 440-430

9.27 Ferrara, Museo Archeologico Nazionale di Spina 44894 (T57 C VP). *ARV²* 1143.1; *Para* 455; *Add.²* 334. Alfieri (1979), 76-8 figs. 174-7. The Kleophon Painter. *c.* 440-430

9.28 Munich, Staatliche Antikensammlungen 2361. *ARV²* 1145.36; *Para* 456; *Add.²* 335. *CVA* II, pl. 74.1. Halm-Tisserant (1986), figs. 1, 6. The Kleophon Painter. *c.* 430

9.29 Bologna, Museo Civico Archeologico 288 (inv. 6990). *ARV²* 1056.86; *Add.²*

322. Schefold (1981), 283 figs. 400-2. *LIMC* VII Prometheus 534 no. 11. Group of Polygnotos. *c.* 420

9.30 Athens, National Museum 1167 (CC1339). *ARV*² 1104.6. *Para* 451. Beazley (1939), 637 fig. 13. *LIMC* VII Prometheus 534 no. 7. The Orpheus Painter. *c.* 430 **Fig. 29a**

9.31 Syracuse, Museo Regionale 24126(a). Beazley (1939), 635 fig. 12. *LIMC* VII Prometheus 534 no. 8. Manner of the Kleophon Painter. *c.* 430

9.32 Philadelphia, University Museum L 29-45. *ARV*² 1163.33. Beazley (1939), 637 fig. 14. *LIMC* VII Prometheus 534 no. 6. The Painter of Munich 2335. *c.* 430

9.33 Würzburg, Martin von Wagner Museum H 4616 (L 491). *ARV*² 1270.17; *Add.*² 356. *LIMC* II, Aphrodite 129 no. 1359, pl. 133. Schöne (1987), pl. 9.2. The Codrus Painter. *c.* 430-420

9.34 Mytilene, Museum of Antissa. *LIMC* VII Prometheus 534 no. 9. *c.* 430-420

9.35 Athens, Kerameikos Museum HS 198. *LIMC* VII Prometheus 534 no. 10. *c.* 430-420

9.36 Providence, Rhode Island, School of Design 23.324. *ARV*² 1188.1. 1686; *Add.*² 341. Queyrel (1984), 128 fig. 7. The Pothos Painter. Late fifth century

9.37 New York, Metropolitan Museum 574. van Hoorn (1951), 157, pl. 242, no. 742. *c.* 430-425

9.38 Athens, National Museum 1219. *ARV*² 1212.1; *Add.*² 347. *LIMC* III, Dionysos 457 no. 383, pl. 341. Close to the Shuvalov Painter. *c.* 425

9.39 Athens, National Museum 1218. *ARV*² 1212.2; *Add.*² 347. *LIMC* III, Dionysos 457 no. 382, pl. 340. Close to the Shuvalov Painter. *c.* 425

9.40 Berlin, Staatliche Museen 2642; *ARV*² 1336.2; *Add.*² 366. Queyrel (1984), 152 fig. 26. The Pronomos Painter. *c.* 425-400

9.41 Oxford, Ashmolean Museum 1937.983. *ARV*² 1153.13; *Para* 457; *Add.*² 336. Beazley (1939), 619 fig. 1. Trendall & Webster (1971), pl. 31, II.4. Kerenyi (1963), pls. 8-9. The Dinos Painter. *c.* 425-420

9.42 Paris Market; Ex Collection Hamilton, then Feuardent. *ARV*² 1157; *Add.*² 337. Beazley (1939), 621 fig. 2. Kerényi (1963), pl. 10a. *LIMC* VII Prometheus 535 no. 14. Near the Dinos Painter. *c.* 425-420 **Fig. 29b**

9.43 Berlin, Staatliche Museen F 2578. Brommer (1959), 48-9 figs. 45-6. *c.* 425-420

9.44 Berlin, Staatliche Museen 3984. Beazley (1939), 633 fig. 10. *c.* 425-420

9.45 Lipari, Museo Archeologico Eoliano T 207. *ARV*² 1053.41.1680; *Para* 445; *LIMC* VII Prometheus 535 no. 16. The Polygnotos Group. *c.* 420-410

9.46 Gotha, Schlossmuseum Ara 110 (75). *ARV*² 1334.19; *Add.*² 365. Beazley (1939), pl. 14. *CVA* II, pl. 61. *LIMC* VII Prometheus 535 no. 17. The Nikias Painter. *c.* 410

9.47 New Haven, Yale University Museum 1913.129. *ARV*² 1342.3; *Add.*² 367. Beazley (1939), 627 fig. 6. *LIMC* VII Prometheus 535 no. 15. The Painter of Louvre G433. *c.* 410-400

9.48 Ferrara, Museo Nazionale inv. Sequ. Trieste 27.2.28. *ARV*² 1349.6; *LIMC* VII Prometheus 535 no. 18. The Bull Painter *c.* 410-400

9.49 Naples, Museo Archeologico Nazionale H 3240. *ARV*² 1336.1; *Para* 480; *Add.*² 182. *LIMC* III, Dionysos 483 no. 719, pl. 383. The Pronomos Painter. Early fourth century **Fig. 28**

CATALOGUE 10: Nocturnal feasts (pannuchides)

Vases

10.1 Laon Museum 37.1072. *LIMC* VI, Hekate 993 no. 47, pl. 657. *c.* 370-360

Bibliography

Akurgal, E. (1983) *Alt-Smyrna I. Wohnsichten und Athena Tempel.* Ankara.

Alcock, S. & Osborne, R. (1994) eds. *Placing the Gods: Sanctuaries and Sacred Space in Ancient Greece.* Oxford.

Alfieri, N. & Arias, P.E. (1958) *Spina: Die neuentdeckte Etruskerstadt und die griechischen Vasen ihrer Gräber.* Florence.

Alfieri, N. (1979) *Spina, Museo Archeologico Nazionale di Ferrara* I. Bologna.

Allen, T.W., Halliday, W.R. & Sikes, E.E. (1936) *The Homeric Hymns.* Oxford (1904, repr. 1936)

Alroth, B. (1989) *Greek Gods and Figurines: Aspects of the Anthropomorphic Dedications.* Uppsala.

Anderson, J.U. (1955) *Greek Vases in the Otago Museum.* Dunedin.

Anderson, M.J. (1997) *The Fall of Troy in Early Greek Poetry and Art.* Oxford.

Arafat, K.W. (1990) *Classical Zeus: A Study in Art and Literature.* Oxford.

Ashmole, B. (1962) 'Torch-racing at Rhamnous.' *AJArch* 66: 233-4.

Athanassakis, A.N. (1976) *The Homeric Hymns.* Baltimore & London.

Austin, C. (1968) *Nova Fragmenta Euripidea in Papyris Reperta.* Berlin.

Avagianou, A. (1991) *Sacred Marriage Rituals in Greek Religion.* Bern.

Babelon, E. (1932) *Traité des Monnaies Grecques et Romaines.* Vol. 2.4. Paris.

Bailey, D.M. (1975) *A Catalogue of the Lamps in the British Museum,* 1. *Greek, Hellenistic and Early Roman Terracotta Lamps.* London.

Bailey, D.M. (1988) *A Catalogue of the Lamps in the British Museum,* 3. *Roman Provincial Lamps.* London.

Bailey, D.M. (1991) 'Aigina, Aphaia Temple. XIV The Lamps.' *Arch. Anz.*: 3-68.

Bailey, D.M. (1996) *A Catalogue of the Lamps in the British Museum,* 4. *Lamps of Metal and Stone, and Lampstands.* London.

Bammer, A. & Muss, U. (1996) *Das Artemision von Ephesos: Das Weltwunder Ioniens in Archaischer und Klassischer Zeit.* Mainz.

Barber, E.J.W. (1992) 'The Peplos of Athena.' in Neils ed.: 103-17.

Barlow, S.A. (1986) *Euripides: Trojan Women.* Oxford.

Barrett, D. (1970) *Aristophanes: The Wasps; The Poet and the Women; The Frogs.* Middlesex, Baltimore & Ringwood. (1st ed. 1964)

Bažant, J. (1984) 'On Satyrs, Maenads, Athenians and Vases.' *Eirene* 21: 41-7.

Beaumont, L.A. (1992) *The Iconography of Divine and Heroic Children in Attic Red-figure Vase-painting of the 5th Century BC.* Unpublished Diss. University of London.

Beazley, J.D. (1939) 'Prometheus Fire-lighter.' *AJArch.* 59: 618-39.

Beazley, J.D. (1940) 'A Marble Lamp.' *JHS* 60: 22-49.

Benndorf, O. (1879) *Ueber das Kultbild der Athena Nike.* Vienna.

Bennet, J. (1997) 'Homer and the Bronze Age.' in I. Morris & B. Powell eds. *A New Companion to Homer.* Leiden, New York & Köln: 511-33.

Benton, S. (1953) 'Further Excavations at Aetos.' *BSA* 48: 255-329.
Bérard, C. (1974) *Anodoi: Essai sur l'imagerie des passages chthoniens.* Rome.
Bergquist, B. (1973) *Herakles on Thasos: The Archaeological, Literary and Epigraphical Evidence for his Sanctuary, Status and Cult Reconsidered.* Uppsala.
Beschi, L. (1988) 'Demeter.' *LIMC* IV: 844-92.
Beulé, M. (1862) *L'Acropole d'Athènes.* Paris.
Bianchi, U. (1976) *The Greek Mysteries.* Leiden.
Bierl, H.A.F. (1991) *Dionysos und die griechische Tragödie: politische und 'metapolitische' Aspekte im Text.* Tübingen.
Blegen, C.W. et al. (1958) *Troy* 4.2. *Settlements VIIa, VIIb and VIII.* Princeton.
Blinkenberg, Ch. (1931) *Lindos* 1. *Fouilles de l'Acropole 1902-1914. Les petits objets.* Berlin.
Blümel, C. (1966) *Die klassisch griechischen Skulpturen der Staatlichen Museen zu Berlin.* Berlin.
Blundell, S. (1995) *Women in Ancient Greece.* London.
Boardman, J. & Hayes, J. (1966) *Excavations at Tocra 1963-1965. The Archaic Deposits 1. BSA* (Suppl. 4).
Boardman, J. & Hayes, J. (1973) *Excavations at Tocra 1963-1965. The Archaic Deposits 2 and Later Deposits. BSA* (Suppl. 10).
Boardman, J. & La Rocca, E. (1978) *Eros in Greece.* London.
Boardman, J. (1967) *Excavations in Chios 1952-1955. Greek Emporio. BSA* (Suppl. 6).
Boardman, J. (1974) *Athenian Black-figure Vases.* London.
Boardman, J. (1993) *Greek Sculpture: The Archaic Period.* London (1965, repr. 1993).
Boitani, F. (1971) 'Gravisca: ceramiche e lucerne di importazione Greca e ceramice locali dal riempimento del vano C.' *Not. Scav.* 25: 242-85.
Bonnechère, P. (1994) *La sacrifice humaine en Grèce ancienne. Kernos* (Suppl. 3).
Bookidis, N. & Fisher, J.E. (1972) 'The Sanctuary of Demeter and Kore on Acrocorinth.' *Hesp.* 41: 283-317.
Bookidis, N. & Stroud, R.S. (1987) *Demeter and Persephone in Ancient Corinth.* Princeton.
Bookidis, N. & Stroud, R.S. (1997) *Corinth* 18.3 *The Sanctuary of Demeter and Kore. Topography and Architecture.* Princeton.
Bookidis, N. (1993) 'Ritual Dining in Corinth.' in Hägg and Marinatos eds.: 45-61.
Borgeaud, Ph. (1988) *The Cult of Pan in Ancient Greece.* Chicago (1987, Eng. trans. 1988).
Borrmann, R. (1881) 'Neue Untersuchungen am Erechtheion zu Athen.' *MDAI(A)* 6: 372-92.
Bosanquet, R.C. (1904-5) 'Excavations at Palaikastro IV.' *BSA* 11: 307-8.
Bötticher, C. (1862) *Bericht über die Untersuchungen auf der Akropolis von Athen im Frühjahre, 1862.* Berlin.
Bouvrie, S. des (1993) 'Creative Euphoria: Dionysos and the Theatre.' *Kernos* 6: 79-112.
Bovon, A. (1966) *Lampes d'Argos: Études péloponnésiennes* V. Paris.
Bowie, A.M. (1993) *Aristophanes: Myth, Ritual and Comedy.* Cambridge.
Bravo, B. (1997) *Pannychis e simposio: Feste private notturne di donne e uomini nei testi letterari e nel culto.* Pisa & Rome.
Brendel, O.J. (1995) *Etruscan Art.* New Haven & London.
Brommer, F. (1937) *Satyroi.* Würzburg.
Brommer, F. (1949) 'Herakles und Hydra auf attischen Vasenbildern.' *Marburger Winkelmann-Program,* Marburg.

Brommer, F. (1978) *Hephaistos: Der Schmiedegott in der antiken Kunst.* Mainz.

Brommer, F. (1985) *Die Akropolis von Athen.* Darmstadt.

Brommer, F.(1959) *Satyrspiele.* Berlin.

Broneer, O. (1930) *Corinth* 4.2. *Terracotta Lamps.* Cambridge Mass.

Broneer, O. (1938) 'Excavations on the North Slope of the Acropolis, 1937.' *Hesp.* 7: 161-263.

Broneer, O. (1942a) 'The Thesmophorion in Athens.' *Hesp.* 11: 250-74.

Broneer, O. (1942b) 'Hero Cults in the Corinthian Agora.' *Hesp.* 11: 128-61.

Broneer, O. (1977) *Isthmia* 3. *Terracotta Lamps.* Princeton.

Brouskari, M. (1974) *The Acropolis Museum: A Descriptive Catalogue.* Athens.

Brulé, P. (1987) *La fille d'Athènes.* Annales Littéraires de l'Université de Besançon 363. Paris.

Brulotte, E.L. (1994) *The Placement of Votive Offerings and Dedications in the Peloponnesian Sanctuaries of Artemis.* Unpublished Diss. University of Minnesota.

Brumfield, A.C. (1981) *The Attic Festivals of Demeter and their Relation to the Agricultural Year.* New York.

Brumfield, A.C. (1996) '*Aporrheta*: Verbal and Ritual Obscenity in the Cults of Ancient Women.' in Hägg ed.: 67-74.

Bundgaard, J.A. (1976) *Parthenon and the Mycenean City on the Heights.* National Museum of Denmark. Archaeological and Historical series 17. Copenhagen.

Burkert, W. (1983) *Homo Necans: The Anthropology of Ancient Greek Sacrificial Ritual and Myth.* Berlin & New York (1972, Eng. trans. 1983).

Burkert, W. (1985) *Greek Religion.* Oxford (1977, Eng. trans. 1985).

Burkert, W. (1992) *The Orientalizing Revolution: Near Eastern Influence on Greek Culture in the Early Archaic Age.* Cambridge Mass. & London.

Bury, R.G. (1926) *Plato: Laws,* vol. 1. London & New York.

Carpenter, T.H. & Faraone, C.A. eds. (1993) *Masks of Dionysus.* Ithaca & London.

Carpenter, T.H. (1997) *Dionysian Imagery in Fifth-century Athens.* Oxford.

Carratelli, G.P. ed. (1988) *Magna Grecia: Vita religiosa e cultura litteraria filosofica e scientifica.* Milan.

Carter, J.B. (1988) 'Masks and Poetry in Early Sparta.' in Hägg, Marinatos & Nordquist eds.: 89-98.

Carter, J.C. (1994) 'Sanctuaries in the Chora of Metaponto.' in Alcock & Osborne eds.: 161-98.

Casadio, G. (1994) *Storia del culto di Dioniso in Argolide.* Rome.

Caskey, J.L. & Amandry, P. (1952) 'Investigations at the Heraion of Argos 1949.' *Hesp.* 21: 165-221.

Cavanaugh, M.B. (1996) *Eleusis and Athens: Documents in Finance, Religion and Politics in the Fifth Century BC.* Atlanta.

Chantraîne, P. (1968) *Dictionnaire etymologique de la langue grecque.* Vols. 1-2. Paris.

Chrysostomou, P.Ch. (1998) *Hê Thessalikê Thea En(n)odia e Pheraia Thea.* Athens.

Clinton, K. (1974) *The Sacred Officials of the Eleusinian Mysteries.* TAPhS 64.3. Philadelphia.

Clinton, K. (1988) 'Sacrifice at the Eleusinian Mysteries.' in Hägg, Marinatos & Nordquist eds.: 69-80.

Clinton, K. (1992) *Myth and Cult. The Iconography of the Eleusinian Mysteries.* Stockholm.

Clinton, K. (1993) 'The Sanctuary of Demeter and Kore at Eleusis.' in Hägg and Marinatos eds.: 108-24.

Clinton, K. (1994) 'The Epidauria and the Arrival of Asklepius in Athens.' in Hägg ed.: 17-34.

Clinton, K. (1996) 'The Thesmophorion in Central Athens and the Celebration of the Thesmophoria in Athens.' in Hägg ed.: 111-25.

Coldstream, J.N. ed. (1973) *Knossos: The Sanctuary of Demeter. BSA* (Suppl. 8).

Cole, S.G. (1980) 'New Evidence for the Mysteries of Dionysos.' *GRBS* 21: 223-38.

Cole, S.G. (1984) *Theoi Megaloi: The Cult of the Great Gods at Samothrace.* Leiden.

Cole, S.G. (1988) 'The Uses of Water in Greek Sanctuaries.' in Hägg, Marinatos & Nordquist eds.: 161-5.

Cole, S.G. (1993) 'Voices from beyond the Grave: Dionysus and the Dead.' in Carpenter & Faraone eds.: 276-95.

Cole, S.G. (1994) 'Demeter in the Ancient Greek City and its Countryside.' in Alcock & Osborne eds.: 199-216.

Cole, S.G. (1998) 'Domesticating Artemis.' in S. Blundell & M. Williamson eds. *The Sacred and the Feminine in Ancient Greece.* London & New York: 27-43

Collard, C., Cropp, M.J. & Lee, K.H. (1995) *Euripides. Selected Fragmentary Plays* I. Warminster.

Comella, A. (1978) *Il materiale votivo tardo di Gravisca.* Rome.

Constantinidou, S. (1993) *'augê/augai*: Some Observations on the Homeric Perception of Light and Vision.' *Dodone* 21: 98-101.

Conway, G.S. & Stoneman, R. (1997) *Pindar: The Odes and Selected Fragments.* London & Vermont. (1st ed. 1972)

Conze, A. (1880) 'Hermes-Kadmilos.' *Archäologische Zeitung* 38: 1-10.

Cook, A.B. (1914) *Zeus.* Vol. 1. Cambridge.

Cook, E. (1995) *The Odyssey in Athens.* Ithaca & London.

Cook, J.M. & Nicholls, R.V. (1998) *Old Smyrna Excavations: the Temples of Athena. BSA* (Suppl. 30).

Cook, J.M. (1950) 'Laconia. Kalyvia Sokhas.' *BSA* 45: 261-98.

Cook, J.M. (1953) 'Excavations at Mycenae. Part III. The Agamenoneion.' *BSA* 48: 30-68.

Corbett, P.E. (1949) 'Attic Pottery of the Late 5th Century. Appendix. *Phulêi nikôsêi bous.' Hesp.* 18: 346-51.

Craik, E. (1990) 'Sexual Imagery and *Innuendo* in Troades.' in Powell ed.: 1-15.

Crielaard, J.P. (1995) 'Homer, History and Archaeology: Some Remarks on the Date of the Homeric World.' in J.P. Crielaard ed., *Homeric Questions.* Amsterdam: 201-88.

Croissant, F. (1992) 'La produzione artistica.' *Sibari e Sibaritida.* Atti del trentaduesimo (XXXII) convegno di studi sulla Magna Grecia. Taranto: 539-59.

Cronkite, S.M. (1997) *The Sanctuary of Demeter at Mytilene: A Diachronic and Contextual Study.* Unpublished Diss. University of London.

Daffa-Nikonannou, A. (1973) *Thessalika hiera tês Dêmêtras kai koroplastika anathêmata.* Volos.

Dakaris, S.I. (1964) 'Anaskaphê eis to Nekuiomanteion toû Akherontos.' *ΠAE* 1961: 108-19.

Dale, A.M. (1967) *Euripides: Helen.* Oxford.

Daraki, M. (1985) *Dionysos.* Paris.

Daux, G. (1958) 'Thasos, Artemision.' *BCH* 82: 808-14.

Daux, G. (1959) 'Corinth, Galataki.' *BCH* 83: 608.

Daux, G. (1960) 'Thasos, Acropolis: Sanctuaire d'Athéna.' *BCH* 84: 864-6.

Daux, G. (1961) 'Olous.' *BCH* 85: 869.

Daux, G. (1967) *Guide de Thasos.* Paris.

Davies, J.K. (1967) 'Demosthenes on Liturgies: A Note.' *JHS* 87:33-40.

Dawkins, R.M. (1903-4) 'Excavations at Palaikastro III.' *BSA* 10: 220-3.

Dawkins, R.M. (1909) 'Laconia I: Excavations at Sparta, 1910. The Eleusinion at Kalyvia tes Sochas.' *BSA* 16: 12-14.

Dawkins, R.M. ed. (1929) *The Sanctuary of Artemis Orthia at Sparta. JHS* (Suppl. 5).

Deacy, S. (1997) 'The Vulnerability of Athena: Parthenoi and Rape in Greek Myth.' in S. Deacy & K.F. Pierce eds. *Rape in Antiquity*. London: 43-63.

Delcourt, M. (1981) *L'oracle de Delphes*. Paris.

Delcourt, M. (1982) *Hephaistos ou la légende du magicien*. Paris.

Delivorrias, A., Berger-Doer, G. & Kossatz-Deissmann, A. (1984) 'Aphrodite.' *LIMC* II: 2-151.

Dell, J. (1934) *Das Erechtheion in Athen*. Brünn.

Demand, N. (1994) *Birth, Death and Motherhood in Classical Greece*. Baltimore & London.

Demargne, P. (1984) 'Athena.' *LIMC* II: 955-1044.

Desborough, V.R. d'A. (1956) 'Mycenae 1939-1955. Part III. Two Tombs.' *BSA* 51: 129-30.

Detienne, M. & Vernant, J.P. (1991) *Cunning Intelligence in Greek Culture and Society*. Chicago & London (1974, Eng. trans. 1991).

Detienne, M. (1989) 'Culinary Practices and the Spirit of Sacrifice.' in M. Detienne & J.P. Vernant eds. *The Cuisine of Sacrifice among the Greeks*. Chicago: 1-20.

Deubner, L. (1932) *Attische Feste*. Berlin.

Dickins, G. (1906) 'Laconia I. Excavations at Sparta, 1907. A Sanctuary on the Megalopolis Road.' *BSA* 13: 169-73.

Dietrich, B.C. (1962) 'Demeter, Erinys, Artemis.' *Hermes* 90: 129-48.

Dimock, G.E. (1989) *The Unity of the Odyssey*. Amherst.

Dindorff, G. (1855) *Scholia Graeca in Homeri Odysseam*. Vol. 2. Oxford.

Dinsmoor, W.B. (1950) *The Architecture of Ancient Greece*. London, New York, Toronto & Sydney.

Donlan, W. (1997) 'The Homeric Economy.' in I. Morris & B. Powell eds. *A New Companion to Homer*. Leiden, New York & Köln: 649-67.

Dörpfeld, W. (1904) 'Der ursprüngliche Plan des Erechtheions.' *MDAI(A)* 29: 101-7.

Dover, K. (1993) *Aristophanes' Frogs*. Oxford.

Dover, K. (1997) *Aristophanes' Frogs*. Oxford (student ed.)

Dowden, K. (1989) *Death and the Maiden: Girls' Initiation Rites in Greek Mythology*. London & New York.

Droop, J. P. (1929) 'The Laconian Pottery.' in Dawkins ed.: 52-116.

Dugas, C. (1935) *Délos 17. Les vases orientalisants de style non mélien*. Paris.

Dugas, C. (1960) *Recueil Charles Dugas*. Paris.

Dunbabin, T.J. (1962) *Perachora 2. Pottery, Ivories, Scarabs and other Objects*. Oxford.

Durand, J.L. (1986) *Sacrifice et labour en Grèce ancienne*. Paris & Rome.

Dyer, T.H. (1873) *Ancient Athens. Its History, Topography and Remains*. London.

Edlund, I.E.M. (1987) *The Gods and the Place: Location and Function of Sanctuaries in the Countryside of Etruria and Magna Graecia (700-400 BC)*. Stockholm.

Edlund-Berry, I.E.M. (1990) *The Central Sanctuary at Morgantina, Sicily*. Stockholm.

Edmonds, J.M. (1961) *The Fragments of Attic Comedy* 3.A. Leiden.

Edmundson, H.P. (1977) *Aspects of the Prometheus Myth in Ancient Greek Literature and Art*. Unpublished Diss. University of Texas.

Elderkin, G.W. (1941) 'The Cults of the Erechtheion.' *Hesp*. 10: 113-24.

Evelyn-White, H.G. (1929) *Hesiod: The Homeric Hymns and Homerica.* London & New York.

Fairbanks, A. (1912) *Athenian White Lekythoi.* London.

Faraone, C.A. (1992) *Talismans and Trojan Horses.* New York & Oxford.

Farnell, L.R. (1896a) *The Cults of the Greek City-States.* Vol. 2. Oxford.

Farnell, L.R. (1896b) *The Cults of the Greek City-States.* Vol. 3. Oxford.

Farnell, L.R. (1909) *The Cults of the Greek City-States.* Vol. 5. Oxford.

Ferguson,W.S. & Dinsmoor W.B. (1933) 'The last inventory of the Pronaos of the Parthenon.' *AJArch.* 37: 52-7.

Fergusson, J. (1880) 'Das Erechtheion und der Tempel der Athena Polias in Athen.' in H. Schliemann ed. Leipzig.

Filges, A. & Metern, P. (1996) 'Eine Opfergrube der Demeter in Neandria.' *Asia Minor Studies 22 Die Troas. Neue Forschungen zu Neandria und Alexandria, Troas* 2 Bonn: 43-86.

Fol, A. (1993) *Dionysos der Thrakische: Zagreus.* Sofia.

Foley, H.P. ed. (1994) *The Homeric Hymn to Demeter: Translation, Commentary and Interpretative Essays.* Princeton (1977, repr. 1994).

Fontaine, P.F.M. (1986-1995) *The Light and the Dark: A Cultural History of Dualism.* 1-10. Amsterdam.

Fontenrose, J. (1981) *Orion: The Myth of the Hunter and the Hunters.* Berkeley, Los Angeles & London.

Fordyce, C.J. (1990) *Catullus: A Commentary.* Oxford. (repr., 1st ed. 1961)

Foxhall, L. (1995) 'Bronze to Iron: Agricultural Systems and Political Structures in Late Bronze Age and Early Iron Age Greece.' *BSA* 90: 239-50.

Frazer, J.G. (1898) *Pausanias' Description of Greece.* Vol. 2. London.

Frickenhaus, A. (1912) *Tiryns* 1. Athens.

Frickenhaus, A. (1912b) 'Der Schiffsgarten des Dionysos.' *JDAI* 27: 61-79.

Frisk, H. (1960) *Griechisches Etymologisches Wörterbuch.* Vol. 1. Heidelberg.

Frisk, H. (1970) *Griechisches Etymologisches Wörterbuch.* Vol. 2. Heidelberg.

Froning, H. (1971) *Dithyrambos und Vasenmalerei in Athen.* Würzburg.

Frontisi-Ducroux, F. (1991) *Le dieu-masque: une figure du Dionysos d'Athènes.* Paris & Rome.

Fuchs, W. (1959) *Die Vorbilder der Neoattischen Reliefs.* JDAI (Ergänzungsheft 2).

Furley, W.D. (1981) *Studies in the Use of Fire in Ancient Greek Religion.* New York.

Furtwängler, A. (1906) *Aegina. Das Heiligtum der Aphaia.* Munich.

Furtwängler, A. (1980) 'Heraion von Samos: Grabungen im Südtemenos 1977, I.' *MDAI(A)* 95: 149-224.

Furtwängler, W. (1895) *Masterpieces of Greek Sculpture.* London.

Gabrici, E. (1927) *Il santuario della Malophoros a Selinunte. Mon. Ant.* 32.

Gantz, T.N. (1977) 'The Fires of the Oresteia.' *JHS* 97: 28-38.

Gardiner, E.N. (1955) *Athletics of the Ancient World.* Oxford (1930, repr. 1955).

Gardner, E.A. (1902) *Ancient Athens.* London.

Gasparri, C. (1986) 'Dionysos.' *LIMC* III: 414-566.

Gasser, A. (1990) *Die korinthische und attische Importkeramik vom Artemision in Ephesos. Forschungen in Ephesos* 12.1. Vienna.

Gauthier, Ph. (1995) 'Du nouveau sur les courses aux flambeaux d'après deux inscriptions de Kos.' *Rev. Ét. Grec.* 108: 576-85.

Glowacki, K.T. (1998) 'The Acropolis of Athens Before 566 BC.' in K.J. Hartswick & M.C. Surgeon eds. *Stephanos: Studies in Honour of Brunilde Sismondo Ridgway.* Philadelphia: 79-88.

Golden, M. (1998) *Sport and Society in Ancient Greece.* Cambridge.

Goldman, H. (1931) *Excavations at Eutresis in Boeotia.* Cambridge, Mass.

Goodison, L. (1989) *Death, Women and the Sun: Symbolism of Regeneration in Early Aegean Religion. BICS* (Suppl. 53).

Göttlicher, A. (1978) *Materiale für ein Corpus der Schiffsmodelle im Altertum.* Mainz.

Göttwald, O. (1927) *Der Fackellauf in der Antike.* Unpublished Diss. University of Vienna.

Göttwald, O. (1928) 'Zum Fackellauf.' *Mitteilungen des Vereins Klassischer Philologen* 5: 46-74.

Graf, F. (1974) *Eleusis und die Orphische Dichtung Athens in vorhellenistischer Zeit.* Berlin & New York.

Graf, F. (1985) *Nordionische Kulte.* Biblioteca Helvetica Romana 21.

Graf, F. (1993) 'Dionysian and Orphic Eschatology.' in Carpenter & Faraone eds.: 239-58.

Graf, F. (1996) '*Pompai* in Greece: Some Considerations about Space and Ritual in the Greek Polis.' in Hägg ed.: 55-65.

Grene, D. & Lattimore, R.A. (1959) *Euripides III: Orestes, Iphigeneia in Aulis, Electra, The Phoenician Women, The Bacchae.* New York & Toronto.

Griffiths, A. (1972) 'Alcman's Partheneion.' *QUCC* 13: 7-30.

Grose, S.W. (1926) *Catalogue of the McClean Collection of Greek Coins*, II. Cambridge.

Guazzelli, T. (1992) *Le Antesterie: Liturgie e pratiche simboliche.* Florence.

Guimond, L. (1981) 'Aktaion.' *LIMC* I: 454-69.

Gulick, C.B. (1957) *Athenaeus: The Deipnosophists.* Vol. 7. London & Cambridge Mass.

Hadzisteliou-Price, T. (1971) 'Double and Multiple Representations in Greek Art and Religious Thought.' *JHS* 91: 48-69.

Hadzisteliou-Price, T. (1978) *Kourotrophos: Cults and Representations of the Greek Nursing Deities.* Leiden.

Hägg, R. & Marinatos, N. (1993) eds. *Greek Sanctuaries: New Approaches.* London.

Hägg, R. (1992) *The Iconography of Greek Cult in the Archaic and Classical Periods.* Proceedings of the 1st International Seminar on Ancient Greek Cult at the Swedish Institute and the European Cultural Centre of Delphi, 16-18 November 1990. Athens & Liège.

Hägg, R. (1994) ed. *Ancient Greek Cult Practice from the Epigraphical Evidence.* Proceedings of the 2nd International Seminar on Ancient Cult at the Swedish Institute in Athens 22-24 November 1991. Stockholm.

Hägg, R. (1996) ed. *The Role of Religion in the Early Greek Polis.* Proceedings of the Third International Seminar on Ancient Greek Cult, organised by the Swedish Institute at Athens, 16-18 October 1992. Stockholm.

Hägg, R., Marinatos, N. & Nordquist, G. (1988) eds. *Early Greek Cult Practice.* Proceedings of the 5th International Symposium at the Swedish Institute at Athens 26-29 June 1986. Stockholm.

Hall, E. (1996) *Aeschylus: Persians.* Warminster.

Halleran, M.R. (1995). *Euripides: Hippolytus.* Warminster.

Halm-Tisserant, M. (1986) 'La représentation du retour d'Hephaistos dans l'Olympe.' *AK* 29: 8-22.

Halm-Tisserant, M. (1993) *Cannibalisme et immortalité. L'enfant dans le chaudron en Grèce ancienne.* Paris.

Hamilton, R. (1992) *Choes and Anthesteria.* Ann Arbor.

Harris, D. (1995) *The Treasures of the Parthenon and Erechtheion.* Oxford.

Harris, H.A.(1964) *Greek Athletes and Athletics.* London.

Harrison, E.B. (1977) 'Alkamenes' Sculptures for the Hephaisteion. Part I. The Cult Statues.' *AJArch.* 81: 137-78.

Haynes, S. (1985) *Etruscan Bronzes.* London.

Head, B.V. (1889) *Catalogue of Greek Coins.* (British Museum Collection) London.

Hedreen, G.M. (1992) *Silens in Attic Black-figure Vase-painting.* Michigan.

Held, W. (1990) 'Künstliche Beleuchtung und Architektur.' in W.D. Heilmeyer & W. Hoepfner eds. *Licht und Architektur.* Tübingen: 53-60.

Helly, B. (1973) *Gonnoi* 1-2. Amsterdam.

Henrichs, A. (1993) ' "He has a God in Him": Human and Divine in the Modern Perception of Dionysus.' in Carpenter & Faraone eds.: 13-43.

Herbert, S. (1986) 'The Torch-race in Corinth.' in M.A. del Chiaro ed. *Corinthiaca: Studies in Honor of D.A. Amyx.* Columbia: 29-35.

Heres, G. (1969) *Die Punischen und Griechischen Tonlampen der Staatlichen Museen zu Berlin.* Berlin & Amsterdam.

Hermary, A., Cassimatis, H. & Vollkommer, R. (1986) 'Eros.' *LIMC* III: 850-942.

Herrmann, H.V. (1966) *Olympische Forschungen* 6. *Die Kessel der Orientalisierenden Zeit.* Berlin.

Heubeck, A., Russo, J. & Fernandez-Galiano, M. (1992) *A Commentary on Homer's Odyssey.* Vol. 3. *Books 17-24.* Oxford.

Higgins, R.A. (1967) *Greek Terracottas.* London.

Hinz, V. (1998) *Der Kult von Demeter und Kore auf Sizilien und in der Magna Graecia.* Wiesbaden.

Hitzig, H. & Blümner, H. (1896) *Pausaniae Graeciae Descriptio* 1. *Attica.* Berlin.

Hoepfner, W. (1997) 'Probleme der Topographie und Baugeschichte.' in Hoepfner ed.: 152-9.

Hoepfner, W. (1997) ed. *Kult und Kultbauten auf der Akropolis: Internationales Symposium vom 7. bis 9. Juli 1995 in Berlin.* Berlin.

Hogarth, D.G. (1908). *Excavations at Ephesus: The Archaic Artemision.* London.

Hollinshead, M.B. (1985) 'Against Iphigeneia's adyton in Three Mainland Temples.' *Hesp.* 89: 419-40.

Hollis, A.S. (1990) *Callimachus: Hecale.* Oxford.

Holloway, R. (1991) *The Archaeology of Ancient Sicily.* London.

Hoorn van, G. (1924) *De Fackelloop. MNIR* 4.

Hoorn van, G. (1951) *Choes and Anthesteria.* Leiden.

Hornbostel, W. (1980) *Aus Gräbern und Heiligtümern.* Mainz.

Howland, R.H. (1958) *Agora* 4. *Greek Lamps and their Survivals.* Princeton.

Hunt, P. (1998) *Slaves, Warfare, and Ideology in the Greek Historians.* Cambridge.

Jacobstahl, P. (1927) *Ornamente Griechischer Vasen.* Berlin.

Jahn, O. & Michaelis, A. (1901) *Arx Athenarum a Pausania descripta.* Bonn.

Jakovides, S. (1962) *Hê Mykenaïkê Akropolis tôn Athênôn.* Athens.

Jameson, M. (1993) 'The asexuality of Dionysus.' in Carpenter & Faraone eds.: 44-64.

Jantzen U. (1972) *Samos* 8. *Ägyptische und Orientalische Bronzen aus dem Heraion von Samos.* Bonn.

Jantzen, U. & Tölle, R. (1968) 'Beleuchtungsgerät.' in S. Laser ed. *Archaeologia Homerica* 2: P *Hausrat.* Göttingen: 83-98.

Jeppesen, K. (1979) 'Where was the So-called Erechtheion?' *AJA* 83: 381-94.

Johnston S.I. (1990) *Hekate Sôteira. A Study in Hekate's Roles in the Chaldaean Oracles and Related Literature.* Atlanta.

Jones, H.L. (1927) *The Geography of Strabo.* Vol. 4. London & New York.

Jones, W.H.S. (1939) *Pausanias: Description of Greece.* Vol. 3. London & Cambridge Mass. (1st ed. 1935)

Jost, M. (1985) *Sanctuaires et cultes d'Arcadie*. Études Péloponnésiennes IX. Paris.

Jucker, I. (1998) 'Euripides und der Mythos von Orest und Iphigenie.' in B. Zimmerman ed. *Euripides: Iphigenie bei den Tauren*. Stuttgart: 105-38.

Julius, L. (1878) *Ueber das Erechtheion*. Munich.

Just, R. (1989) *Women in Athenian Law and Life*. London & New York.

Jüthner (1924) 'Lampadedromia.' *RE* XII.1, cols. 569-77.

Kagan, D. (1988) *The Fall of the Athenian Empire*. Ithaca & London. (1st ed. 1987)

Kahil, L. (1965) 'Autour de l'Artémis attique.' *AK* 8: 20-33.

Kahil, L. (1977) 'L'Artémis de Brauron: rites et mystères.' *AK* 20: 85-98.

Kahil, L. (1984) 'Artemis.' *LIMC* II: 618-753.

Kahil, L.G. (1963) 'Quelques vases du sanctuaire d'Artémis à Brauron.' *AK* 1 (Beiheft): 5-29.

Kalligas, P.G. (1978) 'Hieron Dêmêtros kai Korês stên Kranê Kephallonias.' Ἀρχ. Ἐφ.: 136-46.

Kannicht, R. (1969) *Euripides, Helena*. Heidelberg.

Kanta, K. (1979) *Eleusina*. Athens.

Karageorgis, V. et al. (1981) *Excavations at Kition* 4. *The Non-cypriot Pottery*. Nicosia.

Karageorgis, V. (1999) 'Notes on Some "Enigmatic" Objects from the Prehistoric Aegean and Other East Mediterranean Regions.' *Arch. Anz.* Heft 4: 501-14.

Karagiorga, Th. (1963) 'Archaia Mantineia.' *AΔ* 18, B': 88-9.

Karagiorga, Th. (1970) '*Gorgiê kephalê; Katagôgê kai noêma tês Gorgonikês morphês eis tên latreian kai tên tekhnên tôn Arkhaïkôn khronôn*. Athens.

Karo, G. (1909) 'Archäologische Funde im Jahr 1908.' *Arch. Anz.* 24: 102.

Karo, G. (1911) 'Archäologische Funde im Jahr 1910.' *Arch. Anz.* 26: 132-3.

Kassab-Tezgör, D. & Sezer, T. (1995) *Catalogue des lampes en terre cuite du Musée Archéologique d'Istanbul* I. *Varia Anatolica* 6.1. Paris.

Kearns, E. (1994) 'Cakes in Greek Sacrificial Regulations.' in Hägg ed.: 65-70.

Kefalidou, E. (1996) *Nikêtês: Eikonographikê meletê tou arkhaiou Hellênikoû athlêtismoû*. Thessaloniki.

Kekulé, R. (1884) *Die Terrakotten von Sicilien*. Vol. 2. Berlin & Stuttgart.

Kennell, N.M. (1995) *The Gymnasium of Virtue: Education and Culture in Ancient Sparta*. Chapel Hill & London.

Kérenyi, I.C. (1963) *Prometheus: Archetypal Image of Human Existence*. London.

Kérenyi, I.C. (1967) *Eleusis: Archetypal Images of Greek Religion* 4. New York & London.

Kern, O. (1890) 'Theoi hiatêres.' Ἀρχ. Ἐφ.: 131-42.

Kilmer, M.F. (1993) *Greek Erotica on Attic Red-figure Vases*. London.

King, H. (1993) "Bound to Bleed": Artemis and Greek Women.' in A. Cameron & A. Kuhrt eds. *Images of Women in Antiquity*. London. (1983, repr. 1993): 109-27.

Knoepfler, D. (1993) *Les imagiers de l'Orestie: mille ans d'art antique autour d'un mythe grec*. Catalogue d'une exposition créée au musée d'art at d'histoire de Neuchâtel. Novembre 1991-Février 1992. Zurich.

Kokkorou-Alevras, G. (1990) 'Herakles.' *LIMC* V: 35-43.

Kokkou-Viridi, K. (1991) *Prôïmes pures thusiôn sto Telestêrio tês Eleusinas. Sumbolê stên meletê tou Eleusiniakoû hieroû*. Unpublished Diss. University of Athens.

Kontoleon, N.M. (1949) *To Erekhtheion ôs oikodomêma chthonias latreias*. Athens.

Kontoleon, N.M. (1961-2) 'Hê genesis toû Dios.' *Krêtika Khronika* 15-16: 283-93.

Korres, M. (1997) 'Die Athena-Tempel auf der Akropolis.' in Hoepfner ed.: 218-41.

Koukouli-Chrysanthaki, C. (1989) 'Thrace. Abdêra.' *Arch. Rep.*: 84-5.

Koukouli-Chrysanthaki, Ch. (1987) 'Anaskaphes sta archaia Abdêra.' *AEMΘ* 1: 407-13.

Kourouniotis, K. (1937) 'Eleusiniakê dadoukhia.' 'Αρχ. 'Εφ.: 223-53.

Kovacs, D. (1994) *Euripides: Cyclops, Alcestis, Medea.* Cambridge Mass. & London.

Kraay, C.M. (1976) *Archaic and Classical Greek Coins.* London.

Kraus, T. (1960) *Hekate.* Heidelberg.

Krauskopf, I. (1990) 'Kapaneus.' *LIMC* V: 952-63.

Kron, U. (1976) *Die Zehn Attischen Phylenheroen, Geschichte, Mythos, Kult und Darstellungen.* Berlin.

Kron, U. (1992) 'Frauenfeste in Demeterheiligtumern. Das Thesmophorion von Bitalemi.' *Arch. Anz.*: 629-50.

Kurtz, D. (1983) *The Berlin Painter.* Oxford.

Kyle, D.G. (1987) *Athletics in Ancient Athens.* Leiden.

Kyle, D.G. (1992) 'The Panathenaic Games: Sacred and Civic Athletics.' in Neils ed.: 77-101.

Lada-Richards, I. (1999) *Initiating Dionysus: Ritual and Theatre in Aristophanes' Frogs.* Oxford.

Lambrinoudakis, V. et al. (1984) 'Apollon.' *LIMC* II: 183-327.

Lane, E.N. (1996) ed. *Cybele, Attis and Related Cults. Essays in Memory of M.J. Vermaseren.* Leiden, New York & London.

Lattanzi, E. et al. (1996) *Santuari della Magna Grecia in Calabria.* Naples.

Launey, M. (1944) *Le sanctuaire et le culte d'Heraklès à Thasos. Études Thasiennes* I. Paris.

Lawall, G.-S. (1986) *Euripides, Hippolytus.* Bristol.

Lee, H.M. (1988) '*SIG* 802: Did Women Compete Against Men in Greek Athletic Festivals?' *Nikephoros* 1: 103-17.

Lefkowitz, M.R. (1996) 'Women in the Panathenaic and Other Festivals.' in Neils ed.: 78-94.

Legrand, Ph. E. (1905) 'Antiquités de Trézène.' *BCH* 29: 302.

Leinieks, V. (1996) *The City of Dionysos: A Study of Euripides' Bakchai.* Stuttgart & Leipzig.

Leipen, N. (1970) *Athena Parthenos: A Reconstruction.* Toronto.

Leonhard, M. (1974) *Die Kreuzfackel: Ein Beitrag zum Kult der Demeter und Persephone in Unteritalien.* Unpublished Diss. University of Innsbruck.

Leventi, I. (1997) 'Zeus.' *LIMC* VIII (Supplementum): 338-46

Levi, D. (1968) 'Gli scavi di Iasos.' *ASAA* 45-6: 537-90.

Levi, P. (1971) *Pausanias: Guide to Greece.* Middlesex, Baltimore & Ringwood.

Lezzi-Hafter, A. & Zindel, C. (1991) *Dionysos: Mythes et Mystères. Vases de Spina.* Zurich.

Lilibaki-Akamati, M. (1989) 'Thesmophoria stên Makedonia.' *Arkhaia Makedonia* 5.2: 809-19.

Lilibaki-Akamati, M. (1996) *To Thesmophorio tês Pellas.* Athens.

Lipka, M. (1997) 'Anmerkungen zu den Weihinschriften der Athena Parthenos und zur Hekatompedon-Inschrift.' in Hoepfner ed.: 37-44.

Lissarrague, F. (1990) 'Why Satyrs are Good to Represent.' in J.J. Winkler & F.I. Zeitlin eds. *Nothing to do with Dionysos? The Athenian Drama in its Social Context.* Princeton: 228-36.

Lissarrague, F. (1993) 'On the Wildness of Satyrs.' in Carpenter & Faraone eds.: 207-20.

Lloyd, A.B. (1976) *Commentary on Herodotus. Book 2.* Leiden.

Lloyd-Jones, H. (1994) *Sophocles: Ajax, Electra, Oedipus Tyrannus.* Cambridge Mass. & London.

Lloyd-Jones, H. (1994) *Sophocles: Antigone, The Women of Trachis, Philoctetes, Oedipus at Colonus*. Cambridge Mass. & London.

Lo Porto, F.G. (1967) 'Stipe del Culto di Demetra in Heraklea Lucana.' *MDAI(R)* 11: 100-80.

Löhr, C. (1997) 'Pausanias und der Verlauf des Panathenäen-Festzuges.' in Hoepfner ed.: 16-21.

Loicq-Berger, M.-P. (1970) 'À propos du "lychneion" de Denys le Jeune. Pour une histoire de la lusterie antique.' *Latomus* 114 (Hommages à Marie Delcourt): 149-61.

Lorber, C.C. (1990) *Amphipolis: The Civic Coinage in Silver and Gold*. Los Angeles.

Lorimer, H.L. (1950) *Homer and the Monuments*. London.

Loucas, I.-E. (1994) 'The Sacred Laws of Lykosoura.' in Hägg ed.: 97-9.

Lowe, N.J. (1998) 'Thesmophoria and Haloa: Myths, Physics and Mysteries' in Blundell & Williamson eds.: 149-73.

Luckerman, F. & Moody, J. (1978) 'Nichoria and Vicinity: Settlements and Circulation.' *Excavations at Nichoria in Southwestern Greece* I: *Site, Environs, and Techniques*. G. Rapp & S. Aschenbrenner eds. Minneapolis: 78-112.

Ma, J. (1994a) 'Black Hunter Variations: I. Damon le chasseur noir (Plutarque, *Cimon*, 1-2).' *PCPS* 40: 49-59.

Ma, J. (1994b) 'Black Hunter Variations: II. Damon of Chaironeia: a Historical Commentary (Plut. *Cim.*, 1-2)' *PCPS* 40: 60-9.

Ma, J. (1994c) 'Black Hunter Variations III. Damon of Chaironeia: Battlelines.' *PCPS* 40: 70-8.

MacDowell, D.M. (1988) *Aristophanes: Wasps*. Oxford (1971, repr. 1988).

Malkin, I. (1987) *Religion and Colonization in Ancient Greece*. Leiden, New York, Copenhagen & Köln.

Mandala, T. (1990) 'To klasiko nekrotapheio tês Amphipolês.' *Mnêmê D. Lazaridê: Polis kai Chora stên Arkhaia Makedonia kai Thrakê. Praktika arkhaiologikou sunedriou, Kavala 9-11 Maiou 1986*. Thessaloniki: 275-7.

Mansfield, J.M. (1985) *The Robe of Athena and the Panathenaic Peplos*. Unpublished Diss. University of California at Berkeley.

Marconi, P. (1926) 'Sicilia. Girgenti: Il tempio di Demetra.' *Not. Scav.* 51: 118-48.

Marconi, P. (1929) *Agrigento: topographia ed arte*. Florence.

Marconi, P. (1933) *Agrigento Arcaica: Il santuario della divinità; chthonia a il tempio detto di vulcano. ASMG* 1931. Rome.

Marconi, P. (1977) 'Studi Agrigentini.' *RIA* 1: 29-52.

Margreiter, I. (1988) *Alt-Ägina 2.3. Die Kleinfunde aus dem Apollon-Heiligtum*. Mainz.

Marinatos, S. (1936) 'Le temple géométrique de Dréros.' *BCH* 60: 219-60.

Mazarakis-Ainian, A. (1995) 'New Evidence for the Study of the late Geometric-Archaic Settlement at Lathoureza in Attica.' in Ch. Morris ed. *Klados: Essays in Honour of J.N. Coldstream. BICS* Suppl. 63: 143-55.

Mazarakis-Ainian, A. (1998) 'Epiphaneiakes arkhaiologikes ereunes stên Kuthno (1990-1995).' *ΠΑΕ* 1995: 137-209.

Metzger, H. (1951) *Les représentations dans la céramique attique du IVème siècle*. Paris.

Metzger, H. (1965) *Recherches sur l'imagerie athénienne*. Paris.

Metzger, I.R. (1985) *Eretria 7. Das Thesmophorion von Eretria*. Bern.

Meuli, K. (1946) 'Griechische Opferbräuche.' in O. Gigon (et al.) eds. *Phyllobolia: für Peter von der Mühl zum 60. Geburtstag am 1. August 1945*. Basel: 185-288.

Michaelis, A. (1877) 'Bemerkungen zur Periegese der Akropolis von Athen. 7. Pausanias Wanderung durch den Tempel der Polias.' *MDAI(A)* 2: 15-37.

Mikalson, J.P. (1975) *The Sacred and Civil Calendar of the Athenian Year.* Princeton.

Miller, H.F. (1979) *The Iconography of the Palm in Greek Art: Significance and Symbolism.* Unpublished Diss. University of California at Berkeley.

Miller, S.G. (1991) *Arete: Greek Sports from Ancient Sources.* Berkeley.

Mingazzini, P. (1971) *Catalogo dei vasi della collezione Augusto Castellani,* 2. Rome.

Mitropoulou, E. (1977) *Corpus 1. Attic Votive Reliefs of the 6th and 5th Centuries BC.* Athens.

Mitsopoulos-Leon, V. (1993) 'The Statue of Artemis at Lousoi: Some Thoughts.' in O. Palagia & W.D.E. Coulson eds. *Sculpture from Arcadia and Laconia.* Oxford: 33-9.

Monro, D.B. (1901) *Homer's Odyssey. Books 13-24.* Oxford.

Moret, J.-M. (1982) 'L'apollinisation' de l'imagerie légendaire à Athènes dans la seconde moitié du Vème siècle.' *Rev. Arch.*: 109-36.

Moretti, M. (1966) *Tomba Martini-Marescotti.* Rome.

Morris, S.P. (1997) 'Homer and the Near East.' in I. Morris & B. Powell eds. *A New Companion to Homer.* Leiden, New York & Köln: 599-623.

Morrison, J.S. & Williams, R.T. (1968) *Greek Oared Ships 900-322 BC.* Cambridge.

Mortzos, Ch. (1985) *Hê anaskaphê Brusôn Kudônias. To Hellêniko hiero A sto Kastello.* Athens.

Mountjoy, P.A. (1981) *Four Early Mycenaean Wells from the South Slope of the Acropolis at Athens.* Miscellanea Graeca, fasc. 4. Ghent.

Mountjoy, P.A. (1993) *Mycenaean Pottery: An Introduction.* Oxford.

Mountjoy, P.A. (1995) *Mycenaean Athens.* Jonsared.

Müller, M. (1966) *Athene als göttliche Helferin in der Odyssee.* Heidelberg.

Murray, A.T. (1995) rev. by Dimock, G.E. *Homer: The Odyssey.* Cambridge Mass. & London.

Mylonas, G. (1961) *Eleusis and the Eleusinian Mysteries.* Princeton.

Mylonas, G.E. & Kourouniotis, K. (1933) 'Excavations at Eleusis.' *AJArch.* 37: 281-2.

Neils, J. (1992) ed. *Goddess and Polis: The Panathenaic Festival in Ancient Athens.* Princeton.

Neils, J. (1996) ed. *Worshipping Athena: Panathenaia and Parthenon.* Madison.

Neils, J. (1997) ' "Lost" and Found: Adam Buck's Wedding of Dionysus.' in J.H. Oakley, W.D.E. Coulson & O. Palagia eds. *Athenian Potters and Painters.* Oxford: 231-40.

Németh, G. (1993) 'Übersetzung und Datierung der Hekatompedon-Inschrift.' *JDAI* 108: 76-81.

Neutsch, B. & Rolley, C. (1981) 'Documenti artistici del santuario di Demetra a Policoro.' in *Siris e l' Influenza Ionica Occidentale.* Atti del ventesimo (XX) convegno di studi sulla Magna Grecia. Taranto: 149-73.

Neutsch, B. (1956) 'Archäologische Grabungen und Funde im Bereich der Unteritalischen Soprintendenzen von Tarent, Reggio di Calabria und Salerno.' *Arch. Anz.* 71: 194-450.

Newton, C.T. (1862) *A History of the Discoveries at Halicarnassus, Cnidus and Branchidae* 2.1. London.

Newton, C.T. (1863) *A History of the Discoveries at Halicarnassus, Cnidus and Branchidae* 2.2. London.

Nick, G. (1997) 'Die Athena Parthenos – ein griechisches Kultbild.' in Hoepfner ed.: 22-4.

Nilsson, M.P. (1950) 'Lampen und Kerzen im Kult der Antike.' *Op. Arch.* 6, Skrifter utgivna av Svenska institutet i Rom XV (Acta Instituti Romani Regni Sueviae). Lund: 96-111.

Nylander, C. (1962) 'Die sog. Mykenischen Säulenbasen auf der Akropolis in Athen.' *Op. Ath.* 4: 31-77.

Oakley, J.H. & Sinos, R.H. (1993) *The Wedding in Ancient Athens.* Wisconsin & London.

Oakley, J.H. (1995) 'Nuptial Nuances Wedding Images in Non-wedding Scenes of Myth.' in E.D. Reeder ed. *Pandora: Women in Classical Greece.* Princeton: 63-73.

Obbink, D. (1993) 'Dionysus Poured out: Ancient and Modern Theories of Sacrifice and Cultural Formation.' in Carpenter & Faraone eds.: 65-86.

Oldfather, C.H. (1939) *Diodorus of Sicily.* Vol. 3. London & Cambridge Mass.

Olmos, R. (1986) 'Eileithyia.' *LIMC* III: 685-99.

Orlandini, P. (1963) 'Gela: la Stipe votiva arcaica del Predio Sola.' *Mon. Ant.* 46: 3-78.

Orsi, P. (1906) *Gela. Scavi del 1900-1905. Mon. Ant.* 17.

Orsi, P. (1911) 'Croton. Prima campagna di scavi al santuario di Hera Lacinia.' *Not. Scav.* 8 (Suppl.): 77-124.

Overbeck, J.C. (1972) 'Some Notes on the interior arrangement of the Erechtheum.' *AAA* 5: 127-9.

Owen, A.S. (1939) *Ion: Euripides. Commentary, Edition and Introduction.* Oxford.

Pachis, P. (1996) ' "*Gallaion Kubelês ololugma*" (Anthol. Palat. VI, 173). L'élément orgiastique dans le culte de Cybèle.' in Lane ed.: 193-222.

Padel, R. (1992) *In and Out of the Mind: Greek Images of the Tragic Self.* Princeton.

Page, D.L. (1951) *Alcman: The Partheneion.* Oxford.

Palagia, O. & Lewis, D. (1989) 'The Ephebes of Erechtheis, 333/2 BC and their Dedication.' *BSA* 84: 333-44.

Palagia, O. (1984) 'A niche for Kallimachos' lamp?' *AJArch.* 88: 515-21.

Palaiokrassa, L. (1991) *To hiero tês Artemidos Mounukhias.* Athens.

Pantelidou M. (1975) *Hai Proïstorikai Athênai.* Athens.

Papachatzis, N.D. (1974) *Pausaniou Hellados periêgêsis* 1. Athens.

Papachatzis, N.D. (1976) *Pausaniou Hellados periêgêsis* 2. Athens.

Papachatzis, N.D. (1979) *Pausaniou Hellados periêgêsis* 3. Athens.

Papachatzis, N.D. (1980) *Pausaniou Hellados periêgêsis* 4. Athens.

Papachatzis, N.D. (1981) *Pausaniou Hellados periêgêsis* 5. Athens.

Papadimitriou, I. (1951) 'Anaskaphai en Braurôni Attikês.' *ΠAE* 1949: 75-90.

Papoutsaki-Serbeti, E. (1983) *Ho Zôgraphos tês Providence.* Athens.

Parisinou, E. (1997) 'Artificial Illumination in Greek Cult Practice of the Archaic and the Classical Periods: Mere Practical Necessity?' *Thetis* 4: 94-102.

Parisinou, E. (1998) 'Lighting Practices in Early Greece, from the End of the Mycenaean World until the 7th Century BC.' *OJA* 117: 327-43.

Parisinou, E. (2000) ' "Lighting" the World of Women: Lamps and Torches in the Hands of Women in the Late Archaic and Classical Periods.' *G & R* 47.1: 19-42.

Parke, H.W. (1977) *Festivals of the Athenians.* London.

Parker, R. (1983) *Miasma. Pollution and Purification in Early Greek Religion.* Oxford.

Parker, R. (1996) *Athenian Religion: A History.* Oxford.

Parry, H. (1992) *Thelxis: Magic and Imagination in Greek Myth and Poetry.* Lanham, New York & London.

Paton, J.M. (1927) *The Erechtheum.* Cambridge Mass.

Payne, H. (1940) *Perachora: The Sanctuaries of Hera Akraia and Limenia* 1. Oxford.

Pelekides, Ch. (1962) *Histoire de l'ephébie attique des origines à 31 avant Jésus-Christ*. Paris.

Pemberton, E. (1989) *Corinth 18.1. The Sanctuary of Demeter and Kore. The Greek Pottery*. Princeton.

Perlzweig, J. (1961) *The Athenian Agora 7. Lamps of the Roman Period*. Princeton.

Perrin, B. (1916) *Plutarch's Lives*. Vol. 4. London & New York.

Perrin, B. (1948) *Plutarch's Lives*. Vol. 1. London & Cambridge Mass.

Persson, A.W. (1942) *New Tombs at Dendra near Midea*. Lund.

Peschlow-Bindokat, A. (1972) 'Demeter und Persephone in der attischen Kunst des 6 bis 4 Jahrhunderts. Demeter und Pesephone in der frühgriechischen Dichtung.' *JDAI* 87: 60-157.

Petrakos, V. (1981) 'Nees ereunes ston Ramnounta.' Ἀρχ. Ἐφ.: 1979: 1-81.

Pfeiffer, R. (1949) *Callimachus 1-2. Fragmenta*. Oxford.

Pfeiffer, R. (1960) 'Die goldene Lampe der Athene.' in W. Bühler ed. *Ausgewählte Schriften*. Munich: 1-7.

Philios, D. (1885a) 'Ekthesis tôn en Eleusini anaskaphôn.' *ΠΑΕ* 1884: 64-87.

Philios, D. (1885b) 'Eurêmata en Eleusini.' Ἀρχ. Ἐφ.: 169-83.

Picard, Ch. (1944) 'Trapézophore sculpté d'un sanctuaire thasien.' *Mon. Piot* 40: 107-34.

Picard, Ch. (1948) *Manuel d'Archéologie Grecque: La sculpture 3*. Paris.

Piérart, M. (1996) 'La mort de Dionysos à Argos.' in Hägg ed.: 141-51.

Pingiatoglou, S. (1981) *Eileithyia*. Würzburg.

Pingiatoglou, S. (1991)19 'To hiero tês Dêmêtras sto Dion.' *AEMΘ*: 145-51.

Pittakis, K.S. (1862) 'To en Erekhtheiô heurethen ploion.' Ἀρχ. Ἐφ.: 91-4.

Pouilloux, J. (1948) 'Lampadédromies thasiennes.' *Rev. Arch.* (Mélanges Picard) 2: 847-57.

Pouilloux, J. (1954) *Recherches sur l'histoire et les cultes de Thasos. Études Thasiennes III*. Paris.

Powell, A. (1990) ed. *Euripides: Women and Sexuality*. London & New York.

Powell, B.B. (1991) *Homer and the Origin of the Greek Alphabet*. Cambridge.

Pritchett, W. K. (1956) 'The Attic Stelai.' *Hesp.* 25: 178-317.

Pritchett, W.K. (1987) 'The Pannychis of the Panathenaia.' *Philia Epê eis Georgion Mylonan, dia ta 60 etê tou anaskafikou tou ergou*, B'. Athens: 179-88.

Queyrel, A. (1984) 'Scènes apolliniennes et dionysiaques du peintre de Pothos.' *BCH* 108: 123-59.

Rangabé, A.R. (1882) 'Das Erechtheion.' *MDAI(A)* 7: 321-34.

Raubitschek, T.K. (1998) *Isthmia 7. The Metal Objects (1952-1989)*. Princeton.

Real, W. (1973) *Studien zur Entwicklung der Vasenmalerei im ausgehenden 5Jh. v. Chr.* Münster.

Redfield, J. (1982) 'Notes on the Greek Wedding.' *Arethusa* 15:181-201.

Reeder, E.D. (1987) 'The Mother of the Gods and a Hellenistic Bronze Matrix.' *AJArch.* 91: 423-40.

Reeder, E.D. ed. (1995) *Pandora: Women in Classical Greece*. Princeton.

Rehm, R. (1994) *Marriage to Death. The Conflation of Wedding and Funeral Rituals in Greek Tragedy*. Princeton.

Reichel, W. & Wilhelm, A. (1901) 'Das Heiligtum der Artemis zu Lusoi.' *JÖAI* 4: 1-88.

Reinmuth, O.W. (1971) *The Ephebic Inscriptions of the Fourth Century BC*. London.

Rhodes, P.J. (1981) *A Commentary on the Aristotelian Athenaion Politeia*. Oxford. (repr. 1993).

Richardson, N.J. (1974) *The Homeric Hymn to Demeter*. Oxford. (repr. 1979)

Ridder de, A. (1896) *Catalogue des bronzes trouvés sur l'Acropole d'Athènes 1*. Paris.

Ridgway, B.S. (1992) 'Images of Athena on the Acropolis.' in Neils ed.: 13-27.
Rieu, E.V. (1965) *Homer: The Odyssey*. Middlesex, Baltimore, Ringwood (1st ed. 1946).
Rizakis, A.D. (1995) *Achaie 1: Sources textuelles et histoire régionale*. Athens.
Robertson, C. M. (1948) 'Excavations in Ithaca V.' *BSA* 43: 1-89
Robertson, C.M. (1975) *A History of Greek Art* 2. Cambridge.
Robertson, D.S. (1954) *Greek and Roman Architecture*. Cambridge.
Robertson, N. (1996) 'Athena's Shrines and Festivals.' in J. Neils ed. *Worshipping Athena*. Madison: 27-77.
Robertson, N. (1996) 'The Ancient Mother of the Gods. A Missing Chapter in the History of Greek Religion.' in Lane ed.: 239-304.
Robertson, N. (1992) *Festivals and Legends: The Formation of Greek Cities in the Light of Public Ritual*. Toronto, Buffalo & London.
Robins, F.W. (1939) 'The Lamps of Ancient Egypt.' *JEg. Arch.* 25:184-7.
Robinson, D.M. & Harcum, C.G. (1930) *A Catalogue of the Greek Vases in the Royal Ontario Museum of Archaeology*, 1-2. Toronto.
Rolley, Cl. (1965) 'Dieux Patrooi et Thesmophorion de Thasos.' *BCH* 89: 441-83.
Rolley, Cl. (1981) 'Siris: Le problème artistique.' *Siris e l'influenza Ionica in occidente*. Atti del ventesimo (XX) convegno di studi sulla Magna Grecia. Taranto: 175-95.
Rolley, Cl. (1990) 'Le sanctuaire d'Evraiokastro mise à jour du dossier.' in *Mnêmê Lazaridê*: 405-7.
Rolley, Cl. (1994). *La sculpture grecque I: des origines au milieu du Ve siècle*. Paris.
Rose, H.J. (1951) 'Athena and the Lamp.' *Classical Bulletin* 28: 1-2.
Rouse, W.H.D. (1940) *Nonnos Dionysiaca*. Books 16-35. London & Cambridge Mass.
Roussopoulos, I. S. I. (1862) 'D. Poikila.' Ἀρχ. Ἐφ.: 39.
Rubensohn, O. (1899) 'Eleusinische Beiträge.' *MDAI(A)* 24: 46-56.
Rubensohn, O. (1955) 'Das Weihehaus von Eleusis und sein Allerheiligstes.' *JDAI* 70: 1-9.
Rüdiger, U. (1967) 'Le stipi votive in contrada Conca d'Oro.' *Not. Scav.* 21: 340-53.
Rüdiger, U. (1969) 'Il santuario di Demeter in contrada Conca d' Oro.' *Not. Scav.* 23: 172-97.
Rudolph, W. (1967) 'Antike Sportgeräte.' *Klio* 48: 80-92.
Rutkowski, B. (1983) 'Lampes sacrées de Gortyne.' *Études et Travaux* 13: 321-4.
Rutkowski, B. (1986) *The Cult Places of the Aegean*. New Haven & London.
Sabbione, C. (1984) 'L'artigianato artistico.' *Crotone*. Atti del ventitresimo (XXIII) convegno di studi sulla Magna Grecia. Taranto: 245-310.
Sarian, H. (1992) 'Hekate.' *LIMC* VI: 985-1018.
Sarian, H. et al. (1986) 'Erinys.' *LIMC* III: 825-43.
Scanlon, T.F. (1990) 'Race or Chase at the Arkteia of Attica?' *Nikephoros* 3: 73-120.
Schauenburg, K. (1964) 'Iliupersis auf einer Hydria des Priamosmalers.' *MDAI(R)* 71: 60-70.
Schefold, K. (1981) *Die Göttersage in der klassischen und hellenistischen Kunst*. Munich.
Scheibler, I. (1976) *Kerameikos 11. Griechische Lampen*. Berlin.
Schilardi, D. (1988) 'The Temple of Athena at Koukounaries.' in Hägg, Marinatos & Nordquist eds.: 41-50.
Schiller Sammlung (1996) *Der Jenaer Maler: Eine Topferwerkstatt im klassischen Athen. Fragmenta attischer Trinkschalen der Sammlung Antiker Kleinkunst der Friedrich-Schiller-Universität Jena*. Lehrstuhl für klassische Archäologie

und Sammlung Antiker Kleinkunst der F. Schiller Universität Jena ed. Wiesbaden.

Schlesier, R. (1993) 'Mixtures of Masks: Maenads as Tragic Models.' in Carpenter & Faraone eds.: 89-114.

Schliemann, H. (1886) *Tiryns. The Prehistoric Palace of the Kings of Tiryns*. London.

Schnapp, A. (1997) *La chasseur et la cité: chasse et érotique en Grèce ancienne*. Paris.

Schöne, A. (1987) *Der Thiasos. Eine iconographische Untersuchung über das Gefolge des Dionysos in der attischen Vasen-malerei des 6 und 5 Jhd v. Chr.* Goteborg.

Schwarz, G. (1972-5) 'Eine Hydria des Berliner Malers in Graz.' *JÖAI* 50: 125-33.

Schwarz, G. (1987) *Triptolemos. Ikonographie einer Agrar- und Mysteriengöttheit.* Zeitschrift für die klassische Altertumswissenschaft. Suppl. 2. Horn & Graz.

Sciarra, B. (1976) *Brindisi. Museo archeologico provinciale.* Bologna.

Scodel, R. (1980) *The Trojan Trilogy of Euripides.* Göttingen.

Seaford, R. (1981) 'Dionysiac Drama and Mysteries.' *CQ* 31: 252-75.

Seaford, R. (1987) 'The Tragic Wedding.' *JHS* 107: 106-30.

Seaford, R. (1988) 'The Eleventh Ode of Bacchylides: Hera, Artemis and the Absence of Dionysus.' *JHS* 108: 118-36.

Seaford, R. (1990) 'The Structural Problems of Marriage in Euripides.' in Powell ed.: 151-76.

Seaford, R. (1990a) 'The Imprisonment of Women in Greek Tragedy.' *JHS* 110: 76-90.

Seaford, R. (1993) 'Dionysus as Destroyer of the Household: Homer, Tragedy and the Polis.' in Carpenter & Faraone eds.: 115-46.

Seaford, R. (1994) *Reciprocity and Ritual: Homer and Tragedy in the Developing City.* Oxford.

Seaford, R. (1996) *Euripides: Bacchae.* Warminster.

Seaford, R. (1997) 'Thunder, Lightning and Earthquake in the Bacchae and the Acts of the Apostles.' in A.B. Lloyd ed. *What is a God? Studies in the Nature of Greek Divinity.* London: 139-15.

Sekunda, N.V. (1990) '*IG* II^2 1250: A Decree Concerning the Lampadephoroi of the Tribe Aiantis.' *ZPE* 83: 149-82.

Sélincourt de, A. (1972) *Herodotus. The Histories.* Middlesex, New York, Ringwood, Ontario & Auckland. (1st ed. 1954).

Sfameni-Gasparo, G. (1986) *Misteri e culti mistici di Demetra.* Rome.

Sfameni-Gasparo, G. (1996) 'Per la storia del culto di Cibele in Occidente: il santuario rupestre di Akrai.' in Lane ed.: 51-86.

Sguaitamatti, M. (1984) *L'offrante de porcelet dans la coroplathie géléenne. Étude Typologique.* Zurich.

Shapiro, H.A. (1992) '*Mousikoi Agônes*: Music and Poetry at the Panathenaia.' in Neils ed.: 53-75.

Sherratt, E.S. (1990) ' "Reading" the Texts: Archaeology and the Homeric Question.' *Antiquity 64*: 807-24.

Siebert, G. (1966) 'Artemis Sôteira à Délos.' *BCH* 90: 447-59.

Simms, R.M. (1980) *Eleusinian-Athenian Cult and Myth; their Nature and Origin.* Unpublished Diss. University of Virginia.

Simon, E. (1963) 'Ein Anthesterien-Skyphos des Polygnotos.' *AK* 6: 6-22.

Simon, E. (1966) 'Neue Deutung zweier Eleusinischer Denkmäler des vierten Jahrhunderts v. Chr.' *AK* 9: 72-92.

Simon, E. (1976) 'Ein nordattischer Pan.' *AK* 19: 19-23.

Simon, E. (1985) *Die Götter der Griechen*. Munich.

Simon, E. (1985b) 'Hekate in Athen.' *MDAI(A)* 100: 271-84.

Simons, L.M.R. (1949) *Flamma aeterna*. Studie over de betekenis van het eewige vuur in de cultus van de Hellenistisch-Romeinse oudheid. Amsterdam.

Sinn, U. (1996) *Sport in der Antike. Wettkampf, Spiel und Erziehung im Altertum*. Würzburg.

Sjöqvist, E. (1964) 'Excavations at Morgantina (Serra Orlando) 1963. Preliminary Report VIII.' *AJArch*. 68: 138-47.

Skias, A. (1918) 'To para tên Phulên antron toû Panos.' Ἀρχ. Ἐφ.: 1-28.

Sokolowski, F. (1971) 'On the lex sacra of the Deme Phrearrhioi.' *GRBS* 12: 217-20.

Sommerstein, A. (1983) *Aristophanes: Wasps*. Warminster.

Sommerstein, A. (1994) *Aristophanes: Thesmophoriazousai*. Warminster.

Sommerstein, A. (1996) *Aristophanes: Frogs*. Warminster.

Sotiriades, G. (1913) *The Acropolis and its Museum*. Part 1. Athens.

Sourvinou-Inwood, Ch. (1988) *Studies in Girls' Initiations: Aspects of the Arkteia and Age Representations in Attic Iconography*. Athens.

Sourvinou-Inwood, Ch. (1991) *'Reading' Greek culture. Texts and Images, Rituals and Myths*. Oxford.

Sourvinou-Inwood, Ch. (1995) *'Reading' Greek Death. To the End of the Classical Period*. Oxford.

Stähler, K. (1980) *Archäologisches Museum der Universität Münster. Heroen und Götter der Griechen*. Münster.

Stanford, W.B. (1958) *Aristophanes: Frogs*. London.

Stark, B. (1868) 'Unerdite archaische Vasenbilder im K. Museum zu Berlin.' *Archäologische Zeitung*: 52-7.

Starkie, W.J.M. (1968) *The Wasps of Aristophanes*. Amsterdam.

Steiner, A. (1992) 'Pottery and Cult in Corinth: Oil and Water at the Sacred Spring.' *Hesp*. 61: 385-408.

Steinhauer, G. (1975) 'Lukokheia Mantineias.' *AΔ* 30, B': 77-9.

Stephanidou, T. (1973) 'Relief votif de Potidée.' *Makedonika* 13: 106-16.

Stephanou, A.P. (1958) *Khiaka Meletêmata*, 1. Chios.

Stewart, A. (1990) *Greek Sculpture*. New Haven & London.

Stiglitz, R. (1967) *Die grossen Göttinen Arkadiens*. Vienna.

Stillwell, R. & Sjöqvist, E. (1957) 'Excavations at Serra Orlando. Preliminary Report.' *AJArch*. 61: 151-9.

Stillwell, R. (1959) 'Excavations at Serra Orlando 1958: Preliminary Report III.' *AJArch*. 63: 167-73.

Stillwell, R. (1963) 'Excavations at Morgantina (Serra Orlando) 1962. Preliminary Reports VII.' *AJArch*. 67: 163-71.

Straten van, F.T. (1995) *Hiera Kala: Images of Animal Sacrifice in Archaic and Classical Greece*. Leiden, New York & Köln.

Stroud, R.S. (1965) 'The Sanctuary of Demeter and Kore on Acrocorinth. Preliminary Report I, 1961-2.' *Hesp*. 34: 1-24.

Svoronos, J.N. (1908-1937) *Das Athener Nationalmuseum*. Athens.

Taaffe, L.K. (1993) *Aristophanes and Women*. London & New York.

Technau, W. (1929) 'Griechische Keramik im Samischen Heraion.' *MDAI(A)* 65: 6-64.

Themelis, P. (1989) 'Bathro anathêmatos stê Bendida.' *Horos* 7: 23-9.

Themelis, P. (1993) 'Ho Damophôn kai hê drastêriotêta tou stên Arkadia.' in O. Palagia & W.D.E. Coulson eds. *Sculpture from Arcadia and Laconia*. Oxford: 99-109.

Themelis, P. (1994a) 'Artemis Ortheia at Messene: The Topographical and Archaeological Evidence.' in Hägg ed.: 101-22.
Themelis, P. (1994b) 'Anaskaphê Messênês.' *ΠAE* 1991: 85-128.
Thompson, H.A. (1933) 'The American Excavations in the Athenian Agora. First Report.' *Hesp.* 2: 195-215.
Thompson, H.A. (1936) 'Pnyx and Thesmophorion.' *Hesp.* 5: 151-200.
Thomsen, O. (1992) *Ritual and Desire: Catullus 61 and 62 and other Ancient Documents on Wedding and Marriage.* Aarhus.
Thomson, G. (1938) *The Oresteia of Aeschylus.* Cambridge.
Threpsiades, I. (1961) 'Anaskaphai en Aulidi.' *ΠAE* 1956: 94-104.
Threpsiades, I. (1961-2) 'Anaskaphai Aulidos.' *AΔ* 17: 137-44.
Threpsiades, I. (1965) 'Anaskaphai Aulidos.' *ΠAE* 1959: 26-33.
Tiverios et al. (1997) 'Zeus.' *LIMC* VIII (Supplementum): 315-38.
Tiverios, M. (1981) 'Saltantes Lacunae.' Ἀρχ. Ἐφ.: 25-37.
Tiverios, M. (1990) 'Apharetides-Tyndarides.' in J.-P. Descoeudres ed. *Eumousia: Ceramic and Iconographic Studies in Honour of A. Cambitoglou.* Sydney: 119-24.
Tölle-Kastenbein, R. (1993) 'Das Hekatompedon auf der Athener Akropolis.' *JDAI* 108: 43-75.
Torelli, M. (1977) 'Il santuario Greco di Gravisca.' *Parole del Passato* 32 (fasc. 172-7): 398-458.
Touchefeu-Mayhier, O. (1997) 'Typhon. *LIMC* VIII (Supplementum): 147-51.
Touloupa, E. (1969) 'Une Gorgone en Bronze de l'Acropole.' *BCH* 93: 862-84.
Travlos, J. (1971a) *Pictorial Dictionary of Ancient Athens.* London.
Travlos, J. (1971b) 'Hê esoterikê diataxis toû Erekhtheiou.' *AAA* 4: 78-84.
Travlos, J. (1976) 'Treis naoi tês Artemidos Aulidias Tauropolou kai Braurônias.' in U. Jantzen ed. *Neue Forschungen in Griechischen Heiligtümern.* Tübingen: 197-205.
Trendall, A.D. & Webster, T.B.L. (1971) *Illustrations of Greek Drama.* London.
Tsountas, Ch. (1928) *Historia tês arkhaias Hellenikês technês.* Athens.
Tzouvara-Souli, Ch. (1979) *Hê latreia tôn gynaikeiôn theotitôn eis tên archaian Épeiron.* Ioannina.
Ure, P.N. & Burrows, R.M. (1911) 'Kothons and Vases of Allied Types.' *JHS* 31: 72-99.
Ussher, R.G. (1986) *Aristophanes: Ecclesiazusae.* Oxford. (1973, repr. 1986).
Valavanis, P.D. (1991) *Panathênaïkoi Amphoreis apo tên Eretria. Sumbolê stên Attikê aggeiographia toû 4ou aiôna.* Athens.
Vanderpool, E. (1970) 'A *lex sacra* of the Attic Deme Phrearrhioi.' *Hesp.* 39: 47-53.
Vankove, D. (1993) ed. *Olympism in Antiquity: Catalogue of an Exhibition held in the Olympic Museum, Lausanne.* Lausanne.
Varvitsas, A.K. (1975) 'Anaskaphes Mesêmbrias Thrakês.' *ΠAE* 1973: 77-82.
Vassits, M. (1899) *Die Fackel in Kunst und Kultus der Griechen.* Unpublished Diss. University of Munich.
Vellacott, Ph. (1959) *Aeschylus: The Oresteian Trilogy.* London, New York, Ringwood, Toronto & Auckland. (1st ed. 1956)
Vellacott, Ph. (1972) *Euripides. The Bacchae and Other Plays.* Middlesex, Baltimore & Ringwood. (1st ed. 1954)
Verdelis, N.M. (1964) 'Anaskaphê eis thesin Spêliôtaki.' *AΔ* 19: 121-2.
Vermaseren, M.J. (1977) *Corpus Cultus Cybelae Attisque. EPRO* 50. Leiden.
Vermeule, E. (1970) 'Five Vases from the Grave Precinct of Dexileos.' *JDAI* 85: 94-111.

Vernant, J.P. & Vidal-Naquet, P. (1988) eds. *Myth and Tragedy in Ancient Greece*. New York.

Vian, F. & Moore, M.B. (1988) 'Gigantes.' *LIMC* IV: 191-270.

Vian, F. (1951) *Répertoire des Gigantomachies figurées dans l'art grec et romain*. Paris.

Vidal-Naquet, P. (1981) 'The Black Hunter and the Origin of the Athenian Ephebeia.' in R.L. Gordon ed. *Myth, Religion and Society: Structuralist Essays*. Cambridge & New York: 147-62.

Vidal-Naquet, P. (1986) *The Black Hunter.* Baltimore & London (1981 repr. 1986).

Vidal-Naquet, P. (1988) 'Hunting and Sacrifice in Aeschylus' Oresteia.' in Vernant & Vidal-Naquet eds.: 141-59.

Vokotopoulou, I. (1993) 'Arkhaïko hiero stên Sanê tês Chalkidikês.' *Arkhaia Makedonia* 5.1: 179-236.

Voutiras, E. (1997) 'Zeus.' *LIMC* VIII (Supplementum): 310-12.

Voyatzis, M.E. (1990) *The Early Sanctuary of Athena Alea at Tegea and Other Archaic Sanctuaries in Arcadia*. Göteborg.

Waldstein, Ch. (1905) *The Argive Heraion* 2. Boston & New York.

Walter, H. (1957) 'Frühe samische Gefässe und ihre Fundlage.' *MDAI(A)* 72: 35-51.

Walter, O. (1923) *Beschreibung der Reliefs im kleinen Akropolis Museum in Athen*. Berlin.

Warren, P. (1969) *Minoan Stone Vases*. Cambridge.

Waywell, G.B. (1970) 'Some Relief Sculptures in the Museum of the British School at Athens.' *BSA* 65: 271-5.

Weller, C.H. (1913) *Athens and its Monuments*. New York.

Welter G. (1941) *Troizen und Kalaureia*. Berlin.

Wesenberg, B. (1995) 'Panathenäische Peplosdedikation und Arrhephorie. Zur Thematik des Parthenonfrieses.' *JDAI* 110: 149-78.

West, M.L. (1978) *Hesiod: Works and Days*. Oxford.

West, M.L. (1983) *The Orphic Poems*. Oxford.

Whitby, M. (1994) 'Two Shadows: Images of Spartans and Helots.' in A. Powell & S. Hodkinson eds. *The Shadow of Sparta*. London & New York: 87-126.

White, D. (1964) *Agnê Thea: A Study of Sicilian Demeter*. Unpublished Diss. University of Princeton.

White, D. (1976) 'Excavations in the Sanctuary of Demeter and Persephone at Cyrene. Fourth Preliminary Report.' *AJArch.* 80: 165-81.

White, D. (1984) *The Extramural Sanctuary of Demeter and Persephone at Cyrene, Libya. Final Reports*, I. Philadelphia.

White, D. (1993) *The Extramural Sanctuary of Demeter and Persephone at Cyrene, Libya. Final Reports*, V. Philadelphia.

Whitman, C. (1958) *Homer and the Heroic Tradition*. Cambridge, Mass.

Wiegand, Th. & Schrader, H. (1904) *Priene. Ergebnisse der Ausgrabungen und Untersuchungen in den Jahren 1895-1898*. Berlin.

Williams II, C.K. (1978) *Pre-Roman Cults in the Area of the Forum of Ancient Corinth*. Unpublished Diss. University of Pennsylvania.

Williams, C.H. (1990) 'Excavations at Mytilene, 1990.' *EMC* 35: 175-91.

Williams, C.H. (1994) 'Secret Rites of Lesbos.' *Archaeology* 47.4: 35-40.

Williamson, Ch. (1993) 'Light in Dark Places: Changes in the Application of Natural Light in Sacred Greek Architecture.' *Pharos* 1: 3-33.

Winkler, J.J. (1990) 'The Ephebes' Song.' in J.J. Winkler & F.I. Zeitlin eds. *Nothing to do with Dionysos? Athenian Drama in its Social Context*. Princeton: 20-62.

Winnington-Ingram, R.P. (1980) *Sophocles: An Interpretation*. Cambridge.

Winter, N.A. (1993) *Greek Architectural Terracottas: From the Prehistoric to the end of the Archaic Period.* Oxford.

Wölke, H. (1978) *Untersuchungen zur Batrachomyomachie. Beiträge zur klassischen Philologie.* Hain.

Woodhouse, W.J. (1929) *The Composition of Homer's Odyssey.* Oxford.

Wright, H. (1972) 'Vegetation History.' in W. McDonald & G. Rapp eds. *The Minnesota Messenia Expedition.* Minneapolis: 188-95.

Wroth, W. (1894) *Catalogue of the Greek Coins of Troas, Aeolis and Lesbos.* (British Museum Collection) London.

Wycherley, R.E. (1978) *The Stones of Athens.* Princeton.

Zagdoun, M.-A. (1977) *Fouilles de Delphes* 4. *Monuments figurés: Sculpture* 6. *Reliefs.* Paris.

Zervoudaki, E.A. (1968) 'Attische polychrome Reliefkeramik des späten 5. und des 4. Jahrhunderts v. Chr.' *MDAI(A)* 83: 1-88.

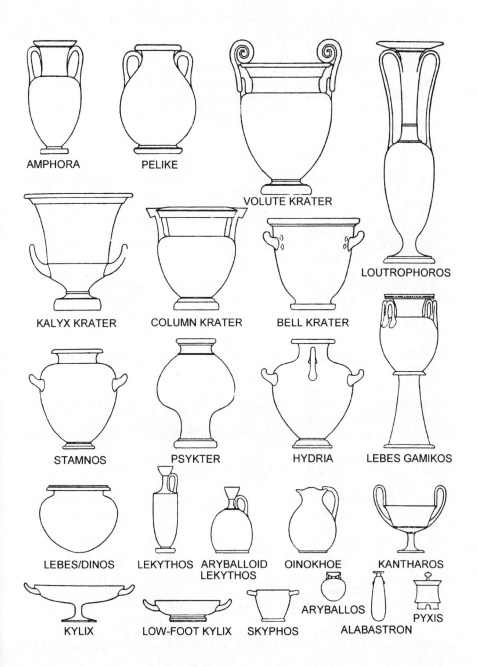

AMPHORA PELIKE VOLUTE KRATER LOUTROPHOROS

KALYX KRATER COLUMN KRATER BELL KRATER

STAMNOS PSYKTER HYDRIA LEBES GAMIKOS

LEBES/DINOS LEKYTHOS ARYBALLOID LEKYTHOS OINOKHOE KANTHAROS

KYLIX LOW-FOOT KYLIX SKYPHOS ARYBALLOS ALABASTRON PYXIS

Glossary

Aduton The most holy room of a temple, often close to the cella; entrance to the aduton would have been permitted only to certain people and/or for special ceremonies.

Aegis Shaggy or scaly skin with a fringe of snakes and a Gorgoneion in the centre; a typical part of the outfit of Athena.

Agelastos petra A rock in the Eleusinian sanctuary where Demeter sat mourning after her restless wanderings in search of Persephone.

Aiskhrologia Use of obscene language during certain rituals. In the Thesmophoria and the Haloa such language was used by the female participants.

Amphidromia A ritual run around the home hearth performed by a father holding his new born baby a few days after the birth.

Amphiphôn Circular cake bearing candles, a common offering to Artemis and Hekate.

Amphora Large two-handled vase, used for transporting liquid or solid goods.

Anaktoron (at Eleusis) A small room possibly in the Telesterion, where the Hiera (sacred symbols of the cult) were kept and from where the Hierophant emerged bathed in bright light on the night of the Mysteries.

Anodos The mythical ascent of Persephone from the Underworld, which was celebrated in the Mysteries.

Anthesteria A festival in honour of Dionysos during which the god's annual marriage was enacted.

Apoptugma Overfold of woman's long garment, usually the peplos.

Arkhon-basileus Magistrate in Athens responsible for chief religious and priestly functions of the state.

Arktoi Girls who served Artemis in her sanctuary at Brauron, Attica, until their coming of age for marriage.

Arrhephoroi Girls who served the godddess Athena on the Akropolis by taking part in certain sacred rites and helping with the preparation of the Panathenaia.

Aryballos Small oil-flask, usually with a globular body.

Bakkhos Wand made of myrtle branches which were carried by the initiates in the Eleusinian Mysteries.

Bothros A sacrificial deposit, often in the form of a pit, with stone-lined borders.

Candelabrum Lampstand or any type of support for a light-container.

Cella The main cult-room of a temple where the image of the god stood.

Daedalic style Early Greek sculptural style of the seventh and early sixth centuries.

Daidoukhousa The torch-bearer in Greek weddings, normally the mother of the bride.

Daidoukhos One of the Eleusinian officials whose main duty was to lead the procession of the initiates on the night of the Mysteries at Eleusis, carrying torches.

Daughter Persephone.

Defixiones Curse-tablets usually inscribed on lead-sheet and shaped in a roll.

Deiknumena The ritual display of the Hiera on the night of the procession and pannukhis at Eleusis.

Diegertikon Part of the epithalamia songs sung by a bride's maiden friends during her first wedding night. They lasted until dawn.

Epaulia The third and last day of a Greek wedding on which gifts were brought to the newlywed couple.

Ependutes A kind of overgarment like a tunic or robe.

Epheboi Adolescent youths aged between eighteen and twenty.

Epiphany Revelation of a god (usually in human form) to a mortal.

Gephurismoi A kind of ritual mockery enacted between the initiates during their crossing of the Kephisos bridge during the procession at the Eleusinian Mysteries.

Gorgoneion The head of a Gorgon used in art, frequently as a centrepiece in circular compositions.

Gunaikon The women's quarters in a Greek house.

Haloa Midwinter festival in honour of Demeter. The celebrations included a nocturnal vigil attended exclusively by women.

Hekataion A type of three-sided statue of Hekate made up of three images of the goddess.

Hekatompedon A temple one hundred feet long.

Hetaira A courtesan; usually a non-citizen woman.

Hierophant A high priest of the Eleusinian cult, responsible for revealing the Hiera to the initiates in the Anaktoron on the night of the Mysteries.

Hieros gamos Sacred wedding, here used for the symbolic annual wedding of Dionysos enacted during the Anthesteria.

Himation Outer garment of fairly rectangular shape, often made of wool, worn over the khiton.

Hubris Excessive pride in one's strength or achievements which was believed to bring down divine punishment.

Hydria Three-handled vase (with two horizontal handles at belly-level and a vertical one on the neck), mainly used for carrying water and wine.

Kalathos Vase in the shape of a basket.

Kantharos Deep drinking cup for wine with two high flung handles and a high foot.

Kernos Ritual vessel with multiple receptacles for multiple offerings to the gods.

Khiton Long female (and sometimes male) dress made of linen or other light-weight fabric, often girded.

Khous Small pitcher particularly used in the celebrations of the second day of the festival of Anthesteria.

Kiste A box which often contained objects sacred to a cult.

Kore General term denoting a maiden; in an Eleusinian context, Persephone is known as Kore (Daughter).

Kothon Deep bowl with incurving rim, low base and occasionally a horizontal handle.

Krater Large vessel used for mixing wine with water, often used in drinking parties.

Kurekion The wand carried by Hermes.

Kylix Shallow, two-handled drinking cup, often with a high foot.

Lampadedromia Torch-race.

Lampter Lighting vessel or brazier.

Lebes gamikos Deep bowl with a stand, often a wedding gift.

Lekythos A narrow-necked flask suitable for carrying oils and perfumes; particularly used in funerary ritual.

Loutrophoros Tall vase with a long neck with two vertical handles, used to carry water for the pre-nuptial bath or as a grave-marker for unmarried persons.

Lukhnoukhoi Supports or stands of lighting vessels (mainly lamps and torches).

Maenad Female follower of Dionysos; a member of the thiasos.

Megaron Pit in which pigs were sacrificed during the Thesmophoria.

Mnesterophonia The killing of the suitors in the *Odyssey*.

Mysteries Cults which involved initiation of **Mustai** (initiates in the Eleusinian or Dionysiac Mysteries).

Narthex Name of the funnel in which Prometheus transported fire to mortals.

Nebris A fawn skin often worn by maenads.

Nike Female personification of Victory.

Nozzle The part of a lamp that accommodates the wick.

Nymphe Bride, nymph.

Oikos House or household.

Oinokhoe Wine-jug with one handle, often with trefoil-shaped 'mouth'.

Omophagia The ritual consumption of raw flesh; one of the mythical activities of the maenads when in a state of divine ecstasy inspired by Dionysos.

Omphalos The mythical navel of the earth which was believed to be at or near the Delphic oracle.

Opaion An opening on the roof of a building for light and air.

Pannukhis All-night vigil including dances and songs in honour of a god.

Parthenos Unmarried maiden.

Pelike A vase with two vertical handles and a belly widening towards the base (similar to an amphora).

Peplos Woman's long garment made of a heavy (often woollen) rectangular cloth, pinned at the shoulders, girded at the waist and open along one side.

Peribolos The wall surrounding a temenos (precinct of a god).

Petasos Hermes' broad-brimmed hat.

Phiale Shallow bowl often with a cental boss inside, used for libations.

Pinax Clay tablet, often used as wall decoration.

Pit-altar see megaron.

Polis City-state.

Polos Goddess's cylindrical headdress.

Pyxis Round box with a lid, often containing cosmetics or other small objects.

Sakkos A bag used to cover the hair.

Satyr Horse-human mythical creature; male participant of the Dionysiac thiasos.

Silenos An aged satyr.

Skyphos A deep drinking cup with two horizontal handles close to rim level.

Sophrosune Dignified and restrained behaviour.

Sparagmos The tearing of a living animal by the maenads when possessed by Dionysos.

Sphurelaton The technique of hammering a bronze sheet over a wooden core.

Telesterion Sacred building of the Eleusinian sanctuary which housed the most sacred part of the rituals of the Mysteries, including the revelation of the Hiera of the cult by the Hierophant.

Temenos Sacred precinct around a temple or a sanctuary.

Theos/Thea Plouton and Persephone (after her 'marriage' with Plouton).

Thesmophoria Autumn festival of Demeter involving the sacrifice of pigs in pits (megara).

Thiasos The mythical company of Dionysos comprising satyrs and maenads.

Thumiaterion Incense burner.

Thursos A wand with a leafy almost cone-shaped end held or shaken by Dionysos or his female followers, the maenads.

Titans Giant opponents of the gods who are defeated by the gods in Hesiod's *Theogony*.

Tumpanon Type of drum or tambourine often depicted in representations of the Dionysiac thiasos.

Volute-krater A krater with two high handles ending in volutes.

Xoanon A primitive image of a god, usually plank-like and made of wood.

Xula Timber or other wood used in sacrificial fires.

Indexes

List of Literary Works Cited

General Index

Women 1, 34, 39, 45, 46, 47, 48, 50, 51, 54, 55, 58, 59, 73, 77, 80, 97, 108-9, 115, 119, 120, 121, 122, 123, 126, 127, 128, 158, 159, 160, 161, 163, 167, 179 nn.73, 74; 182 nn.1, 8; 195 n.37; 202 n.144; widows 34-5

Xula 71, 130, 129, 159
Zeus 4, 48-9, 51, 73, 79, 89-91, 99, 101, 102, 105-8, 110-11, 115, 163, 170 n.12; 173 n.79; 174 n.6; 182 n.126; 182 n.21; 183 n.32; 185 n.67; 190 nn.47-8; 191 n.10; 218

Topographical Index